The Changing Village in India

The Changing Village in India

Insights from Longitudinal Research

EDITED BY
HIMANSHU
PRAVEEN JHA
GERRY RODGERS

OXFORD
UNIVERSITY PRESS

OXFORD
UNIVERSITY PRESS

Oxford University Press is a department of the University of Oxford. It furthers the University's objective of excellence in research, scholarship, and education by publishing worldwide. Oxford is a registered trademark of Oxford University Press in the UK and in certain other countries

Published in India by
Oxford University Press
YMCA Library Building, 1 Jai Singh Road, New Delhi 110 001, India

First Edition published in 2016

ISBN-13: 978-0-19-946186-8
ISBN-10: 0-19-946186-4

Typeset in Dante MT Std 10.5/13
by Tranistics Data Technologies, New Delhi 110 044
Printed in India by Rakmo Press, New Delhi 110 020

Contents

Tables and Figures

Tables

Figures

Preface

In many parts of the world, the village is an indispensable point of departure for research into economic and social change. This is certainly true of India, where urbanization is proceeding apace, but two-thirds of the population still lives in the rural areas. And while village studies go in and out of fashion, studying change at village level can give extraordinary insights into the transformation of social institutions, economic structures, and individual lives.

Change and transformation are the keywords here. The village in India is not timeless and eternal. To be sure, there are continuities. But changes in communications, production methods, incomes, education, social organization, political institutions, and other dimensions all imply that the village evolves. There is a community of researchers who attempt to analyse and understand these processes, in particular by tracking the stories and histories of individuals and villages over long periods of time. This longitudinal approach to village research is the central theme of this book.

This is not just an academic concern. Village studies are directly relevant for a wide range of policy issues, and longitudinal studies are particularly important for their ability to shed light on the practical impact of policies on the ground. While most policy analyses tend to focus on the impact of particular instruments, the greater impact of policy comes through longer term transformations of economic, social, and political life. It is this which can only be properly addressed through repeated studies over long periods of time. Such studies also permit sustained exchange with local social actors and stakeholders, and so permit a greater understanding of the nature and consequences of interactions between external policymakers and local social environments.

This was the background to a conference that was held at Jawaharlal Nehru University (JNU), New Delhi in November 2012. The conference was organized by JNU's Centre for Informal Sector and Labour Studies with the collaboration of the Institute for Human Development (IHD), New Delhi, and supported by the International Development Research Centre (IDRC), Centre de Sciences Humaines (CSH), New Delhi, and Asia Research Centre of the London School of Economics and Political Science. The conference provided a forum for the presentation of a variety of longitudinal village studies and a debate on their methods and their contribution to understanding of development and change. Most of the chapters in this book were first presented at the conference, though the majority has since been extensively revised and some new chapters have also been added. As a result the book includes village studies from a number of different regions of India, as well as a review of comparable studies in Bangladesh, and considers not only current research but also some important historical studies.

In addition to the authors of the chapters included in the volume, we would like to acknowledge the contributions of many other participants in the conference, including Bina Agarwal, Christopher Bliss, Jan Breman, C.P. Chandrashekhar, Basudeb Chaudhuri, Stefan Dercon, Jean Drèze, Jayati Ghosh, Dipankar Gupta, Ruth Kattumuri, Jens Lerche, Sam Moyo, Mridula Mukherjee, Prabhat Patnaik, Utsa Patnaik, V.K. Ramachandran, Ashwani Saith, Abhijit Sen, Pronab Sen, Alakh N. Sharma, Naresh Sharma, Madhura Swaminathan, Sukhadeo Thorat, and Paris Yeros. Many of the chapters have benefited from the debates in which they all participated, and we are most grateful for their help.

We also would like to reiterate a point made by several of the contributors of this book, namely that research of this sort relies heavily on the time and effort given freely by people from villages around India. Unlike large-scale household surveys, village studies, especially if they are repeated over long periods, often involve active participation by villagers in data collection and debate, providing information and insights that are often not available from other sources. We are very grateful for their help.

Abbreviations

AAY	Antyodaya Anna Yojana
AERC	Agro-Economic Research Centre / Agricultural Economics Research Centre
ANM	Auxiliary Nurse Midwife
APL	Above Poverty Line
ARC	Asia Research Centre
ASHA	Accredited Social Health Activist
ASI	Annual Survey of Industries
AWC	Anganwadi Centre
AWW	Anganwadi Worker
BARD	Bangladesh Academy for Rural Development
BDO	Block Development Officer
BMI	Body Mass Index
BPL	Below Poverty Line
BSP	Bahujan Samaj Party
CISLS	Centre for Informal Sector and Labour Studies
CSH	Centre de Sciences Humaines
DFID	Department for International Development
DISE	District Information System for Education
DPT	Diphtheria, pertussis, and tetanus, vaccine against
DUVSG	Dhaka University Village Study Group
EPW	*Economic and Political Weekly*
EUS	Employment and Unemployment Survey
FGD	Focus Group Discussion
FLFP	Female Labour Force Participation
FPS	Fair Price Shop

IAY	Indira Awaas Yojana
ICDS	Integrated Child Development Services
ICRISAT	International Crop Research Institute for Semi-Arid Tropics
IDRC	International Development Research Centre
IFPRI	International Food Policy Research Institute
IHD	Institute for Human Development
IHDS	India Human Development Survey
ILCAA	Research Institute for Languages and Cultures of Asia and Africa
IMR	Infant Mortality Rate
JPS	*Journal of Peasant Studies*
LSE	London School of Economics
LTVS	Long-term Village Studies
MFALDA	Marginal Farmer and Agricultural Labourer Development Agency
MGNREGA	Mahatma Gandhi National Rural Employment Guarantee Act
MGNREGS	Mahatma Gandhi National Rural Employment Guarantee Scheme
MIDC	Maharashtra Industrial Development Corporation
MIDS	Madras Institute of Development Studies
NCCR	National Centre of Competence in Research
NCEUS	National Commission for Enterprises in the Unorganized Sector
NFHS	National Family Health Survey
NICD	National Institute of Community Development
NIEPA	National Institute of Educational Planning and Administration
NIRD	National Institute of Rural Development
NSSO	National Sample Survey Office
OBC	Other Backward Caste
PARI	Project on Agrarian Relations in India
PDS	Public Distribution System
PHC	Primary Health Centre
PPP	Purchasing Power Parity
PRI	Panchayati Raj Institution
RCT	Randomized Control Trial

RTI	Right to Information (Act)
SC	Scheduled Caste
SFDA	Small Farmer Development Agency
SP	Samajwadi Party
SRS	Systematic Random Sampling
ST	Scheduled Tribe
TBA	traditional birth attendants
TNAA	Tamil Nadu Agriculturalists' Association
TNAU	Tamil Nadu Agricultural University
VCACS	Village Community Agricultural Cooperative Society
VJNT	Vimukta Jati and Nomadic Tribes
VLW	Village Level Worker
WHO	World Health Organization

1

HIMANSHU
PRAVEEN JHA
GERRY RODGERS

Introduction

Villages and Village Surveys

The idea of using the village as the lens to understand what is happening in a vast country such as India is not new. In fact, while India is known for its extensive statistical system, it is also well-endowed with village studies, which have had a profound impact on our understanding of the complexities of economic production and social structure in rural areas. It may seem ironic to study villages at a time when India is integrating into the global economy, and the contribution of rural areas to the growth and structural transformation of the economy is declining. But the revival of village studies in recent years, many of them based on repeated visits to the same village, is also a testimony to the usefulness of village studies in providing answers to questions that elude the narrow confines of mainstream theory and large-scale surveys, and in understanding the daily concerns of a majority of India's population.[1] The chapters in this book are an evidence that village studies are alive and well.

[1] For an earlier collection of articles on this subject, see Breman, Kloos, and Saith (1997). A systematic review of village studies was undertaken in the 1970s

One of the reasons for the centrality of the village in studying rural India is because it is the lowest level administrative unit. It has an official identity, which is reflected in land records, population censuses, and state activities, all of which facilitate research. But the advantage of working at the level of the village is that it is also the smallest political and societal unit. Sociologists, anthropologists, and political scientists have often treated the village itself as an object of research—unlike economists who tend to consider the village as a site for research.[2] The differences are obvious but subtle. It is partly to do with the subject of the research and the nature of the research objective—topics such as caste, class, and social relations are centred on the village and can be best observed through studying the village per se. It is true that some economic relations, notably those concerning tenancy, credit, and labour, are also most easily analysed in the limited context of a village economy.[3] But in analysing these relationships, economists tend to treat the village as a representative of 'rural', even though economic studies often use knowledge of the institutional, social, and political structures of the village to help in explaining outcomes. In both the cases, however, the village has been a central locus of research.

What can we learn from village studies that is not already available from other sources? The availability of large-scale data sources such as the socio-economic surveys of the National Sample Survey Office (NSSO), the National Family Health Survey (NFHS), and the India Human Development Surveys (IHDS) have made it possible to undertake a considerable volume of empirical analysis on a variety of issues in rural India. Researchers who work at the village level are often sceptical of the quality of data from these large data sets, but whatever their limitations, they have certainly helped in getting a better idea of the general trend in social and economic outcomes in rural areas. Indeed, if the aim is to estimate

---

by the Institute of Development Studies at University of Sussex; see Dasgupta (1978). See also Lindberg (2012) and studies carried out by the Foundation for Agrarian Studies, such as Ramachandran, Rawal, and Swaminathan (2010).

[2] Although there is no strict compartmentalization of village studies by disciplines, and there are many varieties of economics, such a generalization is not too far off the mark. For a comprehensive survey of village surveys and the anthropological approach, see Harriss (2008).

[3] The ICRISAT village surveys as well as the Palanpur surveys tested many of the existing economic theories of tenancy, credit, and market imperfections.

outcomes and trends at the national level, there is no real alternative to the large-scale survey method. And their contribution in generating testable hypotheses about broad questions of transformation in rural India cannot be ignored. Yet, methodological and measurement issues apart, the lack of detailed information in such surveys on institutional contexts and processes of change limits their contribution both to theoretical formulations and to policy design. In reality, there is some complementarity here, for village studies can go further and deeper, especially if they trace change over time, while large-scale surveys can map out the larger picture and identify patterns and outcomes that need to be better understood.

Another obvious question is whether findings from a single village, or from a few villages, out of six lakh villages in India, can permit us to build a wider understanding of common issues confronting social and economic theory or development policy. That is, how representative is the village, if findings are to be generalized over a large geographical unit such as the state or the country? This has often been a bone of contention, especially since it is not uncommon for different village studies to contradict each other in their findings about similar issues. Needless to say, such differences are inevitable because villages are not homogenous and differ widely in their characteristics and structure. But it is also true that such differences can be embedded in the research process itself, since they may reflect the personal involvement and ideological perspective of individual researchers, the differing objectives of the research, and the use of different instruments of research. Building a reliable overall picture from a heterogeneous set of village studies is definitely an art rather than a science.

India is fortunate to have a large number of village studies, starting from the pre-Independence days. The publication of this book coincides serendipitously with the centenary of the first studies of the 'Slater villages' in Tamil Nadu.[4] The trend of studying villages by sociologists, anthropologists, as well as economists continued after Independence. Notable among these were studies by Bailey (1957) who studied Bisipara village in Orissa, Epstein (1962) who studied Wangala and Dalena in Karnataka, and Hopper (1965) who studied Senapur in Uttar Pradesh (UP). Some of these studies have been used to derive insights for the formulation and understanding of

[4] The Slater villages, as they are popularly known, were some villages in Tamil Nadu surveyed systematically by Gilbert Slater in 1916–17. See Slater (1918) for details and Chapter 2 in this volume.

economic theories while others have been used to validate our existing knowledge of the behaviour of various actors in the closed system of a village. Early Indian anthropology and sociology has produced scholarship on villages, which examined various aspects of villages as units, often combining several in-depth village studies, such as the contributions of Dube (1955) and Srinivas (1963). On the other hand, very few detailed studies are available from this early period which looked at economic issues, such as the functioning of markets and individual behaviour towards risk, savings, investment, and credit. Some of the gaps in this regard were filled by systematic surveys, such as those by the Agro-Economic Research Centres (AERCs) and the Census of India. More than 200 village surveys were carried out by the AERC from the late 1950s to the early 1970s in different parts of the country.[5] These included thematic village surveys centred on the study of agricultural production, labour allocation, cooperatives, and the credit market. While a large proportion of studies in the early 1970s and 1980s focused on the changing dynamics of the agricultural production structure and the labour market in response to the changes brought in by the 'Green Revolution', the subsequent years have seen the agenda broaden to encompass non-farm employment, government intervention, and the impact of urbanization, all of them important drivers of change.

The fact that a large number of village studies were carried out in the first two to three decades after Independence also meant that in many villages there was a baseline, which created the possibility to undertake resurveys, which could measure changes over time. Our particular interest in this volume is in those villages that have been surveyed repeatedly. Many of these longitudinal village surveys, covering either the same villages, or in some cases sampled households in selected villages, have been an important means to understand change in rural India. Of course, they come with their own methodological and conceptual problems. However, the ability to investigate the dynamics of change using the same set of observations, whether of villages or of households, has been a strong point of these longitudinal surveys.[6]

[5] For an analysis of the AERC village surveys, see Dasgupta (1975).

[6] Most of the secondary large-scale data sources, such as the socio-economic surveys of the NSSO and the NFHS are repeated cross-section surveys rather than longitudinal surveys. The IHDS is an exception, since it collects panel data on a sample of some 40,000 households.

While rural areas have seen structural transformation in the different phases of Indian economic development, the nature of change has varied and so have the themes of these longitudinal village studies. The only constant has been the location of the villages: not only has the research agenda changed, but village institutions and relationships have also changed along with the external environment, be it government policy, social structure, or the political dispensation. Villages connect with and are affected by a wider set of regional or national economic and social forces, and these have been transformed over the past few decades. The changing village poses the biggest challenge to any longitudinal village study, conceptually and methodologically, as well as in terms of comparability. The methodological problem is that villages do not just change in response to exogenous forces. Economic changes external to the village may be responsible for migration, for example; but the self-selection of migrants from the village changes the dynamics of the village itself, and this endogeneity raises both conceptual and practical issues. Among the latter, it may not be easy to trace migrants, who are often widely scattered.[7]

Among the many revisit village surveys, the International Crop Research Institute for Semi-Arid Tropics (ICRISAT) surveys hold a special place. ICRISAT's continuous village survey programme, which involved repeated visits to selected villages over a long period of time, has been quite influential because of the nature of the data collected. Eight villages were covered as part of the ICRISAT surveys, and two of them in particular, in Andhra Pradesh, have been used intensively for longitudinal work. A long-term time series is available for these villages, including annual data for six years starting in 2001.[8]

The ICRISAT village surveys were exceptional in the frequency of their data collection. Most longitudinal village surveys have long gaps between revisits. Notable among the long-term longitudinal data sets, the Palanpur village surveys stand out because of the long period covered (1957–8 to 2008–10), but also because of the quality of data collected, involving extended periods of stay in the village (Lanjouw

[7] Some studies, such as the ICRISAT studies, have made painstaking efforts to track down migrants. But these are time- and cost-intensive.

[8] For details see vdsa.icrisat.ac.in (last accessed 15 September 2015) and Walker and Ryan (1990).

and Stern 1998). In Bihar, a dozen villages have been surveyed three times now, starting from the early 1980s (Rodgers et al. 2013). The 'Slater villages' of Tamil Nadu provide a longitudinal picture of the changes in a village for almost a century. These latter three data sets have all been used for articles in this book. There are numerous others that stand out in the list of longitudinal village surveys. Some observers have personally tracked the trends in selected villages over long periods—few longer than Gilbert Etienne (2014). It is not possible to mention all such efforts, but together they have been an important source to enrich our understanding of the complex process of change in rural India.

In a paradoxical way, it is the changing dynamics of globalization and the integration of the world economy that has renewed the importance of villages as the centre of research. The village today, compared with the village of the mid-twentieth century, is less of an autonomous unit with its own dynamics of production and distribution. It is no longer a self-contained closed economy with overdependence on agriculture and limited interaction with the outside world. On the contrary, the village, the neighbouring towns, and the metropolitan centres now form a continuum; the Indian village is not even isolated from the vagaries of the financial markets of London or New York. Agriculture accounts for less than one-fifth of the Indian economy. Even within rural areas, agriculture now contributes only just over half of the economy. So there has been great diversification within the village. But more than the declining importance of agriculture, what makes the study of village economies challenging is the manner in which villages are becoming integrated into neighbouring and distant urban areas through non-farm employment, migration, the spread of telecommunications, and remittances. This is not just an academic issue: it also has major developmental implications. The globalized world and the integration of the local village with the global village has altered social, political, and class structures and relations within the village, and made it a key participant in the dynamics of growth and distribution. The village is also the terrain on which many important development policies are tested. The Mahatma Gandhi National Rural Employment Guarantee Act (MGNREGA) is but one example of this.

A second reason why longitudinal village studies are important, although not necessarily village studies of the old style, is the nature of the complexities that pervade our economic, social, and political structure. A large body of research, quite prominent in the current development discourse, has depended on village surveys to identify crucial variables and behavioural patterns, which are fundamental to our understanding of why some households remain poor and others move up the ladder. And to analyse these dynamics, we need long-term information on assets, education, and other attributes. So this is an important element of longitudinal research. It is particularly important for the separation of issues that concern individual/household behaviour from external factors, such as government policy, urban peripheries, or local sociopolitical structure.

The issue of individual behaviour and the response of individuals has been a dominant theme of another kind of research, which is now gaining currency with a focus on village-level surveys. This is undertaken by researchers who have adopted the technique of Randomized Control Trials (RCTs); they have been at the forefront of village-level studies in recent years (Bannerjee and Duflo 2011). This group of scientists (both economists and other social scientists) has used village surveys to produce empirically based evidence that has nourished some of the longest running debates in development thinking, such as the effects of credit rationing or micro-credit, saving behaviour, determinants of mobility, reasons for persistent malnutrition, and so on. The village provides the ideal space and setting to generate credible evidence on the working of theoretical models. This alone is a valid reason for undertaking village studies, but at the village level we can also produce evidence of a different type of complex interactions in the contemporary economic and social context, whether at the level of consumers, factors, or markets, which have defied conventional theory.

We need to distinguish between surveys in villages and village studies. The RCT approach continues to treat the individual as central to any analysis of change, either as a result of external intervention or due to behavioural change, but uses villages as the site of research because of the usual assumption of village societies being relatively unchanging units of observation, at least in the short run. This runs counter to the general consensus emerging from longitudinal village studies, which have documented and analysed the rapidly changing structure of village societies in a wide range of aspects.

The discourse on development, at least economic development, has moved beyond the traditional questions of the role of economic policy, growth versus development, the role of the state, planning versus market, industrialization, international trade, and savings and capital formation. Issues of market imperfections, institutional structures, and structural changes are now seen to be directly relevant to the analysis of policies in most fields, whether it is the impact of public employment programmes, infrastructure, subsidies, affirmative action, or the development of education and healthcare systems.

The widening recognition of the need to address these complexities is an essential reason for the revival of village studies, since they are an important methodological and empirical tool. Not only can they be used to explore the theoretical underpinnings of various questions that continue to dominate the development discourse, but they also help to find solutions to more vexed problems of policy implementation. The revival concerns both stand alone village surveys, such as the Project on Agrarian Relations in India (PARI) surveys carried out by the Foundation for Agrarian Studies[9], and longitudinal ones. The fact that India is well-endowed with detailed studies on many villages has meant that a wide variety of questions can be addressed. Of course, the nature of evidence generated has also varied depending on the choice of villages and the specific line of enquiry pursued by the researchers. But methodological variations and conceptual frameworks notwithstanding, these longitudinal studies have certainly helped to enrich the understanding of processes of change in rural India.

Some Methodological Questions

So longitudinal village studies can make a unique contribution to the analysis of economic and social change. But they also raise a series of particular methodological issues. Some of these are relevant for village studies in general, but take on a particular character in repeated studies over a period of time. Others are specific to the longitudinal method. In reality, rigorously replicated studies, as Harriss-White and Harriss (2007) put it, may not be possible, for there are always changes in the research

[9] www.agrarianstudies.org (last accessed 27 July 2015).

process and the external environment is not constant. But longitudinal studies have the considerable advantage that they can directly track the evolution of key social and economic factors and outcomes. The central methodological issue is how best to preserve and exploit this advantage.

The Village as an Object of Study

The notion of a village study is, of course, built on the notion of a village, which is itself a constructed concept. The idea that villages are identifiable and separable social or economic microcosms, with their own characteristics and dynamics, is often contested. Villages exist in a wider space, and there is a conceptual tension between the local community with its specific structure and history, and a wider economy in which it is inserted. So choosing a village for a village study is a perilous activity, because depending on its size, location, and social make-up, it may be more or less distinct, at one extreme existing only as a habitat providing labour to the wider economy, at another constituting a complex economic system with its own dynamics.

This issue is particularly relevant in longitudinal work, for as we noted above, the relationship of a village with the outside world changes over time. Improved communications, employment opportunities outside the village, increasing urbanization, greater intervention by the state or other outside agents, the imposition of rules and regulations, but also internal factors, such as increasing education and awareness, all change the nature of the village. In general, villages in India are becoming more integrated with their wider environment. Indeed, some villages are swallowed up by urban areas and are transformed beyond recognition. So in comparing a village at two points in time, one is not really comparing like with like. In some sense, what would need to be compared is the wider social and economic system of which the village forms a part.

A related point concerns changes in the conceptual framework. This is well-illustrated by changes in production relations. In rural Bihar, for example, the semi-feudal structures that lasted until the 1980s have now been transformed by the incursions of the market into production and labour relations. So the class categories used for social analysis have to change, and the comparisons with the past are not exact. Then the longitudinal analysis is not just comparing the situation of different categories of the population, for the categories themselves change. This is also true of caste comparisons, for the role of caste is changing, as well as other social institutions. Social norms and patterns of behaviour evolve. The danger is to continue to make comparisons on the basis of a frame of reference that is no longer relevant, as the village has moved on.

A Variety of Levels

If villages need to be studied in their wider economic and social context, this has implications for the design of longitudinal research. The single village study has the tremendous advantage of depth, but to analyse the impact of external change there is a strong case for examining several villages, or a representative sample of villages, which are positioned differently with respect to that change, for much can be learned by comparing how each evolves. Examples of longitudinal work at both levels are discussed in the chapters of this book. Each has its advantages, reflecting a trade-off between scope and data quality. The village study, carried out by a small team residing for extended periods in the village, can generate high quality information that gives unparalleled understanding of institutional and personal behaviour. Larger surveys call for conventional survey methods, mainly by investigators who are data gatherers rather than researchers. Even with well-trained investigators, the information they collect is constrained by questionnaire design and determined by the nature of their contact with respondents. In reality, these approaches are complementary and should ideally be used in conjunction with each other.

One approach, which is rather underutilized, is the village survey, in the sense of a sample of villages, based on a relatively short period spent gathering information in each. This approach is disdained by economists, who doubt the accuracy of village-level data and prefer to work with households, and by anthropologists who believe that short visits can only generate superficial and often inaccurate information. And it is certainly true that in order to complete village questionnaire schedules, it is necessary to interpret vague and conflicting answers, use key informants without being able to ascertain their credibility or the reality of their knowledge, rely on brief contacts with villagers or on group discussions where answers may be guided by interest groups within the village, use inaccurate secondary data, and so on. Nevertheless, it can be argued that there would be significant returns to a greater investment in this type of approach to the analysis of development patterns, because it is a low-cost approach that is helpful for tracking change.

The Changing Observer

The anthropological and ethnographic literature is replete with discussion of the observer; this is largely absent from the economic literature. But it is certainly true, following Burawoy (2003) among others, that in longitudinal studies it is not only the observed but also the observer that changes, and also the relationship between the two. Of course, in very long-term studies, the research is often done by a succession of different researchers. These different observers bring different disciplines, understandings, and theoretical frameworks to village studies, so some of the reported differences between points in time are in fact due to differences in the observers. This is true even when the same observer is concerned, for people change as they grow older—their theoretical frameworks evolve along with their skills and experience, as well as the issues in which they are most interested. So, observations of differences over time are by their nature composed of differences in both the observer and the observed.

Probably all that one can say on this issue is that the researcher has to be aware of how his or her theorizing evolves in interaction with the contact with the village, and of the disciplinary perspectives of previous generations of researchers. This issue applies both to outsiders and to researchers who themselves originate from the regions that they study, though the problem is slightly different in the two cases. And of course, the village may itself be changed by the research, especially as villagers engage with and build their own understanding of its purpose.

There is another aspect to this latter point, for personal relationships developed in the course of long-term research. The researcher from outside is inevitably viewed in instrumental terms by villagers, but at the same time brings values and perceptions to the village that may or may not be shared but will certainly be discussed—see, for instance, Chapter 3 by Patricia Jeffery in this volume. And often it is hard for the external researcher to maintain strict neutrality when faced with conflicts or actions on which she or he has strong views. Researchers are inevitably engaged to some extent with the subjects they are researching, all the more so when contacts are maintained over long periods of time. This may imply engaging with the struggles of the poor; but at the other extreme, external researchers always face the risk of being identified with local elites, with whom they may be able to communicate more easily, affecting their ability to connect with deprived and disadvantaged groups in the village.

While there are clearly difficulties of bias and consistency here, one should not neglect a major advantage of the longitudinal study—that repeated contact builds up trust and communication between researchers and investigators on the one hand, and villagers at all levels on the other. Large household surveys, in which information is collected in short interviews, suffer from major problems of data quality; but if the investigators are known, the potential for collecting accurate information, even on sensitive subjects, is greatly enhanced. All the more so when there are renewed contacts with successive generations of villagers.

Longitudinal Studies Usually Do Not Start Out That Way

A more practical methodological problem is that longitudinal research is rarely planned in advance. Researchers acquire knowledge of, and an interest in, the areas that they study, and so may well return at a later stage in their careers to investigate change. Or researchers who are interested in change look for earlier studies that can provide them with a baseline. But in neither case is the original study designed in such a way as to provide an adequate base for future work. Harriss's chapter on the Slater villages illustrates this point. It was equally true of the work in Bihar reported in several chapters of this book. The longitudinal nature of that work gradually took shape over time, and as a result, much information from earlier surveys was not securely stored and was lost. In that case some lost data were miraculously recovered from backup files that had survived by chance; others might not be so lucky.

Another point is that very often in longitudinal work, the researcher finds herself wishing that a particular item of information had been collected at an earlier date or that standard definitions had been used for key variables. Concepts and definitions that change from one survey to the next are a constant source of difficulty.

Perhaps these problems are inevitable, since few research projects look decades ahead, but if some simple steps were taken in any surveys that might subsequently be repeated, that would certainly make it easier for longitudinal work to follow on. The most obvious is to maintain full records of households interviewed, to fully document databases, and to retain processed as well as raw data.

The Question of Data Management

Another practical problem concerns data. Longitudinal surveys generate vast amounts of information, whether in the form of researchers' field notes or in terms of quantitative data files. It seems to be frequently the case that data processing and organizing turns out to be a much larger task than originally foreseen. This problem is not confined to longitudinal work, of course, but longitudinal studies multiply the problems, requiring connections between different data sets that have used different concepts or covered different populations. The question is, what are the marginal returns (in the sense of additional knowledge) to additional information? Much information in practice goes unanalysed, as research funding comes to an end before analysis is completed.

The Chapters in This Volume

Many of the methodological points discussed previously, and their theoretical and practical implications, are explored in the chapters in this book. The book consists mainly of contributions that were first presented at a conference on village studies, with a particular focus on longitudinal research, organized by the Centre for Informal Sector and Labour Studies (CISLS) at Jawaharlal Nehru University, New Delhi with support from International Development Research Centre (IDRC), Centre de Sciences Humaines (CSH), London School of Economics and Political Science, and the Institute for Human Development (IHD), New Delhi, in November 2012. The conference brought together leading researchers in this field, many of whom were actively engaged in village studies with recent findings to report. Although the focus of the conference was on India, a few scholars working on other countries also participated, with the objective of connecting with a broader perspective in the developing world at large, particularly with respect to methodological insights. Given the widespread interest in the conference, it was decided to put together a volume which may serve as a reference for research on villages in South Asia, especially research into long-term changes in economic and social relationships using longitudinal methods. To that end, a number of papers from the conference have been revised and expanded for the present volume in the light of the discussions, and some additional papers have been included.

In the following pages, we briefly introduce the contributions to this volume. The aim is not to summarize the papers, which cover a wide range of methodological issues and topics. We merely provide some pointers to the nature of the contributions and the issues that they address.

Three broad areas of concern are addressed in this volume. The first relates to the method and conceptual framework of longitudinal village studies, either in the sense of how information is collected or the relationships between the investigator and the village, or in terms of the ways in which information is used and analysed. The second aims at a broad understanding of the villages across different dimensions of economy and society, offering the reader wide and integrated accounts of particular villages. And the third explores particular themes in some detail within this broader framework. In reality, the papers cannot be rigorously classified in terms of one or other of these concerns, for most touch on all the three areas, and we do not propose any precise categorization. However, in organizing the book we start with chapters that are more methodological in focus, move on to chapters which take a broad brush approach to the village, and finish with chapters that concentrate mainly on particular topics.

The first three chapters after Introduction, by John Harriss, Patricia Jeffery, and Shapan Adnan, all examine methodological issues in depth. Harriss's chapter draws lessons from the repeated surveys of the villages in Tamil Nadu first studied by Gilbert Slater a hundred years ago. These are among the oldest longitudinal village surveys and Harriss's description of the changes in the villages is connected with a discussion of methodological problems of undertaking village surveys at long intervals, with different teams and different methods, which nevertheless provides insights into the changing agrarian structure. Jeffery's contribution is a sensitive and personalized account of the issues that a researcher has to confront in detailed village-level studies, based on her work in Bijnor in UP, and she discusses the fieldwork methods she adopted to address them. This chapter is an important contribution in that the subject of the chapter is the author herself; her reflections enable readers to understand the nature of observer bias, as well as the challenges of doing fieldwork in a patriarchal north Indian state, such as UP.

The third chapter in this group, by Shapan Adnan, provides an overview of a number of long-term village studies in Bangladesh, the methods they have used, the issues they have addressed, and their findings. He offers a critical analysis of the methods used, their strengths and weaknesses, with particular reference to the specific advantages and problems of longitudinal studies. This is the only non-Indian contribution in the book, but his review shows that much can be learned by examining longitudinal village research in a wider South Asian context.

The next group of contributions presents broad empirical patterns and findings for individual villages or groups of villages in different parts of India, aiming at an overall understanding of economic and social relationships over time. These include chapters on Palanpur in UP by Himanshu and Nicholas Stern; on several villages in Bihar by Gerry Rodgers, Sunil K. Mishra, and Alakh N. Sharma; on two villages in Haryana by Surinder S. Jodhka; on a village in eastern UP by Ravi Srivastava; on two villages in northeast Bihar by Praveen Jha and Avanindra Nath Thakur; and a review of a number of village studies in Tamil Nadu, many involving resurveys, by John Harriss and J. Jeyaranjan.

The chapter by Himanshu and Stern provides a large canvas for tracking changes in the UP village of Palanpur, which has been studied intensively since 1957–8. While largely focused on economic changes in the village since that date, it highlights the changes in social and political structure, including dimensions that have been slow to change despite rapid economic progress. The chapter by Rodgers, Mishra, and Sharma draws on longitudinal surveys over four decades from a set of villages in neighbouring Bihar. It portrays the breaking down of semi-feudal structures, and uses longitudinal data on households to explore determinants of changes in their fortunes. Jodhka's description of Haryana villages also highlights the changing agrarian structure and the conditions of agricultural labour in an economy that benefited from high productivity growth following the 'Green Revolution'. Jodhka highlights the obvious but largely ignored link between caste structure and class relations in a changing agrarian economy, and explores some key methodological issues. Srivastava also highlights interactions between class and caste in processes of change in agrarian relations in a UP village, and in particular shows how the labour market has evolved. Jha and Thakur examine similar issues in northeast Bihar, highlighting the important role of migration, and the role of external factors, such as macroeconomic policies. And Harriss and Jeyaranjan bring together results from several long-term studies in Tamil Nadu, which document connections between changes in production structure and changes in social relations.

All these chapters provide integrated overviews of inter-temporal change at the village level, covering a wide range of economic and social issues, although the combination of themes differs significantly from one chapter to the next. Most examine the changing agrarian structures and systems, as well as access to land, livestock, and other resources. All have something to say about the changing landscape of labour and patterns of employment and unemployment. Each study then tries to engage with the dialectics of structural and conjunctural change, including the connections between village-level relationships and overall state policies.

The final group of chapters uses longitudinal data to examine particular topics in greater depth. Contributions include a chapter on non-farm diversification in Palanpur by Himanshu, Peter Lanjouw, Rinku Murgai, and Nicholas Stern; an analysis of education, fertility, and mobility in villages near Coimbatore by Judith Heyer; a study of changes in the rural labour market in Bihar by Janine Rodgers; an application of longitudinal data to the analysis of migration from rural Bihar by Amrita Datta; a chapter on the connections between public services and social structures in Palanpur by Dipa Sinha, Dinesh Kumar Tiwari, Ruchira Bhattacharya, and Ruth Kattumuri; a study of land in a Maharashtra village by R. Ramakumar; and a study of long-term change in urban development and urban–rural relations in Tamil Nadu by Barbara Harriss-White.

While not exhaustive, these chapters demonstrate the value of longitudinal surveys to understand a variety of dynamic relationships. Unlike a traditional village economy with a focus on agriculture and land relations, the growing importance of the non-farm economy in Palanpur is not only changing the distribution of gains from income growth but also changing the way different sections of the village community, particularly the poor and marginalized castes, engage with economic change. Himanshu, Lanjouw, Murgai, and Stern describe and analyse the impact of the non-farm economy in Palanpur, while linking the changes in the village to the larger story of non-farm diversification currently underway in the Indian economy. Judith Heyer highlights the integration of the Gounders in Tamil Nadu into the local industrial economy and how the position of this caste changed over time as a result of both economic and educational strategy. The evolving interaction between social and economic factors can be seen over a thirty-year perspective. The chapter by Janine Rodgers highlights the changing nature of labour markets in rural Bihar. There has been substantial occupational diversification, much of it connected with commuting and migration, and with rising educational levels. But this pattern is highly gendered, and women face more difficulty than men in escaping traditional roles. Longitudinal data also show rising real wages, increasingly dependent on factors external to the village. More details of the migration aspect of Bihar surveys are provided in Amrita Datta's chapter. Longitudinal data permit a much more systematic analysis of migration and its impact, which varies greatly from village to village. Migration is not only changing incomes, but also skills and attitudes. The chapter by Sinha, Tiwari, Bhattacharya, and Kattumuri highlights what is happening to women and social institutions in a village society that is changing in terms of political and social structures. An important issue that the chapter investigates is the lack of development on social indicators despite economic progress. It links this to the inequality in village society, which not only restricts access of vulnerable groups to public services but also results in lack of public action. Ramakumar's chapter looks at the old but important issue of changes in land ownership in a Maharashtra village. Inequality of landholdings persisted even as other aspects of the village economy changed, while landlessness increased.

The final chapter, by Barbara Harriss-White, is different in focus, since it is based on an urban longitudinal study rather than village-level work. But given the growing importance of urban–rural integration in India, this provides a valuable additional perspective. She addresses the evolution of urban–rural linkages in a small town in Tamil Nadu, and the analytical challenges of comprehending these. With the emergence of the non-farm sector as an important driver of rural transformation, the growth of urban–rural interlinkages challenges the notion of villages as a close-knit society, and also affects the evolution of incomes and inequality of income distribution in the villages.

The purpose of the book is not to attempt a comprehensive review of longitudinal research. Rather, by bringing together these different contributions in a single volume, we aim to illustrate the range of analytical and policy issues that can be addressed, highlight the problems and potentials of the longitudinal method, and encourage more work in this tradition. The contributions to the volume are not uniform. They range from what Clifford Geertz called 'thick description', to fine-grained abstract accounts. Nor is there any attempt to squeeze these different studies into a common theoretical framework. What they have in common is a belief in empirical methods at the ground level, a sense that progress in understanding requires an integration between observation and theory in a long-term perspective, implying a broadly heterodox approach to economic and social research, and a shared commitment to progressive socio-economic transformation.

References

Bailey, F.G. 1957. *Caste and the Economic Frontier: A Village in Highland Orissa.* Manchester: Manchester University Press.

Banerjee, Abhijit V. and Esther Duflo. 2011. *Poor Economics*. Noida, India: Random House India.

Breman, Jan, Peter Kloos, and Ashwani Saith. 1997. *The Village in Asia Revisited.* New Delhi: Oxford University Press.

Burawoy, Michael. 2003. 'Revisits: An Outline of a Theory of Reflexive Ethnography', *American Sociological Review*, 68 (5): 654–79.

Dasgupta, Biplab. 1975. 'A Typology of Village Socio-Economic Systems: From Indian Village Studies', *Economic and Political Weekly*, 10 (33/35): 1395–414.

———. 1978. *Village Studies in the Third World.* Delhi: Hindustan Publishing Corporation.

Dube, S.C. 1955. *Indian Village*. Ithaca: Cornell University Press.

Epstein, T.S. 1962. *Economic Development and Social Change in South India.* Manchester: Manchester University Press.

Etienne, Gilbert. 2014. *Indian Villages, Achievements and Alarm Bells, 1952–2012.* Geneva: Graduate Institute Publications.

Harriss, John. 2008. 'Notes on Village Studies from an Anthropological Perspective', paper presented at Studying Village Economies in India: A Colloquium on Methodology, Chalsa, West Bengal, 21–4 December 2008.

Harriss-White, Barbara and John Harriss. 2007. 'Green Revolution and After: The "North Arcot papers" and Long-term Studies of the Political Economy of Rural Development in South India', Queen Elizabeth House Working Paper Series Number 146, Oxford, UK.

Hopper, W.D. 1965. 'Allocation Efficiency in "Traditional Indian Agriculture"', *Journal of Farm Economics*, 47 (3): 611–24.

Lanjouw, Peter and Nicholas Stern. 1998. *Economic Development in Palanpur Over Five Decades.* Oxford: Clarendon Press.

Lindberg, Staffan. 2012. 'Rural India 1970–2005: An Arduous Transition to What?', *The Indian Journal of Labour Economics*, 55 (1): 61–75.

Ramachandran, V.K., Vikas Rawal, and Madhura Swaminathan. 2010. *Socio-Economic Surveys of Three Villages in Andhra Pradesh: A Study of Agrarian Relations.* New Delhi: Tulika Books.

Rodgers, Gerry, Amrita Datta, Janine Rodgers, Sunil K. Mishra, and Alakh N. Sharma. 2013. *The Challenge of Inclusive Development in Rural Bihar.* New Delhi: Manak Publications.

Slater, Gilbert (ed.). 1918. *Some South Indian Villages.* Oxford: Oxford University Press.

Srinivas, M.N. 1963. *India's Villages*. Bombay: Asia Publishing House.

Walker, T.S. and J.G. Ryan. 1990. *Village and Household Economies in India's Semi-arid Tropics*. Baltimore and London: The Johns Hopkins University Press.

2

JOHN HARRISS

The Story of the 'Slater Village' Studies of Agrarian Change in Tamil Nadu, and Methodological Reflections Upon Them

The 'Slater villages' are probably becoming fairly well-known by now, even outside the relatively small group of scholars and researchers who are interested in rural Tamil Nadu. Gilbert Slater, appointed Professor of Indian Economics at the University of Madras in 1915, thought that the understanding of poverty was the most important task for economists working in India, and that a good way of going about it was to study villages. So, he says, '[o]n taking up my appointment as Professor of Indian Economics.... I determined to direct the attention of students towards the study of particular villages.' He published the results of his students' work, carried out in 1916–17, with admirable speed. *Some South Indian Villages* was published in 1918. It includes studies of villages from across the Madras Presidency, five of them in present-day Tamil Nadu.

Twenty years later, in the mid-to-late 1930s, Slater's successor in the Chair of Economics in Madras, P.J. Thomas (later the first Economic Adviser to the Government of India, after Independence) conducted a further round of studies in the same villages in the context of the

Depression (Thomas and Ramakrishnan 1940). Some of the Tamil villages were studied again by the Agro-Economic Research Centre (AERC) in the University of Madras in 1958–60,[1] and Margaret Haswell from the University of Oxford drew on these studies, as well as on her own findings from visits to the villages in 1961, for her book *Economics of Development in Village India* (1967). Another 20 years on, in the early 1980s, the late S. Guhan at the Madras Institute of Development Studies organized a further round of studies, published as Working Papers by the Institute, though one of them—written by Guhan himself with the anthropologist Joan Mencher—on the village Iruvelpattu was published in *Economic and Political Weekly* (Guhan and Mencher 1983a, 1983b). Most recently, in 2008, J. Jeyaranjan, K. Nagaraj, and I embarked on another round of studies (2010 and 2012), though limitations of resources, financial and personal, have meant that thus far we have been able to conduct studies of only two of the five Tamil villages.

Sample Selection

Slater was well aware of the fact that '[n]o single village can be typical of the Presidency of Madras', but he avoided questions of sample design by adopting 'the simple principle of taking those that were most available. I asked students of the University who were willing to help, make surveys of their native villages during the long vacation' (Slater 1918: 1). The consequence of this was that the five Tamil villages studied by his students, reflect a bias towards places that had significant numbers of higher castes, who were quite disproportionately represented amongst the students of the university at the time. Four of them are also villages that are near to big towns, though given that Tamil Nadu has long been the most urbanized and best connected of all India's major states, this is not particularly surprising. They are also fairly well-distributed across the state, from north to south, though there are none in the west. Dusi, located in the old North Arcot district at the northern end of the state, was a Brahmin

[1] I have not seen the AERC studies myself, and am uncertain as to whether all the five villages were studied. Gangaikondan and Dusi certainly were.

village, situated just outside the town of Chengalpattu. Though there were only 66 Brahmin families amongst the 250 or so households in the village, almost all of the rest were tenants or servants of the Brahmins. Further south, in the old South Arcot District, there is a village of Iruvelpattu, situated on the main road a little south of the town of Villupuram, studied by Slater himself with the assistance of E.V. Sundraram Reddi, who was a son of the (Telugu-speaking) Reddiar landlord whose descendants still control the village (Harriss, Jeyaranjan, and Nagaraj 2010). Further south again is a village of Palakkurichi, in Thanjavur—though this is not a 'Brahmin village', as many used to be in the district—but a village dominated by Telugu-speaking Kamma Naidus. Then comes Vadamalaipuram in the old Ramanathapuram District, close to Sivakasi, dominated by Nayakars; and furthest south of all, Gangaikondan, well-connected with the city of Tirunelveli, which was then a Brahmin village, in which Brahmin landlords controlled the village economy. Reddiars, Kamma Naidus, and Nayakars were all communities from amongst the 'forward' non-Brahmins of the old Madras Presidency—those who organized and were organized by the Non-Brahmin Movement in the early decades of the twentieth century.

The Village Questionnaire

Slater worked out a detailed questionnaire for his students, prefacing it with the instruction '[e]mbody in your report the official information which is available but endeavour also to test its accuracy and to correct it when possible' (Slater 1918: 22). His 'Scheme for Survey of a Ryotwari Village' starts with the survey number of the village, a description of its location and geography, and then includes the following sections. Throughout he distinguishes between 'the village' and the *paracheri*, reflecting his view that the worlds of the Dalits and of caste people are quite distinct:

Population

Slater seems not to have expected his investigators to undertake a household census, but rather to refer to 'the last two or more censuses'. He was concerned especially that they should 'ascertain whether the population is increasing or decreasing'. Still, he wanted '[n]umber of families and individuals in each caste' and '[n]umber of children in families (a) Living (b) Dead'. In practice the demographic data included in the five village studies from 1916–17 vary in their precision.

Land

Land use data is taken from the village records, though he says 'some correction may be necessary'. The studies do generally reproduce these data, and provide information on irrigation sources and their condition.

Occupation of Land

Here he sought data on the distribution of landholdings and on the prevailing tenurial contracts, together with a record of the settlement of land revenue. He also wanted information on 'agricultural workers who neither own nor rent land'. The studies generally reproduce data on the distribution of pattas (official records of land ownership), with a descriptive commentary on the concentration of landholdings. No attempt was made to record areas of land held by households; there are quite careful accounts of tenure contracts; and accounts are given of the numbers of *padials* ('attached labourers', at the time of the surveys usually bonded, it seems—Slater says they are 'a sort of serf') and of their conditions of work. In one village, Gangaikondan, it was recorded that there were no padials, and data are given on the employment of wage labour.

Agriculture

Data were sought on cropping patterns; methods of cultivation; costs of cultivation; the organization of irrigation; holdings of livestock and methods of breeding and rearing; cattle diseases and methods of combating them; manuring practices; insect pests and methods of combating them; how and where wood was obtained for different purposes; and description of 'any recent improvement in methods of cultivation'. There is considerable variation across the five studies in the extent to which all these data were supplied.

The Village

This was to feature a description of the village and of its buildings, and of the distances from people's homes to the fields.

Subsidiary Industries

Data were sought on the numbers engaged in weaving and other crafts, together with notes on their economics. Investigators were asked to assess 'whether any village industry is developing or increasing; or, on the other hand dying, decaying ...'

Village Trade

Descriptions were sought of where and how people purchased their needs and sold their products; of the location of the village in regard to roads and railways and markets; of the extent of cooperation, if any.

Economic Condition of Village

Data were sought on wages in cash and kind; prices of staples; savings and debt; the workings of cooperative credit societies, where they existed; village funds (or 'communal income'); land prices; expenditure on festivals; and on the impact of recent legislation regarding agricultural loans.

Sanitary Condition of Village

Data on the prevalence of major diseases; estimated rate of infant mortality; snake bites; water supply and 'insanitary habits'; and customs with regard to infant marriage and purdah were also to be collected.

Education

Data on numbers of schools, and numbers of children attending them, by gender; 'average duration of school life'; literacy levels in both 'the Vernacular' and in English; whether or not people have gone out for education and what has happened to them were also included.

Village Administration

Data on panchayats, village officers, policing, and the history of crime were also sought.

History and Prospects of the Village

Slater asked for evidence on economic progress or deterioration, and on opportunities for improvement

The Findings of the Original Studies and Their Limitations

Slater's questionnaire made for an exhaustive description of the villages (how many village researchers subsequently have gone to so much trouble to record the common diseases of cattle, for instance? Or, if their research concerns have not expressly included questions relating to health, even the diseases most commonly afflicting people.) The published studies are, unsurprisingly, uneven. Those of Vadamalaipuram and of Gangaikondan are the most detailed, and follow the questionnaire most closely. Slater's own study of Iruvelpattu includes less quantitative data than others but has quite a strong focus on poverty and on the low productivity of labour. As he wrote 'various strands of economic, social, and religious conditions and customs are strangely and deftly interwoven in the web of South Indian life, and low wages, low efficiency, and high abstinence are the ground plan of the pattern' (cited by Haswell 1967: 3). He was evidently appalled at the condition of the padials (bonded labourers)—who he thought were probably less well-fed than were men doing 'hard labour' in jail in Madras—and he saw the village as having a 'population problem', relieved by emigration to Ceylon. Emigration is mentioned in three of the other studies as well. Slater was also occupied with problems of sanitation in the villages, and with education; and he paid a lot of attention to innovation of one sort or another. This included a brief account of the effort of two 'well-to-do ryots' to set up a sugar refinery.

In general, the accounts for Gangaikondan, Dusi, and Iruvelpattu show the existence of 'landlordism', with extensive renting out of land and indications that landlords were also moneylenders as well as, some of them, being employers of large numbers of bonded labourers. In the other two villages, both the Naidus of Palakkurichi and the Nayakars of Vadamalaipuram were mostly owner-cultivators, but among them there were also owners of landholdings of considerable size and employers of numbers of bonded labourers. In Vadamalaipuram there were 'only [*sic*] three [landholdings] above 100 acres there being also one of 100 acres' (Slater 1918: 32)—and the 1983 study shows the continuing high concentration of land ownership in the village, describing the Nayakars as 'landlords'. There are clear indications, too, in all the studies of the practices associated with what anthropologists later described as the '*jajmani* system', and all the villages had a fair range of artisans and other specialists—in Vadamalaipuram, for example, goldsmiths, carpenters, blacksmiths, dhobis, barbers, potters, a tailor, flower sellers, and 'Telugu shepherds'. The distinctions between those then labelled as 'the depressed classes', and the caste-people of the main villages is always emphasized. Slater's suggestion, with regard to Iruvelpattu that '[t]o a great extent the village is self-supporting … (an) almost self-contained Dravidian community' (1918: 11), seems reasonable enough—yet it is important to note that all the studies show up both the connectedness of rural society with the towns, and the presence of the state through such institutions as schools and cooperative societies.

The studies might be compared with the rural 'sociography' that was carried on in Eastern Europe in the 1920s and 1930s, detailed descriptive studies such as Gyula Illyes's *People of the Puszta* (1967 [1936])—though this one, at least, is more literary in its presentation. Most critically, for longitudinal research, the surveys—in 1916–17, and again in the Thomas and Ramakrishnan studies in the 1930s—did not extend to enquiries at the household level. They offer no panel data. They offer no precision at all with regard to such crucial matters as the distribution of landholdings (data are given rather on the distribution of pattas, according to the village records), or on patterns of or the regularity of employment. They provide no basis either for the measurement of poverty or for analysis of the conditions of the reproduction of poverty, except at the level of broad description. Still, they seem to represent a significant pioneering effort in agrarian research.

Later Studies—Findings and Limitations

The Thomas and Ramakrishnan studies follow the same pattern as those conducted by Slater's students, though they are rather more consistent and include a lot more quantitative data, including much more data on indebtedness—unsurprisingly so, in the context of the Depression—and also on land values, as well as on both cultivation methods and on costs and returns from cultivation. These suggest stagnation in the agricultural economy and the failure of food supply to keep pace with population growth, but also a decline in real farm incomes. Manikumar, in his 2003 book on the Depression years in Madras, draws attention to the evidence from the village studies of sharply increased absentee landlordism—and the study of Gangaikondan, for example, reports that this tendency 'is taken advantage of by the tenantry, who put forth demands for greater share than the customary one' (Thomas and Ramakrishnan 1940: 70). The Gangaikondan study also shows that the exodus of former Brahmin landlords, who had rarely taken very much direct interest in cultivation, was well under way; and many Brahmin families had left Dusi, too. The increase in absentee landlordism was part of a wider rural exodus. The rural population had generally declined with people having moved to the towns, even though there had also been an influx of repatriates from amongst those who had emigrated for work. Artisans had often left the villages and the remaining weavers had been impoverished in the Depression years. There were apparently increasing numbers of landless agricultural labourers, as well as of tenants-at-will, though in the absence of the more detailed data that are derived from household-level data it is impossible to quantify this trend. There were still significant numbers of padials—the Iruvelpattu study recorded 85 in 1937.

Set against these indications of deterioration or stagnation, there were 'definite improvements that have been made in some aspects of rural life' (Thomas, cited by Haswell 1967: 4). Communications had greatly improved with the advent of the motor bus; educational facilities had improved; more healthcare was available in the villages, even if it was still meagre; rates of interest had fallen and 'professional money-lending was giving way to genuine investment' (Haswell 1967: 4). The villages had become less self-sufficient in respect of some food items, and of manufactures (a change with perhaps both positive and negative implications).

The unpublished AERC studies from 1958–60 are, unfortunately, hard to find, though there are accounts of them, and data from them are recorded in the Madras Institute of Development Studies (MIDS), studies from the early 1980s of Dusi and Gangaikondan. These were the first studies of the Slater villages to have been based on systematic household-level data—though, given that the basic data have not, as far as I have been able to establish, been preserved—they still do not supply material for panel studies.[2] Haswell's accounts of the villages are interesting, but brief, and she was mainly concerned with analysis of particular economic variables, such as land prices and rents. She was, however, on the trail of the Big Landlord of Iruvelpattu, as he was described by Guhan and Mencher in 1983, who reported that he continued to employ 22 of the 36 padials whom they identified in the village (and whom Jeyaranjan, Nagaraj, and I found still to dominate the village in 2008; see Harriss et al. 2010). Her rather fragmented, episodic account includes other such interesting nuggets about agrarian production relations as her explanation for strikingly low levels of literacy in Dusi: 'Absentee landlords owned half the cultivable lands in 1961, and the educated classes were mainly performing the function of Proprietor Investor-cum-Trader[3] in Conjeevaram, leaving a preponderant number of permanent labourers or 'servants' to cultivate their lands in Dusi whose families were ill-educated, or were entirely lacking in formal education' (Haswell 1967: 50). She notes, too, that the real wages paid to agricultural labour were in accord with 'the bold generalization that 3 kg of cereals is the usual reward for a day's work in a subsistence economy, whether it be in India now, Russia at the beginning of the century, or France in the eighteenth century' (1967: 15). Guhan and Mencher thought that the real wage levels obtaining in Iruvelpattu in 1982 showed no change, but the historic level had been

[2] In the case of the old AERC for Eastern India, based at Santiniketan in West Bengal, by contrast, the schedules from different survey rounds in the villages that had been studied, were preserved, certainly up to 1982, when I was able to reanalyse them for the two villages that I studied, and to analyse household mobility.

[3] Here we see evidence of the presence of those later described as 'the provincial propertied class', still with a foot in the agricultural economy, but also much engaged in urbanized economic activity.

broken through by 2008. By that time the daily wage for men was equivalent to 6 kg or more of paddy.

There are glimpses, no more, in Haswell's notes of the impact of agricultural and rural development policies that had been pursued in the 1950s; but then the impact of the 'green revolution' emerged as a major theme running through the MIDS studies in the early 1980s. At last we see some dynamism in the agricultural economy in the findings from the studies. Guhan intended, however, as I know from conversations with him at the time, that the studies should develop the same broad description that was attempted both by Slater and by Thomas and Ramakrishnan. There was, quite deliberately, to be no 'hypothesis testing', and no framing of the research by the sorts of Marxian ideas that informed so much research at that time on agrarian change. The fieldwork for the studies involved detailed household censuses (or in the case of the Gangaikondan study, because of the sheer size of the village, a census of about one-third of the households) and some supplementary studies of the costs and returns from cultivation, as well as limited ethnographic observation. The studies also brought together data from the village records, the census and such other published data as were relevant. It is unfortunate that once again, and to my surprise, the data were not preserved in an archive at MIDS.

Jeyaranjan, Nagaraj, and I proceeded in 2007–8 in the same way as Guhan and his co-workers, undertaking detailed household censuses in Iruvelpattu and Gangaikondan—the latter no mean undertaking given that there are over 1,700 households spread across the many hamlets of this very big revenue village—and supplementing them with ethnographic observation, interviews with key informants (such as both the Big Landlord and the 'the *cheri* intellectual' in Iruvelpattu), and in Gangaikondan a small supplementary survey of employment. In the end, however, whereas Guhan and his co-workers did produce descriptive village monographs, our published articles are more thematic. Each of them, while including a good deal of descriptive material on population trends, education and social services and on agriculture, has an analytical focus on 'Land, Labour, and Caste Politics' (the title of the Iruvelpattu paper)—that is, on caste relations, agrarian structure, and the diversification of employment (we even describe Gangaikondan as being, in a sense, 'post-agrarian'). This was partly because it seemed to us to be unlikely that a descriptive village monograph would be published these days, even in a journal such as *Economic and Political Weekly* (EPW) (and Surinder S. Jodhka [2013] cut out quite a lot of the article, including much of the statistical material, when he reproduced it in his edited collection of village studies from *EPW*). But the thematic focus reflects what seemed to us to be the 'big story' of change in the villages.[4]

If, in the early 1980s, the green revolution was the major story, it was clear that by the early twenty-first century, the agricultural economy of Tamil Nadu had generally stagnated once again. Migration—short and long term—and the diversification of employment and of incomes away from agriculture, even if not necessarily the diversification of rural economic activity, were extremely important trends. They have gone along with increasing complaints about 'labour shortage' in agriculture, which may explain the extensive mechanization that has taken place. Nowadays it is unusual to see ploughing being carried on with bullocks, and harvesting of paddy is almost invariably done with combine harvesters. There is now relatively little demand for male labour in agriculture either in Iruvelpattu or in Gangaikondan, apart from those who are employed as machine operators. Agricultural labour in these villages has become even more feminized, with transplanting, carried on by women, now being the most labour-intensive operation.

Alongside these important trends, there is qualitative evidence of the decline, if not of the demise of landed caste power—though it has persisted to a greater extent in Iruvelpattu than in Gangaikondan—and of the increasing assertion of Dalits. It is important not to over-generalize, however, and to recognize considerable diversity in the fortunes of Dalits both within and between villages and regions of the state. Upward mobility comparable with that which we record in the case of the Pallars of Gangaikondan has not been achieved by the Paraiyars of Iruvelpattu. While poverty persists—more clearly so in Iruvelpattu than in Gangaikondan—we think that there is evidence both of increase in real wage rates and incomes, and of positive effects on livelihoods and well-being from MGNREGA, the availability of rice and other commodities through the PDS, and of functioning schools and primary

[4] It is true, too, that the themes of the two recent studies pretty certainly reflect the fact that I, unlike my two colleagues, or Margaret Haswell, am not an agricultural economist.

healthcare centres—though we are unable to document these with anything like the precision that is to be desired. This could, however, have been achieved only with further survey-based research for which we did not have resources.[5]

Methodological Reflections[6]

1. I believe that the Slater studies constitute a valuable source on the history of rural Tamil Nadu, as is shown in the use made of them by the historians Baker (1975) and Manikumar (2003) in their studies of the 1930s. But the studies offer only snapshots at particular points in time, and for their potential as historical documents to be realized, much more needs to be done to place them in context both historically and geographically. Used in conjunction with data on trends in politics and policy, as well as in population and migration, the structure and growth of the labour force, urbanization, agricultural production, and so on, some of the limitations of the snapshots can be addressed. It is important, too, to contextualize the studies geographically—though there are aspects of the social geography of Tamil Nadu that remain poorly understood. Why, for instance, should the status and living conditions of the (SC/Dalit) Pallars of the south of the state generally be so much better than those of the Paraiyars of the north?
2. The point about the importance of contextualizing village studies is probably a general one, and not simply one that refers to the Slater

[5] This very brief account of trends of change in rural Tamil Nadu, based on our studies of the two Slater villages, may be compared with the generally comparable findings of Staffan Lindberg and his co-workers (Lindberg 2012), and of Isabelle Guerin and her colleagues (Guerin, Venkatasubramanian, and Michiels 2012). Guerin reports sharply increasing internal differentiation amongst Dalits—which is what we would expect in Gangaikondan as well. The only point of difference between Lindberg's and Guerin's findings, and those Jeyaranjan, Nagaraj, and I have reported, is that Lindberg reckons that agricultural labour has become 'masculinized'—though this seems to be because in the villages he describes weeding of paddy is now done with chemicals.

[6] I will not enter here into discussion of the general problems associated with long-term village studies, on which I would refer readers to an analysis in Harriss-White and Harriss (2007).

village studies. All too often village researchers have paid little attention to the context. A cognate point is that scholars have rather rarely sought to study clusters of villages, though the value of this is indicated, I think, in the studies of villages in an irrigation system in Andhra Pradesh by Robert Wade (1998 [1988]), that allowed him to develop an explanation for variations in collective action, and in some of the work of the late Ashok Rudra on the ways in which markets are fragmented by village differences (as, for example, in his contribution to Desai, Rudolph, and Rudra 1984).

3. As I have noted, the first two rounds of the Slater village studies are limited partly by the fact that they were not based on systematically collected household data, whether on a census or sample basis. It is a great shame that data from the household censuses that were completed in more recent studies have not been preserved. The surveys make for no possibilities of taking up panel studies.
4. Slater himself, and later S. Guhan, sought to produce general descriptive studies of villages, the latter expressly rejecting one particular way in which research on agrarian change has often been framed. One can see the point of this, and be sympathetic to the attempt to record village life as a whole at a particular point in time (cattle diseases and all), and then to develop analysis through inference from observation. Yet it must be asked not only whether such 'sociographic' studies are worthwhile, but even whether they are really possible. They are not. Observers, after all, bring to their observations some particular concepts—'data' are constructed by such categories as 'village', 'class', 'household', or 'landholding'; and selection inevitably takes place, even when efforts are made to minimize the role played by the biases of the individual researcher.
5. This rather basic point also affects efforts to use successive studies of particular villages in order to study change over time. As has been recognized, even if the same researcher studies the same place at different points in time, her observations will be subject, at least to an extent, to her changing ideas and concerns. As Harriss-White and Harriss wrote, 'rigorously replicated resurveys of whole villages have never yet been undertaken. They do not seem to be possible. Both researchers and the researched change, and, through both contact and reflection, they each change one another' (2007: 15). I think that Jeyaranjan, Nagaraj, and I have to admit, for instance, that both

we and, to an extent certainly, our respondents were less interested in the economics of agriculture in Iruvelpattu and Gangaikondan in 2008 than we and they might have been in 1984—and more interested in the quality of public services and the availability of non-farm opportunities. Of course, this kind of bias can be guarded against, but particularly when researchers are referring to earlier studies by others it must often be the case that data from different points in time are not strictly comparable.

6. The sorts of broad, descriptive surveys that are the basis of the various 'Slater studies' should probably be regarded as preliminary or reconnaissance studies, and taken as the starting point for more detailed studies. In our Gangaikondan study, for example, we report that '[t]he numbers of households in the village ... report(ing) themselves as depending entirely on agriculture, either through cultivation or through agricultural labour, or a combination of the two, are quite small—no more than 20 per cent at the very most' (Harriss, Jeyaranjan, and Nagaraj 2012: 30). Yet, as I noted whilst undertaking restudies of villages in the North Arcot district of Tamil Nadu in the early 1980s, the ways in which respondents answered questions about their employment, and the ways in which these questions were framed, tended to conceal complexity through such blanket categories as (then) 'agricultural labour'. We really need much more detailed studies of employment patterns and of the allocation of time, as also of household budgets—and ideally we would be able to compare these with comparably constructed data sets from earlier surveys (as some researchers have been able to do, for example, in the 'North Arcot studies': Harriss-White and Janakarajan 2004; and in the studies in villages in the Kaveri delta by Djurfeldt et al. 2008).

In sum, resurveys of the 'Slater villages' over the greater part of a century have created an extraordinary, and probably unique, historical record, but they are a limited instrument for the testing of hypotheses generated from economic theory, or for sociological analysis.

References

Baker, C.J. 1975. *The Politics of South India, 1920–1937*. Cambridge: Cambridge University Press.

Desai, M., S.H. Rudolph, and A. Rudra (eds). 1984. *Agrarian Power and Agricultural Productivity in South Asia*. New Delhi: Oxford University Press.

Djurfeldt, G., V. Athreya, N. Jayakumar, S. Lindberg, A. Rajagopal, and R. Vidyasagar. 2008. 'Agrarian Change and Social Mobility in Tamil Nadu', *Economic and Political Weekly*, 43 (45): 50–61.

Guerin, I., G. Venkatasubramanian, and Sébastien Michiels. 2012. 'Labour in Contemporary South India', paper presented at the conference on Indian Capitalism in Development, Queen Elizabeth House, University of Oxford, UK, July 2012.

Guhan, S. and J. Mencher. 1983a. 'Iruvelpattu Revisited', *Economic and Political Weekly*, 18 (23): 1013–28.

———. 1983b. 'Iruvelpattu Revisited', *Economic and Political Weekly*, 18 (24): 1063–74.

Harriss, John, J. Jeyaranjan, and K. Nagaraj. 2010. 'Land, Labour and Caste Politics in Rural Tamil Nadu in the Twentieth Century: Iruvelpattu 1916–2008', *Economic and Political Weekly*, 45 (31): 47–61.

———. 2012. 'Rural Urbanism in Tamil Nadu: Economy and Society in Gangaikondan 1916–2012. Notes on a "Slater" Village', *Review of Agrarian Studies*, 2 (2): 29–59.

Harriss-White, B. and John Harriss. 2007. 'Green Revolution and After: The "North Arcot Papers" and Long-Term Studies of the Political Economy of Rural Development in South India', Working Paper Number 146, Queen Elizabeth House, UK: University of Oxford.

Harriss-White, B. and S. Janakarajan (eds). 2004. *Rural India Facing the 21st Century. Essays on Long Term Village Change and Recent Development Policy*. London: Anthem Press.

Haswell, M. 1967. *Economics of Development in Village India*. London: Routledge and Kegan Paul.

Illyes, G. 1967[1936]. *People of the Puszta*. Budapest: Corvina Press.

Jodhka, S. (ed.). 2013. *Village Society (Readings in the Economy, Polity and Society Series. Essays from the Economic and Political Weekly)*. Hyderabad: Orient BlackSwan.

Lindberg, S. 2012. 'Rural India 1970–2005: An Arduous Transition to What?' *Indian Journal of Labour Economics*, 55 (1): 61–75.

Manikumar, K.A. 2003. *Colonial Economy in the Great Depression: Madras (1929–1937)*. Hyderabad: Orient Longman.

Slater, G. 1918. *Some South Indian Villages*. Oxford: Oxford University Press.

Thomas, P.J. and K.C. Ramakrishnan. 1940. *Some South Indian Villages: A Resurvey*. Madras: University of Madras, Madras Economics Series No. 4.

Wade, R. 1998 [1988]. *Village Republics: Economic Conditions for Collective Action in South India*. Cambridge and New York: Cambridge University Press.

3

PATRICIA JEFFERY

Plain Tales from the Plains

A Personal Account of Researching in Rural Bijnor over Three Decades

I first visited rural Bijnor in north–western Uttar Pradesh in early 1982 to research the social organization of childbearing, not expecting that it would be the first of several 'punctuated revisits' (Burawoy 2003). The subsequent projects explored women's autonomy in relation to demographic change, fertility and population politics, health, education, and gender politics in general (Jeffery and Jeffery 1996a; Jeffery and Jeffery 1997; Jeffrey, Jeffery, and Jeffery 2008). Communal politics joined this mix over the years (Jeffery and Jeffery 2006). The Bijnor research, then, has spanned from shortly after the Emergency (1975–7) through an era characterized by economic reforms, 'India shining', and increasingly communalized politics. And central to the research trajectory has been the ambition to locate ordinary people's experiences and understandings on this broader canvass of secular changes that have impacted on them in diverse ways.

The first research in Bijnor involved ethnographic fieldwork in 1982–3 with Roger Jeffery and Andrew Lyon, and in 1985 with Andrew Lyon (P. Jeffery, R. Jeffery, and Lyon 1989). Later research entailed lengthy stints of fieldwork in 1990–1 with Roger Jeffery, in 2000–2 with Roger Jeffery and Craig Jeffrey, and my solo fieldwork in 2002–5. Over the years, we have been indebted to our research assistants Swaleha Begum,

Zarin Rais, Shaila Rais, the late Radha Rani Sharma, Chhaya Sharma, and Manjula Sharma.[1]

Hitherto, I have not reflected in print on either the pay-offs or the difficulties that revisits entail.[2] This article, then, is a personal account that focuses on issues that revisiting the same research site have raised for me, rather than on the 'results' of the various fieldwork trips. It does not necessarily reflect the views of my colleagues involved in the research.

Background to the Bijnor Research

In the mid-1970s, I conducted fieldwork among the *pirzāda* of the renowned Sufi shrine of Hazrat Nizamuddin Auliya in Delhi (Jeffery 1979). North Indian Muslims often (but certainly not always) arrange marriages between people who are already closely related (including

[1] The research in Bijnor was funded in 1982–3 and 1985 by ESRC (*The Social Organization of Childbearing in Rural North India*, G00230027 and G00232238) and Hayter Fund (with Roger Jeffery and Andrew Lyon, a doctoral student); in 1990–1 by Overseas Development Administration (*Demographic Transition, Women's Status and Agrarian Change in North India*) and the Rockefeller Foundation (with Roger Jeffery); in 2000–2 by ESRC (*Household Strategies, Schooling Regimes, and Social Exclusion in Western UP*, R000238495), Ford Foundation, and Royal Geographical Society (with Roger Jeffery and Craig Jeffrey). I took full responsibility for the 2002–5 fieldwork funded by Wellcome Trust (*Demographic Change in North India: A Longitudinal Micro-study*, GR067231; Roger Jeffery was co-grantholder). My British Academy/Leverhulme Trust Senior Research Fellowship and Leverhulme Trust Research Fellowship during 2009–10 enabled further work on the Bijnor material. I am also grateful to the many members of the Vira family who facilitated the research; the villagers for their openness, forbearance, and good humour; the research assistants for their energy and enthusiasm well beyond the call of duty; and Edward Simpson, Donald MacKenzie, and the participants and organizers of 'Understanding Change in Rural India', especially Jan Breman and Gerry Rodgers for comments on drafts of this paper. None of them bears any responsibility for what I have written here.

[2] Descriptive accounts of the fieldwork are scattered through publications derived from this work, but they have not explicitly reflected on restudies: P. Jeffery et al. (1989); Jeffery and Jeffery (1996a); Jeffery and Jeffery (1997).

first or second cousins, but also people whose prior links are more complex). Literature on north Indian caste Hindus, however, indicates various prohibitions on marriage between closely related people. North Indian Muslims, then, often marry relatives who are unacceptable marriage partners for their caste Hindu neighbours. I began speculating about the implications for women of being married into a household of familiar kin (as some Muslim brides are), rather than being married into a household of strangers (typically the case among caste Hindus). What impact, if any, did these contrasting marriage practices have on gender politics at the domestic level? Did close-kin marriage empower young married women and enhance their decision-making capacity?

By the late 1970s, second-wave feminism in the global North was spawning feminist theory and academic interest in gender politics. In 1979, I gave birth under highly medicalized conditions in Edinburgh. Not surprisingly, the medicalization of childbirth was one theme in feminist debates that drew my attention, especially the widespread (but problematic) presumption that women in the global South experience more 'natural' and less medicalized birthing (for a critique, see Macintyre 1977). High levels of maternal, neo-natal, and infant mortality were absent from these romanticized portrayals. Around the same time, the World Health Organization (WHO) was advocating worldwide training-programmes for traditional birth attendants (TBAs, known as *dāī* in much of India), that aimed not only to improve birthing conditions and reduce maternal mortality but also to use TBAs as conduits for family planning information and technologies even in remote rural areas.[3] During my research in Nizamuddin, Roger Jeffery was researching health policymaking in India and developed an interest in how policy played out at the local level; for instance, he had discovered that dāī training programmes were not the novelty they were cracked up to be—indeed, they had been repeatedly tried and abandoned when they failed in various parts of British India in the nineteenth century (Jeffery 1988).

Inspired by these and related issues, we homed in on rural Bijnor. The district ranked relatively highly on most economic indicators, but its social indicators, such as literacy, were more modest (Singh 2001: Table VIII.3). Fertility levels—as elsewhere in the rural Gangetic plain—

[3] Jeffery and Jeffery (1993) and Jeffery, Jeffery, and Lyon (2002) contain critiques of this approach, based on the Bijnor research.

remained relatively high. Its other demographic characteristics matched our interests: about three-quarters of Bijnor district's population was rural and the Muslim population was unusually sizeable: about a third of the rural population and over two-thirds of the urban population (Jeffery and Jeffery 2006; Registrar General and Census Commissioner of India 2004). Yet, crucially, it had no history of communal conflicts: accompanied as we would be by a toddler, we did not wish our research to be derailed. And previous fieldwork in Lahore and Delhi had entailed learning Urdu and Hindi, so we could quickly begin communicating with villagers in Bijnor (for more details, see P. Jeffery et al. 1989: Appendix 1).

Obtaining Entry, Gaining Acceptance

Selecting a research location based on its socio-economic and demographic profile is one thing. Actually choosing a specific site and making an entry is quite another. We arrived in Delhi in early 1982 without personal contacts in Bijnor. In the event, at a reception after a seminar, one attendee informed me that her paternal grandmother originated from Bijnor district and that one of her grandmother's brothers, Kunwar Satya Vira, still lived there. The Vira family were prominent local landowners, engaged in local politics and founders of schools and colleges in the area, mainly in Bijnor town. Kunwar Satya Vira managed the family farm in Dharmnagri (about 5 km from Bijnor town). A few weeks later, we visited him and decided to select Dharmnagri and Jhakri, two adjacent villages, for our research. Jhakri had an exclusively Muslim population of nearly 400, whilst Dharmnagri's population of nearly 700 was about 60 per cent caste Hindus (mainly Sahni and Dhimar) and the remainder Dalits (Chamar and Jatab).[4] Within days, we had appointed research assistants (Hindu and Muslim women from Bijnor town) to act as note-takers. Thus far, it had seemed remarkably simple to establish a research base.

[4] Some Bijnor villages have exclusively Hindu or Muslim populations, others are mixed. Over the years, the Bijnor research involved two further villages: Qaziwala (a predominantly Muslim village) and Nangal Jat (a Jat, Chamar, and Muslim village) that were the primary focus of the 1990–1 and 2000–2 projects (Jeffery and Jeffery 1997; Jeffrey et al. 2008). Since we never lived in these villages, the level of engagement was much lower than in Dharmnagri and Jhakri, on which this article focuses.

Yet the first few months of fieldwork were anything but straightforward. Since there was little information on childbearing in rural India, the research entailed first building a picture through informal conversations and observations before gradually engaging in more systematic data collection. The pace, however, was more often dictated by villagers' initial responses to us, the only foreigners residing in the area in living memory.

Kunwar Satya Vira was a major employer of agricultural labour from both villages, so it was imperative to establish some distance from him, despite his crucial role in enabling access to the villages. No other village homes could have accommodated our four-person household, however. Kunwar Satya Vira put in a good word to the District Medical Officer, and we were offered the disused operating-theatre at the Dharmnagri government dispensary—not, of course, a very homely abode. It lacked plumbing and electricity, but was *pakka* and far more robust than village houses, which were mostly still thatched adobe single rooms. We gratefully accepted this offer—but had failed to predict the villagers' responses.

Villagers had fresh memories of the coercive family-planning drive that was integral to the Emergency. People told of village men hiding in the sugar cane fields to avoid being rounded up for sterilization. The operating-theatre had been padlocked since last being used for sterilizations during this period. Villagers feared that we were the vanguard of another sterilization programme, a fear exacerbated by the yellow Mahindra jeep—identical to those used by family-planning workers during the Emergency—that we had for transporting the research assistants from Bijnor town. Many queried our motives. Walking around the villages and stopping to chat, made many villagers apprehensive and suspicious. Our early attempts to create village censuses, or to discuss childbearing and women's maternity histories, met with querulous questions. Some women in Jhakri were frightened enough to run away and hide inside their homes in case we tried to compel them to adopt family planning. For a couple of months in early 1982, these suspicions virtually precluded conversations with the villagers about anything more sensitive than British farming practices and grain prices (about which we were singularly unknowledgeable). It was extremely uncomfortable (it is unpleasant being considered dangerous) and frustrating (we had to soft-pedal on data collection). Then several events shifted villagers' perceptions quite dramatically and helped to reduce the mistrust that was such an obstacle.

Construction of the nearby Madhya Ganga barrage was under way. Compounding villagers' anxieties about family planning were rumours that the government planned to relocate villagers cultivating land by the barrage, and that we were providing the government with information about how many would be affected. Roger Jeffery accompanied a delegation of village men to ask the District Magistrate (DM) in Bijnor town about these rumours but received a severe dressing-down for meddling in government affairs that were none of his business. The men with him were astonished to see a *sahib* treated so curtly. The event became a talking point and the belief that we were government agents intent on causing harm gradually began to recede.

Even more crucially, in April 1982, I was called to observe a delivery in Dharmnagri (P. Jeffery et al. 1989: 114–18).[5] Rajballa had visited the dispensary a few days earlier to consult the Auxiliary Nurse Midwife (ANM), who dealt with her summarily and sent her home. When I arrived at Rajballa's house, the dispensary compounder had already injected oxytocin to augment her contractions. After several hours, no progress had been made and he was summoned again. He was about to administer another injection when I restrained him, fearing that the baby was transverse breech and that an injection would be dangerous.[6] He examined Rajballa (for the first time) and agreed with my diagnosis. Thereupon ensued a lengthy discussion among the compounder, myself, and Rajballa's terrified in-laws about taking her to the hospital. Eventually, they consented to go to the government hospital in Bijnor town. The reception there made me understand why Rajballa's in-laws were so hesitant. I myself was verbally abused for being a pushy Punjabi wanting treatment in the middle of the night. The doctor who performed the caesarean section was courteous if rather patronizing, but Rajballa experienced cruel and abusive treatment from nurses and other staff, both on admission and during her time in hospital. Her husband Rohtash was reduced to cringing servility and he and his female relatives

[5] Personal names in publications derived from the Bijnor fieldwork are pseudonyms.

[6] For more on the dangers of injecting oxytocin, see Jeffery et al. (2007) and Brhlikova et al. (2009). I return to this and other interventions below.

had to remain at Rajballa's bedside to ensure that she received medications on time and that the space around her bed was properly cleaned, which the staff refused to do without payment. For the villagers, this event served to dispel rumours that I wanted to prevent women from having children and would compel them to adopt family planning. It was a watershed in how women in both villages regarded me. For me, this was a hugely chastening episode. Being verbally abused and watching the humiliations meted out to Rajballa and her family members gave me a painful and immediate insight into villagers' encounters with the state.

Later in 1982, Roger Jeffery and I adopted a baby girl, born in a Delhi clinic, and brought her to Dharmnagri.[7] This also served to convince villagers that we were not hostile to children. Moreover, it created talking points about son preferences and childcare: the field notes from the succeeding weeks brim over with people's unsolicited comments and questions. Distributing sweets to villagers generated the rumour that the baby was a boy—and incomprehension that we would celebrate a girl's arrival. Having one daughter already and then opting to have another caused bewilderment. Would the new daughter be educated and her marriage arranged? Would she be provided with a dowry? And how could I be so irresponsible as to feed her mashed banana during the winter as her first solid food? Surely I realized that its *tāsir* (influence) was 'cold' and that she would probably die of a chill?

These episodes enabled the fieldwork pick up pace. They also became launch pads for many spontaneous conversations about family-building, the optimal numbers of sons and daughters, the crucial contributions of sons and their in-married wives to household reproduction, parental anxieties about having daughters who needed to be married and provided with dowries, as well as about household organization and the gender politics of domestic life more generally.

Moreover, villagers' views of the local state in its various guises became a constant through the Bijnor fieldwork. We could begin to comprehend and explore their fearfulness about engaging with the 'state', whether the DM or government hospital staff. Even after agreeing to answer questions, villagers often anxiously enquired if the

[7] To protect her privacy, the only brief reference to this is in P. Jeffery et al. (1989). The conversations that her arrival generated, however, proved crucial for the research.

information would go *ūpar* ('above', to the authorities). Would details of landholdings be reported? Would the number of children become part of official documents? Would there be repercussions if villagers divulged information about their lives?

People talked about needing to give bribes to get their 'work' done and of how money would go from 'the bottom to the very top', with the Prime Minister taking his cut. Given the focus on health, childbearing, and family-building, of course, these comments often revolved around healthcare staff. There was (and still is) cynicism about government doctors whose offensive or desultory behaviour during official working-hours (if they even bothered to report for work) evaporated the instant they began their (technically illegal) private work (Jeffery and Jeffery 2008). People feared going to hospital and often delayed doing so, sometimes with disastrous results (Jeffery and Jeffery 2010), and they complained about the coercive activities of government health staff in relation to family planning or polio (Jeffery 2014; Jeffery et al. 2008). Bijnor villagers did not regard the state as *mā-bāp*.

Beyond that, people began to trust our guarantees of confidentiality. Villagers knew that we were friendly with Kunwar Satya Vira and his wider family and that we sometimes went to their home for meals. Nevertheless, Kunwar Satya Vira's employees soon began talking about their experiences, especially how his accountant cheated workers by paying not in cash but in rice, whilst always claiming he was providing high-value grain. As the villagers often demonstrated to me, the grains were broken and mixed with grit and pebbles. But villagers praised Kunwar Satya Vira for being such a 'big' man that he could veto a police *thana* in the village, for they feared police brutality and extortions. They also reported several occasions when he intervened in disputes about marital violence or dowry to protect the woman involved. Within families, too, women began to realize that their confidences would not go *āge* (further).

One day in 1982, when the *maulvī* used the Jhakri mosque tannoy system to summon a man from the fields to be interviewed by Andrew Lyon, we realized that a sea change had taken place, despite some lingering edginess. Gradually, the fieldwork (mostly) began to proceed more smoothly and subsequent visits have never necessitated the delicate negotiations that slowed the first fieldwork. By 1985, there was a palpable change in villagers' responses during the fieldwork I conducted with Andrew Lyon: between 1983 and 1985, nothing untoward could be attributed to the fieldwork and villagers' confidences were clearly not going ūpar. Most villagers trusted that we were merely trying to understand their lives in their own terms, and began accepting our presence and tolerating our questions—often with good humour and banter on their part.

By the time of my solo fieldwork in the early 2000s, Kunwar Satya Vira insisted that I live in his home rather than establish my own household. This provided a new vista on the village: seeing first-hand how Vira family members could use their local influence in resolving disputes among villagers, or help villagers in their dealings with the sugar cane cooperative and their children's school admissions. Admittedly, village women were diffident about coming to his house, so I was less accessible than when I lived on the dispensary compound. On the other hand, the evidence over time that nothing people said would spread around the village or be despatched ūpar to the authorities, now meant that my questions no longer generated anxieties, even among young people who could hardly have recalled my previous visits. More children were attending school—and clipboards, sheets of paper, and pencils that caused apprehension in 1982 were now commonplace. Some children even peered over our shoulders as my research assistant and I updated household census forms, pointing out their own names or correcting spellings. Young adults were also relaxed about answering questions. For instance, informal moneylending within the villages was a sensitive topic that I had hesitated to address head-on. During the fieldwork in the early 2000s, I learned that Fatima and her husband Farooq engaged in informal moneylending within Jhakri: one day, their older son, who had been a small boy in 1982, patiently explained the intricacies of this process, the interest rates they charged, and so on. Similarly, teaching staff at local *madrasās*—institutions often at the sharp end of Hindu nationalist allegations about Muslim terrorism—openly discussed their fears and frustrations, which reflected the major shift in communal politics since 1982.

'Trained' Informants

In the mid-1970s, my language skills were honed among the Delhi *pirzāda*. I was familiar with the flowery manners of *adab* (etiquette), gracious turns of phrase like *tashrīf rakhiye* (please place your dignity) and the vocabulary of Sufi spiritualism. Rustic speech and manners were rather different. I had to adjust to the blunter *baitho* or *baith* (sit down) and to being addressed as *tum* or even *tu* (the least respectful form of 'you') rather than *āp*, although I could never bring myself to reciprocate in kind. I learned a goodly number of obscenities—often related to women's anatomy and sex—that my research assistants at first were too embarrassed to explain. I needed a vocabulary of ethnobiology for talking about women's anatomy, conception, pregnancy, birth, and the post-partum period. And women married into the area from other villages spoke subtly different dialects.

Having seen the arrogant manner of local urbanites (including medical staff), I exhorted the research assistants to avoid being regarded as threats. We would listen in a non-judgemental and engaged manner, give women space to express their opinions in as much detail as they wished and not be like 'social workers' issuing advice and criticism. We answered women's questions—whether about life in UK and what being in an aeroplane was like, or about childrearing, healthcare, and family planning. To avoid flaunting our status, we wore simple clothing and the minimum jewellery required for properly attired women. Most conversations took place in or around women's homes. Whenever possible we refused to sit on the chairs women often fetched specially from their homes or borrowed from neighbours. Rather, we sat on one of the *chārpāīs* usually sitting outside people's homes, often engaging in banter about who should sit at the 'head' (the position that marked superiority). Sometimes, women visited me in the operating-theatre after consulting dispensary medical staff. Or we met women on the village outskirts in the areas where they prepared dung-cakes (*ūple*) for cooking-fuel. A research assistant and I would each perch on a couple of dried ūple, notebooks to the ready, and talk to women whilst they prepared ūple with fresh dung.[8] Each woman worked in her own patch, somewhat separated from others, and conversations here often became whispered and sensitive, with accusations of marital violence, petty thieving of food, young married women being cheated of wedding jewellery or being bullied by mothers-in-law or *jethānī* (husband's elder brother's wife), and so on.

[8] See R. Jeffery, P. Jeffery, and Lyon (1989, 2012) on the *economic* importance of women's dung-work.

Ceasing to be threatening, however, did not necessarily entail ceasing to be puzzling. Young women were unused to voicing their feelings and opinions and to being taken seriously. They were often amazed that the research assistants and I had nothing better to do than talk with them at length about their upbringing, marriages, dowries, experiences of pregnancy and childbirth, their daily work in their affinal village and how it was negotiated with other women, how (if at all) they obtained respite from work during pregnancy or the post-partum period, or how they managed to obtain leave to visit their natal village. With encouragement, though, women readily began recounting their own experiences, highlighting the vagaries of illness and death, and so on in comparing themselves with other women.

These were relatively straightforward and grounded issues, but other questions continued to perplex. Researching childbearing entailed engaging with local ideas of anatomy and physiology, beliefs about conception, appropriate diet during pregnancy and immediately after giving birth, about how labour should be managed, where babies should be born and who should be in attendance, notions of birth pollution and vulnerability. In Dharmnagri and Jhakri alike, such matters were 'natural', basic, and taken-for-granted knowledge that any adult would have. Village women were astonished to be asked about them by the research assistants. And they were bewildered that an educated foreigner was so ignorant that she continually needed to ask about matters connected with pollution and shame. Surely I was not intending to become a dāī—a far from lucrative means of earning a living and one regarded as thoroughly undesirable by village women?[9] With some persuading, women gradually accepted that my questions made some sense because birthing in the UK was so different. For instance, they patiently answered queries about who helped newly-delivered women with their domestic duties after childbirth. Initially women provided formulaic answers that the *nand* (husband's sister) helps and that a married nand is summoned from her affinal village if necessary. When my observations indicated that this did not always happen, women produced lengthy explanations for why the nand had or had not been called after particular deliveries (P. Jeffery et al. 1989: chapter 7). It even became possible to joke about

[9] For villagers' views of the dāī, see Jeffery et al. (2002), and Jeffery and Jeffery (1993).

these matters, as when I mentioned that cats and dogs are sterilized in the UK; or when I enquired (somewhat facetiously), whether the nand ever helped her brother's wife after *nasbandī* (sterilization operation): no, of course not, as birth is a matter of *khushī* (happiness, celebration), but sterilization is not.

Over a period of time, women began engaging more proactively with the research. Sometimes, women came to the operating-theatre to inform me about something they knew I would find interesting—an imminent delivery, the birth of a girl to a couple who already had several daughters, a dispute about a dowry, a young married woman who sought help from her brothers when she faced marital problems. And in 1990, Fatima, married in Jhakri, insisted on accompanying me to Qaziwala after I mentioned that one of her relatives there was afraid to answer my questions. Fatima steamrollered through the conversation, haranguing her relative, explaining that I would ask simple and totally harmless questions, instructing her to respond politely, and reassuring her that no harm would result. This, of course, was not a means of obtaining 'informed consent' that would be recognized by any ethics committee in a British university. If nothing else, though, it indicates an extraordinary level of trust that Fatima was prepared to intervene so forthrightly on my behalf.

Gradually, then, women in Dharmnagri and Jhakri ceased to consider me a threat, someone who would report what they said to government authorities or to other family members. My questions were often puzzling, sometimes sufficient to cause mirth, but not dangerous. And, whilst some women tended to be rather perfunctory in their answers, many others became proactive facilitators of my work, lively and engaging raconteurs of their own life stories or of events they know I find relevant and intriguing.

Long-term Data and Social Change

The research visits have all combined quantitative and qualitative data collection. The 1982–3 research produced censuses of Dharmnagri and Jhakri and maternity histories of all the ever-married women (recording children's births, immunizations and deaths, and use of family planning techniques to space children or terminate childbearing). At that time, few village women knew their children's birthdates, and trying to arrive at accuracy involved creating an orderliness that was not very meaningful to them. The endeavour often required lengthy discussions of the season if not month of birth, gaps between children, whether specific babies were born before or after children in neighbouring homes, and so on. Trying to fix dates of miscarriages and stillbirths, or the birthdates of children who later died was even more complex (as well as often being painful for the women concerned), especially when these events had occurred some years earlier. Yet, despite initial puzzlement over my interests, women generally responded good-naturedly to my questions. In the early 2000s, for instance, Gulshan told me proudly about a male government employee who had been interviewing women about their children—and how she had systematically recounted all her deliveries and included even children who had died, just as she had earlier done for me.

Using the 1982 village censuses, we selected 22 key informant couples in Dharmnagri and 19 in Jhakri, who became the focus of several rounds of semi-structured interviews: young married couples from differing class, caste, and community backgrounds, in the midst of family-building and more likely than others to recollect women's child-bearing experiences (P. Jeffery et al. 1989: Appendix 1). The qualitative interviews that I conducted with the women ranged over topics such as household organization through time, negotiations and conflicts about property, marriage arrangements and dowry, women's contacts with their natal kin, women's work in their affinal village and relationships with affinal kin, accounts of illnesses and medical treatment, as well as pregnancy, birthing, and the post-partum period. The field notes also include reports of serendipitous conversations, events observed, and so forth.

Each subsequent field trip entailed updating the village censuses and the maternity histories (including for women married into the villages since the previous field trip), with associated field notes recording women's supplementary comments. Updating maternity histories was generally relatively straightforward, since the small children recorded on the previous occasion provided fixed points for any siblings born between field trips, and some parents also began recording birthdates with a view to enrolling children in school. There have also been further rounds of semi-structured interviews, with the original key informants and others, as well as more informal conversations.

There are now several thousand pages of single-spaced typed field notes spanning the years from 1982. It is possible to trace all the households through time, in most detail for the key informants for whom the rich combination of the quantitative and qualitative data furnishes quite rounded accounts of how they have fared since the early 1980s, replete with numerous detailed renditions of their often spicy speech. Alongside these long-term data about the villagers, there is information about the infrastructure and institutions in the villages and their environs.

A major part of the data analysis has been exploring the interplay of villagers' everyday lives with the diverse and significant changes in the social and economic environment in which they must navigate. Between the early 1980s and the early 2000s, alongside numerous continuities, there have been striking alterations in the roles of the state and the market in providing healthcare and schooling, in how economic and demographic factors impact on livelihood options, the costs of child-rearing and schooling and care in old age, in political party issues and the climate of communal politics. And these wider processes impinge on men and women, Dalits, Muslims and caste Hindus, old and young, richer and poorer in distinctive ways.

By the early 2000s, cycle rickshaws plied between Dharmnagri and Bijnor town, more village men owned cycles or 'scooties' themselves, and a row of small shops had sprung up in Dharmnagri. The road across the Madhya Ganga barrage, completed in the mid-1980s, had made Meerut and Muzaffarnagar to the west accessible for medical treatment, jobs, and education. The supply of electricity for lighting and tube wells was rather more predictable than in 1982 (although by no means 24/7). The latrines in Jhakri that had required the removal of night-soil had largely been replaced by 'flush' toilets (squat toilets with septic tanks but without cisterns), and more homes in Dharmnagri now also had 'flush' toilets. Mobile phones had entered the villagers' repertoire of communication technologies.

Whilst the state primary and middle schools had atrophied, non-state educational facilities had expanded, and many more village children were in school. A handful of small private primary schools had opened in the vicinity. In addition to extending their educational institutions in Bijnor town, the Vira family had built a large secondary school between Dharmnagri and Jhakri that catered to several hundred children from the locality, mainly Hindu and Dalit; some girls from Dharmnagri attended this school, though hardly any Muslim girls did. But a madrasā in a nearby village had expanded massively since the 1980s and had a roll of over 1,000 students, more than half of them girls.

As before, villagers did not regard the state's role in healthcare provision as wholly benign. In any case, it remained lamentably inadequate: the dispensary even more rundown, staff attendance erratic, and largely limited to matters such as family planning, tuberculosis (TB), and the pulse polio programme (Jeffery 2014). For curative healthcare, however, villagers could now access a much greater range of non-state facilities, from untrained and unlicensed practitioners working in small roadside kiosks to private clinics in Bijnor town that provided in-patient services. Villagers' expectations about the outcomes of illness episodes had risen strikingly since 1982, when 'fatalism' was often realistic. Now, villagers were more optimistic that a solution was at hand, but they also faced substantially increased outlays when family members were ill (Jeffery and Jeffery 2008, 2010).

Demographic changes within the villages echoed those in north India more generally. The maternity histories indicate how dramatically child-survival improved from the mid-1960s onwards. The Emergency had little direct *demographic* impact and only after a time lag of nearly 20 years did fertility limitation become more widespread. Discussions with village women reflected some shifts since the early 1980s in views on family planning: younger couples in Dharmnagri now tended to presume that the wife would be sterilized once she had two or three children. Yet, largely because of the *political* impact of the Emergency, most Muslims in Jhakri remained nervous about the implications of sterilization for their fate in the afterlife (P. Jeffery et al. 1989: 177–213; Jeffery et al. 2008). Women still hoped to give birth at home, with oxytocin injections more commonplace than in the early 1980s. There were more institutional deliveries, but villagers opted for them only in emergencies, and they still feared the expense as well as poor-quality and demeaning treatment (Jeffery and Jeffery 2008, 2010).

As before, the main crops were sugar cane, wheat, and rice, with some eucalyptus and poplar, but most ploughing was done by tractor rather than teams of oxen, though harvesting was still by hand. Some landless households were allocated land near the Ganga that became cultivable after the flood-controls associated with the barrage. This encroachment on erstwhile *jangal* had reduced access to fodder (and thereby to dung for fertilizer and cooking-fuel) and to free building materials (mud, reeds for thatch). Landowners relied more on commercial inorganic fertilizers and most villagers were locked into the cash economy for pakka bricks, cement, wrought-iron grills, and so forth. More generally, though, the lag between improvements in child survival and the onset of fertility decline had posed challenges to household livelihood strategies. Typically, plots of land inherited by cohorts of brothers born in the 1960s and 1970s were much reduced. Landowners could more readily farm without employing labourers. Men from poorer landowning households needed off-farm employment: as some put it, they were now *nā mazdūr, nā kissān* (neither labourer nor farmer). Given the paucity of employment opportunities, and the need for bribes *(rishwat)* or influence *(sifārish)* to secure a job, many of the more marginalized villagers, especially Dalits and Muslims, were doubting the value of spending money on their sons' schooling. Compared with the early 1980s, more landless and land-poor men were commuting daily into Bijnor town or migrating on a seasonal basis as far away as Chandigarh, Surat, or Kashmir.

Marriages were still arranged by family elders with little or no input from the potential spouses, and women's 'marriage migration' to their affinal homes continued to be an important form of labour migration. Domestic technologies had changed very little since the early 1980s and women's work remained time-consuming and arduous, as well as vital to household well-being. Handpumps continued to provide domestic water-supplies and cooking was still primarily done using ūple and other bio-fuels, though a few households had invested in gas canisters. Yet the declining use of oxen for ploughing had affected women's work providing fodder and processing dung for manure and cooking-fuel, whilst grain was no longer threshed or milled manually. Women's work, however, was still oriented around household reproduction rather than remunerative employment. Although girls' school or madrasā enrolment had increased dramatically since the early 1980s, few girls continued in formal education past puberty and their schooling fed into the marriage market, not employment.[10] The role of schooling either in

[10] For general discussions of girls' education in rural Bijnor, see P. Jeffery and R. Jeffery (1994, 1996b). For more on girls' education in the local madrasās, see Jeffery et al. (2004, 2005, 2006, 2012).

empowering women or affecting childrearing practices (for example, in relation to hygiene) and other domestic practices remained elusive.

Although sex-selective abortions appeared to be uncommon, son preferences continued to be taken for granted and were reflected in the juvenile sex-ratios in the two villages. Arranging marriages continued to generate huge anxieties for parents, whether for fear of deception about the qualities of their children's prospective spouses or the financial outlays that would be required. Dowry was still an issue, but villagers' expectations had changed in manifold ways. In the early 1980s, Dharmnagri residents often alluded to a shift away from previous practices when dowry-giving was (they claimed) based on what people could provide *khushī-se* (out of happiness, voluntarily) to a situation where demands were feared and not uncommonly made. At that time, Jhakri residents did not report such a shift among Muslims, but by the early 2000s dowry demands and expectations about what the dowry should contain had changed substantially for them too. In both villages, a colour TV, 'sofa-set', and various white goods were now virtually essential. Moreover, young men's marriages were often delayed until their households could afford to construct separate pakka rooms for each son and his bride: today's brides, people said, will not tolerate the simple shelters that were standard when their parents-in-law were married. And it is possible to take a more considered longer-term perspective on the conflicts that arise among women within households. In the 1980s, conversations with key informant women often revolved around the controls exercised by mothers-in-law, about household work, when daughters-in-law could visit their parents, or custody of their jewellery, for instance. Conversations with these same women now that they were mothers-in-law themselves displayed a depressing repetitiveness as women moved into the older generation.[11] Mobile phones, however, may be putting young brides into a rather less vulnerable position than previously (Jeffrey and Doron 2013: 165–83).

The long-term data from Dharmnagri and Jhakri, then, can provide a window on the social and economic continuities and changes that villagers have experienced since the early 1980s: improvements in some areas of daily life alongside the resilience of many earlier concerns and difficulties, the continuing son preferences, and anxieties over dowry,

[11] This, of course, brings to mind the TV soap serial *Kyunki Saas Bhi Kabhi Bahu Thi*.

and how, despite demographic shifts, adult women's daily lives continue to revolve around the domestic sphere.

Would that things were as simple as this account might make it seem, however. Revisits to the same research site have undoubtedly furnished numerous rewards, yet there are also complications and pitfalls along the way: among them, ethical issues connected with data management, confidentiality and memory, dilemmas in data analysis and interpretation, and the researcher's inevitable impact.

Confidentiality, Memory, and Long-term Data

Nowadays, UK research funders and universities are much more attuned to the ethical issues raised by social research than they were in the early 1980s. Core ethical concerns include the psychological and/or physical harm that vulnerable research participants might experience, informed consent, confidentiality, preservation of informants' anonymity, ensuring the security of data and vigilance with respect to those who can access the data, and the researcher's safety.[12]

Ethnographic studies—and all the more so ethnographic restudies—pose complex problems for maintaining appropriate ethical standards. Ethnographic data include reports on interviews, observations, conversations, and discussions with several participants, and accounts of episodes involving other people in the research site. Anonymized field notes would hamper the tracking of cross-references and allusions to other people.[13] For the Bijnor research (and I suspect for most ethnographic research), the field notes were stored with people's real names

[12] For examples of recent ethical codes, see those from British Sociological Association, Association of the Social Anthropologists, ESRC and University of Edinburgh/Social and Political Science:
http://www.britsoc.co.uk/media/27107/StatementofEthicalPractice.pdf;
http://www.theasa.org/downloads/ASA%20ethics%20guidelines%202011.pdf;
http://www.esrc.ac.uk/_images/framework-for-research-ethics_tcm8-33470.pdf;
http://www.sps.ed.ac.uk/research/ethics (all URLs mentioned were last accessed 20 August 2015).

[13] By contrast, once-off interviews from surveys can be readily understood when anonymized, since they are not concerned with relationships and processes among the people interviewed.

and anonymization only takes place shortly before finalizing a piece of writing, if specific people are mentioned or quoted.[14] From the initial Bijnor research onwards, we certainly tried to explain our purpose—although this was often hard, since villagers had little experience of formal education or understanding of social science research. So did they comprehend that all conversations and activities are potentially research data? And how should informed consent be obtained from people not from the research site, for instance, medical practitioners encountered when accompanying villagers to urban facilities, or guests at weddings?

Access to long-term data is a crucial advantage of restudies: for new research to benefit fully from the insights of previous studies in the same site, the researchers must be familiar with the data from earlier visits. This, of course, poses issues for secure data storage. But for revisits by the same researcher(s), the lack of anonymization in field notes facilitates the process of updating information and building up a picture, for instance, of the trajectories of particular people and households over time. Researchers revisiting a research site are not just familiar faces, and it is not simply a matter of having built up trust. Over and above this, informants themselves recollect previous conversations and (at some level at least) know what the researcher knows. The returning researcher can prepare for new fieldwork by rereading the earlier field notes—and rapidly become immersed in the intangible benefits of familiarity, as a person who already knows about past *dukh-sukh* (sadness-joy) of individuals and their households. Indeed, re-engaging with informants often entails catching up with family news (in both directions), in which allusions are made to previous events and earlier conversations.

Restudies involving *different* researchers over time would, however, raise further issues for confidentiality and anonymity.[15] How familiar with the original data can new researchers actually be? How familiar *should* they be? What should new researchers reveal about what they

[14] After discussions with people in Dharmnagri and Jhakri, we retained the villages' real names (although I would probably not have done so nowadays).

[15] This is crucial for the ESRC-funded project *Rural Change and Anthropological Knowledge in Post-colonial India*, Edward Simpson (PI), Patricia Jeffery (Co-I), with postdoctoral researchers Tina Otten, Tommaso Sbriccoli, and Alice Tilche, as the original researchers' field notes are available for two of the three sites.

already know? How can they sustain in-depth and enlightening conversations with informants who may or may not understand what they know? The researcher new to the site who is endeavouring to conduct a restudy certainly cannot straightforwardly engage with informants without breaching previous confidentiality.

Moving Targets and Social Change

Even if such ethical concerns are addressed appropriately, restudies raise several further issues. A general account of social and economic change can perhaps be outlined (as above). But long-term data are often a source of frustration rather than completely unalloyed benefits, for some rather important discontinuities and complexities can hobble attempts to account for social change.[16]

Whilst Dharmnagri and Jhakri both still exist as identifiable nucleated villages, they and the world around them have altered in diverse ways since the early 1980s. In practice, though, it is difficult to discern which changes in villagers' lives reflect these wider trends and which are primarily attributable to the inexorable movement of individuals through the 'domestic cycle'. If the key informants and I inhabit (more or less) the same bodies, our lives have also moved on. In 1982, the key informants were selected to reflect the social and economic diversity of the two villages: they had in common being young couples in the midst of childbearing. By the early 2000s, few parents and parents-in-law of the key informants were still alive and some key informants had died or moved away. Men who had been farming jointly with fathers and brothers were running separate enterprises. Women who had been living jointly with mothers-in-law were now cooking at separate *chūlhās* (cooking-hearths) or alongside daughters-in-law. Some daughters were already married and made only occasional visits, with their children in tow. Some sons, too, had wives and small children of their own. In the interim, my own standing had also altered. In 1982, women of around my own age had attached the appellation *behn-jī* (sister) to me. By the 2000s, the sobriquets *auntie-jī* and *nānī-mā* (maternal grandmother) were added to the repertoire by the recently in-married women and small

[16] Burawoy (2003) provides a general discussion of issues that restudies raise.

children, and young married women in Dharmnagri were exhorted to cover their heads with their *sārī ānchal* and press my ankles and lower legs (much to my embarrassment).

On the face of it, it should be possible to track the key informants' households (in particular) and those of the other villagers (in less detail) through this period. But this endeavour is liable to be confounded, for deciding how best to define what households are, leave aside how to map their changing fortunes, is extremely complicated. At any one time, some fathers and sons engage in jointly-organized agricultural work, but others do not. Similarly, mothers and daughters-in-law may organize their work in diverse ways for different tasks, all, some or none sharing a chūlhā, and with complex rotas for any co-owned livestock, for instance. If the father and mother are in the same household, it is not clear that the sons and daughters-in-law necessarily are too: sometimes a household demarcated by men's work and property ownership coincides with one bounded by the women's work—but often it does not. Focusing on men's activities directs attention squarely to landholding and 'class', agricultural and off-farm incomes, labour migration and the wider economy. Focusing on consumption and caring-work foregrounds the collaborations and conflicts over cooking, animal husbandry, and childcare that feature prominently in women's day-to-day lives. So what should the primary rationale be for drawing boundaries around 'households'?

However households are delineated, analysing how they change adds a further layer of complexity. Men may stop working together. Daughters-in-law may separate their chūlhās from their mothers-in-law. Women are married out or married in, children are born, and people die. And although brothers usually begin their adult lives in the same class position, their fortunes can diverge radically and they may reach middle age in very diverse situations. Differing educational levels might have permitted contrasting employment trajectories. Brothers have different numbers of sons and daughters to educate and settle in marriage and/or employment. There may have been deaths and illnesses that caused sudden and sometimes disastrous ruptures to normal budgeting, with distress-sales of land or livestock.[17]

[17] Krishna (2010), for instance, traces household trajectories (albeit through retrospective data) and indicates how household fortunes wax and wane over

Whilst this is all very intriguing, it creates headaches not just for grasping how the village class-profiles (for instance) have changed but also relating these processes to wider shifts in the Indian society. Additionally, with the passage of time, my own interests have altered somewhat, in response to 'real world' trends in India and evolving academic concerns. Grappling with all this, though, presents a dilemma. Sustaining comparability of data over time nudges research towards rigidity and collecting the same kinds of information during each revisit. Yet responding to events and to new academic approaches implies introducing new topics—on which there cannot be systematic information covering the whole time period. True, the earlier field notes include serendipitous conversations and details even on topics that did not seem very important at the time (though a great deal slipped through the net and is long forgotten). Thus, *some* insights can often be gleaned from earlier fieldwork—but the information is rarely sufficiently robust to be satisfying.

The 1982 fieldwork inevitably highlighted some topics and sidelined others. It did not, for instance, explore ritual and religious practices. So am I right to believe that some rituals (such as those connected with *karva chauth*), were being practised by more women and in a more elaborate and commercialized fashion in the 2000s? Or was I simply not paying attention in 1982? Conversely, some topics addressed in 1982 were not explored in detail in subsequent fieldwork. Women's work was central in the nascent gender and development literatures at the time. The 1982 research included my collecting time-use data in the different seasons from the key informant women, to highlight the long hours, multitasking, and evident necessity of their work—for women themselves, leave aside men, often devalued their contributions to household well-being. Women found this boring, despite my efforts at levity and cajoling them to include not only dung-work associated with livestock but also shit-work connected with babies. Resistance set in—and I hesitated to include such detailed questions again. Similarly, comparable information from the key informant men was not replicated in detail in later fieldwork and the village census material provides only sporadic information for the entire villages. Yet men—especially those from land-poor and landless households—enter and exit various employment roles throughout the

---

time, with illness a crucial factor. Snapshot studies of poverty cannot capture the fluctuations *at the household level* that long-term studies can reveal.

seasons, or even play several roles simultaneously. Fluidity, dynamism, and insecurity were central to many men's livelihood strategies in the 1980s, but were they more acute in the early 2000s?

In addition, the census and maternity history data cover all the households and ever-married women, but the qualitative information comes primarily from the key informants. Basically, the research has been a panel or cohort study, with other data supplying crucial background detail. The key informants' changing preoccupations have been explored in some detail since 1982, and in the early 2000s the research concentrated on their concerns then: organizing their children's marriages, their own declining capacities, paying for healthcare and ensuring their own well-being in old age, troubles with daughters-in-law, and the like. This later research, however, could not systematically incorporate (for instance) younger couples preoccupied with childbearing to compare with the original key informants. Certainly, the views of the key informants' children were sought on various matters—including childbearing, family planning, livelihood options, schooling, and healthcare one shot. But this was more ad hoc than the rounds of interviews conducted over the years with the older generation.

Becoming too familiar with a research site is another potential pitfall. Many things that caught my attention, and sometimes took me aback, in the early 1980s have acquired such familiarity that I scarcely notice them now—the body language of *ghunghat* (veiling), for instance. And a flipside of commitment to one research site is not being intensively exposed to other locations and not having to confront new surprise factors. It is, perhaps, all too easy to fall prey to the delusion that rural India is all like rural Bijnor.[18]

On Not Being a Fly on the Wall

Social science research generally entails a direct social engagement between researcher and research subjects. For the researcher, ethnographic research involves navigating a tension between neutral and systematic researcher and involved and concerned human being. Ethnographers

[18] Other projects have taken me to villages elsewhere in India (Assam, West Bengal, Madhya Pradesh, Gujarat, Odisha, and Rajasthan) and to Nepal, but none has entailed long-term residence in the area.

cannot be flies on the wall. Being just a detached 'objective' observer is simply not possible (and, arguably, not even desirable). The researcher inevitably impacts on villagers' lives, sometimes but not always in obvious ways—and it is extremely difficult to ascertain the effects on the nature and quality of the data and on the research process overall.

Endemic and sometimes overt tensions in village life reflect villagers' diverse social and economic locations. Yet the childbearing project in 1982–3 necessitated straddling fissures within the villages to obtain information from Muslims, caste Hindus, and Dalits in differing class positions. This potentially raised anxieties about our loyalties and required our watchfulness and tact, simultaneously nurturing communication with the less powerful to hear their experiences and critiques, while avoiding antagonizing the more powerful so that their enactments of dominance could also be revealed.

For gender politics, the focus on childbearing perhaps seemed 'apolitical' (though, of course, it is not) and this may have permitted some aloofness from other domains of village politics. In any case, potential difficulties were (I think) largely averted by adapting to local gender norms. The female research assistants and I talked to village women; as a foreigner, I could talk to men, including older men, although I rarely did so. Roger Jeffery and Andrew Lyon talked to men and were circumspect in dealing with women, scarcely engaging in eye contact, leave aside conversation. With this arrangement, husbands and wives did not seem to be suspicious about our conversations with the other spouse.

Interactions involving people from different castes or religious communities—Kunwar Satya Vira's employees, dispensary patients, people piling into the jeep for lifts into Bijnor town—generally remained jocular on the surface. People often commented that Bijnor was not famed for communal tensions and had not experienced trouble at Partition. Nevertheless, caste and communal tensions were not far from the surface and negotiating villagers' caste and communal sensibilities has required delicate handling, more or less overtly, throughout the various research visits.

The Hindu (Brahmin) research assistants were acceptable to everyone in Dharmnagri and would take tea from Dalits. They were also acceptable to the Muslims in Jhakri. Yet the Muslim assistants were never warmly greeted in Dharmnagri and the Dharmnagri field notes often record anti-Muslim sentiments voiced in their absence. Consequently, I generally needed to juggle my research schedules in the two villages according to which assistant was free to accompany me. Particularly in the early stages, most caste Hindus did not appreciate our mixing with Dalits and Muslims (and certainly not sitting among them and accepting refreshments). For many Dalits, Muslims were beyond the pale, whilst Muslims often alleged that caste Hindus and Dalits were complicit with the 'Hindu' Raj.

A small illustration of these prejudices arose in 1982, when we were infested with bedbugs *(khatmal)*: the villagers seemingly could not believe that we had imported them ourselves. Rather, our profligate mixing with other people was to blame: the men who sat on our *morahs* on the veranda of an evening must have brought them on their clothing. Who precisely was accused depended on the speaker, though: caste Hindus blamed Dalits and Muslims; Dalits blamed Muslims; and Muslims blamed Dalits.[19] Far more seriously, during 1990–1, several political events on the Indian stage as well as internationally threatened to lay waste to the research. In the second half of 1990, the proposal to implement the Mandal Commission report raised inter-caste tensions within Dharmnagri. Travel to and from Bijnor town was often disrupted by hockey-stick wielding male students. During developments in the Ayodhya campaign, *kar sevaks* tried to make their way to Ayodhya over the Madhya Ganga barrage and through Bijnor town. A procession turned violent and ended in some deaths and arson targeting Muslim-owned businesses. There was a curfew in Bijnor town for over a week (Basu 1995; R. Jeffery and P. Jeffery 1994). In Dharmnagri, some young men from the nearby Bengali refugee village harvested bamboo staves from Kunwar Satya Vira's boundary hedge, sharpened the points and reputedly applied poison—apparently with the intent of attacking Jhakri.[20] For several weeks, the research stalled. The research assistants were extremely anxious and conversations over

[19] This saga has another strand: the bedbug poison applied to the chārpāīs and morahs resulted in a cascade of dead insects onto the floor. Our Dhimar cook swept them into a heap which he surrounded with paraffin. After igniting the paraffin, he pranced around intoning '*Om, shāntī*' in mockery of the village temple pandit.

[20] Kunwar Satya Vira's brother had been Governor of Bengal at the time of the Pakistan civil war in 1970–1 that resulted in the creation of Bangladesh. He arranged for some Hindu refugees from East Pakistan to be relocated in several newly established villages around the Dharmnagri area.

lunch each day highlighted tensions among them that had been masked until then. During the first Gulf War in spring 1991, many Muslims in rural Bijnor mistrusted the 'Hindu' Indian government and foreigners alike (Jeffery and Jeffery 1997: xi–xiii, 1–37). Similarly, communal tensions erupted again with the juxtaposition of the invasion of Afghanistan and the Gujarat carnage during 2000–2.

Over the years, of course, we endeavoured to compensate for the data-extractive mode that fieldwork entails. We generally managed to avoid becoming embroiled in caste and communal conflicts. But we were willingly drawn into many of the villagers' other concerns—although, in truth, the Bijnor research has contributed rather little to the villagers' well-being and the exchange always remains extremely unequal. Villagers often wanted us to sponsor their quests for school admissions and employment, little realizing that we had scant influence in the places that mattered and could not be relied upon to deliver. Other requests were more readily fulfilled, though. The maternity histories and census materials could provide details of births, marriages, and deaths to people who had no written records: in 1990, Rajballa and Rohtash's son born in hospital in 1982 simply wanted to know how old he was, and when Rohtash's youngest brother Punni was arranging his son's marriage in 2004, he requested details of his son's date and hour of birth so that the son's horoscope could be compared with that of the prospective bride. The jeep was available for bridegrooms and their male relatives from Dharmnagri and Jhakri who wished to arrive in the bride's village in style and needed to transport the (often sobbing) brides to their new homes: perhaps the most striking instance was the hilarious occasion of Gulshan's within-village marriage in Jhakri in 1982 (Jeffery and Jeffery 1996a: 216). And the jeep could also take people to hospital in medical emergencies and for routine consultations that frightened them (Jeffery and Jeffery 1996a: 66), transport funeral parties, go on a mission to protect an out-married daughter in distress in her affinal village (Jeffery and Jeffery 1996a: 192–6), or be used to fetch medicines for the dispensary from Meerut during the curfew in Bijnor town. Sometimes, as in Rajballa's case, the intervention was not initiated by the villagers. Rather than watching—fly-on-the-wall style—the almost certainly fatal consequences of Rajballa's mismanaged labour, I prevented a second oxytocin injection being administered, spent a couple of hours cajoling and exhorting her reluctant family members to take her to hospital, and subsequently tried to ensure that her hospital stay was as comfortable as possible. Detachment was not an ethically appropriate option.

Yet in other instances—not immediately life-threatening ones—I adopted a pose of impassive non-intervention. Just what should a researcher do when instances of marital violence come to light, when little girls are walloped and told that their mischief will not be tolerated in their affinal homes, when a sickly girl's mother is consoled with 'don't worry, she will recover and extract a dowry from you', or when the dāī performs an internal examination without washing her hands? Keeping my own counsel was not always possible, however, for women also quizzed me about life in the UK, dowry, and son preferences, care of the elderly, and so forth, which probably prompted them to reflect anew on their own lives. Indeed, one time, several women needled my research assistant to explain why she was not yet married: her spirited riposte that she had no intention of committing herself into slavery (*g͟hulāmī*) sparked off a lively discussion of married life amongst the initially rather startled gathering (myself included) and resulted in one woman's conclusion that 'marriage is a calamity' (*shādī hai barbādī*) (Jeffery and Jeffery 1996a: 134–5).

It is hard to evaluate or control the impact of one's interventions—whether deliberately undertaken after consideration, or more spontaneous. There is surely also a swathe of unintended interventions of which I am unaware, and assessing their impact on the villagers is well-nigh impossible. Moreover, my own rather sporadic stays in Dharmnagri and Jhakri have occurred alongside numerous forces emanating from beyond the villages that have resulted in more or less substantial transformations in village life.

* * *

The 1982–3 Bijnor research involved huge investments of emotional and practical energy on an often troubling experience. Looking back, those first few months were crucial in later decisions not to risk similar experiences elsewhere but to continue returning to a place that became a second home. Rather by default, then, what was planned as a once-off field trip gradually morphed into 'restudies' that have encompassed much of my academic career. I had little realized that substantial chunks of my waking time would still revolve around thinking and writing about the area 30 years later.

Ethnographic restudies entail their own complexities, dilemmas, and concerns, as well as rewards. Building relationships with a wide range of villagers involved time, delicacy, rebuffs, many frustrations, and repeated repair work. Gradually, villagers began reporting our view that everyone was an *insān* (human being) to their guests in apparently favourable tones—but in 1982 our insistence on this point caused widespread puzzlement and even consternation. With hindsight, it is easy (and sometimes disappointing) to appreciate the lack of foresight about what information would become important later and the risks of taking for granted things that had initially surprised me. Sometimes, too, it feels like treading a very narrow line between the richness of long-term data (despite the limitations) and being overwhelmed by information overload. But this is not really a cry of desperation. Indeed, I more than appreciate the blessings of having such detailed material—but keeping track of the key informants over time, leave aside the wider village populations, does tax the grey matter.

Nevertheless, though, the long-term data collection certainly has enhanced my general understanding of how macro-level trends impact on quotidian aspects of rural life at the micro-level, from gender politics to communal politics, from demography and healthcare to education and livelihoods. Undoubtedly, I have gained insights that would have been impossible without repeatedly visiting the area. Albeit through conversation and observation rather than direct personal experience, I now have (a limited and mediated) feel for villagers' dukh-sukh, their hopes and ambitions, their troubles and worries about illnesses and livelihoods, and their strivings in an often hostile economic and political climate. As a woman in Jhakri once commented to me, my heart has been in two places for many years. Rural Bijnor is now under my skin. And I have been immensely privileged to have had the opportunity for the personal enrichment that has also been a by-product of the Bijnor revisits.

References

Basu, Amrita. 1995. 'Why Local Riots Are Not Simply Local: Collective Violence and the State in Bijnor, India 1988–93'. *Theory and Society*, 24 (1): 35–78.

Brhlikova, Petra, Patricia Jeffery, Gitanjali Priti Bhatia, and Sakshi Khurana. 2009. 'Intrapartum Oxytocin (Mis)use in South Asia', *Journal of Health*

Studies, 2 (1, 2, and 3): 33–50. Available at http://www.jhs.co.in/articles/showArticle.aspx?aid=46 (last accessed 20 August 2015).

Burawoy, Michael. 2003. 'Revisits: An Outline of a Theory of Reflexive Ethnography', *American Sociological Review*, 68 (October): 645–79.

Jeffery, Patricia. 1979. *Frogs in a Well: Indian Women in Purdah*. London: Zed Books.

———. 2014. 'Underserved and Overdosed? Muslims and the Pulse Polio Initiative in Rural North India', in R. Jeffery, C. Jeffrey, and J. Lerche (eds), *Development Failure and Identity Politics in Uttar Pradesh*, pp. 46–74 . New Delhi: SAGE Publications.

Jeffery, Patricia, Abhijit Das, Jashodhara Dasgupta, and Roger Jeffery. 2007. 'Unmonitored Intrapartum Use of Oxytocin in Home Deliveries', *Reproductive Health Matters*, 15 (30): 172–8.

Jeffery, Patricia and Roger Jeffery. 1994. 'Killing My Heart's Desire: Education and Female Autonomy in Rural North India', in N. Kumar (ed.), *Woman as Subject: South Asian Histories*, pp. 125–71. Calcutta and Charlottesville: Bhatkal and Sen and Virginia University Press.

———. 1996a. *Don't Marry Me to a Ploughman! Women's Everyday Lives in Rural North India*. Boulder and New Delhi: Westview Press and Vistaar.

———. 1996b. '"What's the Benefit of Being Educated?": Girls' Schooling, Women's Autonomy and Fertility Outcomes in Bijnor', in R. Jeffery and A. Basu (eds), *Girls' Schooling, Women's Autonomy and Fertility Change in South Asia*, pp. 150–83. New Delhi: SAGE Publications.

———. 2006. *Confronting Saffron Demography: Religion, Fertility and Women's Status in India*. New Delhi: Three Essays Collective.

———. 2008. '"Money Itself Discriminates": Obstetric Emergencies in the time of Liberalisation', *Contributions to Indian Sociology*, 42 (1): 61–93.

———. 2010. '"Only When the Boat has Started Sinking": A Maternal Death in Rural North India', *Social Science and Medicine*, 71 (10): 1711–18.

Jeffery, Patricia, Roger Jeffery, and Craig Jeffrey. 2004. 'Islamisation, Gentrification and Domestication: An "Islamic Course for Girls" and rural Muslims in Bijnor, Uttar Pradesh', *Modern Asian Studies*, 38 (1): 1–54.

———. 2005. 'The Mother's Lap and the Civilising Mission: *Madrasah* Education and Rural Muslim Girls in Western Uttar Pradesh', in Z. Hasan and R. Menon (eds), *In a Minority: Essays on Muslim women in India*, pp. 108–48. New Delhi and New Jersey: Oxford University Press and Rutgers University Press.

———. 2006. 'The First Madrasa: Learned Mawlawis and the Educated Mother', in J.-P. Hartung and H. Reifeld (eds), *Islamic Education, Diversity, and National Identity: Dini Madaris in India Post 9/11*, pp. 227–51. New Delhi: SAGE Publications.

———. 2008. 'Disputing Contraception: Muslim Reform, Secular Change and Fertility', *Modern Asian Studies*, 42 (2 and 3): 519–48.

Jeffery, Patricia, Roger Jeffery, and Craig Jeffrey. 2012. 'Leading by Example? Women *Madrasah* Teachers in Rural North India', in M. Bano and H. Kalmbach (eds), *Women, Leadership and Mosques: Changes in Contemporary Islamic Authority*, pp. 195–216. Leiden/Boston: Brill.

Jeffery, Patricia, Roger Jeffery, and Andrew Lyon. 1989. *Labour Pains and Labour Power: Women and Childbearing in India*. London: Zed Books.

———. 2002, 'Contaminating States: Midwifery, Childbearing and the State in Rural North India', in S. Rozario and G. Samuel (eds), *The Daughters of Hāritī: Birth and Female Healers in South and Southeast Asia*, pp. 90–108. London and New York: Routledge.

Jeffery, Roger. 1988. *The Politics of Health in India*. Berkeley and London: University of California Press.

Jeffery, Roger and Patricia Jeffery. 1993. 'Traditional Birth Attendants in Rural North India: the Social Organization of Childbearing', in S. Lindenbaum and M. Lock (eds), *Knowledge, Power, and Practice: The Anthropology of Medicine and Everyday Life*, pp. 7–31. Berkeley: University of California Press.

———. 1994. 'The Bijnor Riots, October 1990: Collapse of a Mythical Special Relationship?' *Economic and Political Weekly*, 29 (10): 551–8.

———. 1997. *Population, Gender and Politics: Demographic Change in Rural North India*. Cambridge: Cambridge University Press.

Jeffery, Roger, Patricia Jeffery, and Andrew Lyon. 1989. 'Taking Dung-Work Seriously: Women's Work and Rural Development in North India', *Economic and Political Weekly*, 24 (17): WS 32–7.

———. 2012 'Taking Dung-work Seriously', in Surinder S. Jodhka (ed.), *Village Society: Essays from Economic and Political Weekly*, pp. 145–56. Hyderabad: Orient BlackSwan. [Abridged version of paper originally published in *EPW* in 1989]

Jeffrey, Craig, Patricia Jeffery, and Roger Jeffery. 2008. *Degrees Without Freedom? Education, Masculinities and Unemployment in North India*. Stanford: Stanford University Press.

Jeffrey, Robin and Assa Doron. 2013. *The Great Indian Phone Book: How Cheap Mobile Phones Change Business, Politics and Everyday Life*. London: Hurst.

Krishna, Anirudh. 2010. *One Illness Away: Why People Become Poor and How They Escape Poverty*. Oxford: Oxford University Press.

Macintyre, Sally. 1977. 'Childbirth: The Myth of the Golden Age', *World Medicine*, 15 (June): 17–21.

Registrar General and Census Commissioner of India. 2004. 'Census of India 2001: Data on Religion'. New Delhi: Office of the Registrar General, India, Ministry of Home Affairs.

Singh, Ajit Kumar. 2001. 'Uttar Pradesh Development Report 2000'. Lucknow: New Royal Book Company.

4

SHAPAN ADNAN

Strengths and Weaknesses of Long-term Village Studies

Reflections on Methods and Research Design from Studies in Bangladesh

The Issues

Village studies involve fieldwork-based data collection to analyse the features of microcosms of rural society. Among these, long-term village studies (LTVS) constitute a special case, which additionally assesses trends over time. The distinctive feature of village studies is that they capture *relationships* and *interactions* between individuals, households, and other units of analysis. Under certain conditions, LTVS can trace and specify *causal* processes among multiple strands of change.

These contributions of village studies are based on the use of particular methods within an overall research design. Viewed in these terms, the village study is characterized by a *toolkit* combining a range of methods suited to the kinds of data that need to be collected and analysed. Correlatively, both short- and long-term village studies have specific weaknesses and disadvantages resulting from the methods and research designs used. These include problems of inadequate coverage and the lack of representativeness. In the case of restudies of the same village, problems may arise due to the inadequacies of the original study, as well as differences in the theoretical outlooks and objectives of the initial and subsequent researcher.

In this chapter, I analyse the strengths and weaknesses of village studies and restudies in general methodological terms, specifying these in relation to particular techniques and research procedures. On this basis, possible ways of overcoming their limitations through compensatory adjustments in the mix of methods and research design are put forward. These general methodological issues and proposals are illustrated by the experience of village studies in Bangladesh.

Defining Features of Village Studies and Restudies

By definition, village studies deal with relatively small residential communities living in bounded settlements. In addition to data for the village as a whole, such studies provide information on their varied constituent units, including individuals, households, lineages, as well as social units such as religious/faith communities, castes, *shamaj*, and factional and clientelist groups. Prevalent relationships among the various social units of the village can be dyadic or polyadic, as well as single-stranded or multi-stranded (that is, multiplex ties) (Wolf 1966). Moreover, such ties and networks may well extend beyond the village, cross-cutting its geographic boundaries (Adnan 1990: 35–7; Bertocci 1970).

The research design (Blaikie 2010) of village studies can be adapted to capture patterns of continuity and change over time. Among these, longitudinal designs involve one or more 'repeat' studies of the same village after the initial ('baseline') study. Thus, restudies of villages generate longitudinal databases with varying degrees of comparability between the baseline and the repeat study or studies (Adnan 1990: 16). Comparison of the findings of the 'baseline' study and one or more subsequent ones provides the basis of assessing continuity and change over the intervening period(s). These can include social, economic, demographic, and other trends affecting a particular community and its members, as well as linkages with the external world. Village restudies can be carried out by the same researcher, or by others who draw upon the initial study as the baseline (Kloos 1997: 435).

However, in anthropology and other social sciences, the notion of restudying a village is fundamentally different from the idea of 'replication' in the experimental natural sciences (Kloos 1997: 429–32). This is because (a) the subject of study itself changes over time, that is, the village and its linkages with the world beyond; and (b) the perceptions of the agent conducting the study—the human person of the researcher(s)—cannot be standardized or calibrated, given irreducible differences in age, sex, identity, experience, theoretical outlook, beliefs, personality, interests, and so on (Kloos 1997: 440).

In exceptional instances, villages have been restudied to cross-check the factual information and theoretical interpretations provided by the original study (Kloos 1997: 432–6). The repeat study may be aimed at subjects and issues missed out or underplayed by the initial study.

Much more frequently, however, village restudies are undertaken to assess continuity and change in relation to the baseline study. Given such concerns, village studies correspond to a special kind of 'historical research', which involves distinct methodological issues and complexities (Kloos 1997: 441–7).

Alternatively, some 'one-shot' studies are designed to capture longer term patterns of continuity and change by 'reconstructing' the past. Researchers have deployed oral history techniques, such as memory recall and analysis of historical documents and artefacts, to piece together the nature and magnitude of inter-temporal trends (Kessinger 1974; Vansina 1985).

In this article, I define LTVS to include both (a) longitudinal studies involving repeat snapshots over time, as well as (b) 'retrospective' one-shot studies that reconstruct inter-temporal trends over a defined period. The LTVS constitute special cases of village studies, which incorporate significant degrees of inter-temporal coverage. The strengths and weaknesses of the methods and research designs used by short- and long-term village studies differ to some extent, as elaborated below.

Objectives and Key Questions

Analysis of the methods, research design, and type of knowledge characterizing village studies focuses upon three key questions, as follows:

1. What are the distinctive strengths and weaknesses of village studies compared to other approaches and methods of analysis in the social sciences?

2. How can the methodological weaknesses and limitations of village studies be overcome or mitigated?
3. What are the distinctive kinds of knowledge that can be generated by both short- and long-term village studies?

These issues are analysed and illustrated by selective references to the methods, research design, and analytical findings of village studies in Bangladesh, as relevant. However, to specify the scope and limits of the discussion, it needs to be stressed that the article is *not* concerned with a *review of village studies in Bangladesh*. Rather, it is primarily directed at assessing the *methods* and *research designs* used in village studies to meet specific aims and overcome particular problems.

The layout of the remaining discussion is as follows. The second section provides a brief introduction to the corpus of village studies in Bangladesh, including those that were conducted prior to its independence in 1971.[1] The strengths and advantages of village studies in terms of methodology and knowledge generation are specified in the third section of this chapter. Correlatively, the fourth section deals with the methodological weaknesses and limitations of village studies as well as possible ways of overcoming them through adjustments in methods and research design. In the fifth and final part, conclusions of the preceding analysis are summarized and integrated with further reflections on the strength and weaknesses of village studies.

Introduction to Village Studies in Bangladesh

Village studies in Bangladesh have been concerned with assessing socio-economic, ethno-demographic, and political structures and trends as well as corresponding linkages and interactions of the village with the world outside its boundaries.[2] These are indicated by the contents of both 'one-shot' and longitudinal village studies, as outlined below.

[1] Present-day Bangladesh formerly constituted the eastern part of Bengal Presidency under British India, and subsequently became the province of East Bengal, and then East Pakistan, within unified Pakistan.

[2] In an earlier publication (Adnan 1990), I have provided a bibliographical listing as well as an analytical review of the socio-economic trends documented in village studies and restudies in Bangladesh and West Bengal of India conducted during the period 1942–88. This review provides a tapestry of thematic

One-Shot Village Studies

During the colonial and the postcolonial periods, there have been occasional descriptions of rural society and 'abstract' villages by a mix of administrators and nationalist writers. However, the first academic village study in the area of present-day Bangladesh was that of Ramkrishna Mukherjee (1948, 1971) who studied six villages in the district of Bogra during 1942–5.[3] This was an exceptional work, and village studies were not undertaken in the area comprising Bangladesh during the next two decades straddling British rule and the emergence of (East) Pakistan.

It was not until the 1960s that significant contributions to village studies in Bangladesh began to be made by a stream of scholars, many of whom belonged to the US-based 'Bengal Studies' group. Some of these monographs were concerned with villages involved in rural development programmes of the Comilla Academy.[4] Notable village studies conducted during this period included remarkable studies of Islam (1974) and Qadir (1960) of land-population adjustments in a Comilla village. A particularly influential study of peasant social organization and change was Peter Bertocci's (1970) doctoral dissertation in anthropology, entitled *Elusive Villages: Social Structure and Community Organization in Rural East Pakistan*.[5]

After the independence of Bangladesh in 1971, there was a remarkable surge in village studies by both local and expatriate scholars.

---

observations based on evidence from this large set of villages. A map showing the geographical locations of these villages in Bangladesh and West Bengal, studied and restudied over the period 1942–88 is also provided (Adnan 1990: 28).

[3] These consisted of a cluster of five contiguous villages in the rural interior and one peri-urban village near Bogra town. The analysis was largely concerned with statistical stratification exercises rather than analysis of roles, relationships, and interactions between individuals, groups, and institutions.

[4] Subsequently known as the Bangladesh Academy for Rural Development (BARD).

[5] As suggested by the title, Bertocci questioned the arbitrariness with which the physical boundaries of the 'revenue' village (*mouza*) in the densely populated Bengal delta were demarcated, given that their geographical limits were typically cross-cut by homestead settlement patterns as well as kinship, community, religious, economic, and political networks.

Between the 1970s and end of the 1980s, a large body of work was produced, including Hartmann and Boyce (1979, 1983), Arens and van Beurden (1977), Westergaard (1980), Cain (1977, 1978), Thorp (1978), Arn (1978), van Schendel (1982), Siddiqui (1982), Islam (1985), and Jansen (1987). During 1974–9, a university-based research programme was undertaken by the Dhaka University Village Study Group (DUVSG) formed by faculty members and students, which studied four villages in distinct agro-ecological zones of Bangladesh, resulting in a stream of working papers and publications.[6] Certain donor-funded development projects also sponsored their own series of village studies in later stages.[7] A Danish-funded project covering Noakhali district produced a series of village monographs and papers including Arn and Mannan (1982), Rahman (1982), and Rahman and Das (1982). After this rich crop of the 1970s and 1980s, the flow of village studies diminished somewhat but continued nonetheless up to the present (2015).

Long-term Village Studies: Longitudinal and Retrospective Studies

Most village studies in Bangladesh have been one-time 'snapshot' exercises, which were not designed to lead to further studies over time. However, a handful of these did reconstruct past trends retrospectively for specific themes and periods. Moreover, some of these one-time study villages were subsequently restudied by others. Both these categories contributed to the corpus of LTVS in Bangladesh, as listed below.

Willem van Schendel (1982) restudied sites originally studied by Mukherjee (1948, 1971) and Qadir (1960), as well as one of the sites he himself had researched earlier. During 1975–6, John Thorp (1978) studied a cluster of 10 contiguous villages (pseudonym Daripalla) in

[6] The research group consisted of four teachers and over twenty students of University of Dhaka. The research outputs were subsequently published as Adnan et al. (1975), Adnan and Islam (1977), Adnan and Mansoor (1977), Adnan et al. (1977), Adnan and Rahman (1978), Rahman (1978), and Adnan (1979).

[7] Other series of village studies in Bangladesh were produced by scholars working in German and Japanese projects. These have not been individually listed here because of limited space; however, a bibliography containing the details of the individual studies is available in Adnan (1990: 204–51).

Pabna, which I restudied during 1985–6 (Adnan 1987, 1997: 278–9). Four villages in Noakhali that had been studied in 1979–80 (Arn and Mannan 1982; de Lasson 1981; Rahman 1982) were briefly restudied by Arn (1988), and subsequently by a host of others. Restudies of their original study villages were conducted in Jessore by Siddiqui (1982, 2000) and in Bogra by Westergaard (1980) and Westergaard and Hossain (2005). Eirik Jansen restudied a village in Dhaka that he had studied earlier (Jansen 1987; Jansen and Rahman 2011). Arens (2011) restudied a Kushtia village (pseudonym Jhagrapur) she had studied earlier (Arens and van Beurden 1977), covering a span of 35 years (1974–2009).

Strengths and Weaknesses of Village Studies

The strengths and weaknesses of village studies in general methodological terms are critically reviewed in the chapter, illustrated by pertinent features and contents of the works on Bangladesh. For this purpose, I have primarily drawn upon village studies conducted during the highly fertile period from the 1970s to the end of the 1980s, while taking note of outstanding studies carried out before and after.

Since LTVS share many features with the one-shot and short-term ones, both categories are reviewed together, with characteristics specific to the former being pointed out in context. I discuss first the strengths and advantages of the village studies approach. This is followed by a critical review of its weaknesses and disadvantages as well as the ways in which these can be compensated for in terms of adjustments in the method-mix and overall research design.

Strengths of Village Studies

In order to assess the approach of village studies, it is useful to compare and contrast it with the questionnaire-based *survey*—a major tool of social science research. The survey instrument collects information from *individual respondents*—subsuming persons, households, and organizations. Crucially, however, it can only capture discrete attributes of the individual units of analysis, such as income and asset-holding of a joint family, or the religion, caste, or status of individual respondents. There is no necessity, in the first place, that elements of the survey population or sample are *interrelated,* or *interact* with each other, in various social arenas. Consequently, this method cannot capture dyadic or polyadic *relations* and *interactions* between individuals, households, and other units of analysis. However, surveys can cover a very large number of villages and their constituent units, such as households, which village studies definitionally cannot, given the much smaller scale at which they operate. This point is taken up later in the context of compensating for the weaknesses of village studies.

In contrast to the survey, the ethnographic method of *participant observation* is integral to village studies. It has the distinctive capacity of being able to capture *relationships* and *interactions* between individuals, households, and other units of analysis. Consequently, this method can provide information on the individuated attributes of the units of analysis, as well as the nature of the relationships and interactions between them.

In the case of village restudies, over and above the baseline observation at the outset, the subsequent studies provide a series of snapshots from which *comparative-static* differences can be assessed. These sequential observations of events and prevalent conditions can provide the basis of inferring trends in the varied *relationships* and *interactions* between individuals, households, groups, and institutions. Taken together, analysis of this ensemble of social entities and their interactive relations over time can help to infer the presence of 'invisible' *structures and dynamics* (Adnan 1987; Arens 2011). Indeed, the extended temporal perspective of LTVS holds the potential of capturing certain kinds of change that would be difficult, if not impossible, with other kinds of social science methods. This applies particularly to *slow-moving processes* and *structural mutations* that may not be discernible from short-term studies.

The distinct forms of knowledge generated by LTVS are illustrated by the reconstruction of inter-temporal trends in the social and economic structure of the Daripalla villages of Pabna over 1947–86. Though the original study (Thorp 1978: 68–74) and the restudy (Adnan 1987) were one-shot attempts, both had reconstructed some elements of the past. By combining their findings, it was possible to work out shifts in the socio-demographic and ethno-religious composition of the village population over four decades (1947–86). Moreover, by comparing the ways in which economic, social, and political relations between peasant households and social groups persisted or underwent change over time, it was possible to assess the nature and extent of the transformation of the agrarian structure and sociopolitical organization of the Daripalla villages (Adnan 1987, 1997, 1999, 2007).

Both the original study and restudy of the Daripalla villages had also reconstructed configurations of the shamaj, the local form of peasant social organization, from an earlier period to the date of their respective fieldworks. Consequently, by integrating the findings of the two studies, it was possible to piece together the changing configuration of peasant social groupings in these villages over 1947–86. In Daripalla, the shamaj group served as the indigenous mechanism of societal maintenance to preserve group cohesion under stress. However, it could disintegrate under exceptional circumstances when such 'tolerance limits' were crossed (Adnan 1997: 289–91). The underlying socio-economic, cultural, and political tensions and conflicts leading to such disintegration (as well as mergers) of shamaj groupings typically took place over a long time. As a result, 'the pace of such shifts in shamaj configuration was usually so slow that there was the deceptive appearance of stability and "changelessness"' (Adnan 1997: 289).

Some of the LTVS in Bangladesh were designed to capture micro-level trends over extended periods of time. For instance, detailed accounts of historical changes in village-level landholdings and property rights during the nineteenth and early twentieth centuries were reconstructed by a number of researchers. These included villages in Comilla by Qadir (1960), in Rangpur by van Schendel (1982), and in Sylhet by Islam (1985) (Adnan 1990: 55–7). In particular, Qadir (1960: 75–6, Table 9, Map 2) was able to trace three successive phases of land-population adjustments in village Dhanishwar in Comilla between the nineteenth and twentieth centuries (pre-1878 to 1944) (Adnan 1990: 46). In a restudy of village Dhanishwar (Dhoneshor), van Schendel (1982: 209–10) confirmed Qadir's thesis of a three-phase sequence of 'inmigration/natural growth/outmigration' in land-population adjustments. In a retrospective village study in Sylhet, Islam (1985) reconstructed the history of human inmigration and settlement processes in its *haor* basin over the nineteenth and twentieth centuries (Adnan 1990: 37).

Significantly, some of these LTVS not only reconstructed past trends of continuity and change but also postulated the causal processes underlying them, based on the maxim that *causes must precede consequences in time*. These demonstrate that complex forms of knowledge, such as *structures of causation*, can be generated by the village studies approach in combination with other methods of social and historical research.

At a practical level, long-term acquaintances with key informants and other residents through fieldwork can help to rectify initial misperceptions of the researcher and obtain more accurate and reliable information. Thus

> ... an advantage of such a long-term village study is that it is an opportunity to study the issues more deeply, establish more personal contacts and get more acquainted with people's lives and problems. This creates mutual familiarity and friendship and builds trust; it certainly helped in collecting reliable data and assessing these correctly. Besides, by studying the village over a longer period it was possible to check and cross check information. Another advantage is that not only a picture ... can be given at particular moments in time, but also of changes that have taken place over time. (Arens 2011: 5)

Weaknesses of Village Studies and Compensating Adjustments

Given the small scale of such micro-level research, the most common criticisms of village studies are those of (a) incomplete coverage; and (b) lack of representativeness. In the special case of longitudinal village studies, there are particular problems related to the comparability of the original baseline and the subsequent restudies, as well as differences in the objectives, priorities, and personalities of the respective researchers. The specific nature of such weaknesses, as well as the ways in which these might be compensated for, are taken up below.

Inadequate Coverage

There are two senses in which village studies cannot provide complete coverage of the object of research. First, they can at best cover a few microcosms of rural society, so that the data sets generated by them are partial and limited. Second, some kinds of macro-economic and macro-social data involve much more than the mere aggregation of individual attributes. Such data cannot possibly be generated by village studies, even if a very large number of them are undertaken.

Specifically, such macro- or *meso*-level data may be necessary for contextualizing the findings of a village study. The data and insights generated by participant observation may need to be supplemented by information obtained through alternative methods so as to provide a comprehensive picture of rural society and change. In practice, village studies typically make use of *multi-method tool kits*, combining participant observation with other techniques of primary data collection, such as interviews and group discussions, as well as secondary data sources, such as census and survey reports, documentary records, and websites on the internet.

The widespread use of such techniques can be illustrated by village studies in Bangladesh. Most researchers supplemented participant observation with other fieldwork methods like surveys, interviews, and group discussions to varying extents (Arens 2011). For instance, Westergaard and Hossain (2005: 3–4) used interviews and quantitative surveys in addition to their ethnographic observations in the restudy of a Bogra village. A few exceptional studies collected data from a wide variety of sources, such as national and regional reports, large-scale surveys, newspapers, documents on property rights and policy changes, and so on. In his study and restudy of a Jessore village (pseudonym Jagatpur), Siddiqui deployed a whole range of methods in addition to participant observation to ensure that all relevant information was collected. These included 'community survey, complete household surveys, non-structured interviews, structured direct observation, participant observation, focus groups, diaries, biographies, perusal of official and private records and maps, community meetings and continuous cross-examination sessions with selected informants' (Siddiqui 1982, 2000: 64).

Such additional data obtained with multiple methods have helped to construct the overall analytical framework within which the findings of the village study have been situated. They have also been used to fill up the gaps in subject areas that could not be covered by the village study itself. For instance, while restudying a Kushtia village, Arens (2011: 6–7) situated the findings of participant observation in a wider context by drawing upon her the knowledge of Bangladesh and global issues and making use of her role as an activist involved in a variety of networks. She also conducted several quantitative surveys to supplement the findings of participant observation.[8]

[8] One survey was conducted between December 1998 and January 1999 to assess the changes in the socio-economic position of the households that had existed during Arens' original study in 1975 (Arens and van Beurden 1977).

In these varied instances, the overall *research design* (Blaikie 2010) of the village study or restudy was adapted to compensate for the weaknesses and limitations of coverage of participant observation. These involved incorporation of complementary methods and techniques such as surveys, interviews, document analysis, as well as knowledge and insights gleaned from interactions with wider networks.

Lack of Representativeness

Lack of representativeness is another widely cited shortcoming of village studies (and other forms of micro-level analysis). It has been noted that 'fieldworkers often too easily extrapolate the results of research in one village to a whole region' (Kloos 1997: 436), leading to unwarranted generalizations.

Conscious of this problem, Arens (2011) notes that the proximity of the village she was studying in Kushtia district to India made it subject to the influences of border trading and other interactions that were not typical of villages in the interior of Bangladesh. More generally,

> ... a disadvantage of village studies is that it is difficult to generalise findings, especially in a country with more than 60,000 villages, a total population of some 160 million people and some regional variations from coastal and river areas to relatively dry areas, such as the Jhagrapur area, which is only seldom hit by floods. Similarly the proximity of the District [and village] to the Indian border creates different dynamics than in Districts that are in the middle of the country or that are close to the capital Dhaka. (Arens 2011: 6)

In order to deal with this problem, it is useful to make a distinction between *representativeness* of (a) the *units of study*, for example, villages, households, and individuals; and (b) the *relationships* and *interactions* between them. The *range of variations* among the latter—that is, differences in the types of village-based relationships and interactions—is far less compared to the variations in the traits of millions of social

---

This enabled her to take account of the growth in the number of households, changes in their economic activities, and thereby 'map the new village settings in my mind again' (Arens 2011: 7). She conducted another survey in 2006–7 on women's land ownership in accordance with the specific objective of her restudy.

units, such as peasant households. To illustrate, most of the 65,000 or so villages of Bangladesh have their respective units of social organization (for example, shamaj) and mechanisms of conflict resolution (for example, *shalish* or *bichar*) (Adnan 1997). These institutions exhibit some degree of variation in terms of location-specific names and different local practices in terms of their operational *rules and procedures*. However, the *system of rules* characterizing these institutions of peasant society in Bangladesh can be grouped into a handful of major types, as compared to the much more wide-ranging diversity among thousands of villages and peasant households (Adnan 1990: 154–80).

Since the distinctive contribution of ethnographic village studies as a methodological approach lies in capturing *relations* and *interactions*, it is significant that the degree of variance among these is much lower compared to that among the units of analysis. Moreover, the possible lack of representativeness of the relations and interactions prevailing in a particular village can be balanced and mitigated by taking account of variations in the corresponding features in other types of villages. To illustrate, agro-ecological conditions of villages are known to influence the kind of livelihood activities and production relations in which its households are involved. Consequently, systematic biases in the social relations and interactions between inhabitants of a given village can be partially balanced by a research design that compares them with those of villages chosen from contrasting agro-ecological zones. This is precisely the approach that was followed by the DUVSG when it selected four villages to study in different *agro-ecological* zones of Bangladesh in 1974 (Adnan et al. 1975).

However, relations and interactions characterizing the social units of a village can be influenced by factors other than agro-ecological conditions. In such cases, *typologies* of such differentiating factors can be used to design a correspondingly balanced selection of villages to be studied to reduce and correct for possible lack of representativeness. As noted above, given the concern that the village she was studying was close to the international border and hence subject to its peculiar influences, Arens (2011: 6) tried to 'balance this disadvantage to some extent' by going beyond the boundaries of the village and covering 'a wider area of social networks and issues with wider relevance'. She also regularly visited other villages in the vicinity and collected relevant information from their inhabitants.

In addition to selecting a mix of villages in their own study, researchers concerned with representativeness can also compare and contrast their findings with those of other researchers studying villages in *distinct* agro-ecological zones or other typological domains. In this way, by comparing and cross-checking with the corpus of available village studies, conducted in different typological domains by many independent researchers, it may be possible to prevent or rectify possible biases in the data on social relations and interactions from a particular village study. The use of such a research design, aimed at ensuring representativeness and balanced coverage, is illustrated by the analytical review comparing the findings of all available village studies in Bangladesh and West Bengal (Adnan 1990; Ludden 2011: 236–7).

Long-term Village Studies: Specific Limitations and Compensatory Adjustments

Longitudinal or repeat village studies are characterized by specific methodological features and limitations that call for judicious handling. While their findings indicate continuity and change between two or more snapshots at particular points of time, these do *not map dynamic trajectories* of inter-temporal trends but *comparative-static* differences. As Kloos (1997: 446) observes: 'A comparison between two points in time cannot logically tell us about the process of continuity and change which historically speaking connects both points'. This is echoed by Arens (2011: 5) in the context of her restudy of a Kushtia village: 'the time-span between snapshots taken at different points of time cannot be taken as linear; it does not say anything about the process in between'. The procedure of 'inferring' the intervening trajectory in terms of a simple linear projection between the points of observation is not warranted because, in the general case, the trajectory of ongoing processes is likely to be non-linear, with ups and downs corresponding to particular events and shocks.

Furthermore, the baseline study itself may not be adequate or appropriate for answering the questions motivating the restudy, that is, the 'problem definitions' of the two studies can be very different (Kloos 1997: 444). Correlatively, the *findings* of the restudy of a village may vary considerably with those of the original study for a number of reasons (Kloos 1997: 436–8). The restudy may be initiated after substantive changes have already taken place in the study area. A village may be subject to structural or cyclical factors of change over time and hence the difference between the original and the subsequent studies would be influenced by the specific conjunctures and phases in which these were respectively undertaken (Kloos 1997: 438). In other words, if the object of study itself has undergone substantive change, and/or is subject to periodic fluctuations, it would not be surprising if the findings of the original and the restudy differ considerably.

The findings may also vary because of differences in the theoretical concerns and research questions, as well as the priority given to them, by those undertaking the original study and the restudy.[9] For instance, differences in theoretical orientation between the original and the subsequent researchers may explain divergences in their village studies. Correspondingly, the political outlook and commitment of the original researcher might have been very different from that of the subsequent one, such that issues of concern to the latter were not covered by the former.

Interestingly, comparable problems may arise even when the *same* researcher, who did the original study, undertakes a restudy later with *different* concerns and objectives (Kloos 1997: 445–6). As Arens (2011: 6) notes: 'A disadvantage of a village re-study [by the same researcher] is that it may be more difficult to look critically at one's own previous work, potentially resulting in repeating errors. Moreover, the researcher as researcher and as a person may have changed and therefore may look at things differently, consciously or unconsciously'.

In general terms, the lack of any standardization of the core data set of village studies implies that the scope of comparison may be *limited by differences in research design*, for example, because variables and issues of significance to the restudy were not included in the original study in the first place. Given such 'problematic' aspects of the original study in terms of the lack of appropriate baseline data with which to compare later observations, the only option open to the subsequent researcher would be to 'go back in time' and independently reconstruct the past in

[9] The differences in the findings of the studies of the same Mexican village, Tepoztlan, by Redfield and Lewis are attributed to the very different ('hidden') research questions as well as their contrasting predisposition towards the research objects and the questions to be asked (Kloos 1997: 436–9).

a form suitable for answering the questions of concern to the restudy (Kloos 1997: 444–5).

In effect, it would be necessary to create a 'virtual baseline' that would provide a benchmark of past conditions to fill up the gaps in the original study, as well as assess subsequent changes on that basis. If there is insufficient documentary evidence for the period between the original and the repeat study, the only method of reconstructing the past would be to analyse oral histories based on memory recall of respondents who had witnessed that period at first-hand or had heard their stories, as well as group memories based on transmission of the original narratives among the following generations (Vansina 1985). Incorporation of these methods in the research design may enable overcoming the limitations of the original study by reconstructing the virtual baseline and the intervening trajectory up to the time of the restudy.

The circumstances leading to adoption of such an approach can be illustrated by the restudy of the Daripalla villages which had been originally studied by John Thorp in 1975–6. His work contains 'a detailed account of the metaphysical beliefs, world-views and ritual practices of the Muslim peasantry' of these villages (Adnan 1997: 278). Ironically, even though the title of Thorp's published volume is *Power Among the Farmers of Daripalla*, it does not provide any concrete details identifying powerful individuals and groupings, prevalent power relations, and political contentions that are indispensable for comparative assessment during a restudy (Thorp 1978). Instead, his account of social organization and local politics in Daripalla is highly abstract and stylized, remaining confined to generalized statements about anonymous and ideal-type individuals (for example, the *malik*) and social groupings (for example, the shamaj). Correspondingly, the economic data cited by Thorp, taken from official sources, are incomplete and often aggregated in ways that preclude tracing of the trajectory of particular cohorts of individuals and households through time (Adnan 1987).

In this instance, therefore, the 'baseline' study did not provide adequate benchmark data about the economic and social organization and political structure of the Daripalla villages at the time of Thorp's research. When initiating the restudy in 1985, I realized that there was no option but to independently reconstruct the social, political, and economic structure of the Daripalla villages and subsequent trends from the time of the 'baseline' study, given the serious inadequacies of the latter. Accordingly, such a 'virtual baseline' was constructed through a review of available written records and oral history techniques, such as interviews and group discussions with those key informants who could still provide recollections of the key events of the preceding period (Adnan 1987). Interestingly, the adapted research design and mix of methods yielded information about the past which, in some instances, pertained to periods earlier than the dates of the original study in 1975–6. While such a reconstruction of the past, based on critical evaluation of oral testimonies and documentary records, was by no means perfect, it served to provide 'some history' as contrasted to the stark choice of having 'no history' at all (Adnan 1987, 1997, 1999, 2007).

* * *

The real strength of ethnographic villages studies lies in capturing multiplex relationships and social interactions between individuals, households, and other social units of analysis. The subset of LTVS has the potential of tracing patterns of persistence and change by reconstructing past events and trends, for example, through the use of oral history techniques and document analysis. Such insights on *relationships, interactions,* and *processes* of change within the smallest communities of rural society cannot be obtained through methods such as the survey and census enumeration.

Moreover, LTVS hold the possibility of discovering and specifying *causal* relationships between multiple strands of change that influence each other. This involves integrated analysis of interlinkages and interactions between political, demographic, economic, and other social processes taking place in parallel. Generation of such knowledge about the interactive sequence of events and processes can provide the basis of inferring the underlying *structures of causation.*

Correlatively, village studies have their shortcomings in terms of lack of adequate coverage and representativeness. Ethnographic participant observation cannot necessarily provide *comprehensive* analysis of social and economic structures and trends of the concerned area and population. Such limitations can be partly compensated by including complementary methods, such as surveys and document analysis, within the framework of the overall research design.

The small scale of village studies means that their findings may lack representativeness in terms of the overall range of variations of the units of analysis, as well as of the structures, relations, and processes interconnecting the former. However, adaptation of the research design and judicious choice of methods can enhance representativeness by ensuring that different types of the units of analysis, as well as structures and relationships, are covered. This may require formulation of a typology of the key differentiating factors in order to select villages with diverse characteristics in appropriate sites, with the aim of capturing the maximum possible range of diversity across the different types. Moreover, LTVS could enhance reconstruction of continuity and change over time through the judicious 'combination of anthropological and historical approaches' (Kloos 1997: 446–7).

Reconstruction of past events, relations, interactions, and processes through memory recall techniques and analysis of written records is not always perfect. The very nature of such tools, respectively involving retrospective recollections and documents produced for other purposes, inevitably imparts a degree of subjectivity and distortion. Nonetheless, an imperfect and limited historical reconstruction may be better than having 'no history' at all by providing a provisional 'map' of the past.

In this context, it is important to note that the inter-temporal perspectives emerging from village restudies at successive points of time may also change as new developments and latter-day outcomes serve to modify initial understandings of past trends. Shifting time-horizons can redefine the significance and impacts of antecedent events and processes and thereby alter the cumulative perspective.

To conclude, in this chapter I have critically reviewed the methodology and research design of both one-shot and longitudinal village studies, highlighting their strengths and weaknesses. The conclusions of the analysis have provided considered responses to the key questions posed in the introduction, as follows.

First, I have specified the methodological problems and limitations generally afflicting all village studies. The focus of the analysis has been on the lack of adequate coverage and representativeness pertaining to the units of analysis, as well as the interrelations, interactions, and processes interconnecting them. In the special case of longitudinal village studies, distinctive problems have been identified in terms of deficiencies of the baseline study in relation to the objectives of the restudy as well as differences in the theoretical outlook and priority concerns of the original and the subsequent researchers.

Second, ethnographic participant observation, the principal method used in village studies, has the unique capability of capturing *relationships* and *interactions* between the units of analysis such as individuals, households, lineages, and other social groupings. However, participant observation also has its limitations, which can be compensated to some extent by the use of additional methods and instruments of research. In this context, I have cited innovative ways of overcoming such limitations by actual village studies through a judicious choice of methods and compensatory adjustments in the research design.

Third, I have highlighted the distinctive *forms of knowledge* that can be generated by LTVS, involving the analysis of parallel and interactive processes of economic, social, and political change. In particular, this approach can lead to postulation of the *structures of causation* underlying multiple strands of change over time.

These general analytical points about the strengths and weaknesses of village studies have been selectively illustrated by the experience and findings of such research in Bangladesh. In this context, it is pertinent to note that much of what is known about rural society in Bangladesh today is based on the findings and interpretations of a large body of scholars undertaking village studies and restudies over the last five decades (Adnan 1983, 1988, 1990). This applies particularly to social, political, and economic relations and processes at the micro-level, as well as the causal factors underlying their persistence and change over time. Such contributions can be significantly attributed to the distinctive strengths of village studies and restudies in terms of their methodology and research design.

References

Adnan, Shapan. 1979. 'Class Structure and Fertility in Rural Bangladesh: Reflections on the Political Economy of Population Growth', in *Economic and Demographic Change: Issues for the 1980s*, vol. 2, pp. 87–118, Proceedings of the IUSSP Conference in Helsinki, 1978. Liege: International Union for the Scientific Study of Population (IUSSP).

———. 1983. 'The Conditions of the Peasantry in Bangladesh', in Joan M. Mencher (ed.), *Social Anthropology of Peasantry*, pp. 313–19. Bombay: Somaiya Publications.

Adnan, Shapan. 1987. 'The Roots of Power: A Re-study of Daripalla in Rural Bangladesh', unpublished manuscript, Chittagong, University of Chittagong.

———. 1988. 'Peasant Ideology and Societal Maintenance: Conflicting Patterns from Bangladesh', *ADAB News*, XV (4): 11–19.

———. 1990. *Annotation of Village Studies in Bangladesh and West Bengal: A Review of Socio-Economic Trends Over 1942–88*. Comilla: Bangladesh Academy for Rural Development (BARD).

———. 1997. 'Class, Caste, and *Shamaj* Relations among the Peasantry in Bangladesh: Mechanisms of Stability and Change in the Daripalla Villages, 1975–86', in Jan Breman, Peter Kloos, and Aswini Saith (eds), *The Village in Asia Revisited,* pp. 277–310. New Delhi: Oxford University Press.

———. 1999. 'Agrarian Structure and Agricultural Growth Trends in Bangladesh: The Political Economy of Technological Change and Policy Interventions', in B. Rogaly, B. Harriss-White, and S. Bose (eds), *Sonar Bangla? Agricultural Growth and Agrarian Change in West Bengal and Bangladesh,* pp. 177–228. New Delhi: SAGE Publications.

———. 2007. 'Departures from Everyday Resistance and Flexible Strategies of Domination: The Making and Unmaking of a Poor Peasant Mobilization in Bangladesh', *Journal of Agrarian Change*, 7 (2): pp. 183–224.

Adnan, Shapan, Kamal A. Khan AM, and Mohammad M. Khan AM. 1975. 'The Preliminary Findings of a Social and Economic Study of Four Bangladesh Villages', *Dacca University Studies*, 23 (Part A): 111–27.

Adnan, Shapan and Rushidan Islam. 1977. 'Social Structure and Implications for Resource Allocation in a Chittagong Village', *Proceedings of the Seminar on Integrated Rural Development,* vol. 1. Dacca: The Institute of Engineers.

Adnan, Shapan and A.H. Mansoor. 1977. 'Land, Power and Violence in Barisal Villages.' *Political Economy,* 2 (1): 125–43.

Adnan, Shapan, H.Z. Rahman, and M. Khan. 1977. 'Differentiation and Class Structure in Char Shyamraj', mimeo, Working Paper No. 8, Dacca, Village Study Group.

Adnan, Shapan and H.Z. Rahman. 1978. 'Peasant Classes and Land Mobility: Structural Reproduction and Change in Rural Bangladesh', *Bangladesh Historical Studies*, III: 161–215.

Arens, Jenneke. 2011. *Women, Land and Power in Bangladesh: Jhagrapur Revisited*. Amsterdam: Universiteit van Amsterdam (Academisch Proefschrift).

Arens, J. and J. van Beurden. 1977. *Jhagrapur: Poor Peasants and Women in a Village in Bangladesh*. Amsterdam/Birmingham: Third World Publications.

Arn, Ann-Lisbet. 1978. *A Case-Study from Bangladesh: An Integrated Village in Mymensingh District*. Copenhagen: Centre for Development Research.

Arn, Ann-Lisbet. 1988. 'Noakhali Villages–9 Years Later: A Re-study of Ramapur, Hasanpur, Madhupur and Yussufpur Villages 1979/88', Noakhali, NRDP/DANIDA Monitoring and Evaluation Unit.

Arn, Ann-Lisbet and M.A. Mannan. 1982. 'Lakshmipur Thana: A Socio-Economic Study of Two Villages', Copenhagen, Centre for Development Research (Project papers, A. 82.6).

Bertocci, Peter J. 1970. 'Elusive Villages: Social Structure and Community Organization in Rural East Pakistan', PhD thesis, Michigan, Michigan State University.

Blaikie, Norman. 2010. *Designing Social Research: The Logic of Anticipation*. Cambridge: Polity Press.

Cain, Mead. 1977. 'The Economic Activities of Children in a Village in Bangladesh', *Population and Development Review*, 3 (3): 201–27.

Cain, Mead. 1978. 'The Household Life Cycle and Economic Mobility in Rural Bangladesh', *Population and Development Review*, 4 (3): 421–38.

de Lasson, Aksel. 1981. 'A Socio-Economic Study of Hasanpur Village, Noakhali, Bangladesh', Copenhagen, BIDS-CDR Joint Noakhali Development Study, CDR Project Paper.

Hartmann, B. and J. Boyce. 1979. *Needless Hunger: Voices from a Bangladesh Village*. San Francisco: Institute for Food and Development Policy.

———. 1983. *A Quiet Violence: View from a Bangladesh Village*. London: Zed Publishers.

Islam, A.K.M. Aminul. 1974. *A Bangladesh Village: Conflict and Cohesion: An Anthropological Study of Politics*. Cambridge, Massachusetts: Schenkman Publishing Company.

Islam, Sirajul. 1985. 'Villages in the Haor-basin of Bangladesh. Studies in Socio-Cultural Change in Rural Villages of Bangladesh no. 4', Japan, Institute for the study of language and cultures of Asia and Africa (ILCAS).

Jansen, Eirik G. 1987. *Rural Bangladesh: Competition for Scarce Resources*. Dhaka: University Press Limited.

Jansen, Eirik G. and M. Nazibor Rahman. 2011. 'Revisiting Bhaimara', *The Daily Star*, 12 January.

Kessinger, Tom G. 1974. *Vilayatpur 1848–1968: Social and Economic Change in a North Indian Village*. Berkeley: University of California Press.

Kloos, Peter. 1997. 'Restudies in Anthropology: Modalities, Limitations and Alternatives', in Jan Breman, Peter Kloos, and Aswini Saith (eds), *The Village in Asia Revisited*, pp. 429–50. New Delhi: Oxford University Press.

Ludden, David. 2011. *An Agrarian History of South Asia*. Cambridge: Cambridge University Press.

Mukherjee, Ramkrishna. 1948. 'Economic Structure of Rural Bengal: A Survey of Six Villages', *American Sociological Review*, 13 (6): 660–72.

Mukherjee, Ramkrishna. 1971. *Six Villages of Bengal*. Bombay: Popular Prakashan.

Qadir, S.A. 1960. *Village Dhaniswar: Three Generations of Man-Land Adjustment in an East Pakistan Village*. Comilla: Pakistan Academy for Rural Development.

Rahman, Hussain Zillur. 1982. 'Report from Raipur Thana', Copenhagen, Centre for Development Research (CDR Project Papers A. 82.2).

Rahman, H.Z. and S.P. Das. 1982. 'The Rural Labour Market in Noakhali', Copenhagen, Centre for Development Research (CDR Project Paper A.82.14).

Rahman, Rushidan Islam. 1978. 'In Search of a Peasant: A Case Study of Char Shyamraj', Mimeo, Dacca, Bangladesh Institute of Development Studies.

Siddiqui, Kamal. 1982. *The Political Economy of Rural Poverty in Bangladesh*. Dhaka: National Institute of Local Government.

———. 2000. *Jagatpur 1977–87: Poverty and Social Change in Rural Bangladesh*. Dhaka: University Press Ltd.

Thorp, John. 1978. *Power among the Farmers of Daripalla*. Dhaka: Caritas-Bangladesh.

van Schendel, Willem. 1982. *Peasant Mobility: The Odds of Life in Rural Bangladesh*. New Delhi: Manohar Publications.

Vansina, Jan. 1985. *Oral Tradition as History*. London: James Currey.

Westergaard, Kirsten. 1980. *Boringram: An Economic and Social Analysis of a Village in Bangladesh*. Bogra: Bogra Rural Development Academy.

Westergaard, K. and A. Hossain. 2005. *Boringram Revisited: Persistent Power Structure and Agricultural Growth in a Bangladesh Village*. Dhaka: University Press Ltd.

Wolf, E.R. 1966. *Peasants*. Englewood Cliffs, NJ: Prentice-Hall.

HIMANSHU
NICHOLAS STERN

How Lives Change

Six Decades in a North Indian Village*

Motivation, Method, and the Survey

Palanpur, a small village in Moradabad district, is not particularly unusual among India's half a million or so villages in its social and economic structure, although no one village could be seen as 'representative'. But what makes Palanpur important for understanding the broad changes in rural India is that it is 'uniquely endowed' with data and studies. It is this uniqueness of longitudinal data, covering six decades, that has allowed a small village of over 1,000 people to be an observatory of

* This work is based on a programme of work in Palanpur, a village located in Moradabad district of Uttar Pradesh. There have now been six surveys of the village, one for every decade since Independence. The most recent covers 2008–10 and is the most detailed and comprehensive. The analysis of the new data is under way in Delhi and London. This article is largely based on an earlier paper by the authors (Himanshu and Stern 2011). We are very grateful to Jean Drèze, Ruth Kattumuri, Peter Lanjouw, Abhiroop Mukhopadhyay, Dipa Sinha, and Naresh Sharma, and all the Delhi team for guidance, advice, and support. The work is supported by a grant from the Department for International Development (DFID) to whom we are very grateful.

the myriad ways in which the rural economy of India is affected by and, in turn, affects the broader economic policies and outcomes. In many ways, the motivation for the studies and the choice of the village were guided by the same questions, controversies, and objectives that have worried policymakers and analysts in the intense debates over possible paths of transition of the rural economy. They were also influenced by specific turns in the history of independent India, which are crucial in understanding the responses of village economies to both policy and what is happening in India. Some of these changes in the structure of rural markets and the transformation of the village economy have required the nature of the survey itself to change.[1] These changes, and the attention to detail over the long period of the surveys in the village, have allowed our work on Palanpur to reflect not only on the changes in rural India in general and in villages in particular in terms of policy imperatives, but also on underlying theoretical questions, which have been crucial in explaining change in a rural society. We are economists and have brought that discipline to our study: at the same time one cannot think about and analyse change over half a century in a complex society without reflecting on issues and ideas beyond those of economics narrowly understood.

Palanpur was first studied by the Agricultural Economics Research Centre (AERC) of the University of Delhi in 1957–8 and then again by the AERC in 1963–4 to examine the impact of the integrated cooperative marketing scheme: cooperative farming was seen in many official planning documents as essential for enhancing the agricultural productivity in a country with many villages and small landholdings. Both these surveys were part of the continuous village survey programme of the AERC, which used to undertake such surveys in different parts of the country. The specific reason for choosing Palanpur by the AERC was that the village was already endowed with a cooperative bank and a cooperative seed store; and importantly, since its agricultural economy consisted primarily of smallholdings, it was seen as an ideal setting to observe the functioning of a cooperative

[1] We note that, while maintaining continuity in the survey design and structure, the survey has seen both intensification of data collection on existing issues to extending the scope of the survey to cover new areas of interest in trying to explain changes in the village economy and society.

scheme.[2] The 1957–8 survey was meant to be a baseline survey for this purpose; subsequent surveys were anticipated and the 1963–4 survey followed. Of these two surveys, the 1957–8 survey was fairly detailed and the data collected was generally of very good quality.

Christopher Bliss and Nicholas Stern returned to Palanpur in 1974–5 because, inter alia, they sought baseline data for examining some of the context, processes, and impacts of the 'green revolution', which was focused on wheat in North India, and for examining some theories of land tenancy and the formation of wages.[3] Whilst the focus of the survey in 1974–5 was primarily agriculture, in particular the functioning of factor markets and tenancy, the survey also collected data on various aspects of the village economy, including features of the non-farm economy. Stern returned in 1983–4 for a more intensive study, in which Jean Drèze and Naresh Sharma played leading roles; this had more detailed information on income; Drèze and Sharma also undertook a smaller-scale study in 1993. There was continuity with the first two studies in that S.S. Tyagi Jr, the brother of S.S. Tyagi Sr who carried out the first 1957–8 study, was central to the data collection in 1974–5 and continued to advice for 1983–4.

The 1983–4 data set has been the baseline for the subsequent study, not only because of the depth of the survey, which went beyond standard agricultural questions, but also the quality of data collected, which was cross-checked and verified in great detail. The 1983–4 data are also enriched not only by the extensive qualitative data collected for specific purposes but also by the diary kept by one of the investigators, Jean Drèze. The 2008–9 and 2009—10 data collection was still more detailed than 1983–4. Also for the first time we have two consecutive years. It is the richest data set of the six. Its collection was led by Himanshu. Nicholas Stern was directly involved in all four of the studies since 1974–5. Thus we have a detailed 100 per cent sample study of key variables for every decade since Independence, and strong continuity of the researchers involved.

[2] It is interesting to note the interest even in the early years of Indian independent history of a systematic way of evaluating the efficacy of government interventions in rural areas. While these may not have been as formal in structure and rigour as the modern day Randomized Control Trials (RCTs), these did provide valuable information on the changes associated with interventions.

[3] The 1974–5 survey also served as a testing ground for many theories of market functioning and wage formation prominent in the mainstream economic literature of the 1970s.

The 1974–5 and 1983–4 studies involved residence in the village for nearly a year in the former case and more than a year in the latter. The 2008–9 and 2009–10 data collection involved residence for two years. These extended periods of residence allow for much more detailed checking of data (often from 'both sides' of transactions, such as land, credit, tenancy shares, and wages), knowledge of the institutional and political context, and direct understanding of the specific circumstances of individual households. This is surely a unique data set.

One lesson we have learned is that our presence in the village and constant cross-checking and subsequent verification is vital to data quality. It induces a certain amount of scepticism about the possibilities for and accuracy of data collection from short visits. That includes aspects of national sample surveys. But we should emphasize that such surveys are nevertheless indispensable for understanding economic development of the country as a whole. Their contribution to understanding development is greatly enhanced by the availability of more detailed studies, such as Palanpur, especially where they track changes over time.

The two most detailed data sets (1983–4 and 2008–10) can be compared most deeply and that is a particular focus of this article. But there are many variables for which we have a time-series of cross-sections with data from all six surveys covering the half-century 1957–2010. The period 1983 to 2010 is especially interesting because it was a period of such rapid change in India. And a key purpose of this article is to begin setting out some of the characteristics of the changes in India and in Palanpur in that period and to examine some of the links, parallels, and hypotheses concerning changes in India and in its villages.[4]

The collection of the data has only recently been completed. The process of careful cleaning is of great importance because of the quality of data being collected and the magnitude of the investments we have made in assembling the data. This includes further work on the earlier data sets to make them as comparable as possible on key dimensions. Such work was itself a major task, in part because some of the earlier data sets were collected for different purposes. This task gives us confidence in those earlier data sets, which are of high quality, and our ability to make comparisons over time.

[4] But we should not forget that the first three decades since Independence brought profound changes too, including democracy, zamindari abolition, and the green revolution.

We do not apologize for spending much of this introduction on the data: its nature and quality are vital to the study and a major part of its distinctiveness. It also reflects a view that much of modern economics focus too little on data quality and jumps too quickly into technique, vital though that is to analytical investigation.

This article presents initial ideas from the early examination of the data. It will, therefore, contain a number of impressions and analyses that suggest further analyses of the data and further hypotheses: it should be seen as a first pass at the data analysis. Nevertheless, it is already revealing some very interesting outcomes for and perspectives on Palanpur, particularly in relation to its integration with India and changes in India.

With this context as the background, both our preliminary conclusions and our subjects for further research fall into three broad categories. First, describing and highlighting economic and social change—for example, the integration of Palanpur into the overall economy of Moradabad, Uttar Pradesh, and India, the changing nature of agriculture and associated capital equipment, the changing social status of some of the poorer groups, and so on. Second, an examination of what has been happening to social and political institutions and how public services have performed. Third, asking how the results and observations in Palanpur fit with various economic, social, and development theories and hypotheses. Further, we shall try, over the course of the analysis, to draw out some possible implications for public policy in India.

Population and Caste in Palanpur

The key drivers of change in Palanpur have been threefold: population and demographics, agricultural change, and non-farm opportunities. In the 1950s, 1960s, and 1970s, it appears that the first two were of particular importance. Over the last 25 years or so, activity off-farm and outside agriculture appears to have become the dominant driving force for change in the village of Palanpur. Evidence from elsewhere suggests this is true of India as a whole. The detail of how this manifests itself is of great importance in understanding economic and social change in India.

The population of Palanpur has grown at a similar rate to the population of India as a whole, as we can see from Table 5.1. The rate of population growth for Palanpur is slightly above that for India in the

1950s and 1960s and substantially below in the last 25 years; although adjusted for outmigration from Palanpur, it is very similar to India for that period.

In Palanpur, caste exercises not only an important social function but also has a bearing on economic behaviour and outcomes.

TABLE 5.1 Basic Population Indicators of Palanpur

	1957–8	1962–3	1974–5	1983–4	1993	2008–9
Population	528	585	790	960	1133	1265
Number of households	100	106	117	143	193	231
Average household size	5.3	5.5	6.8	6.7	5.9	5.5
Female–male ratio	0.87	0.87	0.85	0.93	0.85	0.98
Annual growth rate of population	–	2.2	2.5	2.2	1.7	0.74
Migration-adjusted growth rate		2.3	2.7	1.9	2.2	1.9
Age distribution of the population (%)						
0–14	39	38	46	44	41	38
15–24	21	19	15	20	21	21
25–44	23	25	25	23	22	26
45–64	14	13	12	10	12	11
65 +	3	5	2	3	4	4
Proportion of the population in different caste groups (%)						
Thakur	17	17.9	22.3	20.9	24.9	24.5
Murao	21	23.6	25	18.2	22.8	23.6
Muslim	10	9.5	13.4	14.2	13	12.4
Jatab	16	12.3	12.5	12.8	12.4	16.7
Other	36	36.7	26.8	33.9	26.9	22.8
Proportion of households of different types						
Single-person	6	6	3	3	3	6.4
Nuclear	45	44	41	44	54	60.2
Stem	28	28	29	33	31	20.3
Joint	21	22	28	20	12	13.1

Source: Based on survey data.

Notes: A *single-person* household is a household consisting of a single person. A *nuclear* household is a household with several members, but only one basic couple (husband and wife). A *stem* household has two basic couples, with one husband being the father of the other husband. A *joint* household is a household with two or more basic couples.

In Palanpur there are three main castes in the village accounting for about two-thirds of the population: Thakurs, Muraos, and Jatabs.[5] Relations between these three castes evolved in significant ways between 1957–8 and 2008–10. Highest in the village social hierarchy are the Thakurs, who traditionally had the largest landholdings in the village which, in part perhaps because of an apparent aversion to manual labour, they usually leased out or cultivated with hired labour. Declining land endowments and rising real wages have gradually compelled most of them to take up cultivation. Thakurs are also keen to take advantage of employment opportunities outside the village. Politically, the Thakurs remain the most powerful caste in Palanpur in 2008–9, but they have become less and less the unquestioned leaders of the village. Political reforms introduced in Uttar Pradesh in the 1990s, reserving the position of village headman for Scheduled Castes, have prevented the Thakurs from directly exercising their political power. This has not resulted in a withdrawal from village politics, but has required the Thakurs to engage in coalition building and in enlisting proxies to act on their behalf. In economic terms, Thakurs have seen their supremacy challenged by Muraos, whose rising prosperity—particularly during the 1970s and 1980s—has inspired much respect in the village.

The Muraos are the only caste in Palanpur whose traditional occupation is cultivation. In 1957–8 their per capita land endowments were roughly the same as those of the Thakurs, but over the survey period, they have accumulated land, and have ended up with the best land endowments in the village. Good land, hard work, sustained thrift, and excellent farming skills, at least compared with the village average, enabled the Muraos to take advantage of technological change in agriculture. They have generally been so successful in this regard that they have tended to eschew involvement in non-agricultural activities. The economic status of the Muraos improved considerably over the survey period, and this carried over into some rise in their social status as well. The most recent round of survey data suggest that by 2008–9, agriculture may have become somewhat less potent a driver of income growth and that this may be contributing to an erosion of the economic status of the Muraos.

[5] Details on caste relations are presented in an accompanying chapter in this volume. See Chapter 15 of this volume.

An examination of evolving caste relations based on a scrutiny of the Muraos and Thakurs would suggest considerable caste dynamism in Palanpur, with the Muraos gradually coming to rival the Thakurs at the top of the village hierarchy. At the bottom end of the hierarchy, however, the situation of the Jatabs had long seemed frozen in place. Historically, the Jatabs were socially and economically the most deprived caste in Palanpur. They owned little land, lived in a cluster of shabby mud dwellings, and earned most of their income from casual labour and subsistence farming. Illiteracy among Jatabs had been near universal throughout the survey period, and till 1993, few Jatabs had ever succeeded in obtaining regular employment outside the village. Indeed, Lanjouw and Stern (1998) indicate that in the period upto 1983–4, Jatabs were unlikely to find regular employment in the non-farm sector, even after controlling for wealth position and education levels. In these earlier survey rounds, there was little sign of growth in per capita income for the Jatabs. So, in relative terms, their incomes were declining: in the 1957–8 and 1962–3 survey years the average per capita income of Jatab households was about 70 per cent of the village average. In the 1974–5 and 1983–4 survey years the corresponding proportion had declined to barely 50 per cent. In terms of access to land, the Jatabs also experienced little advancement. Even though the Jatabs were as involved in cultivation as the Muraos and Muslims, unlike those two groups they did not succeed in increasing their land endowments. In fact, between 1983–4 and 1993, Jatabs lost 10 per cent of their land, mainly due to one household selling most of its land to repay mounting debts.

One of the key findings emerging from the 2008–9 survey data, is that the circumstances of the Jatabs is showing significant improvement, both absolutely and relative to the rest of the village. This process is paralleled by a clearly discernible expansion of non-farm employment in the village economy. The important point is that Jatabs appear now to be enjoying greater access to non-farm opportunities than in the past, and this is translating into rising per capita incomes and upward mobility. We provide some preliminary documentation of this trend further in the companion chapter in this volume (see Chapter 11 in this volume).

The population shares of caste groups over the years are also presented in Table 5.1. The Muslim group consists of Telis and Dhobis,

Thakurs (a sub-group of Kshatriyas or 'warrior' group) are generally ranked highest and the Muraos (a sub-group of Sudras or cultivators) are ranked next. The sharp reduction in the population share of others represents mostly Passi outmigration. All other population shares have increased with the increase for Muslims being the largest. Table 5.1 also shows an increase in the proportion of nuclear households and a decline in stem and joint households, comparing 1983–4 with 2008.

The data also show the beginnings of outmigration over the last two decades. It is an important feature of our study and we have managed to collect some data concerning the identity and activity of outward migrants. The information is in its nature only partial, tracking people is not easy, and it is currently being analysed. However, some details are available in Mukhopadhyay (2011) and these suggest a tendency towards increasing access to outside opportunities by Palanpur residents, although not equally by all caste and income groups. We anticipate this to be an important feature of Palanpur's economy in the coming years.

But primarily because of the outward mobility of Palanpur residents, the ways in which population acts as a driver of change have themselves seen change. Unlike a primarily agrarian economy, where population both acted as a source of labour, a 'reserve army', and created pressure on agriculture, the growing importance of non-farm and outside opportunities for those in the village also means that the influence of population pressure on the incomes of Palanpur residents has been muted to a large extent. This is not to deny the impact of population pressure, which has seen a decline in per capita land availability, a feature also influenced by land sales. On the other hand, it has led to the increasing importance of education, we presume, at least in part, as a means, for the next generation to access better livelihoods. It seems that experience plays a role in 'next steps'. Thus those with regular outside jobs seem more likely to migrate. And those with experience as labourers in some trade seem more likely to set up as self-employed entrepreneurs.

The past 15 years have seen a dramatic increase in access to education across most household categories. Table 5.2 summarizes literacy figures by caste and gender. Not only has literacy increased sharply in this period, there is also evidence of a decline in the gender gap. Particularly remarkable is the increase in literacy rates for Muslims (Dhobi and Teli). Even for 'traditionally conservative' castes, such as

TABLE 5.2 Literacy Rates by Caste and Gender

Caste	% of literates (7+) (Male)					
	1957–8	1962–3	1974–5	1983–4	1993	2008
Thakur	38.6	54.7	59.2	59.3	62.6	82.0
Murao	10.4	27.8	40.0	46.3	45.9	72.7
Dhimar	4.2	20.0	19.2	26.5	37.8	71.4
Gadariya	0.0	22.2	30.8	40.0	25.7	67.6
Dhobi	0.0	0.0	0.0	10.0	30.8	50.0
Teli	4.8	20.8	10.3	30.4	22.9	67.8
Passi	8.0	34.5	26.7	47.2	57.1	75.0
Jatab	3.0	9.1	5.4	7.5	16.9	42.7
Other	55.6	60.0	62.5	53.3	60.9	71.4
All Castes	14.1	31.2	33.4	39.8	42.5	68.5
	% of literates (7+) (Female)					
Thakur	0	8.9	12.7	13.8	15.4	46.6
Murao	0	0.0	3.1	1.3	1.4	28.3
Dhimar	0	0.0	0.0	0.0	5.4	35.7
Gadariya	0	0.0	0.0	13.2	9.1	29.3
Dhobi	0	0.0	0.0	0.0	0.0	0.0
Teli	0	0.0	0.0	0.0	2.0	29.2
Passi	0	7.1	5.3	9.1	6.7	36.4
Jatab	0	0.0	3.1	2.6	0.0	20.3
Other	25.0	0.0	33.3	56.3	27.3	41.7
All Castes	1.1	3.0	5.5	8.6	7.0	32.0

Source: Based on survey data.

the Muraos, the increase in female literacy rates is striking. However, notwithstanding this improvement, they are still far below the national average, although fairly similar to the average for rural Uttar Pradesh (UP). For those with more land, the rates are somewhat higher than for rural India and for those with less, somewhat lower (Figure 5.1).

There is a sharp variation across caste in the school attendance of children, with the ordering across caste following closely that of social status (Figure 5.2). Passis are the exception—a small caste that came to the village 60 or so years ago from east UP and for whom outward migration has recently been important. The Telis are the largest Muslim group and about three-quarters of the 6–14 years old children attend

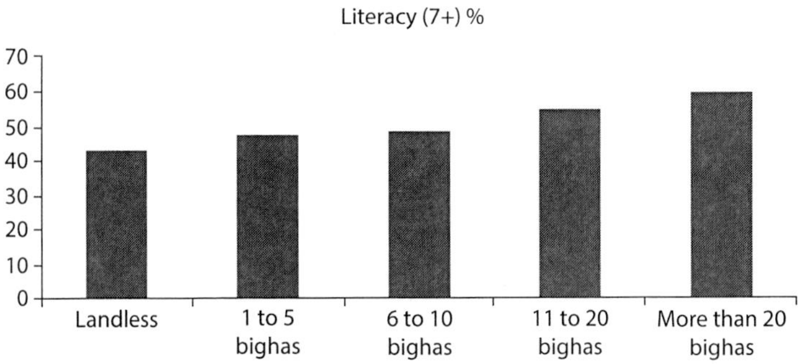

FIGURE 5.1 Literacy by Landholding (2008)
Source: Based on survey data.

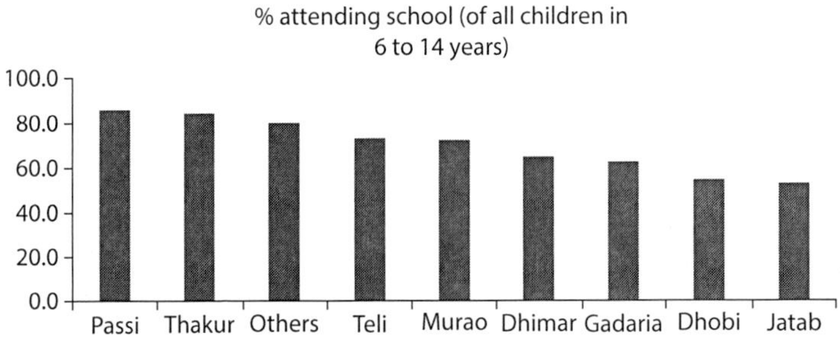

FIGURE 5.2 School Attendance by Caste (2008)
Source: Based on survey data.

school. For the Jatabs (seen as Chamars or leather workers in terms of traditional occupation) the lowest in social status of the substantial groups, attendance is only just over 50 per cent.

Education is the first point in our discussion in this article where we have presented issues of caste, social structure, and other related issues. We have much more detail on these issues and they will form an important contribution of this work.[6] One of the key conclusions, for example, is that the greater opportunities for Jatabs to get outside jobs have raised their bargaining power and social status

[6] See Chapter 15 in this volume.

in Palanpur.[7] This has been complemented by the political rise of Ms Mayawati as Chief Minister of Uttar Pradesh and policies that favour disadvantaged groups, including in local politics.[8] For some further details on education and literacy, see Chapter 15 of this volume.

Agriculture and Tenancy

Land, Assets, and Agricultural Output

The last two and half decades have seen major changes in the role played by agriculture in determining rural incomes. Despite the declining share of agriculture in national GDP, agriculture continues to remain an important source of livelihood for the majority of the rural population. This is also true for Palanpur with 84 per cent of households reporting income from agriculture. But within these households, only 23 per cent of the households were earning their income from agriculture alone while the rest have non-farm activities also contributing to the income of the household. Although population pressure, along with land sales, has continued to lead to a lowering of land owned per capita, Palanpur agriculture also shows elements of dynamism with the agrarian economy taking advantage of the new markets domestically as well as internationally.[9] With the consolidation of the gains of technological progress, such as mechanization and the introduction of high-yielding varieties in the agrarian economy of the village, the rate of increase in yields per hectare has also shown improvements but at a slower rate than that in the peak green revolution period. Tables 5.3 and 5.4 give some basic indicators of the agrarian economy of the village.

Land owned per capita has gone down from 5.2 bighas in 1957 to 2.7 in 1983 to 1.6 in 2008 as a result of population growth and some selling of the land to those outside the village. The latter arose in large

[7] For details, see Chapter 11 in this volume.

[8] Ms Mayawati was the chief minister of Uttar Pradesh from May 2007 to May 2012. She is the leader of the Bahujan Samaj Party (BSP), a party representing the interests of Dalits (Scheduled Caste).

[9] For example, mentha is a new cash crop, which has gained prominence in the last decade and is primarily cultivated for the export market. The prices of mentha are traded in the futures market also and it has seen high price volatility due to international price fluctuations.

TABLE 5.3 Palanpur 1957–2009: Selected Indicators

	1957–8	1962–3	1974–5[a]	1983–4	1993	2008–9
Number of households	100	106	117	143	193	218
Population	528	585	790	960	1133	1265
Average household size	5.3	5.5	6.8	6.7	5.9	5.8
Owned area	2747	2331	2498	2596	2380	2075
Operational area[b]	2723	2783	2438	2650	n.a.	2264
Number of landless households	14	12	17	27	44	42
Land owned per capita (bighas)	5.2	4.7	3.3	2.7	2.1	1.6
Land cultivated per capita[b] (bighas)	4.1	4.8	3.2	2.8	2.1	1.8
Proportion of leased-in land to cultivated land (%)	10	12	22	28	26	36
Proportion of irrigated land to owned land (%)	52	46	96	96	96	100
Gini coefficient: land owned per capita	0.49	0.47	0.49	0.5	0.52	0.52
Gini coefficient: land cultivated per capita	0.48	0.45	0.44	0.51	0.52	0.47
Ownership of selected productive assets (number per 1,000 persons in parentheses)						
Bullocks and male buffaloes	124 (235)	138 (236)	157 (199)	141 (147)	104 (92)	51 (40)
Cows and she-buffaloes	89 (169)	79 (135)	109 (138)	129 (134)	156 (138)	242 (191)
Persian wheels[c]	11 (21)	17 (29)	22 (28)	22 (23)	0 (0)	0 (0)
Pumpsets	0 (0)	0 (0)	7 (9)	27 (28)	40 (35)	85 (67)
Tube wells	0 (0)	0 (0)	0 (0)	1 (1)	n.a	13 (10)
Tractors	0 (0)	0 (0)	0 (0)	0 (0)	9 (8)	13 (10)

(Contd.)

TABLE 5.3 (*Contd.*)

Source: Tyagi and Himanshu (2011a).

Notes: One bigha=0.16 acres.

[a] The 1974–5 reference population excludes 6 households discarded by Bliss and Stern (1982), who restricted their sample to households with at least some involvement in cultivation;

[b] 'Land cultivated' or 'Operational area' is calculated as (land owned) + (land leased in) — (land leased out). The figures for leased area are based on the rabi season; since most leases in Palanpur last for a whole year, this can be taken as representative for the full agricultural year.

[c] Including non-functional or unused Persian wheels (quite common in 1983–4).

Table 5.4 Cultivation Details for Selected Major Crops in Palanpur[1]

Crop	1957–8[a]	1962–3[b]	1974–5	1983–4	2008–9
1. Wheat					
a) Area cultivated (bighas)	879	767	1030	1573	984 (1438)
b) % of total cultivated area[2]	52	48	46	57	48 (71)
c) Yield (kg/bigha)	41	41	114	101	224 (223)
d) 'Normal' yield (kg/bigha)	40–50	50	100	150–60	230
e) Real output value/bigha[3]	16	22	41	27	69 (69)
2. Mentha					
a) Area cultivated (bighas)	0	0	0	0	226 (728)
b) % of total cultivated area[2]	0	0	0	0	11 (36)
c) Yield (litres/bigha)	n/a	n/a	n/a	n/a	3.9 (2.9)
d) Real output value/bigha[3]	n/a	n/a	n/a	n/a	62 (47)
3. Paddy					
a) Area cultivated (bighas)	70	274	125	266	493
b) % of total cultivated area[2]	5	17	6	12	24
c) Yield (kg/bigha)	11	26	103	130	186
d) Real output value/bigha[3]	2	10	33	34	96
4. Sugar cane					
a) Area cultivated (bighas)	391	430	463	886	214 (388)
b) % of total cultivated area	28	27	22	39	11 (19)
c) Yield (quintal/bigha)	n/a	n/a	21.3	12	31
d) Real output value/bigha[3]	34	34	72	43	99
Price Index (CPIAL) (1960=100)	1.07	0.98	3.78	5.28	30.95
Index of agricultural productivity[c]	25.1	24.6	57.3	34.6	40.55

(Contd.)

TABLE 5.4 (*Contd.*)

Source: Tyagi and Himanshu (2011a).

Notes: [1] The figures in brackets show the total figure, including plots sown with mixed crops. In these cases the area figures are upper bounds on the effective areas.

[2] The proportion of the area cultivated refers to the percentage of area under the specified crop for the relevant season (rabi for wheat and mentha; kharif for paddy; kharif has also been taken as the reference area for sugar cane).

[3] Real values are obtained by deflating with price deflators based on the Consumer Price Index for Agricultural Labourers (CPIAL) for Uttar Pradesh. All values are in 1960–1 rupees.

[a] The 1957–8 figures are based on direct calculations from the household questionnaire, and are consistent with the corresponding figures given in Ansari (1964), reported in Bliss and Stern (1982).

[b] The average yield figures for 1962–3 in this table are somewhat misleading in that they exclude cases of zero output, which were not uncommon in that year due to total crop failure on a number of plots. The true average yields, inclusive of cases of zero output, would be lower. For the record, 1962–3 and 1983 were bad agricultural years whereas 1957–8, 1974, and 2008–9 were normal agricultural years.

[c] Value of agricultural production at 1960–1 prices divided by land cultivated.

measure as a result of problems with debt. Thus pressure on land has changed dramatically over 50 years. However, overall the Gini coefficient has stayed close to 0.52 for land owned; there is a decline in the Gini coefficient for land operated largely through the leasing back of land that was sold to outsiders. Preliminary calculations suggest that farm income per capita in the village has stayed roughly constant in the last 25 years; thus the revenue per bigha has had to rise sharply as bighas per person has declined (from 2.7 to 1.6). This rising revenue per bigha has come about in part through an intensification of agriculture associated with productive assets and the increase in cropping intensity. The number of diesel pumping sets doubled from 1993 to 2008, electric tube wells rose from 1 in 1983 to 13 in 2008, and tractors from 0 in 1983 to 8 in 1993 to 13 in 2008.

Agricultural intensification has brought strong increases in yields for some crops, particularly wheat and paddy. It has also been associated with some new crops, particularly mentha, for oil, which arrived in the late 1990s. However, the income per household has risen less quickly than wheat and paddy yields because of the decline in per capita land owned and also because costs have increased (and there has been greater monetization of some input costs). Agricultural intensification in terms of extra capital and more intensive use of land has, therefore, offset population growth and allowed labour to be released into non-farm activities—see in the following sections. As we shall show in further work, the intensification has to do with individual initiatives and the availability of new crops and techniques of cultivation in the neighbouring districts rather than agricultural extension provided as part of public services.

Tenancy

The difference between net area owned and area operated for the village as a whole is explained by the net leased in area from owners outside the village. For 1962, 1974, and 1983 this area was small, representing only 2 per cent of village land, but for 1957 and 2008 it was respectively large and negative (18 per cent of land) and large and positive (13 per cent). In 1957, soon after the abolition of zamindari, some larger landowners associated with zamindars may have been leasing to cultivators from outside the village. We can be more confident of events between 1983 and 2008, as we have tracked land sales. A number of households got into trouble with debts and, as a result, their land was sold to outsiders and leased back to them. In some cases, migrating households have sold land to those outside the village. Extensive details on land sales and purchases have been collected and will form the basis of subsequent analysis.

Preliminary analysis of trends and characteristics of tenancy are available in Tyagi and Himanshu (2011a). Preliminary results show support for the hypothesis that decisions on taking land and tenancy are influenced by the difference between land-owned and desired cultivated area, which depends on agricultural aspects of the household (assets and workers) that may be immobile in the short term. Household labour is important among these aspects and, as Bliss and Stern (1982) showed, for 1974–5 draught animals owned (bullocks and he-buffalos). In 2008–9 the vast majority of ploughing was done by tractors and the role of draught animals was largely irrelevant. Now the more relevant assets are mechanical, such as pumping sets, tube wells, threshers, and tractors; and these are not necessarily fixed in the short term for households as they can be rented in or out. See Tyagi and Himanshu (2011b) for a description of these investigations.

The integration with the broader economy and changes in agricultural assets deployed has brought substantial change in the type of tenancy contract. In earlier years, land tenancy contracts were dominated by *batai,* 50–50 sharecropping, with cash costs for non-labour inputs shared 50–50. The tenant was required to supply the labour. Decisions on cropping patterns and inputs were jointly taken by landlord and tenant. Discussions with participants indicated that risk-sharing, supervision, and liquidity issues exerted a powerful impact on contract choice.

In the last 25 years, with the increased influence of outside jobs and markets, there has been a striking change, as is shown in Table 5.5. Batai has dropped from more than three-quarters of contracts in 1983 to less than half now. *Peshgi*—fixed cash rent—has risen to more than a quarter of contracts and *chauthai*—payment of a quarter of output to the tenant with no cost sharing—has risen to 15 per cent. Peshgi seems attractive to someone with outside commitments who can spend little time in supervision. Chauthai is much more like wage labour and seems attractive to a landlord who can accept risk, perhaps because someone in the family has an outside job, but wishes to leave some incentive to perform, that is, the quarter share, with the tenant or labourer. The emergence of

TABLE 5.5 Tenancy Contracts: 1983–4 and 2008–9

Contracts		Area under specified contracts		Proportion of leased-in area under specified contract[a]	
		1983–4	2008–9	1983–4	2008–9
Peshgi	Advanced Cash Rent	83.3	151	11 (3.1)	20 (6.7)
	Fixed Kind RentAv	23	53	3 (0.9)	7 (2.3)
Batai		564	351	76 (21.3)	47 (15.5)
Chauthai[b]		31.7	118	4 (1.2)	16 (5.2)
Other Contracts		45	78	6 (1.8)	10 (3.4)
Total		747	751	100 (28.2)	100 (36.2)

Source: Tyagi and Himanshu (2011a).
Notes: [a] Figures in brackets indicate leased in area under the specific contract as a proportion of total operated area in percentages.
[b] Chauthai could be seen largely as a sharecropping contract in 1983–4 but mainly as a labour-contract in 2008–9.

chauthai shows the changing nature of the tenancy market in Palanpur. Preliminary analysis suggests that this is partially a result of the tightening of the labour market for agricultural activities in the village and partly a response to supervision problems. There is also some evidence to suggest that the balance of supply and demand for land under tenancy in Palanpur is changing with demand beginning to outstrip the supply of tenanted land. There is some evidence that the bargaining power of tenants may have weakened with more potential tenants emerging. Jatabs, for example, with their increased resources and liquidity, are emerging as potential tenants where earlier they may have been seen as, and seen themselves as, only labourers. And they do not find it necessary to have draught animals as tractor services can be hired.

These observations indicate institutional and contractual arrangements, which respond to a changing economy and society, in other words, they are not immutable traditional aspects of life. And they generate hypotheses about the changing features of an increasingly market-oriented economy which influence the changing contract forms.

A traditional question or hypothesis in the examination of share-tenancy is whether the share, here 50–50, dampens incentives since the worker does not get the full value of the marginal product. The so-called Marshallian view was that output per unit of land would be lower on share-tenanted relative to cash-rented or owner-cultivated land. Marshall, however, was sensitive to this issue and saw that share-contracts would be likely to cover more than just the share and would extend to crops and obligations (see Bliss and Stern 1982).

As in an earlier work, the results for 2008–9 show that this 'Marshallian' hypothesis would be rejected—see the detailed work described in Tyagi and Himanshu (2011b).[10] Cropping patterns, contractual agreements, productivity and influence of risk, and incentives in agricultural choice and arrangements will be a major part of further work. In particular, this will include an examination of household portfolios of activities (agriculture, outside jobs, etc.).

Income and Outside Jobs in Palanpur

The third driver of change in Palanpur after population and agricultural techniques has been the work outside the village. Such work outside the village includes most of the non-farm income, as there is little non-farm income, as conventionally measured, in Palanpur inside the village; of course intra-household activities are always of importance but have not been counted within income here. Outside jobs and income have become ever more important to Palanpur.[11] Most of the activity and income from outside jobs is associated with commuting. As with many villages on the densely populated Indo-Gangetic Plain, there are medium-sized towns within an hour or so of travel time. In Palanpur's case, Chandausi (around seven miles away) and the large town of Moradabad (around 16 miles away) are particularly important as commuting destinations.

Migration over longer distances for longer periods has been increasing, but quantitatively commuting is substantially more important. Most migrants belong to richer classes; there is very little migration amongst the Jatabs (we have already noted the special case of the Passis). Further,

[10] Analysis of crop yield on owned versus tenanted land has not shown any significant differences throughout the survey in Palanpur.

[11] Details on the trend towards non-farm diversification are presented in the accompanying chapter in this volume. See Chapter 11 in this volume.

those households that were already in some regular job or in outside casual jobs seem to have a higher tendency to move out. But even for those who have stayed in the village, a larger percentage is working outside. The increase of work outside Palanpur over the period from 1983 is shown in Table 5.6. The number of persons working outside Palanpur has increased from 95 in 1983 to over 129 in 2008. Details on migrants and the occupational profile of those migrating out is available in Mukhopadhyay (2011).

Preliminary analysis also suggests that the integration with the outside world is no longer the preserve of the upper castes alone. Closer integration with the outside labour markets has made the main lower social group, the Jatabs, better off. Most of their houses have been changed from *kachha* (mud) to pukka (brick). They are explicit about how the increase in their bargaining strength associated with outside jobs has enabled them to raise the agricultural wage in the village substantially; moving from Rs 60 per day in 2005–6 to Rs 100 per day in 2008–9. Real wages for casual labourers in the village are presented in Figure 5.3. The relatively low rate of growth of wages until the 1980s has already been noted earlier in the case of Palanpur. However, the acceleration in growth rate of wages, consistent with all-India trends after 2006, does require more analysis. We shall have more to say about these processes in subsequent chapters. At this stage of our work, the timing of the increases and the analysis by the Jatabs themselves and others suggests that it is the outside employment rather

TABLE **5.6** Occupation Profile of Persons Working Outside

	1983	1993	2008
Skilled self-employed	3 (3)	4 (5)	7 (5)
Unskilled self-employed	5 (5)	2 (2)	22 (17)
Regular (skilled)	5 (5)	3 (4)	10 (8)
Regular (unskilled)	39 (40)	20 (24)	14 (11)
Semi Regular (skilled)	1 (1)	1 (1)	7 (5)
Semi Regular (unskilled)	17 (18)	19 (23)	9 (7)
Unspecified casual labour	25 (26)	35 (42)	53 (41)
TOTAL	95 (100)	84 (100)	129 (100)

Source: Mukhopadhyay (2011).

Note: Figures in parentheses are percentages of total.

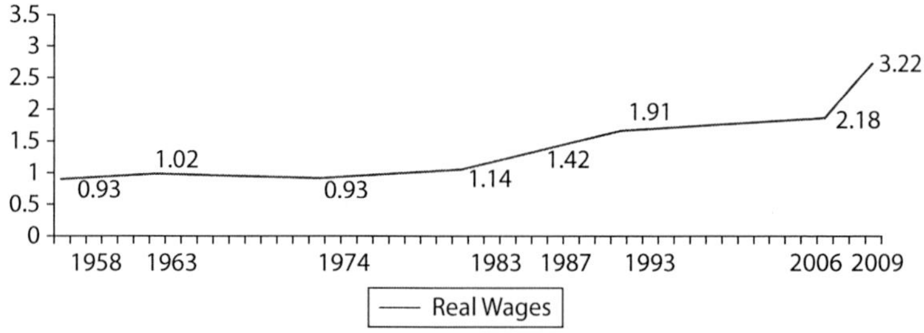

FIGURE 5.3 Real Wages of Casual Labourers in Palanpur (1960–1 prices)
Source: Based on survey data.

than MGNREGA-led intra-village work opportunities that have been the most important influence.[12]

Table 5.7 provides basic indicators of income, consumption, and inequality in Palanpur. For the first time, data on the consumption expenditure of households were also collected.[13] Estimates of consumption expenditure suggest that the poverty ratio of Palanpur at 33 per cent is similar to the average of rural areas of the state. Although not strictly comparable to income poverty estimates of previous years, these also suggest a gradual decline in poverty, even though particular years can be strongly affected by harvest fluctuations.[14] Similar to the trend in rural India and rural Uttar Pradesh, this appears to be a result of significant growth of incomes, which have increased by more than double, but which have been accompanied by some increase in household inequality. The increase in inequality is confirmed by the measure of income inequality but even for consumption expenditure,

[12] MGNREGA, in principle, gives workers the right to work for 100 days a year on public projects at a specified local wage—in Palanpur in 2009 this was Rs 100 per day.

[13] Although the 1958 and 1964 rounds also have some details on consumption expenditure collected as part of household transactions, the 2008–9 survey is the first attempt at collecting consumption expenditure in a systematic manner comparable to the NSSO consumption surveys.

[14] As mentioned earlier, 1958, 1974, and 2008–9 were good agricultural years, whereas 1964 and 1983 were bad agricultural years in terms of rainfall.

TABLE 5.7 Basic Indicators of Income and Inequality in Palanpur

	1957–8	1962–3	1974–5	1983–4	2008–9
Gini (income)	0.336	0.39	0.253	0.307	0.40
Gini (consumption)					0.35
Poverty HCR	47	55	13	40	32.9
Income per capita	161.3	152	274.8	194.2	398.2
Consumption per capita (month)					426.8
Daily product wages (kg wheat/day)	2.5	2.25	3.1	5	9
Annual growth rate		57–62	62–74	74–83	83–08
Per capita income		–1.18	5.06	–3.78	3.19
Product wages		–2.09	2.71	5.46	2.38

Source: Himanshu, Bakshi, and Dufour (2011).
Note: Income and consumption per capita are rupees per month in 1960/61 prices. Poverty line is the Tendulkar Committee poverty line adjusted by CPIAL for rural Uttar Pradesh (Planning Commission 2009).

the Gini coefficient of the locality is very similar to the Gini coefficient of the state. Some idea of the increase in incomes is also available by looking at the product wages, which have almost doubled in the last 25 years.

The distribution of income sources by caste is shown in Table 5.8 for 1983 and 2008. Within-caste inequality contributes more to overall inequality than between-caste inequality (for details, see Chapter 11 in this volume). Over this period, village per capita income roughly doubled but village per capita agricultural income was roughly constant. However, non-farm income rose by a factor of around four. The result was that the share of farm income decreased from two-thirds to one-third. This is a remarkable change of a fundamental nature and we shall be looking at the numbers, consequences, and causations more carefully in the subsequent work. It is interesting to note that similar phenomena have occurred in many other cases across India, for example, the International Crops Research Institute for the Semi-Arid Tropics (ICRISAT) villages in other states: this ICRISAT reference is based on oral communication from Hans Binswanger and we shall be making more careful comparisons in future work.

TABLE 5.8 Per Capita Income

	Number of Households		Per Capita Income (1960/1 Rs)		Share of Income from Non-farm Sources (in %)	
	1983–4	2008–9	1983–4	2008–9	1983–4	2008–9
Thakur	30	56	200	451	32	71.6
Murao	27	58	231	360	14	37.6
Dhimar	13	18	181	380	51	93.0
Gadariya	12	16	202	614	41	68.5
Dhobi	4	8	159	205	2	31.6
Teli	16	21	147	488	47	90.0
Passi	14	6	218	292	69	71.8
Jatab	19	38	85	253	17	68.1
Other	8	9	185	395	58	96.4
Total	143	230	194	398	34	67

Source: Himanshu et al. (2011).

Health, Nutrition, and Status of Women

Improvements on the economic dimensions of prosperity have been associated with improvements in human development outcomes in Palanpur in the last 25 years. We have discussed increases in educational attendance and literacy rates. The last 25 years have also seen improvements in access to health services and improvements in the nutritional status of children as well as adults. A preliminary analysis of some aspects of the nutritional status of children and adults is available in Sinha (2011). Some indicators of the nutritional status of children by caste and economic status are given in Table 5.9. Compared to the national average or the state average, malnutrition among children in Palanpur appears to be on the high side. Although comparison with previous surveys on child malnutrition are not entirely valid because of the small sample size in 1983 (the only previous year for which some information on nutrition is available), comparison of adult body mass index (BMI) suggests that there has been some improvement over the years.[15]

[15] For details, see Sinha (2011).

TABLE 5.9 Child Malnutrition Status by Caste and Economic Status

	Underweight		Stunted	
	N	%	N	%
Caste				
Thakur	17	53.1	20	62.5
Murao	22	62.9	25	71.4
Jatab	20	69.0	21	72.4
Muslims	11	52.4	16	76.2
Others	8	47.1	10	58.8
Total	78	58.2	92	68.7
Asset quintiles[16]				
1 (Lowest)	21	75.0	20	71.4
2	19	73.1	18	69.2
3	12	63.2	15	79.0
4	12	44.4	16	59.3
5 (Highest)	14	48.3	20	69.0
Total	78	60.5	89	69.0
Land ownership (household total)				
No land	13	68.4	16	84.2
1–5 bigha	28	66.7	30	71.4
6–10 bigha	13	50.0	17	65.4
11–20 bigha	18	56.3	19	59.4
20+ bigha	6	40.0	10	66.7
Total	78	58.2	92	68.7

Source: Sinha (2011).

However, a comparison of the nutritional status of children by caste and economic status also suggests large inequalities. Jatabs continue to have the highest percentage of malnourished children. Thakurs do relatively well on these indicators. However, there is also clear evidence that richer households have on an average a lower percentage of malnourished children compared to poorer households (measured by asset quintiles or land owned). There has been slow improvement nationally on these dimensions.

[16] The asset quintiles are based on data on ownership of the household of various productive and non-productive assets using Principal Component Analysis. For details, see Himanshu et al. (2011).

We had detailed surveys on access to health and the health-seeking behaviour of the residents of Palanpur. While the data are yet to be analysed on these issues, qualitative discussions have shown that weakness in public provision have forced reliance on private expenditure on health; sickness and injury continue to remain an important source of vulnerability for poorer households. Our survey on credit also confirms the vulnerability of poorer households to such shocks, with many of them falling into debt after a major illness of a family member. The relatively slow improvement in the supply of health services, such as public health centres (until recently, the nearest health centre was 15 km away), has also meant low improvements in the number of institutional deliveries (only two institutional deliveries of babies were reported in the entire sample of women who have delivered in the last five years).

Women in Palanpur continue to have low access to education and health. We have seen earlier that literacy and school attendance is much lower for girls and women (also see Kattumuri et al. 2011), although we have noted some recent advances in the participation of girls. Problems with the empowerment of women are manifested in the very low participation of women in the labour market. Historically, Palanpur did not have many women participating in paid work; the 2008 survey paid special attention to this issue. Table 5.10 provides the distribution of women by their employment status. Nineteen per cent of women reported working outside the household in a paid job with associated payments (not very different from the state average based on Census 2001). Those who do participate in the labour market mostly belong to lower castes, such as Jatabs (plus some Murao women). However, regular employment, such as that of school teachers, *anganwadi* (nursery) workers, and Accredited Social Health Activist (ASHA) is still dominated by upper caste women.

TABLE 5.10 'Outside' Work by Women in Palanpur in 2008

Work	Freq.	Percent
No paid job	176	81.1
Paid in kind	25	11.5
Paid in cash	16	7.4
Total	217	100

Source: Sinha and Coppoletta (2011).

The surveys on women in Palanpur covered various aspects of the status of women in Palanpur society using various indicators of autonomy, decision-making, and mobility. Preliminary results confirm the low mobility, in the sense of frequency of travel outside the village, of Palanpur women, on average, with the moderately higher mobility of Jatab women compared to Thakur women. Three out of four women reported having some say in household expenditures but only 8 per cent have land in their own name and 18 per cent have access to a bank account. Issues such as domestic violence are sensitive. Fifty-four per cent of women in Palanpur reported having ever been beaten by their husbands, of which 11 per cent were beaten regularly and 36 per cent sometimes. These are far higher than the rural India average of 36.1 per cent and the Uttar Pradesh average of 42.4 per cent (International Institute for Population Sciences and Macro International 2007). However, given that our survey was done at a later stage during our stay, when we had gained the confidence of the women in Palanpur, these numbers could also be higher because of better reporting.

Government Institutions and Politics in Palanpur

Some of the external stimuli, such as the opening up of markets, access to outside jobs and greater connectivity and communication, have also affected the functioning and evolution of village institutions. Some institutional responses in economic dimensions, such as tenancy, have already been highlighted above. On social and political dimensions too, there is some evidence of a changing institutional response. While some of the existing institutional barriers, such as patriarchy, show some sign of weakening with the greater participation of women in higher education, there has been some strengthening of participative and collective action for the common public good of the village. This has been mediated through various forums, including the panchayat. This has been partly a response to the internal dynamics of the village, with the greater participation of lower castes in political processes, but also through external factors, such as the emergence of the BSP as a strong political force in the state.

There has also been a significant increase in the spending by the central and state governments on education and health. However, the increased spending has not yet materialized into corresponding improvements in schools and public health facilities in Palanpur. While the number of classrooms has increased from three in 1983 to more than five in 2008, the number of teachers in the village primary school has come down from five in 1983 to only one in 2008. Although there are two para-teachers in the village, the quality of teaching in the school leaves much to be desired. Similarly, the village anganwadi (Integrated Child Development Scheme centre for pre-school children) has never been functional. The village anganwadi workers sit at the primary school but there are very few pre-school children present there. We have also not seen any reliable and systematic effort to provide supplementary nutrition to pre-school children in the village. Even the midday meal school programme was non-functional for almost one year of our presence in the village. The most ambitious programme of the central government, MGNREGA, was initiated when the survey team was in the village, but hardly functioned in the initial months of its implementation. We also did not find any substantial evidence of the functioning of the Public Distribution System (PDS), designed to distribute subsidized and ration 'essentials'. For almost six months, the PDS shop in the village was closed because of corruption charges against the PDS dealer.

What was also unfortunate was that there was no effort to maintain even the existing institutions. The seed store and the cooperative bank in the village were important village institutions and played a role in the green revolution in the village up to the 1970s. The seed store building has almost collapsed, along with its functioning, and the cooperative bank was hardly functional. The brother of the cooperative bank manager is also the main money lender in the village, leading to a problematic nexus of the institutional and non-institutional credit market.

Some of these problems were related to the failure or absence of collective effort by the village community. Ironically, most of the decay in village institutional structure had taken place during the tenure of the first Dalit (Scheduled Caste) pradhan (headman) of the village. However, during our stay in the village, there were signs of change, which are worth emphasizing here. Two instances of village collective action are mentioned. The first was the impeachment of the erstwhile pradhan by the village community. The requisite number of signatures to require a new election was collected and he was defeated. This was unprecedented in the history of the village. The second was the villagers' efforts to get rid of the monkey menace in the village through collective action.[17]

Fortunately, after the impeachment of the old pradhan and the election of a new pradhan, there have been improvements in the functioning of most of the village institutions. There is a new permanent teacher who has been appointed in the school. The midday meal programme, which was non-functional, has started functioning. A new PDS dealer was appointed in the village. During the last election for a village pradhan (this was later than the by-election after the impeachment of the old pradhan), the seat was reserved for women and the village now has a woman pradhan.[18]

* * *

The high growth rates in the Indian economy for 15 years from the mid-1990s have generated considerable attention. In addition to the issue of the sustainability of such growth, it is questioned whether this growth is also shared by rural India, still home to almost three-quarters of the population. It is in this context that this chapter has looked at the changes happening in Palanpur in the last six decades. The basic story of Palanpur over the years, and in particular the last three decades, the particular focus of this chapter, has been a story of continuity with change. The continuity is in terms of the three primary drivers of change, which have remained population, technology, and outside jobs. However, there are very important elements of change in the way these factors have influenced the village, including the growth of incomes and the way institutions have responded to these forces, including in land and labour markets.

Population growth continues to exert pressure on the resources of the village. However, in contrast to earlier periods, the pressures have in part been accommodated by the mobility of the residents of Palanpur.

[17] Although the survey team was staying in the village, we decided not to intervene in the local politics of the village and in both instances, the survey team kept out of the affairs of the village community.

[18] Although the current pradhan of the village is a woman, she lives in Moradabad and the activities related to the panchayat are handled by her husband and other relatives in the village.

Some have migrated out, in greater numbers than previous years, but also the population has been able to avail itself of the opportunities outside the village. The second factor has also contributed to an easing of some of the pressure of population on land and agriculture. Even though the land owned by the village residents has declined, yields per hectare have seen substantial improvements; the tenancy market has adapted itself to the new challenges with no decline in the absolute area under tenancy. Along with the intensification of mechanization, the introduction of new crops and the integration with outside commodity markets have brought benefits to the farming community. However, this has also made them more vulnerable to the volatility of international markets, particularly in the case of mentha, a cash crop adopted in the village since late 1990s.

The increase in non-farm employment opportunities has also meant that the labour market is no longer dependent overwhelmingly on agriculture. Mechanization and technological change are leading to a (relative) decline in labour demand in agriculture; wages continue to increase. The access to outside jobs and markets has also been a factor in changes in the distribution of income and changes in the social status of different caste groups. While Jatabs, the poorest caste group, remain at the bottom of the caste hierarchy, there is evidence that they have gained socially and economically as a group. But even though Jatabs have seen improvements in their social and economic status, overall inequality in the village has continued to increase, in a manner similar to national trends.

Notwithstanding incomes increasing and institutions adapting to economic changes, there has not been strong improvements across the board in human development indicators. Literacy has increased and there has been significant improvement in school enrolment. We should emphasize, however, that these are largely driven by increase in demand. On the supply side, there seems to be some deterioration in the quality of teaching and of the presence of teachers. Other public services, such as the anganwadi and health services, hardly function. Existing institutions, such as the seed store and the cooperative bank, are no longer functional. However, some of these problems appear to be temporary; with the change in village headman there is some improvement in the quality of public services. The collective action by the villagers in impeaching the earlier village headman does suggest a rise in sensitivity of the village community to these issues.

Overall, Palanpur over the last six decades shows a mixed picture of change and continuity. Understanding the nature of change in Palanpur and making use of its rich data, can make a powerful contribution to our understanding of the nature of development processes in the rural areas of the country. Such understanding is also important, in turn, for an understanding of the structural responses and bottlenecks for the sustainability of growth in the country as a whole. The uniqueness of the Palanpur data lies not only in its longitudinal nature, spanning over six decades, but also in the extent and nature of data collected, covering almost all aspects of the village economy. These features together with the quality of the data, and the care with which they were collected, will allow various analytical exercises, which are not only crucial to the examination of relevant economic theories but also for lessons on policy.

References

Ansari, N. 1964. 'Continuous Village Surveys 1958–59 No.41: Palanpur, District: Moradabad, State: Uttar Pradesh, a Study of its Economic Resources and Economic Activities', Agricultural Economics Research Centre (AERC), University of Delhi, New Delhi.

Bliss, Christopher and Nicholas Stern. 1982. *Palanpur: The Economy of an Indian Village*. New Delhi: Oxford University Press.

Himanshu, Ishan Bakshi, and Camille Dufour. 2011. 'Poverty, Inequality and Mobility in Palanpur: Some Preliminary Results', Asia Research Centre Working Paper Number 45, London School of Economics and Political Science, UK.

Himanshu and Nicholas Stern. 2011. 'India and an Indian Village: 50 Years of Economic Development in Palanpur', Asia Research Centre Working Paper Series, London School of Economics and Political Science, UK.

International Institute for Population Sciences and Macro International. 2007. 'National Family Health Survey (NFHS-3) 2005–06: India', vol. 1, IIPS, Mumbai.

Kattumuri, Ruth, Dinesh Tiwari, Diya Bhatnagar, Hemendra Ahirwar, and Gajanand Ahirwar. 2011. 'Literacy, Education levels and Related Services in Palanpur', Asia Research Centre Working Paper Number 46, London School of Economics and Political Science, UK.

Lanjouw, Peter and Nicholas Stern. 1998. *Economic Development in Palanpur Over Five Decades*. Oxford: Clarendon Press.

Mukhopadhyay, Abhiroop. 2011. 'Stepping Out of Palanpur: Employment outside Palanpur', Asia Research Centre Working Paper Number 46, London School of Economics and Political Science, UK.

Planning Commission. 2009. 'Report of the Expert Group to Review the Methodology for Estimation of Poverty', New Delhi, Planning Commission, Government of India.

Sinha, Dipa. 2011. 'Nutrition Status in Palanpur', Asia Research Centre Working Paper Number 51, London School of Economics and Political Science, UK.

Sinha, Dipa and Rosalinda Coppoletta. 2011. 'The Invisible Half: Women's Status in Palanpur', Asia Research Centre Working Paper Number 50, London School of Economics and Political Science, UK.

Tyagi, Ashish and Himanshu. 2011a. 'Change and Continuity: Agriculture in Palanpur', Asia Research Centre Working Paper Number 48, London School of Economics and Political Science, UK.

——— 2011b. 'Tenancy in Palanpur', Asia Research Centre Working Paper Number 47, London School of Economics and Political Science, UK.

GERRY RODGERS
SUNIL K. MISHRA
ALAKH N. SHARMA

Four Decades of Village Studies and Surveys in Bihar*

Longitudinal Data on Bihar Villages

This article is based on longitudinal village research that has been carried out in rural Bihar over several decades. A brief history of that research is given in the following pages. The second section discusses the databases that have been constituted, the questions that they have been designed to address, and some of the practical issues that have been faced in survey implementation. There have been several projects at different points in time, which have adopted quite diverse approaches. The third and fourth sections then show how these

* This article draws on work carried out jointly with Janine Rodgers and Amrita Datta under the IHD research programme on Inclusive Development in Bihar, and has been revised to take into account their comments and contributions. Comments by participants in the international conference on 'Understanding Change in Rural India: Perspectives from Longitudinal Village Studies', held at Jawaharlal Nehru University in November 2012, where an early version of this article was presented, are also gratefully acknowledged.

longitudinal data can illustrate different aspects of village development; the third section considers changes in the agrarian system, and the fourth section looks at the how the living standards of individuals and households have changed over time.

The research in Bihar had two origins.

The first was work that Pradhan H.S. Prasad conducted at the A.N. Sinha Institute of Social Studies in Patna in the 1960s and 1970s. Prasad was a participant in the mode of production debate that then prevailed, and one of the protagonists of a model of semi-feudalism, which he used to explain agricultural stagnation and persistent poverty in the post-zamindari era. He undertook a number of field studies in rural Bihar in that period to document the workings of his model of the agrarian system.

The second was some studies that Gerry Rodgers undertook in a small number of villages in Bihar in 1969–71. This was in the early Green Revolution days, and a group from the University of Sussex was studying the implications for agricultural and rural development in the Kosi area. Rodgers' research was on the effectiveness of policy against poverty, and that involved fieldwork among poor households in several villages in Purnia district. This research showed that policy was not being designed in the light of village realities—especially labour markets, which functioned in particular ways at very low income levels.

In the late 1970s, Pradhan Prasad and Rodgers decided to study patterns of change in rural Bihar more systematically. Prasad was interested in the dynamics of the mode of production and the forces preventing or promoting the emergence of capitalist agriculture; Rodgers was interested in the persistence of poverty and the role of labour market institutions and demographic change. We decided to study these subjects by collecting fresh data at the village and household level. The study ended up with a sample of 36 villages, chosen through a mix of purposive and random techniques, and designed to be as far as possible representative of rural Bihar.

In the period 1981 to 1983, a survey was carried out in these 36 villages by the A.N. Sinha Institute of Social Studies, and household data collected from 12 villages selected among them (a census of 2,531 households and a sample survey of 564). Detailed information was collected on production and employment, on assets and investment;

there were surveys of women, anthropometric measures of children, questions on village institutions, on health and mortality, on education and other topics. More data were collected than could be analysed at the time, but a number of papers were prepared on topics such as the relative importance of caste and class, poverty, demographic change, regional variation, the impact of government policy and other issues, and a detailed report was issued by the A.N. Sinha Institute on findings from early rounds of data collection (Prasad et al. 1988).

In this same period, Janine and Gerry Rodgers returned to some of the villages of the earlier study in Purnia, in the first truly longitudinal element of this research, and reinterviewed a small sample of households after a ten-year gap. They found economic stagnation and intensification of poverty. But tracking individual households also showed how they moved in and out of poverty, often as a result of life cycle effects or accidents. This is an important application of longitudinal work, which adds a new dimension to poverty estimates (see, for instance, Baulch and McCulloch [2002] on Pakistan), since a much higher proportion of households is vulnerable to poverty than is below the poverty line at any one point in time (Rodgers and Rodgers 1984).

In the late 1990s, Alakh N. Sharma, who had participated in the A.N. Sinha Institute study, decided to resurvey the 36 villages, as one of the first projects of the newly founded Institute for Human Development. The broad objective was to investigate whether there had been significant economic and social change since the early 1980s. It was not possible to cover the same households, because the data needed to permit individual identification had been lost. However, this project undertook in-depth surveys of households in the same 12 villages as before, covering production, incomes, credit, gender inequality, and other issues. The survey found that there had been considerable change since the early 1980s. Poverty had declined, migration had increased, the middle castes were reinforcing their position, and the agrarian system was evolving rapidly (Institute for Human Development 2004; Sharma et al. 2001).

About the same time, Janine and Gerry Rodgers revisited some of the villages studied earlier in Purnia, and documented the breakdown of semi-feudal agrarian relations in the face of increasing migration. They traced and reinterviewed some households that had been interviewed in earlier visits, and documented both rising incomes and occupational diversification (Rodgers and Rodgers 2001).

Since 2009, there has been another series of surveys in the same villages. These examine whether new production relations and institutional frameworks have emerged, and their implications for production and incomes. There is a particular focus on state policies, weak at the time of the earlier surveys, but politically much more visible and effective in 2009. Both village-level and household data were collected; there were now some 5,498 households in the 12 core villages. This time, the survey traced the same households as had been surveyed earlier. Of the 891 households surveyed in 1998–9, 761 were recovered, giving rise to a sample of 941 households after household division and formation. Another round of data collection was carried out in 2011.

In addition to the household survey, more detailed studies of individual villages (selected from among the 12 core villages) were undertaken in order to explore the mechanisms of economic and social change. This included open-ended interviews with selected households for which data exist from 1998–9 (sometimes in the shape of extended interviews).

Types of Data and Their Applications

This series of projects has generated a wide variety of data, collected through methods of different types.

a) There are conventional household survey data, collected at different dates in the selected villages. The intention was to be able to say something about each village, as well as about the population as a whole. Within each village a random sample of around 20 per cent of households was taken, stratified by class. In both 1998–9 and 2009–10, a basic questionnaire was canvassed for a sample of households from all 36 villages, but in-depth household data came from 12 villages. These data have been applied to the analysis of change in the agrarian system, patterns of poverty and employment, levels of living, and the impact of state policy. Much of this is about describing patterns, trends and their correlates, treating the sample as broadly representative of rural Bihar as a whole, or at least capturing the main features of rural Bihar. The fact that the same villages were surveyed in each round makes it possible to be reasonably confident about the measurement of change. Complementary data were also collected at the village or *tola* level, notably including a survey of gender issues. Some results were reported in Rodgers et al. (2013).

b) There are two types of panel data: on households (between 1998–9 and 2009–10) and villages (since 1981).

Household panel data offer many possibilities for analysis. As noted above, it is possible to measure not only the incidence of poverty, but also vulnerability to poverty over time, and the same is true of other household measures. Panel data also permit the investigation of how a household's characteristics at a point in time affect its future trajectory, or whether government policy at one point in time has a continuing impact on the households concerned.

Village panel data come both from secondary sources and key informants, and from aggregating household characteristics from the sample. They can be used to analyse development patterns in unconventional ways. For instance, it may be possible to both develop typologies of village development paths and explore how far initial endowments (land, irrigation, population density, and education) or agrarian structures affected subsequent outcomes.

c) There are more detailed village studies involving multiple visits and wider contacts. These studies cannot attain the in-depth knowledge achieved by anthropologists, since they are based on short visits and interactions with selected households and social actors. Nevertheless, they provide a great deal of information on labour markets and livelihoods, on social relations and patterns of behaviour, to expand on that available from household and village surveys. This can be used for comparative analysis of development paths. For example, a detailed comparative study was undertaken of two villages (among the 12 core villages), which represented two different development models (Datta et al. 2014).

In addition to in-depth studies of the villages of the main survey, there have been several revisits to two villages in Purnia district first surveyed in 1970. These have documented trends and provided ideas and hypotheses for subsequent investigation, for example, the intensification of poverty in the 1970s, the shift of the agrarian system towards market relationships in the 1990s, and more recently the contrast between successes in the implementation of social policy on the one hand, and a lack of dynamism in the rural economy on the other.

d) Case studies of individual households at different points in time. Only a few of these have been done, but they provide additional insights in much the same way as village studies. In particular, they help to understand the strategies of households and their perceptions of outcomes.

An important issue with panel data is the completeness of coverage at different points in time. In our case the main question was the recovery rate in 2009–10 of sample households from 1998–9. Table 6.1 gives the details for the 12 core villages, broken down by caste and community. Of the 891 households in the 1998–9 sample, 761 were recovered in 2009–10 (85 per cent). It can be seen that recovery rates for Muslim households and Other OBC-II are low (the same is true of Scheduled Tribes but there are very few cases). Recovery rates for OBC-I, Brahmins, and Koeris are higher.

TABLE **6.1** Panel Data in Rural Bihar. Recovery Rate for Sample Households, 1998–9 to 2009–10, by Caste and Community

Caste/ community	No. of hhds 1998–9	Hhds recovered 2009–10	Recovery rate	Total no. of hhds 2009–10	Ratio 2009–10 to 1998–9 among recovered hhds	Overall ratio
Brahmin/ Kayasta	164	150	0.91	175	1.17	1.07
Bhumihar/ Rajput	87	72	0.83	89	1.24	1.02
OBC-I	163	148	0.91	190	1.28	1.17
Kurmi	27	23	0.85	29	1.26	1.07
Yadav	53	45	0.85	56	1.24	1.06
Koeri	33	31	0.94	34	1.10	1.03
Other OBC-II	65	51	0.78	64	1.25	0.98
Scheduled Caste	197	163	0.83	211	1.29	1.07
Scheduled Tribe	3	2	0.67	2	1.00	0.67
Upper Muslim	28	22	0.79	27	1.23	0.96
Lower Muslim	71	54	0.76	64	1.19	0.90
Total	891	761	0.85	941	1.24	1.06

Sources: IHD Bihar Survey, 1998–9; IHD Bihar Survey 2009–10, Household Sample (12 villages).

Table 6.2 gives the reasons for the failure to cover the missing households. This information was collected in the course of a special follow-up tracking survey in 2013, which involved recontacting the majority of surveyed households and obtaining additional information. In particular, direct or indirect information was obtained on households that had not been captured in the resurvey (indirect information being provided, when possible, by neighbours or relatives when the household concerned could not be contacted). In addition, the follow-up survey provided an opportunity to check on some errors and inconsistencies, notably in demographic data and land ownership.

It can be seen that almost 30 per cent of these cases were accidental omissions. This was sometimes due to the absence of all members of the household at the time of the 2009 survey for social or personal reasons, sometimes investigator error, sometimes relocation of the household within the village. A further 17 per cent were cases where the wrong household was interviewed in the second round of data collection, usually because several household heads had the same name. Another 8 per cent were not traceable. Sometimes this appears to be because the name was incorrectly recorded in 1998–9. In addition, when the household head is female, the common practice is to write the surname as 'Devi' rather than to write the surname

TABLE 6.2 Major Reasons for Omission of 1998 Households in 2009

Reason	Number of households	Percentage of households
Accidentally omitted (in 2009 and 2011)	37	28.5
Household disappeared through death of all members	15	11.5
Household disappeared because all remaining members joined another household	8	6.2
Long-term or permanent outmigrant (including return migrant)	38	29.2
Wrong household surveyed in 2009	22	16.9
Could not be traced	10	7.7
Total	130	100.0

Source: IHD Bihar Survey 2009–10, Household Sample.

of the husband. In this case it can be impossible to determine which household is concerned. So altogether, about half of the missing households reflected survey problems of one sort or another. The remaining cases were legitimate changes. Just under 30 per cent of the missing households had permanently migrated (including a small number who had since returned from 'permanent' migration). In the remaining cases, the household had disappeared because of the death of all members, or because after the death of some members the remaining members (often the widow) joined some other household (often the son). We can see that the overall permanent migration rate is very low—38 households out of 891 over 11 years, or about 0.4 per cent per year.

These 761 households from 1998–9 grew to 941 households in 2009–10 because of household division. The highest rates of household formation were found among Kurmi, OBC-I, and SC households. Taking both the recovery rate and the rate of household formation into account, in the 2009–10 sample there was a range from less than 100 per cent of the 1998–9 sample size for Muslims and other OBC-II to almost 120 per cent for OBC-I (neglecting the small number of ST households). There may be some biases as a result, but the overall pattern is broadly maintained over time.

It should be recognized that in data of this type, collected and processed by different teams over long periods of time, it is impossible to eliminate all errors and biases. The goal has been to keep such errors to a minimum through repeated checking and updating of data files and through renewed field visits. The present article is mainly based on the data base as of late 2013, but some later revisions of 1998–9 data files have also been taken into account.

The Changing Agrarian System

An important application of longitudinal research in Bihar is to understand the changing agrarian economy. At the time of the surveys in the 1980s, the agrarian system was understood in terms of a semi-feudal mode of production, as described by Pradhan Prasad (1979, 1987), Bhaduri (1973), and others. In this system, caste, class, and landholding were intertwined, an issue that we have examined in other writings (for example, G. Rodgers 2012). Here we use the longitudinal data to track the changing class structure.

Table 6.3 shows the changing distribution of households in terms of class categories that were used to capture semi-feudal differentiation in 1981. The following categories were used:

- *Agricultural labour households* (all households in which some agricultural work was done for wages). These were divided into four groups according to whether they were also cultivating some land as owner or sharecropper and whether they were attached or tied to a single employer.
- *Peasant (cultivating) households,* divided into three groups: poor or small peasants, who neither hired in nor hired out labour; middle peasants who hired labour in and where both male and female family members also worked in agriculture: and big peasants who hired in labour and who used only male family labour. Notice that gender roles were built into the definition of class: whether or not women engaged in cultivation was seen as a key dividing line in 1981.
- *Landlords renting out land and landowners who only supervised cultivation on their land* (but did not work on the land themselves)
- *Non-agricultural households,* in 2009–10 divided into wage labour and self-employment. These are defined as households that did no agricultural work.

It can be seen from the Table 6.3 that attached agricultural labour all but disappeared between 1981 and 2009–10. Attached labour is a central feature of the semi-feudal model, and its disappearance a clear indicator of the change in the agrarian system. On the other hand, the share of casual agricultural labour households rose by more than the decline in attached labour, so overall the share of agricultural labour slightly increased. By far the biggest increase concerned landless agricultural labour. There was also a substantial increase in the proportion of households that only did non-agricultural work, especially non-agricultural wage work (which in 2009–10 accounted for 10 per cent of households). Among the cultivating and landowning classes, there was some increase in the share of poor peasants and a decline in the number of big peasants, but the shifts among different groups of cultivators were fairly small, and seemed to reflect the increase in population pressure on land. The main exception concerned landlords, whose share declined sharply, reflecting the declining numbers of large landowners renting out their land, another indicator of the disappearance of semi-feudal production relations.[1]

[1] However, the definition of a landlord was more restrictive in 2009. In 1981 it included all those who leased land out or who only supervised agricultural

TABLE 6.3 Distribution of Households by Class: 1981 and 2009–10 (%)

Class	1981	2009–10
Agricultural wage labour, cultivating, attached	13.6	1.1
Agricultural wage labour, cultivating, casual	14.5	16.8
Agricultural wage labour, landless (not cultivating), attached	3.0	0.5
Agricultural wage labour, landless, casual	21.1	35.4
Poor peasants, neither hiring labour in, nor out	7.6	11.2
Middle peasants hiring labour in, both male and female family members work in agriculture	4.5	4.4
Large peasants hiring labour in, only male family members work in agriculture	21.3	16.9
Landlord/supervision of agriculture only*	8.8	1.1
Only non-agricultural work, self-employment	5.6**	2.9
Only non-agricultural work, wage employment		9.8
Total	100.0	100.0

Sources: ANSISS-ILO Bihar Survey, 1981–3, Household Census (1981, 12 villages); IHD Bihar Survey 2009–10, Household Sample.

Notes: * Definition more restrictive in 2009–10; ** All non-agricultural work was combined in 1981.

The longitudinal data makes it possible to explore the implication of this structural change for individual households, at least since 1998–9. Table 6.4 shows the distribution of households by class in 2009–10 according to their class, or the class of their households of origin, in 1998–9, and so shows the individual transitions.[2]

There were fairly substantial shifts between classes from one survey to the next. Tied labourer households, of whom there were still a fair number in 1998–9, had largely shifted to casual agricultural labour by

work; in 2009 it did not include those who leased out land if this was not their main economic activity. This implies that the decline in the numbers of landlords is exaggerated in the table (overall some 4.5 per cent of households were leasing out some land in 2009–10).

[2] The class distribution in 2009–10 in Table 6.4 does not correspond exactly to Table 6.3, because in the former the numbers are unweighted. Weighting is needed to obtain an overall estimate (as in Table 6.3) because the sample is stratified, but is not appropriate when we are tracking individual trajectories.

2009–10. But those tied labourers who were previously cultivating some land were more likely to remain in that category, and some moved out of agricultural labour altogether into one of the peasant categories.

Similarly, two-thirds of casual agricultural labour households in 1998–9 remained in the same category in 2009–10. A few moved into cultivation, but there was a larger move down into landlessness among those agricultural labour households that had previously been cultivating some land. There was some movement from all agricultural labour categories into small and medium peasant categories, and even a few large peasants, but not very many shifted to the non-agricultural category.

Among the peasant categories, the most stable was that of the large peasants, with 53 per cent unchanged. Small and middle peasants in 1998 were more scattered across all categories in 2009, including a significant move out of agriculture, suggesting that the smaller peasant categories were quite unstable. Larger peasants showed less movement out of agriculture, but the opposite was true of landlords—over 20 per cent of landlords made this shift. On the other hand, among non-agricultural households, many moved towards agricultural labour or the smaller peasant categories. On the whole, then, there was a lot of class mobility, more than the aggregate figures in Table 6.3 show.

One problem in interpreting these shifts is that the class categories have become less appropriate as the production system has changed. In particular, the way class is defined understates the growth in importance of non-agricultural occupations. In the tables discussed previously, a non-agricultural household is one that does no agricultural work; as soon as any household member does any agricultural work, even as a secondary occupation, they are placed in one of the agricultural categories. This was reasonable in 1981, but no longer reflects the realities of rural Bihar. This occupational shift is explored further by Janine Rodgers in Chapter 13 of this volume.

Alongside these large changes in class structure, the distribution of land ownership also shifted. Landlessness increased slightly between 1981 and 2009–10, which is not surprising given growing population pressure on land; indeed a larger increase could have been foreseen since the number of households increased by some 117 per cent. In fact, much of the adjustment to increased population pressure came through the subdivision of small plots, rather than through loss of all land, but the shift was uneven; there was a sharp decline in the largest

TABLE **6.4** Class Transitions, 1998–9 to 2009–10. Per cent Distribution of Households by Class in 2009–10, for Each Class in 1998–9

Class in 2009–10	Class in 1998–9								Total	No. of Obs.
	Ag. Lab. Landless, Tied	Ag. Lab. Landless, Casual	Ag. Lab. Cultiv-ating, Casual	Small Peasant	Middle Peasant	Large Peasant	Land-lord/ super-vision	Non-ag. Empt (self/ wage)		
Ag. Lab. Landless, Tied	6.3	1.1	1.6					1.6	1.1	10
Ag. Lab. Landless, Casual	41.7	67.4	35.0	6.9	6.6	6.0	2.3	25.8	27.5	258
Ag. Lab. Cultivating, Casual	27.1	14.4	33.3	20.7	18.0	4.9	5.4	12.9	15.9	149
Small Peasant	12.5	6.1	15.8	10.3	18.0	15.2	12.4	9.7	12.4	116
Middle Peasant	6.3	2.2	3.8	17.2	19.7	2.7	5.4	4.8	5.2	49
Large Peasant		1.1	6.6	27.6	23.0	52.7	39.5	6.5	20.4	192
Landlord/supervision						3.3	7.8		1.7	16
Non-ag. Wage empt	6.3	5.0	3.3	13.8	14.8	10.9	20.9	25.0	11.6	109
Non-ag. Self empt		2.8	.5	3.4		4.3	6.2	13.7	4.3	40
Total	100.0	100.0	100.0	100.0	100.0	100.0	100.0	100.0	100.0	
No. of Observations	48	181	183	29	61	184	129	124		939

Source: IHD Bihar Survey, 1998–99; IHD Bihar Survey 2009–10, Household Sample.

Notes: 939 households rather than the 941 reported in Table 6.1 because of the omission of two households with unresolved data problems at the time of preparation of this article.

TABLE 6.5 Land Transitions, 1998–9 to 2009–10. Per cent Distribution of Households by Land Ownership Class in 2009–10 for Each Land Ownership Class in 1998–9

Land ownership category in 2009–10	Land ownership category in 1998–9						Total	No. of observations
	Landless	0.01 to 0.99 acres	1.00 to 2.49 acres	2.50 to 4.99 acres	5.0 to 9.99 acres	10 acres or more		
Landless	77.1	27.6	9.3	5.4	3.1		41.3	388
0.01 to 0.99 acres	17.2	56.3	35.2	21.6	21.9	5.6	29.4	276
1.00 to 2.49 acres	3.2	10.6	42.9	37.8	29.7	5.6	17.0	160
2.50 to 4.99 acres	1.7	4.0	9.9	31.1	18.8	11.1	7.5	70
5.0 to 9.99 acres	.5	1.0	2.2	4.1	20.3	22.2	3.0	28
10 acres or more	.2	.5	.5		6.3	55.6	1.8	17
Total	100.0	100.0	100.0	100.0	100.0	100.0	100.0	
No. of observations	402	199	182	74	64	18		939

Sources: IHD Bihar Survey, 1998–9; IHD Bihar Survey 2009–10, Household Sample.

landholdings, but also some decline in the smallest. In contrast there was some increase in the 1 to 2.5 acre range, which might be regarded as a viable family farm in Bihar conditions. So the overall distribution of land, among those who owned some, became somewhat less unequal.

The direction of change for households in the survey can be seen in Table 6.5, which shows transitions between land ownership groups between the surveys in 1998–9 and 2009–10.[3] It is striking that the pattern of land ownership is a great deal more stable than the pattern of class. There is an unsurprising tendency for a downward shift in landholding (unsurprising because of population growth), particularly noticeable in the larger landholding categories—though the majority of those owning more than 10 acres in 1998–9 still reported owning more than 10 acres in 2009–10, just as almost 80 per cent of the landless in 1998–9 were still landless in 2009. Given that there are well known problems in obtaining accurate information on land ownership in household surveys, the pattern is remarkably strong.

[3] As in Table 6.4, this table is unweighted.

Overall we can see both continuity and change here. The end of semi-feudal relations did not have a noticeably adverse impact at the top of the village social hierarchy, as new non-agricultural opportunities (largely outside the village) provided an economic alternative for the previously dominant groups. Agricultural labour households also had access to non-agricultural occupations through migration (see Chapter 14 by Amrita Datta in this volume), but few abandoned agricultural work altogether; while the men migrated, women continued to work in agriculture. And there was quite a lot of movement between the agricultural labour and small peasant groups, suggesting that class was not set in stone but varied with individual fortunes.

The Pattern of Change at the Household Level

Because the same households were surveyed in 1998–9, 2009–10, and 2011, it is possible to track the trajectories of these households and the individuals within them over time—and in particular, to examine what happened to the households in this interval of 10 to 13 years, in relation to their characteristics in the earlier year. Household data also exist for 1981, but since the same households were not tracked we cannot carry out this exercise for the longer period.

In looking at changes over time, we have to bear in mind that the households themselves change. Table 6.6 gives the distribution of households in the 2009–10 survey, according to the nature of their relationship with the 1998–9 household.

More than half the households were unchanged, but many had divided or had otherwise changed. Clearly this affects the pattern we observe—land is divided when households split, and when a son separates from the household of his parents he will usually start out with few assets, though he may have new qualifications and new patterns of economic activity. Note that the patrilineal system in Bihar implies that households normally need to be tracked through the male members. Young women marry out into other households, usually in other villages, and these are not included in the sample.

We studied the following indicators of change in the economic status of the households concerned:

TABLE 6.6 Distribution of Households in the 2009–10 Survey by Relationship with 1998–9 Household

Relationship of household in 2009–10 to household in 1998–9	Frequency	Per cent
No change (same head and same household)	520	55.4
Same head, but one or more sons have left to form new household	117	12.5
Head has died, but otherwise same household, wife or son has become head	100	10.6
Head has died, there is a new head, but also one or more sons has left to form a new household	42	4.5
New household head, formed by separation from an existing household, old household still exists	154	16.4
New household head, formed when old household splits—old household no longer exists	6	0.6
Total	939	100.0

Sources: IHD Bihar Survey, 1998–9; IHD Bihar Survey 2009–10, Household Sample.

Change in Income and Consumption

- Ratio of household income recorded in 2011 to income recorded in 1998–9 (including remittances from migrants but not their incomes).

The change in household income is the most obvious indicator of economic status. Per capita estimates may be better, but only if they are adjusted for the number and ages of children and economies of household scale. For the purposes of this chapter, household income was considered an adequate first approximation. Household income, including remittances from migrants, was available for both years. We refer to this as 'narrow income' below.

- Ratio of household income recorded in 2011, including the incomes of migrants, to total household consumption recorded in 1998–9.

An alternative indicator of economic status is household income, including the income of migrants. Many migrants stay away for long periods, and have high incomes in village terms, but their wives and children stay in the village. Whether this is considered as one household or two is a question of definition, but certainly one alternative measure of household welfare is to treat this as a single household and add these external incomes to local incomes. This was possible for 2011 but not for 1998–9. Rather than compare this 'broad income' in 2011 with 'narrow income' in 1998–9, we used total consumption expenditure in 1998–9 as a proxy for the overall economic status of the household in that year (noting these are not directly comparable, since on average expenditure will be less than income).

Changes in Assets

- Change in household mobile assets (that is, all domestic and productive assets except land and housing), using value in rupees in 2009–10 and 1998–9.
- Changes in household land ownership over the same period.

We did not include housing in the value of assets. This is in reality the second most important asset after land, but there is no real housing market in rural Bihar and the values of houses quoted by respondents appear to be arbitrary.

We used 2009–10 asset data, because more information on assets was collected in that round of the survey (income data were collected in 2011).

Tables 6.7 to 6.14 present these indicators.

- The first column gives consumption per household in 1998–9, in rupees, in order to provide a baseline.
- The second column gives the ratio of (narrow) household income in 2011 to 1998–9. This is calculated in two different ways. The first is the ratio between the two years of mean income aggregated across all households in each subgroup in the table. For a ratio of this type, the mean ratio for individual households is not a reliable indicator, because errors or random variations in the first year generate large variations in the ratio, in particular biasing the mean upwards. It is better to take the overall income of the group. The best measure of central tendency for the individual households in the group is the median, which is given in brackets.
- The third column gives the ratio of mean broad income (that is, including incomes of migrants) in 2011 to mean consumption expenditure in 1998–9, for each of the subgroups in each table.
- The fourth column gives the ratio of the mean household assets in 2009–10 to the mean in 1998–9, again for each of the subgroups in each table.

- Columns 5 and 6 give the percentages of households gaining and losing land between 1998–9 and 2009–10. Column 6 is defined only for those who owned land in 1999.

These indicators are in current prices. We do not need to adjust for price changes because we are confining ourselves to relative rather than absolute relationships; that is, we are comparing these indicators across different groups of the population rather than over time. However, for reference purposes one can note that the consumer price index for agricultural labourers in Bihar rose from 282–91 in the first half of 1999 to 538–41 in the first half of 2011 (1986–7=100), which gives a deflator of 1.88.[4] No good price series exists for land or other assets, so the consumer price index may be considered a point of reference, though the price of land has probably risen faster than consumer goods.

We use 1999 as a shorthand for 1998–9 from here on, since the data mainly refer to the year 1999; and 2009 as a shorthand for 2009–10, for a similar reason.

Income and Asset Changes by Type of Household

Table 6.7 presents these indicators according to the change in the type of household between 1999 and 2011. In order to keep a sufficient number of observations in each category, the different situations in Table 6.6 can be divided into two groups:

1. 'Old household'—the first three categories, which imply the least change (78.5 per cent of sample households)
2. 'New household'—the last three categories, all of which imply new household formation (21.5 per cent).

For the sample as a whole, the median ratio of household income in 2011 to 1999 is 2.83, or more than 50 per cent higher than the increase in the price index, so it is clear that there has been a large increase in living standards.[5] The difference between the broad income measure in 2011

[4] Source: Labour Bureau, Ministry of Labour, Government of India. The 2011 survey was in the field from April to August, with a one-year reference period. The consumption survey was carried out in 1999, with a one-month reference period for current consumption and a six-month reference period for larger items.

[5] This is a per household measure, which should also be adjusted for changes in household size and composition.

TABLE 6.7 Income, Consumption, and Assets 1999–2011, by Whether New Household*

Whether new household in 2009/11	Annual consumption from 1999 survey (Rs)	Ratio of 'narrow' household income 2011 to 1999**	Ratio of 'broad' household income in 2011 to consumption 1999**	Ratio of mobile assets in 2009 to 1999**	Whether gained land between 1999 and 2009 (%)	Whether lost land between 1999 and 2009 (%)***	N****
Old household	22,260	3.53 (3.27)	4.84	3.01	28	63	728
New household	32,198	1.64 (1.71)	2.15	1.15	14	82	175
Total	24,390	2.98 (2.83)	4.08	2.49	25	67	903

Sources: IHD Bihar Survey, 1998–9; IHD Bihar Survey 2009–10, 2011, Household Sample (12 villages).

Notes: *Results in this and subsequent tables are weighted to compensate for unequal sampling fractions.

** This is the ratio of the total income/assets aggregated across households in each subgroup. The 'narrow' income ratio also gives the median ratio for individual households (in brackets).

***The percentage losing land is only calculated for those owning land in 1999, 537 observations out of 939.

**** Number of observations refers to income measures (income data for the two years were available for 903 out of the 939 households in Table 6.6). For asset measures all 939 observations were included.

and consumption in 1999 is even greater, though of course these two measures are not strictly comparable.

Mobile assets have increased by a factor of about 2.5; again, this can be compared (very approximately) with the increase in consumer prices of 1.88. This suggests that there has also been a modest real increase in the value of assets, although it is less than the increase in income.

Landholding averaged 1.11 acres in 1999 (across all households) and 0.85 acres in 2009, a decline of about 23 per cent. Since the number of households has increased by about 24 per cent (Table 6.1), we would expect the average farm size to come down by almost 20 per cent, so the results are broadly consistent. Twenty-five per cent of households show a gain of land, against 67 per cent that show a loss (the latter among those who had land in 1999).

It makes a great deal of difference whether or not the household has been newly formed. The income gain between 2011 and 1999 is around twice as high in old as in new households, land loss is much lower, and the increase in assets is much greater. This of course is not surprising. New households are being compared with the income and assets of their household of origin, and assets tend to stay with the old household, or are divided in new ones, and the new households are generally small. We can also see from the average consumption levels in 1999 that new households have been formed from households that were, on average, relatively larger or better off. Poorer households are less likely to divide.

Income and Asset Changes by Village

An important feature of rural Bihar is variability between villages. Table 6.8 gives the details. There has been a greater increase in income in North Bihar than in the South, which shows up in both the income ratios, but most consistently in the narrow income ratio. The South is on the whole more developed, but the North has benefited more from long-distance migration, and the difference in income gains is largely due to migrant incomes and remittances. Another notable result is that several villages, where consumption was relatively low in 1999, have on the whole, done relatively well on the wide income measure (Mahisan, Belabadan, and Rupaspur Salempur), while other villages where consumption was high in 1999 have gained less from migration (Alalpur

Bishunpur, Amarhi, and Samhauti Buzurg), suggesting some role for push factors in migration, and some equalization of incomes across villages. But the pattern is not uniform, since it does not apply to the first two villages in the table, located in the relatively more advanced agricultural district of Gopalganj.

There are also substantial differences between villages in the accumulation of assets, though in contrast to income, South Bihar does at least as well as the North in mobile assets. The high increase for Belabadan reflects exceptionally low assets in 1999 rather than a particularly large absolute gain. Changes in land ownership were much more variable from village to village, though in most villages the majority of households reported loss of land.

Clearly, many local factors are involved in these changes. In reality, the overall development process in rural Bihar is a composite of many different village patterns, which often reflect local factors, such as development of irrigation or communications, the dynamism of a particular community, the agrarian structure, violence and conflict, political favouritism, the impact of flood and drought, and many other factors.

Change by Class

A key dimension of the agrarian structure is the class pattern. This too differs from village to village; as we have seen above, it is changing over time. However, it is interesting to see the overall relationship between class in 1999 and subsequent change in living standards. Table 6.9 illustrates the pattern. We do not have strong hypotheses about the expected pattern of change—there is some expectation that landlords will have lost out in agriculture, but may have gained elsewhere. Whether peasant farmers have gained will depend on the extent to which they have innovated and diversified. Agricultural labour may have benefited from a tightening of the labour market due to migration.

The first column of Table 6.9 shows the difference between classes in consumption in 1999—substantial but not enormous compared with inequalities elsewhere in the economy. Large peasants and landlords report consumption levels about double those of agricultural labourers and non-agriculturalists. In the subsequent 12 years it is the non-agricultural group that has done best overall, but they were starting from

Table 6.8 Income, Consumption, and Assets 1999–2011, by Village*

Village	Annual consumption from 1999 survey (Rs)	Ratio of 'narrow' household income 2011 to 1999	Ratio of 'broad' household income in 2011 to consumption 1999	Ratio of mobile assets in 2009 to 1999	Whether gained land between 1999 and 2009 (%)	Whether lost land between 1999 and 2009 (%)	N
North Bihar							
Dewan Parsa	31,103	2.40 (2.34)	4.87	3.13	27	75	72
Paharpur Deyal	31,896	4.45 (4.35)	5.02	5.97	19	80	20
Khangaon	21,484	3.88 (3.82)	4.16	1.93	20	71	99
Mahisan	18,972	2.90 (2.54)	5.06	3.22	28	45	132
Belabadan	16,737	3.84 (3.41)	5.08	9.40	40	54	82
Jitwarpur	23,338	3.61 (3.06)	3.68	1.51	17	76	181
South Bihar							
Alalpur Bishunpur	36,423	2.64 (2.91)	2.52	3.90	36	64	39
Rupaspur Salempur	19,355	3.76 (2.30)	7.15	3.15	23	71	57
Chandkura	23,852	2.10 (1.99)	3.57	1.33	20	75	80
Mohiuddinpur	20,477	3.48 (2.72)	4.45	3.11	26	53	24
Amarhi	46,597	1.87 (2.01)	2.50	2.67	36	57	47
Samhauti Buzurg	36,972	2.30 (2.35)	2.90	3.14	29	73	70
Total	24,390	2.98 (2.83)	4.08	2.49	25	67	903

Sources: IHD Bihar Survey, 1998–9; IHD Bihar Survey 2009–10, 2011, Household Sample (12 villages).

Note: * For notes, see Table 6.7.

the lowest incomes. Otherwise the pattern is mixed. Large peasants and landlords do worst on the narrow income measures, but better than average when the incomes of migrants are taken into account. For agricultural labourers the reverse is true. Small and medium peasants do relatively well on both measures. This suggests that within the village, the labouring and poorer peasant classes have done relatively better, but the upper classes have more than compensated with high incomes from migration outside the village. While all classes migrate, the returns on migration are much greater for the upper classes.

This picture is broadly reflected in the asset data. All groups increased their assets by more than the increase in the price index. Agricultural labour had the lowest increase; this group also reported the highest land loss and the lowest land gain. There is not much to choose between small/medium peasants and large peasants/landlords. Once again, the non-agricultural group has done well, but starting from a low base.

On the whole, one has to conclude that no group has done spectacularly well, or spectacularly badly. The relatively good performance of small and medium peasants supports the hypothesis of growing productivity among this group; that of landlords and large peasants suggests high incomes among migrants from these households, and non-agricultural households have closed the gap with other groups and are no longer particularly deprived as a group. Clearly, they were relatively well placed to take advantage of the growth of non-farm occupations over the last decade.

Income and Asset Changes by Caste

The caste pattern (Table 6.10) is in some respects foreseeable from the class pattern; the upper castes have a pattern quite similar to that of the large peasants and landlords to which many of them belong. Variations in the narrow income ratio among other caste and community groups are small—all castes seem to have benefitted to a similar extent—but this is not true of the wider income measure, for then Muslims and upper castes do better than the others. Scheduled Castes (SCs) do somewhat better than average on the narrow measure, and slightly less well on the wider measure. Scheduled Tribes (STs) do badly but the sample is small.

The asset figures broadly confirm the pattern of the wide income measure. The large increases in assets for Muslims, especially upper

TABLE **6.9** Income, Consumption, and Assets 1999–2011, by Class

Class in 1999	Annual consumption from 1999 survey (Rs)	Ratio of 'narrow' household income 2011 to 1999	Ratio of 'broad' household income in 2011 to consumption 1999	Ratio of mobile assets in 2009 to 1999	Whether gained land between 1999 and 2009 (%)	Whether lost land between 1999 and 2009 (%)	N
Agricultural labour	19,061	3.05 (2.95)	3.64	2.16	21	71	397
Small/medium peasants	24,420	3.22 (2.66)	4.82	2.47	32	64	92
Big peasants and landlords	39,300	2.74 (2.37)	4.39	2.63	30	66	294
Non-agricultural	17,723	4.19 (4.03)	4.57	5.70	31	30	120
Total	24,390	2.98 (2.83)	4.08	2.49	25	67	903

Sources: IHD Bihar Survey, 1998–9; IHD Bihar Survey 2009–10, 2011, Household Sample (12 villages).

Note: * For notes, see Table 6.7.

TABLE **6.10** Income, Consumption, and Assets 1999–2011, by Caste Group

Caste group	Annual consumption from 1999 survey (Rs)	Ratio of 'narrow' household income 2011 to 1999	Ratio of 'broad' household income in 2011 to consumption 1999	Ratio of mobile assets in 2009 to 1999	Whether gained land between 1999 and 2009 (%)	Whether lost land between 1999 and 2009 (%)	N
SC	17,778	3.01 (3.30)	3.99	2.81	15	78	197
ST	21,655	2.14 (1.94)	3.46	1.72	20	89	13
OBC-I	21,556	3.19 (2.72)	3.58	2.01	19	65	188
OBC-II	31,127	2.54 (2.65)	3.51	2.06	39	61	163
Lower Muslim	19,620	3.81 (2.91)	4.36	3.05	23	69	67
Upper Muslim	24,551	3.63 (3.67)	4.84	13.88	56	45	22
Upper Caste	32,030	3.01 (2.54)	4.81	2.75	28	69	254
Total	24,390	2.98 (2.83)	4.08	2.49	25	67	904

Sources: IHD Bihar Survey, 1998–9; IHD Bihar Survey 2009–10, 2011, Household Sample (12 villages).

Note: * For notes, see Table 6.7.

caste Muslims, are surprising and may reflect underestimates in 1999, since the absolute 2009 figures are in line with comparable Hindu groups (OBC-II for upper Muslims, OBC-I for lower Muslims). However upper Muslims also show some improvement in landholding. Otherwise the largest proportionate gains are to be found among upper castes and SCs. A fairly high proportion of OBC-II—mainly Koeri, Kurmi, and Yadav—show gains of land, but there is nevertheless a net loss overall.

Apart from the relatively large gains of Muslim households, there is not much sign here of a concentration of the benefits of growth. The fact that upper castes and SCs both do relatively well may result from different mechanisms—in the case of the latter, this may well reflect the end of bonded labour and the opening up of opportunities for migration. They were also starting from the lowest income levels in 1999. In the case of the upper castes, it probably reflects gains from migration into a higher paid, regular labour market.

Income and Asset Changes by Land Ownership

Another way to break down the data is in terms of land ownership in 1999 (Table 6.11). This shows a stronger and clearer pattern than either class or caste. There is some expectation that those with more land should have done relatively better, but this is not the case. In fact, the group that shows the highest proportional gain in the narrow income measure is the landless. They also show a fairly high proportional increase in assets. This is not due to the acquisition of land (only 19 per cent) but presumably because of the diversification of employment opportunities and a rise in the real wage. But in absolute terms their assets remained small.

Above this level, there is a marked tendency for the increase in narrow income and in assets to decline with increasing landholding in 1999. Those who had less than one acre of land in 1999 had the highest propensity to gain land, but a smaller rise in other assets, perhaps indicating an attempt to reach a viable farm size. Above 2.5 acres, the proportionate increase in assets was smaller and the loss of land greater. However, in absolute terms, those with more than 5 acres still had vastly more assets than the landless or those with small holdings, and the loss of land in these households is probably the result of household

TABLE 6.11 Income, Consumption, and Assets 1999–2011, by Landholding

Land ownership Class 1999	Annual consumption from 1999 survey (Rs)	Ratio of 'narrow' household income 2011 to 1999	Ratio of 'broad' household income in 2011 to consumption 1999	Ratio of mobile assets in 2009 to 1999	Whether gained land between 1999 and 2009 (%)	Whether lost land between 1999 and 2009 (%)	N
Landless	16,732	3.71 (3.24)	4.44	3.15	19	n.a.	386
0.01 to 0.99 acres	21,928	2.94 (2.85)	3.65	2.35	40	59	196
1.00 to 2.49 acres	31,045	2.92 (2.52)	3.66	3.23	26	68	172
2.50 to 4.99 acres	31,895	2.49 (2.06)	5.67	2.86	19	79	68
5.0 to 9.99 acres	60,963	2.31 (1.69)	3.52	1.79	12	88	63
10 acres or more	59,955	2.16 (2.12)	4.64	1.61	26	74	18
Total	24,390	2.98 (2.83)	4.08	2.49	25	67	903

Sources: IHD Bihar Survey, 1998–9; IHD Bihar Survey 2009–10, 2011, Household Sample (12 villages).

Note: * For notes, see Table 6.7.

division rather than any real deterioration in the position of this group. Moreover, in terms of income growth, the same pattern can be seen as in the previous tables by caste and class, in that once migrant incomes are included in the wide income measure the top landholding group does better than average.

Income and Asset Changes by Educational Level in 1999

There is, of course, a strong relationship between income and education; consumption levels in 1999 were three times higher in households with post-secondary qualifications than in households with no more than primary education. But education also changes the dynamics. Table 6.12 shows the relationship between income change between 1999 and 2011, and the highest level of education in the household in 1999. This relationship shows opposite patterns for narrow and wide income measures. In the former case, it was the least educated who gained proportionately most; in the latter case it was the most educated.

Once again, this is clearly connected with the pattern of migration. Since the wide measure of income includes the incomes of migrants, it was clearly the households with the highest education levels that were able to gain most from migration for work outside the village. Households with low education levels were also gaining from migration, because of remittances, but migrants from these households were clearly confined to lower income jobs in their areas of destination.

The asset pattern was consistent with the wide income measure. The increase in assets was greatest among those households with some post-secondary education in 1999; moreover, this group was more likely to gain land and less likely to lose it. So even for this more educated group there is no sign of movement away from land.

Presumably those households with higher education levels in 1999 were more likely to invest in the education of the next generation, and this will also be part of the story. That however will require more detailed analysis.

Income and Asset Changes in Relation to Indebtedness in 1999

Another interesting relationship concerns the impact of indebtedness. In the old agrarian system, indebtedness to landlords and money-

Table 6.12 Income, Consumption, and Assets 1999–2011, by Highest Educational Level in 1999

Highest educational level in household, 1999	Annual consumption from 1999 survey (Rs)	Ratio of 'narrow' household income 2011 to 1999	Ratio of 'broad' household income in 2011 to consumption 1999	Ratio of mobile assets in 2009 to 1999	Whether gained land between 1999 and 2009 (%)	Whether lost land between 1999 and 2009 (%)	N
Primary or less	17,605	3.49 (3.13)	3.82	2.19	20	71	426
Secondary or vocational	24,064	2.93 (2.59)	4.21	2.59	29	66	309
Higher	52,169	2.49 (2.10)	4.29	2.64	32	65	168
Total	24,390	2.98 (2.83)	4.08	2.49	25	67	903

Sources: IHD Bihar Survey, 1998–9; IHD Bihar Survey 2009–10, 2011, Household Sample (12 villages).

Note: * For notes, see Table 6.7.

lenders was an important means of exploitation. Insofar as this was still important in 1999, one could expect that it would affect income growth for the households concerned. On the other hand, institutional loans could be expected to support investment and income growth.

Both these patterns can be seen in the data (Table 6.13), though different measures tell different stories. Those who reported large traditional loans in 1999 also reported a much slower increase in income subsequently. This pattern is quite strong for income, but it does not carry over to assets. Smaller traditional loans do not show the same relationship. This would be consistent with large traditional loans being used for exceptional expenditures, such as medical treatment and ceremonies, and persistent indebtedness then acting as a drag on subsequent income growth. On the other hand, the pattern for institutional loans is quite mixed. Those with the largest institutional loans showed the highest income increase, the reverse of the pattern for traditional credit, for broad income, and also for the median narrow household income. However, this does not carry over to the mean ratio for narrow household income (which shows a ratio of 2.42, as compared with 3.97 for the median). The large difference between the mean and the median might be explained if a few households with large incomes in 1999 were able to obtain institutional loans but did not put them to productive use. However, this would need to be confirmed. What is clear is that those with large institutional loans showed a very slow accumulation of assets, suggesting that these loans did not go into productive investment. There was no consistent relationship with land gains and losses for either type of loan. Multivariate analysis is required to work out exactly what is going on here.

Income and Asset Changes by Migration Status in 1999

Finally, we should look more specifically at the role of migration.[6] Outmigration can have many causes, but there are reasons to believe that outmigration should help increase incomes and the capacity to accumulate assets. Migration status in 1999 should therefore have a

[6] For a more detailed analysis of migration using these data, see Datta (forthcoming).

TABLE 6.13 Income, Consumption, and Assets 1999–2011, by Type and Amount of Debt in 1999

Debt in 1999 (Rs)	Annual consumption from 1999 survey (Rs)	Ratio of 'narrow' household income 2011 to 1999	Ratio of 'broad' household income in 2011 to consumption 1999	Ratio of mobile assets in 2009 to 1999	Whether gained land between 1999 and 2009 (%)	Whether lost land between 1999 and 2009 (%)	N
Traditional							
None	25,452	2.96 (2.92)	4.35	2.30	27	66	546
1–5,000	18,868	3.51 (2.87)	4.11	3.18	17	74	199
5,001+	28,228	2.55 (2.44)	3.22	2.78	28	65	158
Institutional							
None	23,217	3.04 (2.77)	4.01	2.77	25	66	796
1–5,000	29,278	3.20 (3.05)	3.94	1.80	20	79	42
5,001+	37,769	2.42 (3.97)	4.79	1.55	25	66	65
Total	24,390	2.98 (2.83)	4.08	2.49	25	67	903

Sources: IHD Bihar Survey, 1998–9; IHD Bihar Survey 2009–10, 2011, Household Sample (12 villages).

Note: * For notes, see Table 6.7.

significant influence on the subsequent household trajectory. But when we look at the overall pattern of change in income and assets (the total rows in Table 6.14), we see a relationship with income that is mixed.

On the narrow income measure, households with migrants in 1999 do worse than non-migrants in the subsequent period whether we take the median (a ratio of 2.55 against 3.24) or the mean (2.65 against 3.33). On the wider income measure, on the other hand, the reverse is true (4.44 against 3.74) and this also carries over to the accumulation of assets, including land. We can see that migration in 1999 has a positive impact on the subsequent income trajectory only if it leads to substantial incomes of migrants outside the village, and not just remittances to the village.

This becomes clearer when we break the data down by class. The only class category for which migration in 1999 has a payoff in terms of subsequent increases in narrow income is the big peasants and landlords—precisely the group most likely to have access to the higher paying regular jobs outside the village. On the broad income measure, which includes the incomes of migrants, this group shows a ratio between the two years of 5.69 in migrant households, as against 3.46 in non-migrant households. For other classes the pattern is weak or the reverse. This pattern also carries over to the gain in assets.

These patterns lend themselves to the following interpretation: Migration among agricultural labour households in 1999 did not generate much return in terms of real incomes (consumption levels of migrant and non-migrant households were similar in that year); nor did it make much difference to the subsequent income trajectory. Average incomes rose fairly substantially for both migrant and non-migrant households over the next decade, but migrants from agricultural labour households mainly had access to the same sort of casual unskilled work outside the village as inside. Nevertheless, migration rates increased, and migrants could take advantage of an expanding labour market outside the village. By 2011, the median income in agricultural labour households with one or more migrants (at that date) was almost 50 per cent higher than in non-migrating agricultural labour households. So migration played an increasing important role for this group, but those who were already migrating in 1999 were not particularly advantaged.

Migration from large peasant and landlord households in 1999, in contrast, was associated with income gains in the subsequent period. This was clearly related to the type of migration. In these households,

TABLE 6.14 Income, Consumption, and Assets 1999–2011, by Migration Status and Class in 1999

Migration status of household in 1999	Class in 1999	Annual consumption from 1999 survey (Rs)	Ratio of 'narrow' household income 2011 to 1999	Ratio of 'broad' household income in 2011 to consumption 1999	Ratio of mobile assets in 2009 to 1999	Whether gained land between 1999 and 2009 (%)	Whether lost land between 1999 and 2009 (%)	N
Household with migrant(s)	Agricultural labour	19,209	2.58 (2.60)	3.69	2.12	21	64	184
	Small/medium peasants	29,520	2.04 (2.05)	4.00	1.93	31	66	44
	Big peasants and landlords	36,249	2.80 (2.35)	5.69	3.24	38	60	135
	Non-agricultural	19,483	4.06 (3.87)	4.34	5.90	27	47**	80
	Total	23,956	2.65 (2.55)	4.44	2.65	26	63	443
Household without migrant(s)	Agricultural labour	18,915	3.63 (3.77)	3.59	2.20	20	76	213
	Small/medium peasants	19,410	5.63 (3.44)	6.04	3.17	33	62	48
	Big peasants and landlords	41,837	2.69 (2.46)	3.46	2.27	23	72	159
	Non-agricultural	14,393	4.44 (4.34)	5.17	5.40	37	0**	40
	Total	24,817	3.33 (3.24)	3.74	2.37	23	72	460

Notes: * For notes, see Table 6.7; **Very few observations.

it is likely that at least one male household member remained in the village, while a son or brother migrated to a longer term, higher income job elsewhere. That would explain why the addition of migrant incomes changed the picture. This group also showed a much greater gain in assets where there was a migrant, so some of the migrant incomes certainly returned to the village; probably this means that remittance flows are underestimated for this higher income group.

The pattern was different for small and medium peasant households. For this group, migration in 1999 was not an advantage. Income rose faster for households that were concentrating their work in the village, and they were less likely to lose land. Nevertheless, this may have been a temporary pattern. Data from 2011 show that by then this group too was benefiting substantially from migration.

Finally, non-agricultural households in 1999 were mainly in traditional occupations with a local base and were generally poor. Their incomes rose more than the average in the period up to 2011, but this was not primarily due to migration, more because of the diversification of the rural economy and the increasing demand for non-agricultural occupations. Non-agricultural households also benefited from increasing incomes around them in the village, which must have increased demand for their services, and they reduced the income and asset gaps with other groups in the village.

The Overall Picture

The growth in narrow income, that is to say local income plus remittances from migrants, is clearly in some degree equalizing. First of all, it is higher in the villages of North Bihar, which were relatively backward. In addition, the longitudinal data suggest that the less well-off groups in 1999 did at least as well as and usually better than average in the following decade—by landholding, where the landless and smaller landowners did better than large landowners; by class, where agricultural labour and poorer non-agricultural groups did relatively well, and the large peasants and landlords relatively badly; by education, where the growth of income was highest among the least educated; and, less clearly, by caste, where SCs did better than upper castes.

The broad measure of income change, which includes incomes earned by migrants outside the village, shows a much less equalizing pattern. The relative improvement in North Bihar remains, but now agricultural labour and lower castes do less well, and upper castes and Muslims do best. The impact of education is reversed, with higher education now delivering the highest increase in income. The landless continue to do relatively well, but so do those with the largest landholdings. Migration in 1999 is now associated with faster income growth in the following decade, but this is concentrated on the large peasant and landlord group, and is smallest for agricultural labour households. Clearly, what is happening is that the upper groups in the village hierarchy can place migrants in better, higher paying jobs, and once those incomes are taken into account they do much better. It should perhaps be considered that these households have divided, as these are migrants in regular jobs who spend little time in the village. That would be the conventional statistical procedure. But they are considered by the family in the village to be part of the household, and this is the way the better-off households maintain their economic position, through long-term employment of family members outside the village, rather than through circular migration and remittances.

The pattern of change in assets is less clear than for income, and this may reflect the difficulty of collecting good asset data. There is some sign that the upper echelons of the village do better than average for increases in mobile assets (big peasants, upper castes, and upper Muslims, the better educated); also there is a positive impact of migration on asset accumulation, which is important only for large peasants and landlords. On the other hand, large landowners show the lowest increase in assets, and SCs improved their position (but from a very low base). As for landholding, gains and losses of land do not show a strong regional pattern, although there are considerable differences between villages. But there are significant differences between groups. Agricultural labour, SCs, the landless and the uneducated—overlapping groups, of course—all show low gains of land, while agricultural labour and SCs both showed a higher than average tendency to lose land. So the polarization between the landed and the landless has been growing. Groups gaining land included OBC-II and upper Muslims. There was no sign that migration was strongly associated with either gain or loss of land—though there was some weak indication that households with migrants in 1999 were less likely to lose land, and more likely to gain. On balance there is some evidence here that asset inequality was increasing, at least between the poorest and the rest.

★ ★ ★

The results reported above are only the first stage of analysis of a large set of longitudinal data. They should be regarded as tentative, as some relationships can only be fully understood with a finer breakdown of households in terms of composition and change over time. But they do illustrate the value of longitudinal data. It is possible to explore the dynamics of income, assets, and agrarian structure in relation to other changes in the rural economy and society, in ways that would be much more difficult with cross-section data. It is also possible to explore the diversity of individual and household experiences over time, on which there is otherwise not much evidence. Some of these issues are discussed further in Chapters 13 and 14 of this book. Further analysis of this data set on rural Bihar should provide more insights into the nature of economic and social change and its consequences for the women and men concerned.

References

Baulch, Bob and Neil McCulloch. 2002. 'Being Poor and Becoming Poor: Poverty Status and Poverty Transitions in Rural Pakistan', *Journal of Asian and African Studies*, 37 (2): 168–85.

Bhaduri, Amit. 1973. 'A Study of Agricultural Backwardness Under Conditions of Semi-Feudalism', *Economic Journal*, LXXXVI (329): 120–37.

Datta, Amrita. forthcoming. 'Migration, Remittances and Changing Sources of Income in Rural Bihar (1999–2011), Some Findings of a Longitudinal Study', revised version of a paper presented at a seminar on Migration, Care Economy and Remittances at the Centre for Development Studies, Thiruvananthapuram, 17–19 September 2014.

Datta, Amrita, Gerry Rodgers, Janine Rodgers, and B.K.N. Singh. 2014. 'Contrasts in Development in Bihar, A Tale of Two Villages', *Journal of Development Studies*, 50 (9): 1197–208.

Institute for Human Development. 2004. 'Dynamics of Poverty, Employment and Human Development in Bihar', Report of a project sponsored by NABARD, New Delhi, Institute for Human Development.

Prasad, Pradhan H. 1979. 'Caste and Class in Bihar', *Economic and Political Weekly*, XIV (7–8): 481–4.

———. 1987. 'Towards a Theory of Transformation of Semi-Feudal Agriculture', *Economic and Political Weekly*, XXII (31): 1287–90.

Prasad, Pradhan H. and Gerry Rodgers. 1983. *Caste, Class and Landholding in the Analysis of the Rural Economy,* Population and Labour Policies Working Paper 140, Geneva, International Labour Office, August.

Prasad, Pradhan H., Gerry Rodgers, Shaibal Gupta, Alakh N. Sharma, and Bachhoo Sharma. 1988. *The Dynamics of Employment and Poverty in Bihar.* Patna: A.N. Sinha Institute of Social Studies.

Rodgers, Gerry. 2012. 'Understanding Unequal Economic and Social Outcomes in Rural Bihar, The Importance of Caste, Class and Landholding', Working Paper 01/2012, New Delhi, Institute for Human Development.

Rodgers, Gerry and Janine Rodgers. 1984. 'Incomes and Work Among the Poor of Rural Bihar, 1971–1981', *Economic and Political Weekly*, XIX (130): A-17–A-28.

Rodgers, Gerry and Janine Rodgers. 2001. 'A Leap Across Time, When Semi-feudalism Met the Market in Rural Purnia', *Economic and Political Weekly*, XXXVI (22): 1976–83.

———. 2011. 'Inclusive Development, Migration, Governance and Social Change in Rural Bihar', *Economic and Political Weekly*, XLVI (23): 43–50.

Rodgers, Gerry, Amrita Datta, Janine Rodgers, Sunil K. Mishra, and Alakh N. Sharma. 2013. *The Challenge of Inclusive Development in Bihar.* New Delhi: Manak Publishers.

Rodgers, Janine. 2012. Labour Force Participation in Rural Bihar, A Thirty-Year Perspective Based on Village Surveys, Working Paper 04/2012, New Delhi, Institute for Human Development.

Sharma, Alakh N. 2005. 'Agrarian Relations and Socio-Economic Change in Bihar', *Economic and Political Weekly*, XL (10): 960–72.

Sharma, Alakh N., Sandip Sarkar, Anup K. Karan, V. Gayathri, and Pushpendra. 2001. 'Poverty and Livelihoods in Rural Bihar', Report of project sponsored by ActionAid, New Delhi, Institute for Human Development.

Sharma, Alakh N., Amrita Datta, and Joyita Ghose (eds). 2011. *A Decade of Development Research on Bihar: A Compendium (2000–2010).* New Delhi: Institute for Human Development.

7

SURINDER S. JODHKA

A Forgotten 'Revolution'

Revisiting Rural Life and Agrarian Change in Haryana

The success of Green Revolution technology during the 1960s and 1970s, though confined only to some pockets of India, generated a great deal of excitement. Even when critiques pointed to its limited spread and possible social and ecological 'side effects', it produced a sense of pride in the Indian development community and among the newly emergent rural elite. Looking back, it appears as though it was a surprising thing to have happened. Deliberations on Indian agriculture in development circles until the middle of the 1960s were hopelessly negative and centred mostly on subjects like technological backwardness of Indian agriculture and the social conservativeness of the peasantry. It was this economic and social context that was held responsible for the prolonged stagnation of the rural economy. The perpetual scarcity of food, which produced frequent famines and social disparities, were all consequences of this state of backwardness. Initiatives taken by the Government of India soon after Independence to ameliorate the depressing scenario had not been very successful. The land reform legislations had by and large been thwarted by vested interests and the community development programme had almost completely failed to achieve its professed objectives.

One of the representative conceptualizations of this mainstream discourse on Indian agriculture during the 1950s could be found in the early writings of Daniel Thorner. The backwardness of Indian agriculture, he argued, could be attributed to the historically evolved structure of social and power relations in the countryside, which were unique to India. Conceptualizing the stagnating effects of the structural framework of an Indian village, he argued:

> ... complex of legal, economic, and social relations uniquely typical of the Indian countryside served to produce an effect which I should like to call that of *build-in 'depressor'*. Through the operation of this multifaceted 'depressor', Indian agriculture continued to be characterized by low capital intensity and antiquated methods. Few of the actual tillers were left with an efficacious interest in modernization .... The pattern of land-holding, cultivation, and product-sharing operated to hold down agricultural production. (Thorner 1956: 12, emphasis added)

Seen in this context, Byres sounds quite right in saying that the success of the Green Revolution brought the discourse on Indian agriculture out of the 'limbo of cow dung economics' and 'dismissive contempt' with which development professionals saw it (Byres 1972: 100). As the agrarian economy began to show some dynamism, new types of questions began to be raised and debated. Scholars started collecting empirical data on various aspects of the changes taking place on the ground. Though everyone did not turn into its admirer, or became a 'green revolutionary', the fact that something hitherto unknown was happening in the pockets where the new agrarian technology had been introduced was widely recognized.

The growing use of high-yielding varieties of seed, chemical fertilizers, pesticides, and new machines raised the productivity of the land several fold and nearly solved India's national problem of food scarcity in a rather short time. From the simple concerns of elementary economics, such as who benefited from the new technology and who did not, to the complex questions of social and cultural change in the Indian countryside, all were examined empirically and debated with passion in the pages of journals like the *Economic and Political Weekly* (EPW) and *The Journal of Peasant Studies* (JPS). The famous 'mode of production debate' among economists and anthropologists of Marxist persuasion on the nature of emerging social relations of production in Indian agriculture, was a direct outcome of this growing new interest of social science scholars in the changing rural scenario in the wake of the Green Revolution.

The face of the Indian countryside in the Green Revolution pockets started changing very rapidly. In terms of social groups, the most visible beneficiaries of this change were the substantial landowners from the locally dominant caste groups, who had traditionally been landowners and cultivators. The locally dominant castes consolidated their position in the regional power structure and acquired a new sense of confidence. The rise of dominant caste farmers in the 1970s also set in motion a phase of populist politics at the regional and national levels. The newly emerged agrarian elite did not speak only for 'his' own caste or class. He spoke on behalf of the entire village. His identification with the village was not just political or that of a representative of a section of the village. He saw himself to be the natural spokesperson of the village.

However, this excitement about the Green Revolution and modernization of Indian agriculture did not last long. By the mid-1980s the Indian countryside began to show a new kind of restiveness. Interestingly, this restiveness was pronounced particularly in the pockets that had experienced the Green Revolution. The surplus-producing farmers began to mobilize themselves into unions, demanding subsidies on farm inputs and higher prices for their produce. The market economy, they argued, was inherently against the farm sector and favoured the urban industry and middle-class consumer. Given the unequal power relations between the town and countryside, they argued, the agricultural sector suffered from unequal terms of trade, the evidence of which could be seen in the growth of indebtedness among the cultivating/farming classes.

Farmers mobilized themselves in different parts of India quite successfully for over a decade. Though the movements had a local character in terms of leadership and strategies of mobilization, they coordinated their activities across regions. In a sense, they were quite successful in getting their agenda accepted at the level of the national politics. The farmers' movements of the 1980s also signalled the rise of a new social category of rural people who had prospered because of the Green Revolution, were connected closely to the market economy, saw their fate being conditioned by the market, but also aspired to go beyond the village. The agrarian economy could not satisfy their aspirations for social and cultural mobility. They began to move out of the village, from their local seats of power to legislative assemblies in the state capitals. The surplus they generated from agriculture went into education, urban trade, and other non-agricultural activities (Omvedt 1992; Rutten 1995; Upadhya 1988). By the early 1980s, the social profile of this class had begun to change. The following lines of Balagopal provide a lucid account of this process of growing diversification:

> ... a typical family of this class has a landholding in its native village, cultivated by hired labour, *bataidar*, tenant or farm servants and supervised by the father or one son; business of various descriptions in town managed by other sons; and perhaps a young and bright child who is a doctor or engineer or a professor. It is this class that is most vocal about injustice done to the village. (Balagopal 1987: 1545)

The Indian village was undergoing a social and cultural transformation which had been unprecedented. However, it was not simply a story of economic growth but also of social transformation wrought with difficulties and contestations.

Twenty Years Ago

It was around this time, when agrarian issues had been intensely worked on by the social sciences for nearly a decade and a half and had become politically sensitive, that I initiated my doctoral research on rural indebtedness and the changing nature of debt-dependencies in three villages of the Karnal district of Haryana. Karnal had been a successful IADP district and typically represented the prosperous agrarian terrain of northwest India. I began my fieldwork in March 1988 and completed it by the middle of 1989.

There were three sets of questions that interested me. First, there were general questions relating to the nature of changes taking place in the structure of rural credit markets. My second set of questions related to the nature of indebtedness among the farmers, particularly their growing involvement with the market and how did their relations with the *arhtiyas* in the marketing centre structure their choices on farming? The third set of questions related to the role that credit played in institutionalizing certain kinds of dependency relations of the labouring classes with their employer farmers.

Though the Indian village had been an important and fashionable area of research for the sociologists and social anthropologists, they rarely looked at the kind of questions I had identified for my research. Most of the empirical work on agrarian change in India had been done by the economists, mostly using the framework of political economy. While the economists researching on agrarian change worked with the category of 'class' for classifying and analyzing rural social structure, sociologists and social anthropologists were preoccupied with 'caste'. Even when caste seemed a relevant factor in the study of rural social structure and change, it was rarely seen in relation to the agrarian social structure. Economists found it meaningless to talk about caste and the sociologists/social anthropologists saw its core lying in the ritual domain and the value framework of social hierarchy. Castes were also seen to be functionally integrated and ideologically over-determined in a manner that questions of power and social inequality or marginality and exclusion either seemed secondary or simply irrelevant for understanding the 'essence' of Indian rural life.

This textbook conceptualization of caste did not make much sense to me. On the other hand, I found the economists' writings on the political economy of agrarian change much more useful and inspiring. Unlike the sociologists and social anthropologists, the economists in India had also been preoccupied much more with state policy and development related questions. Though the mainstream economists did not focus too much on relational structures, questions of poverty and social disparities had been among their core concerns.

Most of my doctoral work was published in *EPW* (Jodhka 1994, 1995b, 1995c, 1995d). The first paper I published was on the changing nature of debt dependencies in relation to the various forms of labour relations. My specific focus was on the changing patterns of attached labour. Social science literature had looked at the phenomenon of attached labour in post-Green Revolution agriculture from several different perspectives. First were those who believed that with the development of capitalism in agriculture and modernization all forms of traditional structures and dependency relations would disappear. Jan Breman had described this as a process of de-patronization where labourers were not only freed from traditional ties but they also lost the security of patronage they had earlier enjoyed (Breman 1974). Some others looked at it as a process of formalization or casualization of labour.

However, empirical research showed that attached labour not only did not disappear from Green Revolution pockets but in some cases it actually became more pronounced, albeit in different forms. Similarly the phenomenon was also interpreted differently. Terence Byres, for example, did not find anything wrong with it and argued that this form of labour only fulfilled the changing demands of the new agrarian economy, and could work as a means of differentiating labour. Attached labour, he speculated, will be required when greater mechanization will reduce the need for employing causal labour and instead the capitalist farmer would prefer 'one attached labourer, who is paid a regular and probably high wage and who is trained to look after the mechanical implement'. This 'privileged class of attached labour', he expected would also get to participate in the prosperity of the 'Green Revolution' (1972: 105–9). Several years later, Rudra made a similar argument when he compared the semi-attached labour employed by the capitalist farmers of West Bengal with the regular employees of the organized sector (Rudra 1987).

Another set of scholars saw it as a form of unfreedom. Attached labour was for them a form of bondage and slavery. Amit Bhaduri, for example, saw in it an evidence of continuity of pre-capitalist relations of production, even in the Green Revolution pockets of India. Some others, such as Brass, underlined the point that their presence in post-Green Revolution agriculture was simply an evidence of the fact that capitalism can be pretty comfortable with slave labour as long as it helps in accumulation. Brass had, for example argued that the employer farmers in post-Green Revolution Haryana actively worked towards decomposing labour through the mechanism of debt, using short and long-term labour-tying arrangements, which amounted to a process of what he described as 'deproletarianization' (Brass 1990).

Attached labour indeed existed in my study villages, though the form and content of relationship had changed substantially and had become quite formalized, a point that had also been made earlier by Sheila Bhalla (1976). The attached labourers rarely saw themselves as being a 'privileged class' or as 'permanent employees' of the organized sector. Elements of unfreedom were also present in their relationship with the farmers. However, I could not agree fully with Brass on his conceptualization of attached labour as a form of slavery, or that labour-tying was a growing phenomenon. The overall change in the social framework of agricultural production had opened up several choices for the labouring classes.

There were many cases where, after working as attached labourers for some time, the labourers had been able to move out of the relationship. The growing integration of the village in the broader market economy, the increasing availability of alternative sources of employment outside agriculture, along with the changing political and ideological environment, had weakened the hold of the landowner over the labourers. Labourers intensely disliked working in an attached relationship and chose to work only when they had no other source of mobilizing credit. They also tried to come out of the relationship as soon as they could. There was also a general decline in the number of labourers willing to work on annual contracts in the three villages.[1] Recognizing the significance of these processes and their influence on relations on the ground I conceptualized the contemporary forms of attached labour as a system of 'labour mortgage', an unfree relationship, but internally fragmented and frequently contested in nature (Jodhka 1994).

The New Context and Research Questions

The shift in India's economic orientation during the early years of the 1990s had several implications for the agricultural sector. Apart from other things, it marginalized agriculture in the development discourse on India. Social science research on rural and agrarian economy also declined. Agrarian questions no longer generated excitement in university seminars, or in the popular media. Unfortunately, it was only when incidents of farmers' suicides began to be reported from different parts of India in quick succession during the late 1990s that agriculture returned to academic and political platforms.

By the early years of the twenty-first century, a new discourse on Indian agriculture began to take shape. The preoccupation this time was with 'crisis'. While the Indian economy was growing at a much faster pace, the agricultural sector was experiencing stagnation. The relative share of the agricultural sector in the national economy began to decline quite steadily. Rural India once again appeared as a site of gloom and depression where real incomes were declining and farmers committed suicide all the time.

[1] This article also generated an interesting debate with Tom Brass (see Brass 1995, 1996; Jodhka 1995a, 1996).

Interestingly, in this new discourse of 'crisis of agriculture', only occasionally were any references made to internal inequalities in agrarian India, not even by those who swore by the political economy framework and had participated in the debate on agrarian class relations and mode of production. In fact very little research was being done on the internal dynamics of the political economy of agriculture. Most of their formulations also seemed to be emerging from analysis of journalistic reports, or the large data sets produced by official agencies, such as the NSSO. It was in this context that I decided to revisit two of my three study villages.

However, the questions I had in mind during my 'revisit' to the Haryana villages were not quite similar to the ones with which I had gone to these villages 20 years ago. Over the last twenty years, the face of social science research had changed significantly in India and globally and so had my orientation to social science research. For example, I now look at the question of caste much more seriously than I did earlier. My questions were rather obvious: what exactly was happening to the village and agriculture? Has the village really been socially and economically stagnant over the last 20 years or has it continued to change? If it has been changing, what has been the nature of this change and how has this change affected different categories of the rural population? How do the cultivating farmers of different categories relate to agriculture as an occupation? Who has moved out of agriculture over the last 20-odd years and why? What kinds of changes have come about in the patterns of labour/production relations? What kinds of changes have come about in caste relations? How do Dalit groups relate to agriculture? How has the rural power structure changed over the last two decades?

The Fieldwork

I began my fieldwork with open-ended interviews with some individuals and groups of villagers in different localities. After getting an idea of the villages I hired three local researchers. Two of them were school teachers and one taught in a local college. I had a few sessions with them on the objectives of the study and the kind of information I was looking for. I asked them to begin with a listing of the households while I worked on preparing a village schedule and a household schedule.

With the help of the household schedule we did a household census survey of the two villages. After completing the survey, I again did interviews with villagers from different social categories. Some of these interviews, such as with the attached labourers, were done individually and some others in groups settings.

A good proportion of my respondents recognized me and remembered the time I had spent in these villages 20 years ago. I introduced myself as a university professor who is hoping to write a book on the social and economic changes taking place in the villages. However, the villagers have a particular understanding of researchers like me, who ask them development-related questions. They do see some possibility of state policy emerging out of such researches and tend to fashion their responses accordingly. I could not speak to some of my core informants, talking to whom had been very useful last time I was there. Some of them were not alive any longer and some had left the village.

The Two Villages

The idea of a typical Indian village, which represented the traditional social structure and cultural values of the Indian society in a microcosm, is a complete misnomer. It was a construction of the colonial ethnography and served their political interests (Cohn 1987; Inden 1990). The project of village studies initiated by social anthropologists during the 1950s and 1960s further reinforced this idea (Jodhka 1998). Historically, Indian villages varied significantly in size and in their social fabric. Their character is determined more by the regional agrarian histories and the local trajectories of social, economic, and ecological processes. No single village, or a group of villages, can represent the entire rural India.

The two villages selected for the study represent a particular type of rural setting, which is becoming increasingly common in different parts of the Third World. These are villages that are actively connected to urban centres and are being changed very rapidly by the processes of industrialization and technology. Though the two study villages are still sufficiently far from urban centres to be treated as urban-peripheries, they are certainly not economically 'backward' or socially and culturally 'traditional'. Of the two study villages, village-I is located at a distance of around 9 kilometres from the town of Panipat and the other (village-II) around 17 kilometres. Both are multi-caste villages with diverse caste communities living within the villages and both experienced the Green Revolution during the 1970s.

It was around mid-1970s that the Government of Haryana decided to set up a thermal power station close to Panipat. Some of the farmers from village-I lost a part of their agricultural land to the power project. However, it did not directly affect the agrarian economy of the village very much. The villagers whose land was acquired were considered for jobs in the thermal power station and some of them managed to get regular employment in the plant. It also generated a lot of new employment for casual labour. Over the years, the plant has been expanding and new ancillary industries have also been developing in the area. The Panipat oil refinery, which came up during the 1990s, is also located close to the two villages, within a distance of around 4 to 7 kilometres. However, so far the two villages have not lost much land to the refinery project. But quite like the thermal power station, it has generated a lot of new employment for casual labour for the villager.

Demographics and Changing Social Ecology

As I walked around the villages, the first thing that struck me was the growth in size of the two villages. They looked quite different from the way they did 20 years ago. There were many more streets and the villages had grown on all sides. Though there were cases of outmigrations, the absolute population of the villages had grown quite a bit, certainly by more than one and a half times.

The physical and demographic expansion of the villages also has several long-term sociological implications. Though most of the *baras* (localities) were still around caste lines and most people lived in the *bara* of their own caste, the village had lost its old residential pattern. For example, Dalit communities no longer lived away from the village, or in segregated quarters. The villages had grown on all sides and in some cases non-Dalits had come to live quite close to Dalit households. In village-II, for example, in one of my group interviews I met respondents from four different caste groups living next to each other. Though none of them was from a landowning dominant caste of Jat or Ror background, they were not all Dalits. In fact one of them was a Brahmin. Another one was Jhimmar (a local OBC caste) and yet another one from another non-Dalit caste. They all lived in close proximity to the extent that a non-Dalit's house shared a wall with a Dalit house.

Both the villages have grown demographically but the growth of village-I has been more than village-II. Whereas twenty years ago, village-II was slightly bigger than village-I, village-I is now bigger both in terms of the number of houses as well as the total population. This can perhaps be attributed directly to its proximity to the thermal power station. Also, proximity to the town has kept back even those households within the village who have their businesses and jobs in the town. Of the two villages, increase in the Scheduled Caste (SC) population was relatively higher in the village I. This has happened because of the inclusion of an additional community of Badis or Bajigars into the list of SCs.

Demographics has interestingly become a contested subject and this contestation has larger implications in the context of the new development regimes of the postcolonial world. Development and underdevelopment do not remain mere structural locations but they also become sources of identity for the common people. Demographics is part of the state enterprise used actively for formulating and implementing development strategies. As Akhil Gupta writes, '... underdevelopment is also a form of identity, something that informs people's sense of self. Who people think they are, how they got that way and what they can do to alter their lives have been profoundly shaped by the institutions, ideology, and practices of development' (Gupta 1998: ix).

Residents of the two villages have come to recognize the crucial significance of numbers and modes of representing themselves to the state in the larger discourse of development and underdevelopment. It is not only the administrative categories of SCs and OBCs that have become part of the local parlance of self-description but even categories like family and household are increasingly defined and described keeping the state processes in mind. This was quite evident from my field experience of trying to estimate the number of households.

When I first inquired from the village *sarpanch*s and some other knowledgeable informants about the approximate numbers of households in the two villages, I was given an estimate of around 900 to 1,000 households for each of the villages. It sounded much higher than what I had expected it to be. I asked my field assistants to begin the process of listing households. Given their local context, they too were sure that the figure will not be very far from the numbers suggested by the village officials. However, when we completed the listing process we discovered that the number of households in village-I was around 550 and in village-II around 540, lower than the numbers reported to the census enumerators in 2001. Of these, we were able to interview 503 and 491 respectively from the two villages.

Why does this *demographic inflation* happen? The local administration had recently undertaken a survey of the rural households for the purpose of identifying poor families so that they could be given ration cards of appropriate colours. Being listed as a family 'below poverty line' (BPL) entitles them to certain benefits; the amount of benefits would obviously go up if the units are reported in large numbers. Interestingly, the operational category used by the local administration for poverty survey was 'family' and not 'household'. However, the earlier survey being fresh in their mind, the subtle distinction between the two categories was of little significance, and could not be reported to 'outside' enumerators.

Communities and Their Social Profile

Twenty years ago, when I worked in these villages, I presumed land ownership and non-ownership was the most important factor in determining the structure of opportunities and socio-economic well-being of households in rural India. Thus, I worked with the category of social class loosely defined through landownership. This was perhaps partly an effect of my own academic orientation and the fact that much of the literature I read on agrarian social structures had been produced by economists.

However, over the years, the social sciences in India have become much more sensitive to several other social variables and indicators of development. While the mainstream economics has moved from simple calculations of income and productivity to the complex realities of 'human development', sociologists and other social scientists have rediscovered 'communities' (Jodhka 2001) and have begun to give much more importance to other forms of subjectivities, the manners in which people construct their own notions of 'well-being'.

As I began to speak to different people in the villages, I realized that my respondents though were quite knowledgeable about the larger processes of change and economic realities, they looked at the experience of the last 20 years through the prism of communities, particularly caste communities. They classified the village population through communities and viewed the economic experience of the rural population in terms of communities. Some communities had done very well while some others had not done so well and still others had done badly and over the years were seen to have either gone down, or remained where they were 20 years ago.

Village-I has two main communities, the 'locals' and the Punjabis. This village had a large Muslim population, a majority of which migrated to Pakistan at the time of Partition in 1947 and the land and homes vacated by them were allotted to Hindus and Sikhs who had to migrate out of western Punjab because of the Partition related violence. The term 'locals' was thus coined by the Punjabi settlers for the 'native' inhabitants of the village who spoke the local Haryanvi dialect. The natives of the village referred to the Punjabis as 'refugees'. This was particularly so 20 years ago. However, over the years the term refugee had been replaced by Punjabi. Only some older respondents still used the term refugee for the Punjabis.

The Punjabis are all from one caste community, Aroras, and they all came from one district of western Punjab. Of the 503 households surveyed, 67 are Punjabi Arora households. However, they have varied economic profiles. A small number of them (around 15 households) can be classified as big farmers with holdings ranging from 20 acres to 60 or more. Except for one, all big landowners of the village are Punjabis. Another 20 to 25 households can be classified as middle and small or marginal landowners. A small number of them are also poor. They own no land and have been working as sharecroppers and wage/attached labourers in the village. A good number of them (nearly 30 households) have members employed in non-farm occupations. Either they have small grocery shops in the village or have businesses outside the village, mostly in the neighbouring town of Panipat. Punjabis are also the most occupationally diversified group.

The second major caste community of the village is that of Gujjars (97 respondent households). Though they have now been listed among the OBCs, they qualify to be a 'dominant caste' (Srinivas 1959). They are mostly landowners and farmers. They are substantial in numbers, locally and in the region; they are ritually far above ex-untouchables and have enough members of the community educated and connected to the town. They too are internally differentiated but not as much as the Punjabis.

The village also has a good number of Brahmin households (30). With the exception of one family, which came to the village from western Punjab, they are all 'locals'. The Brahmins of the village do not see themselves as being superior to the other two dominant communities of the village. Ritual ideology has been quite weak in the region and being a Pandit is rarely seen as a dignified identity (see Jodhka 2002; Saberwal 1972, 1973; Tandon 1961). Most of them are small landowners and tend to see themselves as such, closer to the *chhote log* (the poor and the marginals) of the village than to the *bade log* (rich and powerful).

The largest chunk of the population is in the category of 'backward castes' (nearly 125), which are now listed amongst the OBCs. While the term 'OBC' has not yet become a popular category of description in these villages, the word 'backwards' has been in usage for a long time. The state government has had a quota of jobs for the designated 'backward caste' for quite some time, which was introduced much before the Mandal commission recommendations came into effect. However, it is very critical to make a distinction within the 'backwards', between those who have traditionally been landowners/cultivators and those who have been predominantly landless. Apart from the Gujjars, the Malis (or Sainis, as they are now called) have also been landowning cultivators, though the average size of their landholdings has been smaller than those of the Gujjars.

Jhimmars (who now like being called Kashyap Rajputs) are the largest caste group in the category of OBCs in village-I. In fact, with 99 respondent households they are the single largest caste group in the village. Since a large majority of them are landless, they work as casual labourers in the village or outside in the neighbouring towns and industries. Some of them are also employed in regular jobs outside the village. They are among the poorest of the communities in the two villages.

The second major community in this category is that of the Kumhars. They now call themselves Prajapats. Traditionally, they were the potters. They also kept donkeys for carriage work. Their traditional occupations have, over the years, become redundant and they too have mostly been landless. But unlike the Jhimmars, they have been more enterprising. While some of them have been leasing-in land on a share basis from the local farmers, others have invested in carts and trucks. However, the success stories are not too many and a majority of them continue to be struggling on the borderlines of poverty.

The village has several SC communities. The most prominent of them are the two traditional communities of the scavengers (the Balmikis with 48 households) and the Chamars (36 households). Quite like the 'lower' OBCs, the Dalits too have changed their names. The Balmikis were earlier known as Chuhras. Though non-Dalit villagers still used their old caste names in conversations with me, they are mostly addressed as Balmikis. Similarly, the Chamars are increasingly called Harijans by the villagers. They too prefer the title of Harijans over Chamar, though they have increasingly begun to call themselves as Ravidasis. Many of the villagers are familiar with the category Dalit, but very few of them use it in everyday conversation. Apart from these two major groups, there are also some other SCs. Most prominent of them are the Badis or Bajigars. Unlike the other SC communities, Badis have never been an untouchable caste. They have been living in a settlement away from the village but interact with all castes without hesitation.

The village also has several small groups listed as OBCs and SCs. They include the Dhobis, Jogis, Nais, Badhais, and several other Dalits and non-Dalit servicing castes.

Village-II too has a similar caste profile. Quite like village-I, it has two major landowning caste communities, the Jats (92 households) and the Rors (104 households). Much of the agricultural land in the village is owned by these two 'dominant castes'. Like the Punjabi Aroras of village-I, the bigger landowners of the village-II too belong mostly to one community, the Jats. However, unlike the Punjabis, the Jats have always been living in the village. Village-II too had a few households of migrant Punjabis but they moved out to neighbouring towns during the 1980s. Village-II also has a much larger number of Brahmins (60 households). Here too Brahmins are small cultivators and lived closer to the OBC communities of the village than to the dominant castes.

Among the non-landowning OBCs, the largest population is that of the Jhimmars (43 households) though they are not the largest community in the village. Jogis (36 households) and Kumhars or Prajapats (25 households) are the other major OBC caste groups of the village. The social and economic profile of these communities in village-II is quite similar to their status in village-I. The case is the same with Dalit groups. Here too the two major communities are those of Balmikis (40 households) and Chamars (50 households).

For the purpose of analysis, I have clubbed caste communities into four categories. First, the Dalits or SCs; second, the Backward Castes (BCs); third, the Dominant Castes (DCs); and fourth the ritually upper castes (UCs), which includes the Brahmins, Banias, Aroras, and Rajputs. I have clubbed Gujjars with the DCs because of their local status. Table 7.1 gives us an idea about the caste composition of the village population as shown in our survey and as per our categories. The proportion of Dalits is more or less equal in both the villages. However, the proportion of BCs is significantly larger in village-I. The proportion of ritually upper castes is also larger in village-I, which is primarily because of the Punjabi Aroras in the village, who can also be clubbed with the dominant caste because a good number of them are cultivators.

Family, Gender, and Some Other Aspects of Social Life

Family continues to be an important institution in the two villages. Almost every one lives in a family. A few individuals live alone but that is rarely out of choice. As expected, most families and households are headed by men. Households headed by women are rare; in most cases, it happens only when the male member dies or leaves home. Unlike some other parts of India, not many men have gone away from home to work. Even when they work outside, they get back home in the evening. The size of the households is also not very small. Nearly 75 per cent households have five or more members living together and 28 per cent household have seven or more members living together. The incidence of joint household is also not insignificant. Nearly 35 per cent of all the households are joint households. Their proportion is a little higher among the landowning dominant castes than for the BCs and SCs.

TABLE 7.1 Village-wise Caste Composition of Respondent Households

Caste	Village-I	Village-II	Total
Dalit	91 (18.09)	92 (18.73)	183 (18.41)
BC	178 (35.38)	131 (26.68)	309 (31.08)
DC	122 (24.25)	206 (41.95)	328 (32.99)
UC	112 (22.26)	62 (12.62)	174 (17.50)
Total	503 (100)	491 (100)	994 (100)

Source: Primary Survey by the Author.

The two villages typically represent the patriarchal landscape of northwest India. According to the Census data of 2001, the sex ratio in the two villages was 894 and 890 respectively, well below the national average. At first glance nothing much seemed to have changed in the family life. Women continue to be invisible from the public sphere. It was only after a month of interaction with the villagers that I came to know that a woman had actually won the post of village sarpanch during the last elections in village-I and that it is currently a reserved seat for a SC woman. Whenever I enquired about the sarpanch, I was either told the name of her father-in-law or husband.

However, at a more subtle level, things have changed. For example, fewer women wore purdah and educating a girl child has become much more acceptable. Sending daughters to school is much more common across communities than it was 20 years ago. In fact, there are several families who have sent their daughters out of the village for their education. They live in hostels on their own and aspire for careers, and/or a more dignified middle-class urban life.

Education is valued. Both villages have government schools up to class 12. Village-I also has a separate school for girls up to class 8. These villages also have private schools run by religious trusts. A good number of children also go to neighbouring towns to study. As per the official data of 2001, the literacy rate for village-I was 66 per cent (77 per cent for men and 55 per cent for women) and for village-II 67 per cent (78 per cent for men and 54 for women). Though nearly 30 per cent of our respondents were still illiterate, there were only 4 per cent households with no educated members and nearly 80 per cent of the households had three or more educated members in the family.

Economic Life

Until sometime ago, rural life was almost completely identified with agriculture and activities that supported agriculture. Though there were a large number of households that never owned land, they too largely depended on agriculture for their livelihood. They either worked as casual/attached labourers with the cultivators or provided other supporting services to the cultivators. Mediated through the institution of caste, the rural society of Haryana had a system of patron–client relations within which the agrarian economy was socially organized.

This system of jajmani ties had begun to weaken with the introduction of commercial agriculture during the colonial period (Bhattacharya 1985) and had nearly completely disintegrated by the 1980s. However, twenty years ago, the two villages still had a predominantly agrarian character. Agriculture was at the centre of the rural social life. It provided employment to a majority of the working population of the village and it gave them their primary identity. Poor Dalits and other landless villagers looked up to the big farmers for employment, and occasionally for credit. Through credit, the farmers tied the labouring poor for work on land and at home. Those who owned big plots of land also controlled political institutions at the local level and commanded respect and authority in the village.

This has almost completely changed. The change was more visible in village-I than it was in village-II, but the pattern was similar. Less than 30 per cent of all households identified cultivation as their primary occupation. This was even lower in village-I (23 per cent). As is evident from Table 7.2, the largest proportion of the households is in the category of labourers. However, they are not necessarily agricultural labourers. In fact, a large majority of them earn most of their livelihood from working outside the agricultural sector and only occasionally work on land, a point I will return to later.

More important perhaps is the number of people who have employment outside the village (17.20 per cent). This becomes particularly interesting when we see it in relation to caste. Landownership and cultivation continues to be a prerogative of the dominant and UCs in the two villages. Nearly 92 per cent of all the cultivators were from these

TABLE 7.2 Primary Occupation of the Respondent Households

Primary occupation	I	II	Total
Cultivators	117 (23.26)	172 (35.03)	289 (29.07)
Labourers	206 (40.9)	153 (31.16)	359 (36.11)
Shopkeepers/Business	39 (07.75)	45 (09.16)	84 (08.45)
Regular service/ Government job	108 (21.4)	63 (12.8)	171 (17.20)
No clear arrangement	33 (06.55)	58 (11.8)	91 (09.15)
Total	503 (100)	491 (100)	994 (100)

Source: Primary Survey by the Author.

caste communities. In contrast, more than 80 per cent of those who reported their primary occupation as labourers were either Dalits or were from 'backward castes'.

However, diversification had occurred among all the caste groups. As is evident from Table 7.3, a good proportion of households in each category have primary occupations outside agriculture. Interestingly, proportionately the number of Dalits with regular jobs is the highest and that of the BCs the lowest. Though they have both been poor and lacking in social and cultural capital required for securing a regular job, Dalits have been able get these jobs partly because of their statutory quotas in education and employment being more effective than that for the BCs.

Apart from the economic activity, the number of working members in a household also determines its social and economic well-being. Notably, nearly half of our respondent households have more than one full-time working member in their households and in some cases the number of working members in the household is as high as five. Further, the pattern across caste groups is almost the same. There are also some households where there is no full time working member in the household.

TABLE 7.3 Caste-wise Primary Occupation of the Respondent Households

Caste	Cultivator/ Farmer	Labourer	Shopkeeper/ Business	Regular service/ Government job	No regular job	Total
Dalit	7	106	0	51	19	183
	(3.8)	(57.9)		(27.86)	(10.38)	(100)
BC	17	202	14	42	34	309
	(5.5)	(65.37)	(4.5)	(13.5)	(11.0)	(100)
DC	201	25	23	55	24	328
	(61.28)	(7.6)	(7.01)	(16.7)	(7.31)	(100)
UC	64	26	47	23	14	174
	(36.78)	(14.94)	(27.01)	(13.21)	(8.04)	(100)
Total	289	359	84	171	91	994
	(29.07)	(36.11)	(8.45)	(17.20)	(9.15)	(100)

Source: Primary Survey by the Author.

TABLE 7.4 Number of Working Members in the Respondent Households

Caste	1	2	3	4	5	None	Total
Dalit	82	65	24	5	4	3	183
BC	144	109	37	10	6	3	309
DC	162	99	40	13	6	8	328
UC	95	46	15	4	2	12	174
Total	483	319	116	32	18	26	994

Source: Primary Survey by the Author.

An important aspect of this is the fact that the households in rural Haryana are increasingly becoming pluri-active (Jodhka 2006a; Lindberg 2005). Different members of the household pursue different occupations. Further, more than 15 per cent (152 households) of the respondents also reported having a secondary occupation either within the village or outside. In most cases, the secondary occupation is a small business, either some kind of shop within the village, or outside in the neighbouring village.

A striking change in the two villages over the last two decades is a manifold expansion of the local market. Twenty years ago, the number of shops in each of the villages was around 15 to 20 and most of them were grocery shops, which provided almost everything the villagers needed for their daily consumption. Most of these shops were owned and run by the local Banias or the Punjabi Aroras. This has changed significantly over the years. The number of shops in village-I is 78 and in village-II is 64. More significantly, the local market has also witnessed diversity and differentiation of various kinds. They are being run by

TABLE 7.5 Caste-wise Shop Ownership in Study Villages

Caste of Shopkeepers	Village-I	Village-II	Total
UC	35	11	46 (32.39)
DC	17	19	36 (25.35)
BC	22	25	47 (33.09)
Dalit	4	9	13 (9.15)
Total	78	64	142 (100)

Source: Primary Survey by the Author.

members of all castes and communities. Only 32 per cent of all the shops are now owned and run by the UCs that used to have a near complete monopoly over the local market in the past. Interestingly, even though none of our Dalit respondents reported of shopkeeping as the main occupation of the household, there were a few shops being run by the Dalits. However, the caste element continues to be significant in the local market. Not only is the proportion of Dalit shopkeepers much lower than their numbers, their shops are also either located in Dalit localities or they provide some specific kinds of manual services, such as cycle or shoe repair.

TABLE 7.6 Types of Services Provided by Local Shops in the Study Villages

Types of shops	Village-I	Village-II	Total
Barber shops	4	6	11
Cobbler shops	1	2	3
Ration shops	32	27	59
STDs	3	4	10
Cement/Brick Shops	2	1	3
Liquor shops	1	1	2
Tent Houses	1	0	1
Mechanical (cycle repair)	2	4	6
Electric shops	3	2	6
Vegetable shops	4	0	4
Jewellery shops	2	1	3
Cloth stores	2	0	2
TV/radio repair shops	3	1	4
Tailors	4	3	7
Photo studios	1	1	2
Medical stores	1	2	3
Clinics	2	0	1
Cable networks	1	0	1
Sweet shops	4	1	2
Hardware shops	2	3	3
Flour mill	3	1	1
Furniture shop	0	1	1
Tea stall	0	1	1
Fertilizer store	1	1	1

Source: Primary Survey by the Author.

The villages now have all kinds of odd services available within the village, ranging from fertilizers and pesticides to jewellery and electrical goods and their repairs. This indeed reflects the growing consumer culture in the villages and the fact that villagers have more disposable income. The growth of the local market is also a consequence of the near complete disappearance of the traditional jajmani economy. Though ideologically the jajmani system had lost its appeal long ago and I could see it disintegrating twenty years ago, the services traditionally provided by local caste groups had not become completely commodified as is the case today. Now there is a shop for almost every service and there are newer services and commodities for which there are specialized outlets. Some shops provide multiple services and keep different categories of goods under one roof. For example, one could buy shoes from the kirana shop, or fertilizer bags from a shop that also sells cement bags.

Agriculture

Technologically speaking, there has not been much change over the last two decades in the manner in which the agrarian economy is organized in the two villages. Despite the growing shadow of industry over the two villages, not much land has been lost to 'outsiders', so far. On the contrary, land under cultivation has grown in size as the *banjar* land is improved for cultivation. In village-I, most of the panchayat land, which was lying fallow, has also been encroached upon by the local farmers and is being regularly cultivated.

As was the practice two decades ago, the two main crops in the region are still wheat and paddy. Some villagers used to also grow sugar cane but not any longer. Some farmers also grow a third crop, peas or lentils. Use of fertilizers and pesticides has continued to grow. Farmers have almost completely stopped making their own seeds and depend entirely on the market for supply of hybrid seeds. Their irrigational needs are met by the canal water (around one-third) and tube wells (two-third). Though the water table has not gone down much, the farmers install tube wells using a new technology, the submersible pumps. These are more expensive but they provide a better flow of water.

The mechanization has also grown. A large number of farmers owned tractors even during the late 1980s; a good number of villagers also kept bullocks. In fact I came across some cases where the relatively smaller farmers, after working with tractors for some time, had gone back to bullock farming, finding it more economical for their size of holdings. This is no longer the case. There are no bullocks in the two villages any longer. The small and marginal farmers who could not afford to buy tractors hired it from tractor owning farmers for ploughing their fields. There are 72 tractors in village-I and nearly 90 in village-II.

The use of combine harvesters had grown at the cost of threshers for the harvesting of wheat. Initially there was some resistance to their use, because combine harvesters only picked up the seed and left the plant on the field, which is a useful source for cattle fodder. Threshing machines were preferred because they also processed the plant and converted it into hay (used for cattle fodder). However, the arrival of a new machine called a reaper has to an extent solved this problem. The reaper plucks the plant left behind by the combine and processes it into hay. Mechanical harvesting machines are available for paddy as well, but they do not work for the longer plant of Basmati rice, which is popular with most of the farmers in the two villages. One of the implications, and perhaps also a reason, for this second phase of mechanization is a steady decline of demand for human labour for agriculture.

Landholdings and Agrarian Social Structure

Despite the declining significance of agriculture in the national life, agriculture continues to employ the largest numbers of working Indians. Though this holds true for the two villages, there is clearly a declining trend in the number of people working on land. As mentioned above, less than 30 per cent of the households in the two villages reported agriculture or farming as their primary occupation. Also, there are significant disparities in the land ownership patterns. As evident from Table 7.7, 66 per cent of the households in village-I and 48 per cent in village-II reported owning no land at all. On the other hand, a small number of households owned large plots of land.

When seen in relation to caste, this picture of disparity becomes even more significant. Despite many radical changes in the rural social life over the last century or so, the agrarian economy of the village continues to be almost exclusively under the control of dominant and upper castes, those who have traditionally been the landowning and agrarian communities. As is evident from Table 7.8, nearly 95 per cent of the

TABLE 7.7 Patterns of Land Ownership in the Two Study Villages

	No land	Less than two acres	2–5 acres	5–10 acres	10–25 acres	25–50 acres	50+ acres	No response	Total
Village-I	333	25	101	30	7	5	1	1	503
	(66.2)	(4.97)	(20.1)	(5.96)	(1.39)	(0.99)	(0.19)	(0.19)	(100)
Village-II	235	36	130	50	30	7	2	1	491
	(47.9)	(7.33)	(26.5)	(10.2)	(6.10)	(1.42)	(0.40)	(0.20)	(100)
Total	568	61	231	80	37	12	3	2	994
	(57.1)	(6.13)	(23.2)	(8.04)	(3.72)	(1.20)	(0.30)	(0.20)	(100)

Source: Primary Survey by the Author.

Note: The number of farming households owning and cultivating more than 10 acres of land appears to be under-reported for the obvious reasons.

TABLE 7.8 Landownership Patterns across Caste Groups

	No land	<1 acre	2–5 acres	5–10 acres	10–25 acres	25–50 acres	50+ acres	No response	Total
Dalit	174	2	6	0	0	0	0	1	183
	(95.08)	(1.09)	(3.28)					(0.55)	(100)
BC	293	4	9	3	0	0	0	0	309
	(94.82)	(1.29)	(2.91)	(0.97)					(100)
DC	39	27	156	61	35	7	2	1	328
	(11.89)	(8.23)	(47.56)	(18.6)	(10.67)	(2.13)	(0.60)	(0.3)	(100)
UC	62	28	60	16	2	5	1	0	174
	(35.63)	(16.09)	(34.48)	(9.19)	(1.14)	(2.87)	(0.6)		(100)
Total	568	61	231	80	37	12	3	2	994
	(57.14)	(6.13)	(23.24)	(8.05)	(3.72)	(1.21)	(0.3)	(0.2)	(100)

Source: Primary Survey by the Author.

Dalits and BCs are completely landless. On the contrary, only around 12 per cent of the DC households are landless.

However there have been very important changes in the agrarian social structure, both in terms of relations across caste groups and class categories, as also in the attitudes of the landowners towards their occupational callings.

Land, Labour, and Caste

Twenty years ago, agrarian relations in these villages had already changed quite radically. Farmers no longer gave their land on lease to tenants on a long-term basis. The relationship with attached labourers had also become completely formalized (Bhalla 1976; Jodhka 1994). Most of the labour needs of the farmers were fulfilled by casual and contractual labour, mostly on a fixed cash rate. Though a good amount of peak-season work was done by the migrant labour from Uttar Pradesh and Bihar, local Dalits and other landless labourers also worked on farms. Most of the middle and big farmers, who owned more than 15 acres of land, also employed attached labourers. Some of the big farmers employed up to five attached labourers. With the exceptions of one or two, all attached labourers came from the village. Only the locals could be trusted with an advance wage.

Though the process of mechanization was part and parcel of the Green Revolution technology, it did not lead to labour displacement. In fact, demand for labour went up considerably with the new agrarian technology making it possible to intensify cropping patterns and considerably expanding land under cultivation. Even when labour came from outside during the peak harvesting sowing seasons, local labour also had enough work available on the farm.

This has changed considerably over the last twenty years. First and foremost, there has been a clear decline in the demand for labour over the last 20 years and this has happened because of the second phase of mechanization. Decline has not only been on the demand but also of the supply. The local Dalits have nearly completely withdrawn from the local agrarian economy. Nearly all of the Dalits have been landless and they no longer like working as labourers on the farms. As I had earlier observed in the villages of Punjab, Dalits do not wish to work on land with cultivating farmers primarily for social and political reasons (Jodhka 2002).

Working with farmers implies accepting their domination and power. By refusing to work on land, Dalits express their dissent against the traditional structure of patron-client ties. Even if it means cycling to the town for casual labour and no higher wage or secure income, a Dalit does not like working on land. Some of them also told me that work on a farm was much more demanding and the number of working-hours invariably exceeded eight hours.

This distancing of the Dalit from the agrarian economy has of course been made possible by the availability of alternative sources of employment in the industries nearby and the vibrant urban centre of Panipat not being so far off.

As communities also, Dalits seemed to be consolidating themselves. They have been quite successful in getting regular jobs due to the caste-based quotas for them in government service. As mentioned earlier, nearly 28 per cent of Dalit households reported regular jobs outside the village as their primary occupation. This would have also helped them to decrease their dependence for short-term credit on the local cultivating farmers. In contrast, the economic position of those from landless BCs seemed more vulnerable. They also worked as wage and attached labourers with the local farms.

The two villages still had attached labourers and they were mostly employed by big farmers. However, their numbers had considerably declined. This was particularly the case with village-II. The total number of attached labourers in the village was not more than 15 or 20. Two decades ago, there would have been nearly 70 such labourers. Village-I still has around 25 to 30 attached labourers. Most of them are employed by Punjabi farmers. Gujjar farmers no longer hire attached labourers. During the late 1980s, a large majority of attached labourers were local Dalits. Twenty years later, not even one of them was a local Dalit. However, the terms of their hiring and the nature of their relationship has not changed much (see Jodhka 2012).

Tenancy Arrangements

Though the land market has been rather sluggish, not all landowners are cultivating farmers. Two sets of landowners have been moving out of direct cultivation; the first are those who are left with small plots of land, where the main working members have either found a job outside or there is no one in the family with the capacity to work on the land. The second is the category of relatively bigger farmers who have diversified into other occupations but continue to live in the village, or want to keep an active relationship with the land. Such landowners lease out their lands, invariably to smaller enterprising landowners. In such cases land is mostly leased out on an annual cash rent, which has recently gone up from around 13,000 or 14,000 to around 18,000 to 20,000 rupees. This phenomenon has come to be known as 'reverse tenancy' (Brar and Gill 2002), which is a misnomer, because the land is leased out not only by the big landowners to small landowners but also by small and marginalized land owners to enterprising farmers. Apart from being enterprising, such farmers also require sufficient funds to pay cash to the landowner in advance for the year. They also have to have some risk bearing capacity. A bad crop due to weather or pests can mean a complete disaster. A rough estimate suggests that nearly 20 to 25 per cent of all the land is being cultivated under such arrangements.

Another form of tenancy arrangement, which is preferred by relatively more active landowners, is what can be described as labour sharecropping. Many of the middle-size farmers, and some big farmers, preferred leasing their lands out on share basis to the labouring households, which work on the farm with their family and get one-fourth share of the entire yield. Such arrangements are mostly for a single crop, paddy, which requires intensive input of labour. The labourer in this arrangement has to also share one-fourth of the expense, which is invariably paid by the farmer and deducted from the total yield at the end of the season. Some of these labourers are also indebted to the farmers whose lands they cultivate but they are not tied to the farmer like an attached labourer. The farmer, though continuing to take interest in the farm, does not have to worry about the everyday work.

Future of Agriculture and Rural Life

The two villages have experienced some very important economic and social changes. However, there is no clear indication of a classical type of capitalist development taking place where a few farmers are able to buy large plots of lands and the rest are proletarianized (Lenin 1956). Also there was no move towards corporate agriculture or contract farming. Only occasionally were some farmers contracted to produce seeds by seed companies. But there was no sign of this emerging as a trend in the two villages. Not much land is being sold or purchased, unless it is acquired by industry or the state. The smaller farmers, who find their holdings unviable, are getting out of agriculture but without selling off their land. Land sales happen only when the entire family moves out and is unable to keep in touch with the village. Some of the middle and bigger landowners, who have found viable urban employment, also prefer leasing their land out to selling it.

Interestingly, even though there is still a strong sense of attachment to land, agriculture is not seen as a desirable occupation. The younger generation across caste groups dislikes farming. When we asked our respondents about their preferences for practicing agriculture by their children and grandchildren, only around 8 per cent of our respondents answered in the affirmative. Surprisingly, responses to the question were quite similar across caste and occupational categories. Dalits and UCs (5 to 6 per cent) were least interested in their families staying in the farming occupation but even cultivating farmers of DCs (9 per cent) did not want their children to practice agriculture. Only among BCs, there was some desire to continue with agriculture (11 per cent).

However, these villagers are less opposed to living in the village (see Table 7.9). Many of the households, or individual members of the households who have jobs outside, in the neighbouring towns, continue

TABLE 7.9 Perceptions on Preferred Place of Residence for Children and Grandchildren

Caste	Village	City	No response	Total
Dalit	92	85	6	183
	(50.27)	(46.44)	(3.27)	(100)
BC	236	68	5	309
	(76.37)	(22.0)	(1.61)	(100)
DC	180	140	8	328
	(54.87)	(42.68)	(2.43)	(100)
UC	85	86	3	174
	(48.85)	(49.42)	(1.72)	(100)
Total	593	379	22	994
	(59.65)	(38.12)	(2.21)	(100)

Source: Primary Survey by the Author.

to live in the village. Cities are invariably seen as polluted and expensive to live in.

Not only has social and economic organization of the village changed, but the meaning of the village for its residents has also undergone a complete change. Choosing to live in the village does not imply any kind of commitment to, or identification with the village and its ethos. The social order of caste hierarchy is a thing of the past and the collective identity of the village is fragmented.

Local Power and Panchayats

How could we talk about the nature of power relations in the two villages? The social science literature on the subject has invariably pointed to 'land' and 'caste' as being the two major sources of power in rural India (Dumont 1970; Srinivas 1959). The introduction of the democratic political process and adult franchise helped the landowning middle-level agrarian caste groups to acquire dominance at the local and regional levels during the post-Independence period (Kothari 1970; Srinivas 1962). Over the years, scholars have also pointed to new emerging trends, which assign greater importance to the growing role of individual political entrepreneurship (Krishna 2001) and growing political mobilizations among Dalit castes (Jodhka 2006b).

Twenty years ago, the dominance in the two villages was clearly located in caste and land. The big landowners (the *chaudharies*) were also the most powerful individuals in the two villages and they were all members of the dominant/upper castes. With the introduction of competitive politics, operationally the power of dominant individuals had to be institutionally reproduced through electoral politics. Universal adult franchise also gave a new sense of identity to Dalits. 'Every individual began to matter and everyone had a single vote', was the way one of my Dalit respondents articulated the change in the local politics 20 years ago.

However, on the ground, the local democratic politics worked through factional alliances. Factions were always vertical in nature, with some members of all castes being loyal to the leader, who was always a substantial landowner. Even after the introduction of a representative system of electing local leaders came into force, the big landowners, the chaudharies, of the village continued to enjoy influence in the local setting. However, they had to be constantly aware of the need to keep partners in the faction together.

There have been some interesting changes in this over the last 20 years.

Coupled with changes in the agrarian political economy and caste system, the democratic electoral system has radically transformed the authority structure of the village. 'A *Chaudhari* is a thing of the past', was a statement made by several of the big landowners. Another respondent from a BC community articulated the general feeling of the landless castes towards the changing power structure in following words:

> No one cares for anyone simply because he thinks he is a *chaudhari*. *Chaudharies*, if they are, they must be in their homes. We do not care.

In other words, there has been a clear decline in power of the 'individual' and 'individual's family' in the local politics. 'Power' has become much more fluid and no more seems to be determined, or shaped by caste and land alone. Though Jats are the big landowners in village-II, the sarpanch is from the caste of smaller landowners, Rors, who owns around 6 acres of land. Village-I has had even a more interesting trajectory. As mentioned above, the big landowners of the village are all Punjabi Aroras. A Punjabi landowning family commanded a lot of authority in the village. Mr S. Ram, patriarch of the family was also the sarpanch of the village for nearly twenty years. After he died, his eldest son became the sarpanch. However, over the last 10 years or so, the sarpanch has neither been from this family or from any other family of the Punjabi big landowners. If the post is not reserved for SCs, the sarpanch is likely to be a small landowner from a caste like the Gujjars or Brahmins.

What has brought this change about? What is the nature of the new power structure of the village? Does it have any influence on the development process?

Perhaps the most important factor that has brought this change about is the general disintegration of the 'village community'. As I have argued elsewhere in relation to rural Punjab (Jodhka 2002), here also one could observe the processes of dissociation, distancing, and autonomy. With the exception of a small number of those from the scavenging community, Dalit families of the village were no longer engaged in traditional caste occupations. They go out of the village for work, and many of them have regular employment (see Table 7.3). Their dependence on local landowners for credit has also declined. They have also moved away or distanced from the agrarian economy of the village and they rarely, if ever, participate in the ritual life of the village, or that of the other caste groups on any occasion. In other words, they no longer see themselves as being a part of the social order of caste. This has also given them a sense of independence and political agency.

The other 'poor' communities of the village, the so-called BCs, also have alternative sources of employment outside agriculture and many of them indeed go out of the village for work. However, a smaller number of them have regular government employment.

Do the local poor feel politically empowered? The answer is both 'yes' and 'no'. As I have discussed previously, the disintegration of the traditional hierarchical structure has indeed given them a sense of citizenship and they are quite aware of their political rights. They interact and participate in the larger world of caste and community politics at the regional level, which gives them a set of political resources they can use in times of crisis. However, they are also acutely aware of their vulnerabilities that come with poverty and marginality. When I asked a respondent from the Jhimmar community why they did not contest elections and become sarpanchs? His answer was very candid:

> ... We are poor people. We know our votes are more than any other caste community of the village. However, we also know our limits (*aukat*). I want to live in this village. If I were to take your words seriously, I may even have to leave the village.

Some other respondents also pointed to the money one has to spend to contest an election for the position of sarpanch, '... at least a few lakhs ..., who is going to fund it?'

Who has inherited power from the traditional patriarchs? The village politics today is integrated much more with the regional politics and the bureaucratic structure and is shaped by a large number of factors. A new class of 'political entrepreneurs', who are not necessarily rich but are invariably from upper or dominant caste groups, seem to be the main actors in the emerging political scenario. Invariably young, in the age group of 25 to 45, they are required to have skills of coordinating with the outside world of politics and development bureaucracy. But at the same time, they also have to link themselves organically with different caste communities and demonstrate to them their leadership abilities. Given their sense of pride and arrogance, the old chaudharies find it difficult to do such a thing.

While some villagers complained about the local sarpanchs being implicated in corruption cases and one of the sarpanchs was in fact suspended on some charges of corruption in the month of April 2008, they do have to be much more accountable and performance-oriented. Development programmes indeed have better chances of being implemented in the emerging atmosphere of competitive politics at the village level.

Mobility and Marginalities

Who is rich and who is poor in the villages today? What are the patterns of social and economic mobility? How are the processes of social and economic change affecting different categories of the rural population?

Even when the social and political grammar of the village life has changed a great deal, land continues to be economically the most valued asset in the rural northwest India.

Over the last ten years or so, land prices have escalated by more than 10 times. An acre of land, which could be sold for around 3 lakhs sometime in the late 1990s, now sells for 25 to 30 lakh rupees or even more. Not only has the value of land gone up, but the value of land products has also gone up. All this has happened very recently with the sudden increase in the prices of wheat and rice. Though their incomes and values of their assets have seen a sharp rise, the big landowners were never poor. After the Green Revolution big landowners generated enough surpluses from their lands. Even after they invested in the required agricultural machinery they had surplus. Where were these surpluses invested?

Their main aim has been to diversify the household economy. The first and foremost priority for most of them has been to invest in the education of their wards. Over the years, many of their children have been to schools, colleges, and universities. Having studied outside, they have also found employment outside the village. While most of them continue to own their agricultural lands, they do not have the time or the inclination to even be part-time farmers. The third generation of 'Green Revolutionaries' does not want anything to do with agriculture.

Even when they have not done well in their education, they want to stay away from agriculture. The younger kids seemed very clear about their dislike for agriculture. They want to move ahead in life, out of the village and beyond, to the life of the urban middle class and the comforts of consumer goods.

Even while living in the village, they have become urbanized. They own cars, television sets, refrigerators, and mobile phone. Nearly 4 per cent of the households owned cars for personal use. More than 35 per cent of the households owned motorbikes. Nearly 40 per cent had refrigerators and LPG connections. Television sets and mobile phones were even more popular. More than 50 per cent of the households had mobile phones, and nearly 70 per cent had television sets.

However, there are significant variations across different caste groupings in ownership of luxury goods. Interestingly, despite the disparities, ownership of these 'middle-class luxuries' is not completely absent among the Dalits and BCs. Even though proportionately much lower than the DCs and UCs, a good number of Dalit and BC households also own motorbikes, refrigerators, LPG connections, and mobile phones. Inequalities are much more pronounced in 'hard assets', such as land ownership and urban property.

Expanding Vulnerabilities

The nature of changes taking place in the rural economy and social setting over the last 20 odd years has also created grounds for a new set of vulnerabilities. An important source of these vulnerabilities

TABLE 7.10 Caste-wise Ownership of Luxury Goods

Caste communities	Car	Motor cycle	Refrigerator	LPG	TV	Tele-phone	Mobile	Computer
Dalit	0	24	25	44	86	9	53	1
BC	1	32	50	61	171	11	97	2
DC	26	215	214	238	283	52	255	11
UC	12	96	114	142	151	31	138	6
Total	39	367	403	485	691	103	543	20

Source: Primary Survey by the Author.

is the gradual but near complete disappearance of village common lands. Almost all the cultivable land is under cultivation in both the villages. Even the land owned by village panchayats has been brought under cultivation. Nearly 1,000 acres of land in village-I owned by the village panchayat has apparently been encroached upon by farmers and is being cultivated privately. As has been argued by Jodha, the disappearance of common lands makes the poor more vulnerable (Jodha 1988).

An evidence of this process could be seen in the changing patterns of cattle ownership in the two villages. Haryana has traditionally been a land of milk and ghee (clarified butter). A popular slogan describes Haryana as a land of milk and curd (*deshan mein desh Haryana, jit doodh dahi ka khana*). Twenty years ago, when I first did my fieldwork in these villages, keeping milk cattle was a norm in these villages. The bigger farmers kept a large number of cattle, ranging from 5 to 40. This was an important source of income for the rural households. Apart from being a source of nutrition, the milk produced at home was also sold to the milk-vendor. Some of the farmers also raised calves and sold cattle to add to their incomes. The poorer households purchased buffaloes with IRDP schemes to add to their incomes. Only around 10 per cent of the households did not keep cattle. Besides, some of the poorer households also raised sheep and made a living out of it.

Twenty years later, this has completely changed. None of the households in any of the two villages keep sheep now. Cattle ownership has also come down significantly. As is evident from Table 7.11, nearly 42 per cent of all the households did not keep any cattle. This figure is much larger for the Dalit and BC households. Another 35 per cent of the households have only one animal. Twenty years ago, more than 70 per cent households had more than two cattle and more than 40 per cent of them had more than five cattles.

What has brought about this change? While there are several factors responsible for this change, the most critical is the disappearance of the commons. 'Where do we take them for grazing? There are no grazing grounds left any more in the village and where do we have the money to buy fodder for them?' was the typical response of the poorer respondents. The relatively well-off respondents also complained about the disappearance of the common lands but their main problem was the difficulties in taking care of them. 'They stay tied up at home all

TABLE 7.11 Caste-wise Cattle Ownership among Respondent Households

	Nil	1	2–3	4–6	7–10	11–15	25+	Total
Dalit	126	50	6	1	0	0	0	183
	(68.85)	(27.32)	(3.27)	(0.54)				(100)
BC	175	111	22	1	0	0	0	309
	(56.63)	(35.92)	(7.11)	(0.32)				(100)
DC	29	127	134	32	2	3	1	328
	(8.84)	(38.71)	(40.85)	(9.75)	(0.60)	(0.91)	(0.30)	(100)
UC	85	61	23	4	0	0	1	174
	(48.85)	(35.07)	(13.21)	(2.29)			(0.57)	(100)
Total	415	349	185	38	2	3	2	994
	(41.75)	(35.11)	(18.61)	(3.82)	(0.20)	(0.30)	(0.20)	(100)

Source: Primary Survey by the Author.

day. Our women do not like working in the cattle shed any longer. The scavengers do not come to clean the dung. The younger generation does not even come close to this kind of work.'

The implications of these changes are very important. Apart from providing nutrition and additional income to the household, milk cattle also worked as important buffers in the times of crisis. For the landless poor, a cow or a buffalo was a source of additional income. The small/marginal farmer also earned additional income from selling milk but equally important was the additional income they earned from selling a home-raised cow or buffalo. They were particularly useful in times of crisis. If a crop failed or they needed money for a wedding, they sold a cow or buffalo and raised the additional money. The decline in cattle ownership expands the vulnerability of the poor and not-so-poor.

The Disappearing Community

It is not only the physical commons that have disappeared; the social and emotional commons are also rapidly disappearing from the rural landscape. Though the Indian village never had a community in the sense in which the category is understood in the western social sciences, there was a sense of collective identity that the villagers shared. The disintegration of caste and hierarchical social order has also weakened this sense of collective identity significantly. It has different implications for different sets of populations and there can be different ways of looking at these changes. For those on the margins, particularly the ex-untouchable Dalits, this change has only been for the good. It has freed them from the oppressive normative order of caste and the traditional valued frame of hierarchy. For the dominant and the upper castes, this has meant an end of their power and privilege. Not surprisingly, they are the ones who complain the most about the change. But, as discussed earlier, they want to move out of the village and their younger generation is ready to move out to other occupations. Many of them have in fact already done so.

At another level, these changes have also generated a new sense of individuation in the village society and in the absence of viable economic opportunities and social support structures, it has generated a new sense of anxiety and ontological insecurity. One of the visible manifestations of this is rapidly growing popularity of some religious cults in the area. I was quite surprised to hear from several respondents about the extent of following that some of the babas and *deras* have in these villages. The two most popular religious sects in these villages are the Dera Sacha Sauda, located in the Sirsa town of Haryana, around 100 kilometres from the villages; and the Radha Soami Dera, located in Beas in Punjab, around 350 kilometres from the village. However, these deras have local branches, in the working of which the villagers take a lot of interest. Dera Sacha Sauda has nearly 500 followers from different caste groups from village-I, most of them relatively poor.

References

Balagopal, K. 1987. 'An Ideology of the Provincial Propertied Class', *Economic and Political Weekly*, XXI (36–7): 2177–8.

Bhaduri, A. 1984. *The Economic Structure of Backward Agriculture*. Delhi: Macmillan.

Bhalla, S. 1976. 'New Relations of Production in Haryana Agriculture', *Economic and Political Weekly*, XI (13): A26–A30.

Bhattacharya, N. 1985. 'Agrarian Change in Punjab 1880–1940', Unpublished PhD thesis, New Delhi, Jawaharlal Nehru University.

Brar, J.S. and Sucha Singh Gill. 2002. 'Tenancy Reversal and Operational Enclosures', in Sucha Singh Gill (ed.), *Land Reforms in India Intervention for Agrarian Capitalist Transformation in Punjab and Haryana*, pp. 215–37. Delhi: SAGE Publications.

Brass, T. 1990. 'Class Struggle and the Deproletarianization of Agricultural Labour in Haryana (India)', *The Journal of Peasant Studies*, 18 (1): 36–67.

———. 1995. 'Unfree Labour and Agrarian Change: A Different View', *Economic and Political Weekly*, XXX (13): 697–9.

———. 1996. 'Misinterpreting Unfree Labour in Contemporary Haryana', *Economic and Political Weekly*, XXXI (33): 2362–4.

Breman, J. 1974. *Patronage and Exploitation—Changing Agrarian Relations in South Gujarat, India*. Berkley: University of California Press.

Byres, T.J. 1972. 'The Dialectics of India's Green Revolution', *South Asia Review*, 5 (2): 99–106.

Cohn, B.S. 1987. *An Anthropologist among Historians and other Essays*. New Delhi: Oxford University Press.

Dumont, L. 1998[1970]. *Homo Hierarchicus: The Caste System and its Implications*. New Delhi: Oxford University Press.

Gupta, Akhil. 1998. *Postcolonial Developments: Agriculture in the Making of Modern India*. New Delhi: Oxford University Press.

Inden, R. 1990. *Imagining India*. Cambridge: Blackwell.

Jodha, N.S. 1988. 'Poverty Debate in India: a Minority View', *Economic and Political Weekly*, XXIII (45–7): 2421–8.

Jodhka, S.S. 1994. 'Agrarian Changes and Attached Labour: Emerging Patterns in Haryana Agriculture', *Economic and Political Weekly*, XXIX (39): A102–6.

———. 1995a. 'Agrarian Changes, Unfreedom and Attached Labour', *Economic and Political Weekly*, XXX (31–2): 2011–13.

———. 1995b. 'Who Borrows? Who Lends?: Changing Structure of Informal Credit in Rural Haryana', *Economic and Political Weekly*, XXX (39): A123–31.

———. 1995c. 'Bureaucratisation, Corruption and Depoliticisation: Changing Profile of Credit Co-operatives in Rural Haryana', *Economic and Political Weekly*, XXX (1): 53–6.

———. 1995d. 'IRDP and Changing Agrarian Relations: A Study of the Unintended Consequences', *Journal of Rural Development*, 14 (1).

———. 1996. 'Interpreting Attached Labour in Contemporary Haryana', *Economic and Political Weekly*, XXXI (29): 1286–7.

———. 1998. 'From "Book-View" to "Field-View": Social Anthropological: Constructions of the Indian Village', *Oxford Development Studies*, 26 (3): 311–32.

———. (ed.) 2001. *Community and Identities: Contemporary Discourses on Culture and Politics in India*. New Delhi: SAGE Publications.

———. 2002. 'Caste and Untouchability in Rural Punjab', *Economic and Political Weekly*, XXXVII (19): 1813–23.

———. 2006a. 'Beyond "Crises": Rethinking Contemporary Punjab Agriculture', *Economic and Political Weekly*, XLI (16): 1530–7.

Jodhka, S.S. 2006b. 'Caste and Democracy: Assertion and Identity among the Dalits of Rural Punjab', *Sociological Bulletin*, LV (1): 4–23.

———. 2012. 'Agrarian Changes in the Times of (Neo-liberal) "Crises": Revisiting Attached Labour in Haryana Agriculture', *Economic and Political Weekly*, XLVII (26–7): 5–13.

Krishna, Anirudh. 2001. 'What is happening to Caste? A View from Some North Indian Villages', Terry Sanford Institute of Public Policy Working Paper SAN01-04, Duke.

Kothari, Rajni. 1970. *Caste in Indian Politics*. Hyderabad: Orient Longman.

Lenin, V.I. 1956. *The Development of Capitalism in Russia: The Process of the Formation of a Home Market for Large-Scale Industry*. Moscow: Foreign Languages Publishing House.

Lindberg, Steffan. 2005. 'Whom and What to fight?: Notes and Queries on Indian Farmers Collective Action under Liberalisation and Globalisation', Unpublished seminar paper, Punjab University, Patiala.

Omvedt, Gail. 1992. 'Capitalist Agriculture and Rural Classes in India', in B. Berberogly (ed.), *Class, State and Development in India*. New Delhi: SAGE Publications.

Rudra, A. 1987. 'Labour Relations in Agriculture: A Study in Contrast', *Economic and Political Weekly*, XXII (17): 757–60.

Rutten, M.A.F. 1995. *Farms and Factories: Social Profile of Large Farmers and Rural Industrialists in West India*. New Delhi: Oxford University Press.

Saberwal, S. 1972. 'Status, Mobility, and Networks in Punjabi Industrial Town', in S. Saberwal (ed.), *Beyond the Village: Sociological Explorations*. Shimla: Indian Institute of Advanced Studies.

———. 1973. 'Receding Pollution: Intercaste Relations in Urban Punjab', *Sociological Bulletin*, 22 (2): 234–59.

Srinivas, M.N. 1959. 'The Dominant Caste in Rampura', *American Anthropologist*, 61 (1): 1–16.

———. 1962. *Caste in Modern India and Other Essays*. Bombay: Media Promoter and Publishers

Tandon, P. 1961. *Punjabi Century 1857–1947*. New York: Harcourt, Brace and World.

Thorner, D. 1956. *Agrarian Prospect in India*. New Delhi: Oxford University Press.

Upadhya, Carol B. 1988. 'The Farmer-Capitalists of Coastal Andhra Pradesh', *Economic and Political Weekly*, XXIII (27 and 28): 1376–82 and 1433–42.

8

RAVI SRIVASTAVA*

Assessing Change

Land, Labour, and Employment in an Eastern Uttar Pradesh Village, 1994–2012

This article traces the changes in land and labour relations and social relations in an eastern Uttar Pradesh (UP) village first surveyed by me with G.K. Lieten in 1994 as part of a larger six-village study, and resurveyed recently by me in 2012. The analysis based on the first survey has been published in Lieten and Srivastava (1999), in Lieten (1994), and Srivastava (1999).

Belapur, the Village

Belapur, a pseudonym for one of the two villages forming a *gram panchayat*, which was surveyed in 1994, is on the border of Pratapgarh and Jaunpur districts in UP. The river Sai forms the border between the two districts in the proximity of the village. Although the village has

* I am grateful to Sharad Chandra and Kishori Lal for providing research assistance and to the villagers of Belapur for giving us their support and cooperation once again. Financial assistance for carrying out the resurvey was provided by G.B. Pant Social Science Institute and the Indian Institute for Dalit Studies, New Delhi. I thank them for their support.

six hamlets, Brahmins constitute the largest chunk of its population in the main habitation and have also traditionally been the dominant landowners, several among them owning land in a number of villages on both sides of the river. The other numerically important caste groups were Pasi and Chamar (both belonging to the Scheduled Castes or SC category),[1] and Yadav, Maurya, and Pal (all belonging to the Other Backward Castes or OBCs).[2]

Brahmins dominated the formal and informal institutions in Belapur in 1994. The *gram pradhan* was a Brahmin, but their writ ran well beyond the formal institutions of governance, although cracks had begun to appear in their dominance, sometime before 1994. We had noted that several changes were already under way in Belapur, well before our last survey. The *jajmani* system had begun to collapse, and although a few *halwahs* (ploughmen) remained, these ploughmen were no longer the mainstay of the agricultural production system, which relied more on hired casual labour, or leasing out by the larger upper caste landowners. SCs were refusing to follow 'unclean' hereditary occupations, which was a source of tension between them and the upper caste landowners. In fact, their dependence on agricultural labour and traditional services had declined, with more self-employment, and greater possibilities of non-agricultural employment, both locally and through emigration. Education had begun to make inroads, and some men belonging to SC were already in government service. Following a rise in agricultural wages in nearby villages, labourers in Belapur were also demanding an increase in wages from 3 kg to 4 kg of grain per day.

[1] The Scheduled Castes (SCs) are historically disadvantaged former untouchable castes, who along with the Scheduled Tribes (STs) are entitled to positive discrimination, including reserved electorates, in the Indian Constitution, and are listed in Schedule 1 of the Constitution.

[2] The Indian Constitution entitles educationally and socially backward classes, other than SCs and STs, to positive discrimination in certain matters in order to remove the historical vestiges of backwardness from which they might suffer. These (other) socially and educationally backward classes have been considered to be belonging to certain caste groups, which are referred to in this article as Other Backward Castes or OBCs, All castes, other than SCs, STs, or OBCs are referred to as 'General' or 'Upper' caste or by their specific nomenclatures.

A major rupture took place in 1993, a year before our survey, following an altercation between SC youth and some Brahmins near the festival of Holi, and the refusal of SCs to apologize for their role in the incident. Matters came to a head when Brahmins attacked the main SC hamlet to the north of the village, destroyed property and assets, including rickshaws and carts, and the SCs retaliated in self-defence, with injuries on both sides, and the demise of one of the SC men. Criminal cases were lodged against individuals on both sides, but the incident also led to an economic retaliation by Brahmins, who forcibly harvested the crops on lands leased out to the SC households in this hamlet, and imposed an economic boycott on them, preventing them from collecting fodder, grazing their cattle on fields with crop residues, and not giving them wage employment.

When we surveyed the village in 1993 and 1994, the boycott was still in operation. SC labourers in the northern hamlet were not offered agricultural employment or lease land. Their livestock could not venture even on fallow fields of the Brahmin landowners. Since their rickshaws and carts had been destroyed in the altercation, SC men and women had to seek other forms of employment. Our fieldwork results on leases and labour employment pertained to 1993–4 and were affected by the ongoing boycott. The results have to be interpreted with this caveat in mind.

At the same time, the events both preceding and following the 1993 incident indicated a coming together of backward and SCs, reflecting in part the formation of a coalition government in UP, in which the Bahujan Samaj Party (BSP) of Ms Mayawati and the Samajwadi Party (SP) of Mr Mulayam Singh Yadav held power together. It also showed a greater articulation of local SC youth with BSP politicians at higher levels of the polity.

Our interest in carrying out the resurvey was to see the course in which socio-economic relations in the village had developed after the 1994 survey, and in the wake of the shifting alliances in the state polity, which saw three major political parties (BSP, BJP, and SP) enter into different kinds of relationships, and independently try to attract a broader support base among the social groups in UP.

This article, however, is mainly an attempt to explore the changes in land ownership and land relations, and the changing pattern of employment and labour relations. It does not focus on the changing social and political landscape, which is mentioned only in passing.

Fieldwork

The 1993–4 survey was carried out over several months, in three phases in 1993 and 1994, by a team of investigators led by G.K. Lieten and myself. The survey was carried out in three panchayats and six villages in the Muzaffarnagar, Rae Bareli, and Jaunpur districts of UP. In Jaunpur, the survey was of three revenue villages, which formed part of the gram panchayat, but since for all practical purposes, the smallest revenue village among the three was considered to be a hamlet of village Belapur, we refer to two villages in our study viz. Belapur and Birpur. Belapur served as our headquarters and both of us, along with some of the field investigators, stayed in the village, Lieten for periods much longer than myself.

The 1993–4 survey used a number of research instruments and questionnaires. These included semi-structured interviews of panchayat members; a census survey of all the households in the villages; a questionnaire that focused on land, labour, and credit relations; a questionnaire relating to participation in the panchayat and perceptions relating to the Panchayati Raj Institutions (PRIs); and a questionnaire canvassed among beneficiaries of government poverty reduction programmes. In addition, we also carried out open-ended discussions with villagers on changes in socio-economic and political relations in the village.

The 2012 resurvey is much more modest in scope. It has been carried out over a month in September–October 2012, by this author, with 2011–12 as the reference year and with the assistance of two research assistants, both of whom were also part of the original survey. We focused only on three field instruments—the village census survey; the questionnaire on land, labour, and credit and interlinkages; and open-ended interviews with villagers on socio-economic and political relations. Additionally, we also concentrated on studying the Mahatma Gandhi National Rural Employment Guarantee Act (MGNREGA) and its impact on labour markets, mainly through interviews with the present and former pradhans, labourers, and farmers, and an examination of job cards and records, to the extent that we could find these.[3]

Demographic and Education Profile

The census survey indicates that Belapur had 292 households in 1994 and this number had increased to 389 (Table 8.1). Brahmin households comprised 40.1 per cent of households, followed by SC (29.05 per cent) and OBC (28.05 per cent). There were nine Muslim households in the village and one upper caste (Bania) household other than Brahmin. The reduction in the percentage of Brahmin households is due both to a lower rate of partitioning and a few households leaving the village and settling in urban areas. As can be expected, SC households show a higher rate of partitioning.

Table 8.2 shows that the overall sex ratio (female: male) is 1.15, as one might expect in a village where there is male selective outmigration. The ratio is high for Muslims, OBCs, and Brahmins. It is also the highest in the prime migration age group (15 to 34 years). But the sex ratios in the 0–14 year age group are highly adverse in the case of Brahmins (0.68) and OBCs (0.68).

[3] The sample survey and land, labour, and credit linkages in 1994 were based on a sample of about 15 per cent households selected through systematic random sampling. In Belapur, we had surveyed 47 households. Of the households, five had left the village by 2012. Of the remaining 42 households, 12 had been partitioned. We selected all the unpartitioned households, as well as one randomly selected segment in each of the partitioned households of the old sample. In the intervening period, the number of total households in Belapur had increased from 292 to 388. In order to take a 15 per cent sample in 2012, we selected 19 households through systematic random sampling (SRS) after excluding the households already selected, increasing the sample size to 61. Of this sample then, 30 households were directly comparable to the old sample, 12 were partitioned old sample households, 18 were new sample households, and one was an entirely new household, which had moved into the village in this period.

The qualitative interviews and Focus Group Discussions (FGDs) carried out in 2012 were much more extensive than 1994. We re-interviewed all individuals who were available, and had been interviewed in 1994. In all, more than 50 open-ended interviews and about ten FGDs were conducted on the changes between 1994 and 2012, and on the MGNREGA, which was of special interest to us.

TABLE 8.1 Number and Percentage of Households by Social Group

Social Group	1994	2012
Brahmin	42.47	40.1
Other Forward Castes	0.68	0.26
Other Backward Castes	26.71	28.28
SCs	26.03	29.05
Forward Muslim	1.37	1.03
Backward Muslim	2.74	1.29
N	292	389

Source: Household census survey, Belapur, 1994 and 2012.

Nearly two-third of the households are linear or collateral joint households. The tendency towards joint households appears to have increased in this period and may be due to higher male outmigration over the period. As a result, as Table 8.3 shows, the average household size in the village is large (9.6) and has increased between 1994 and 2012. The largest household sizes are among Brahmin and OBCs whereas SCs have the smallest household size (which has also not increased between the years).

A notable factor is the increasing education level among both males and females. The presence of an undergraduate college in the vicinity has facilitated access to higher education among relatively deprived households. Better-off OBC and Brahmin households are prepared to make significant investments in education and send their (male) children to Allahabad, a major educational centre in the region, to study and prepare for competitive examinations, which are required to compete for public services.

TABLE 8.2 Female–Male Ratio, 2012

Caste	0–14 years	15–34 years	35–60 years	61 and above years	All ages
Brahmin*	0.62	2.05	1.10	1.33	1.13
OBCs	0.68	1.79	2.00	2.00	1.23
SCs	1.07	1.46	0.75	0.67	1.04
All**	0.76	1.76	1.20	1.20	1.15

Source: Sample Household Survey, Belapur, 2012.

Notes: * includes one other forward caste household; ** includes Muslim households.

TABLE 8.3 Average Household Size

Caste	1994	2012
Brahmin	6.7	11.0
OBCs	9.2	11.1
SCs	7.2	7.1
Muslim	5.5	7.7
Total	7.6	9.6

Source: Sample Household Survey, Belapur, 2012.

Table 8.4 presents the educational attainment level of the main working-age population. It can be seen that, in two decades, the education level of the population has improved considerably, with half the population in this age group having studied up to the secondary level. While Brahmins retain an edge over other groups, the OBCs, who were behind the SCs in 1994, have caught up. The education level among the SCs has also improved and two-fifth of adults have secondary level achievements. The Muslim households continue to have the lowest attainment levels. The implications of the changing educational levels go well beyond employment structure and the labour market.

TABLE 8.4 Education Attainment of Sample Population (15 to 60 years)

Caste	Illiterate	< Primary	Primary	Middle	Secondary and above	Total
			1994			
Brahmin	28.6	1.3	16.9	32.5	20.8	100.0
OBC	61.8	1.5	8.8	19.1	8.8	100.0
SC	63.6	0.0	9.1	9.1	18.2	100.0
Muslim	60.0	10.0	20.0	10.0	0.0	100.0
Total	49.2	1.5	12.6	21.6	15.1	100.0
			2012			
Brahmin	9.9	1.9	10.6	21.1	56.5	100.0
OBC	32.4	1.0	6.7	8.6	51.4	100.0
SC	37.7	2.9	4.3	14.5	40.6	100.0
Muslim	42.9	7.1	0.0	28.6	21.4	100.0
Total	23.5	2.0	7.7	16.3	50.4	100.0

Source: Sample Household Surveys, Belapur, 1994 and 2012.

Agriculture in Belapur

The development of productive forces in agriculture is no doubt influenced by a number of factors in any region, ranging from the region's agro-climatic potential, public investment in irrigation, land improvement, etc., the range of technologies available, and the possibilities and constraints on investment by different classes of cultivators, the last being determined by the prevailing agrarian structure and agrarian relations.

Agriculture in Belapur was fairly prosperous in 1994, with a main paddy-wheat rotation, but other crops, such as sugar cane, pulses, oilseeds, vegetables, and potatoes, were also important. Most of the land was irrigated by diesel pumpsets and a public tube well. Small cultivators belonging to the OBCs and a few SC cultivators also owned pumpsets.

In the intervening years, there has been further levelling down of operational holdings, with large landowners either losing land or leasing out parcels, and smaller landowners gaining land through purchases. At the same time, all classes of farmers have access to more cash income, which can be ploughed back into agriculture, depending on the extent of their non-agricultural sources of income. Although labour endowments still differ across different classes of farmers, no class can be considered as having abundant labour, although the upper caste landowners continue to be more constrained. Thus, the propensity to mechanize key operations is across the board.

The main external constraint on agriculture comes from underground water scarcity. The number of tube wells and diesel pumpsets has grown enormously since the last survey, but in most of the areas, the water table has gone down, and the pumpsets run dry after a few minutes. Deep-well submersible pumps, which require much higher investment, are seen as an option, but these require electricity, which is not available for more than one and a half to two hours at a stretch and four hours per day. This is insufficient to make these pumps economically viable, although four farmers (all Brahmins) have already invested in them. Some farmers have also invested in generators, pumpsets, and pipes to draw water from the river and bring it to their fields.

This has led to changes in the cropping pattern and a decline in the area under paddy and sugar cane. The main kharif crops grown now are bajra, oilseeds (sesame), and pulses, whereas in the rabi season, the main crops grown are wheat, gram, barley, mustard, and potato.

In the fields near the river bed, the other major problems was the crop destruction by blue bulls and wild boar, the latter also destroying tuber crops, such as potato.

Land Ownership

The distribution of land ownership among social groups is shown in Table 8.5. In 1994, Brahmins, who constituted 42.5 per cent of all households, owned 77.9 per cent of the cultivable land. There were significant variations in Brahmin land ownership with 14.5 per cent Brahmin households owning more than 7.5 acres each and 44.3 per cent Brahmin households owning less than 2.5 acres of land. OBCs (Maurya, Yadav, and Pal) comprised 26.7 per cent of the households but owned only 17.3 per cent land. Only one OBC household owns more than 7.5 acres. SC households comprised 26.7 per cent but owned only 4.5 per cent of land. Over a period of time, land transfers were reported to have been slowly taking place from the Brahmins to other groups, mainly the OBCs. According to a Yadav cultivator, the Brahmins have been slowly selling their land and renting out their trees to contractors, and in the process, have lost some of their clout.

TABLE 8.5 Percentage Distribution of Land across Social Groups

Caste	Landless (<0.5)	Petty (0.5–2.5)	Small (2.5–5.0)	Medium (5–10.0)	Large (> 10 acres)	Total
			1994			
Brahmin	1.1	52.4	73.3	87.6	100.0	77.9
OBC	32.0	33.7	26.7	12.4	0.0	17.3
SC	56.5	13.3	0.0	0.0	0.0	4.5
Muslim	10.5	0.5	0.0	0.0	0.0	0.4
Total	100.0	100.0	100.0	100.0	100.0	100.0
			2012			
Brahmin	12.7	56.1	84.1	83.5	100.0	74.6
OBC	24.5	34.6	15.9	16.5	0.0	19.8
SC	57.9	9.3	0.0	0.0	0.0	5.3
Muslim	4.9	0.0	0.0	0.0	0.0	0.2
Total	100.0	100.0	100.0	100.0	100.0	100.0

Source: Household census survey, Belapur, 1994 and 2012.

These changes have continued to occur after 1994. Brahmin landowners, who once owned land in six or seven villages around Belapur, have gradually been disposing off land in far-flung areas, while retaining plots closer to home. The main reason given by the Brahmin landowners for the sale of land was their inability to supervise cultivation (directly or through leasing out) in the distant plots, which were therefore often left permanently fallow, and the requirement of cash for marriages. Land has mainly been purchased by cash-rich OBC cultivators with incomes from migration-based occupations in Belapur and neighbouring villages. The census survey shows that land owned by the upper caste (Brahmin) households declined from 493 to 415 acres in this period, while land owned by OBC and SC households increased by very small amounts (an acre each).

Even with the land sales and whittled down holdings, Brahmins remain the dominant landowners in the village, owning three-quarters of the cultivable land. But near-landlessness among Brahmin households has also increased with 12.7 per cent households owning less than 0.5 acres of land.

Tenancy Systems

We have shown the changing pattern of land leasing in Table 8.6. In 1994, tenancies had declined abruptly following the dispute between the Brahmins and the SCs. But by 2012, these had again re-emerged as an important form in which upper caste Brahmin landowners organized production on their lands. Not all lease transactions have been captured in our survey. However, analysis shows that the upper castes had leased out 14.2 per cent of their owned holding, while OBCs and SCs had leased in land equal to 32.1 per cent and 28.7 per cent of their owned holdings.

Since data was collected on the caste origins of both lessors and lessees, these results have been combined in a lease transaction matrix, which is shown in Table 8.7. The final row and column summarizes the results in percentages. All (100 per cent) of leased-out land belonged to upper caste land owners. OBC households accounted for nearly half (48.2 per cent) of the land leased in, while SC households accounted for 34.5 per cent of the leased-in land. Muslim households accounted for 17.3 per cent of leased-in land.

TABLE 8.6 Per cent to Owned Land Leased In/Out

Caste	Leased in	Leased out	Mortgaged in	Mortgaged out
		1994		
Brahmin	0.9	1.5	0.0	0.0
OBC	4.0	0.0	0.0	0.0
SC	36.0	0.0	0.0	0.0
Muslim	0.0	0.0	0.0	0.0
		2012		
Brahmin	0.0	14.2	0.0	1.2
OBC	32.1	0.0	0.0	0.0
SC	28.7	0.0	0.0	0.0
Muslim	1562.5	0.0	0.0	0.0

Source: Sample Household Survey, Belapur, 2012.

Cash-rich tenants, both among the OBCs and the SCs, state that they prefer cash rents (locally known as *pataon*). Cash rents differ, depending on the type of land and bargaining power of the tenants and landlords and could vary from Rs 3,000 an acre to Rs 12,000 an acre. But landowners still prefer to lease out on crop share, generally bearing half the cost of the share of fertilizer and water (in a few cases, also of seeds). Although cash tenancy was discussed and reported in qualitative interviews, we did not find any case of cash rents in our sample.

TABLE 8.7 Lease Transaction Matrix, 2012

	Land leased out (acres)						
	CASTE Brahmin	Brahmin	OBC	SC	Muslim	Total	Percent
Land leased in (acres)	Brahmin	0	0	0	0	0	0.0
	OBC	6.98	0	0	0	6.98	48.2
	SC	5	0	0	0	5	34.5
	Muslim	2.5	0	0	0	2.5	17.3
	Total	14.48	0	0	0	14.48	100.0
	Per cent	100	0	0	0		

Source: Sample Household Survey, Belapur, 2012.

Tenancies are generally rotated every two to three years. Depending upon the spread of landholdings, landowners may prefer to lease out plots of land to both OBC and SC cultivators, the latter because they may also supply labour to the landlord's self-cultivated holdings. The crop-share tenancy is usually of the half-half kind and landowners generally share 50 per cent of the cost of fertilizer and water. Variations exist in the sharing of other inputs (seed) and by-products.

Changes in Employment Structure and Labour Relations

When we last surveyed the village in 1994, the dominant upper castes were largely divorced from agricultural work and were involved principally with management and supervision of agricultural operations. Land was either self-cultivated with the help of farm-servants (in a few cases), or casual labourers, or leased out. Labour relations between the dominant landholders and SC labourers were characterized by features of extra-economic coercion. There were few possibilities of local employment in non-agricultural activities. A number of households from each of the castes had taken recourse to employment in urban areas, primarily in other states, through migration. Upper castes and OBC households had accessed jobs in the service sector, or in trade. There were a few workers in manufacturing enterprises.

By 2012, by far the most significant change that had taken place was the increased direct participation of upper caste households in agricultural operations. Both males and females in upper caste households had increased their participation in agriculture and allied activities. OBC and SC households often noted with glee how upper caste males and females—especially the latter—would participate in agricultural operations almost surreptitiously.

> *They go out and harvest their fields at night so that they cannot be seen.*
>
> —an OBC cultivator

This change was brought about by the breakdown of personalized labour relations and relations of dominance, unavailability of labour at the employers' beck and call, and labour costs.

The other major changes related to the changes in the nature and quantum of non-agricultural jobs. The villagers increased their search

TABLE 8.8 Percentage of Households Reporting Indicated Sources of Income

Caste	Agriculture	Ag. Labour	Migration	Non-ag Labour	Farm Business Income	Non-farm Business Income	Other Income	Salary/ Pension
					1994			
Brahmin	89.5	5.3	63.2	0.0	5.3	5.3	5.3	10.5
OBC	92.9	9.1	71.4	7.1	0.0	14.3	21.4	0.0
SC	72.7	45.5	54.5	45.5	0.0	0.0	9.1	9.1
Muslim	33.3	33.3	33.3	0.0	0.0	33.3	0.0	0.0
Total	83.0	14.9	61.7	12.8	2.1	6.4	10.6	6.4
					2012			
Brahmin	95.8	0.0	95.8	0.0	0.0	16.7	4.2	16.7
OBC	94.1	5.9	88.2	5.9	5.9	5.9	17.6	11.8
SC	52.9	23.5	41.2	64.7	5.9	5.9	5.9	11.8
Muslim	66.7	33.3	66.7	0.0	0.0	33.3	0.0	0.0
Total	82.0	9.8	77.0	19.7	3.3	11.5	8.2	13.1

Source: Sample Household Surveys, Belapur, 1994 and 2012.

for jobs outside the village as livelihood possibilities within the village declined. These mostly utilized the bridgeheads built by early migrants, from Belapur or nearby villages, and there was a dramatic increase in worker migration, already quite high in 1994. One needs to note that the possibility of salaried jobs locally has not increased, although the educated workforce in the village had increased. At the same time non-agricultural labour employment did increase in and around the village, mainly due to private construction activities.

The changing pattern of activities in Belapur is summarized in Tables 8.8 and 8.9. Agricultural income was the most broad-based source of income for households in Belapur in 1994, providing some sustenance to 83 per cent of households. This was followed by migrant work (61.7 per cent of households). All other sources were relatively insignificant. For SC households, however, agricultural and non-agricultural labour were sources of income for 45.5 per cent households in each case. Salaried incomes or pension was available to one in ten upper caste and SC households.

In 2012, migrant work increased as a source of livelihoods and income, particularly for upper caste and OBC households; the significance of agricultural labour declined while that of non-agricultural labour

TABLE 8.9 Average Number of Workers per Household across Social Groups

Caste	Ag. Labour	Non-ag. Labour	Migrant work	Salary	Other
		1994			
Brahmin	0.0	0.0	0.8	0.1	0.1
OBC	0.2	0.1	1.1	0.0	0.2
SC	0.9	0.5	0.5	0.1	0.0
Muslim	0.3	0.0	0.3	0.0	0.0
Total	0.3	0.1	0.8	0.0	0.0
		2011			
Brahmin	0.0	0.0	1.8	0.2	0.2
OBC	0.1	0.1	1.9	0.2	0.4
SC	0.4	0.8	0.6	0.1	0.2
Muslim	1.0	0.0	1.0	0.0	0.3
Total	0.2	0.2	1.5	0.1	0.2

Source: Sample Household Surveys, Belapur, 1994 and 2012.

increased. Income from salaried employment became available to 13 per cent of households overall and 16.7 per cent households among upper castes.

Table 8.9 gives the average number of workers per household in some major occupation groups. Agricultural production is not covered here. There were 0.8 migrant workers per household already in 1994 but this increased to 1.5 workers per household in 2012. The maximum increase in worker participation in migration took place for Brahmin and OBC households, in the former from 0.8 to 1.8 workers per household, and in the latter from 1.1 to 1.9 workers per household. Only SC households had a higher number of workers in another occupation (non-agricultural labour).

One needs to note the gendered implications of changes in the labour market. Apart from a handful of salaried jobs created by growth in social sector employment opportunities, women have no access to non-agricultural jobs locally or through migration. The participation of upper-caste women in agricultural activities has increased while that of lower-caste women in agricultural wage labour has declined. Overall, women's participation in agriculture has increased, but has become more difficult to measure, and is also likely to be under-reported in the case of OBC and upper-caste women.

We revert to some issues raised by the changing structure of employment and livelihoods in later sections.

Agricultural Wage Employment

Two decades ago, we had already noticed a decline in traditional labour relations. The system of halwahi (hereditary plough men) had virtually disappeared by then but a few farm servants still worked for large farmers. The struggle for higher wages (from three kilos to four kilos of grain) was at the root of the discord between the SC labourers and the Brahmin land owners. Between 1994 and 2005, wages rose from 3 kilos of grain (wheat) to 5 kilos (about Rs 50–5 in nominal terms).

The MGNREGA was introduced in the district in 2006. Both landowners and labourers confirm that the MGNREGA wages (which had been raised from Rs 58 to Rs 80) were used by labourers in the construction sector as a reference wage to demand higher wages from their contractors.

Higher demand for labour in construction activities and in other employment (wood and bamboo cutting is an important wage employment activity), further led to an upward pressure on wages outside agriculture, currently Rs 150 for an eight-hour day, although wages can be lower (Rs 120 per day, where outside contractors are involved).

In agriculture, employment has seen significant changes in the last two decades, both on the demand and supply sides.

On the demand side, landowners have adjusted cropping patterns and agricultural practices to reduce labour demand. This has also been reinforced by the lack of stable irrigation. Paddy and vegetable crops occupy small acreage. The use of tractors has cut down on labour for ploughing, while the use of weedicides has reduced demand for interculture. Labour is now mainly in demand during the harvesting season. Second, the deployment of family labour has increased even among upper castes. Upper caste women now cut and collect fodder and engage fairly routinely in animal husbandry, which was not the case earlier.

On the supply side, male labourers have by and large withdrawn from a number of operations in agriculture. Their involvement is now restricted to agricultural operations that are of very short duration (threshing) or irregular (hoeing, field bunding). The reduction of area under paddy cultivation has led to a reduction of labour requirement for transplanting, while the use of weedicides has resulted in reduced employment in weeding. Wherever family labour does not suffice, labour is required during harvesting and potato digging. But harvesting labour is now predominantly female, so that as a result, agricultural labour has become a considerably more predominantly feminized activity.

The reduction in employment in agriculture labour between the survey years is shown in Figure 8.1, which also shows the average days of employment for labourers from each caste group. In 1994, the average days of employment for males and females were already low at 62 days and 39 days per year respectively. We have already mentioned that these were lower than normal figures due to the boycott. In 2012, this had shrunk to 17 and 18 days per year respectively. No OBC female in the sample was reported to be working as agricultural labour in 2012.

As mentioned earlier, discussions and data attest to the reported *feminization* of agricultural labour in the village. The share of the female labourers in total agriculture labour days increased from 38 per cent

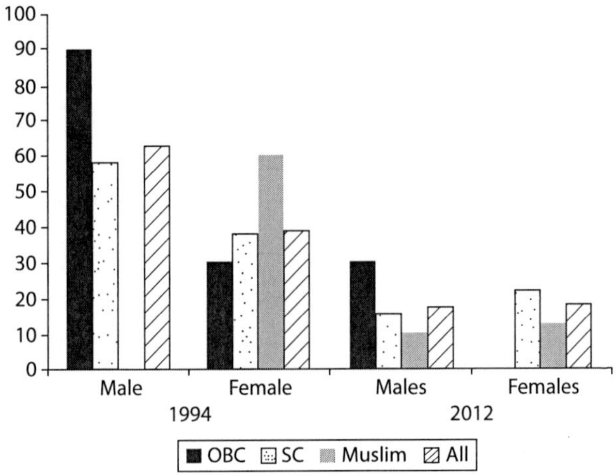

FIGURE 8.1 Average Days of Employment per Labourer in Agriculture by Social Group
Source: Sample Household Surveys, Belapur, 1994 and 2012.

in 1994 to 51 per cent in 2012. Alongside this change, there also has been a *Dalitization* of *casual* labour, both in agriculture and outside it. Although sample data confirms that a high proportion of agricultural labour continues to be supplied by Dalit households, it does not show a trend towards use of more Dalit labour (see Figure 8.2). This is because of the presence of two of three poor Muslim households and some of the few OBC labour households in the sample.

However, our discussions with both employer and labour households suggest that with the withdrawal of the major OBCs (Yadav and Maurya) from agricultural labour, and with only a handful of other OBC and Muslim households still working as agricultural labourers, SC households supply an overwhelming proportion of labour days in agriculture.

Almost all categories of employers assert that labourers have been in short supply and prefer to work outside agriculture and that they use a variety of strategies to meet labour requirements. This includes deployment of family labour, exchange labour (other members of the community), good or long-standing relations with a labouring family so that it remains on tap; using the labour of their share-croppers; labour

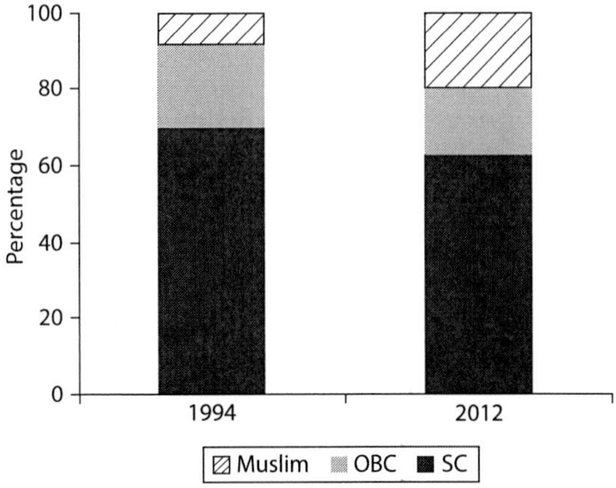

FIGURE 8.2 Percentage of Agricultural Wage Labour Days across Social Groups, 1994 and 2012

Source: Sample Household Surveys, Belapur, 1994 and 2012.

importation; good relations with the labouring community; advances, and financial cash or kind premiums/incentives.

Both employers and labourers mentioned 'good behaviour' as something that was valued by labourers and a criterion on which they 'chose' their employer. Women labourers said that they were unwilling to work on the fields of employers who 'did not behave well' with them. Labourers repeatedly asserted that 'dominance (*dabangai*) had become much less of a factor in influencing the way labour markets functioned in the village'. Employers said that they had to demonstrate good relations with the labourers so that they would come and work in their fields:

> *We call them brothers and gentlemen (Bhaiya, babu), and then on top of that give them food or snacks and good wages, then only they agree; they come to our fields.*

These features signal a change from the way in which the labour market operated earlier when, as one SC labourer had put it to us then:

> *The poor fraternity live under the domination of the Brahmins. If we do not go to work at their bidding, they abuse our sisters and mothers and so we are compelled to work for them. Earlier we lived under their shadow. Although their domination is less now, if we refuse to work for them they abuse us. All the*

> *Brahmins in the village think no end of themselves. They have ample resources and they are capitalists.*

The erosion of paternalistic ties and dominance is attributed to the cataclysmic changes that took place in social and political relations following the dispute between Brahmin landowners and Dalits in the hamlet to the south of the village. But it is also due to the fact that labourers also exercise greater choice over employment options compared to earlier years. But large farmers still enjoy an advantage, over smaller farmers from non-Brahmin castes; remnants of clientelism remain vis-à-vis small sharecroppers and Dalit/OBC households that are spatially segmented and are more embedded in proximity to the upper caste localities. These households were also not part of the earlier labour and Dalit struggles in the village. As a result, (some) labour is available to these relatively dominant households on tap, and at lower than prevailing rates.

For male agricultural labourers, the reference wage in agriculture is the non-agricultural unskilled wage prevalent in the construction sector (Rs 150 per day). But actual wages may vary from Rs 100 to 150 per day depending on the factors mentioned above, work intensity, and demand (one employer said that he had imported a group of labourers at a daily wage rate of Rs 200 per day). Hoeing, land levelling, and field bunding fetch a wage closer to the high end of the wage band, whereas irrigation is closer to the lower end. Male wages are usually paid in cash but on occasion, wages in kind can also be given for these operations—currently at a prevailing rate of 10 kg grain (wheat). Threshing wages are hourly—Rs 40 to 45 an hour, but farmers may also hire a daily worker to also assist in the transportation and storage of grain and straw. The daily rate in this case is higher—around Rs 200.

Female labourers earn 7 kg of grain per day on average in harvesting or transplanting operations. In peak seasons, wages may rise to 8 kg. But the range of wages paid to women varied in the reference year from 5 kg (for weeding and in the case of dominant landholders) to 7 kg. Wages in kind were valued at Rs 10 per kilo in the reference period, although currently these are being valued at Rs 15 per kilo. Thus, a wage of 7 kilos can be valued at Rs 70 to Rs 105 depending on the assumed price of grain. In either event, wages paid to women are lower than the MGNREGA wage (Rs 120 per day) and a male–female wage gap continues to persist in the village. Average wages received by labourers in the reference year are shown in Figure 8.3.

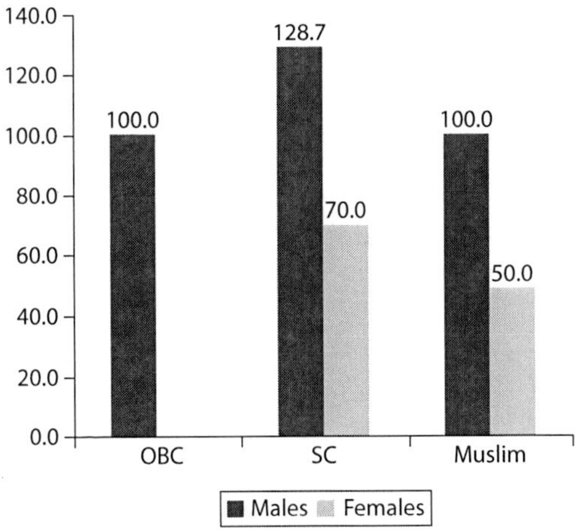

FIGURE 8.3 Average Agricultural Wage per Labourer, 2012
Source: Sample Household Survey, Belapur, 2012.

Thus, between 1994 and 2012, several important changes have taken place in the agricultural labour market in Belapur. First, the size of the agricultural labour market has shrunk much further and agricultural employment is no longer the mainstay for any household in the village. Second, the characteristics of the labour market have changed with the greater *Dalitization* and *feminization* of agricultural wage labour, reduction in paternalism, and reduction in the influence of dominant upper caste landholders. Third, real wages have increased for both men and women but there is a persistent wage gap between the sexes.[4]

Non-agricultural Employment

When we surveyed Belapur in 1994, opportunities for local non-agricultural labour were negligible. Only six individuals (all males) reported participation in non-agricultural labour, four of them as

[4] Cash wages that are generally applicable to unskilled non-agricultural work and spade work in agriculture increased at a rate of about 5 per cent a year in real terms while wages in kind increased at about 4 per cent per year over this period.

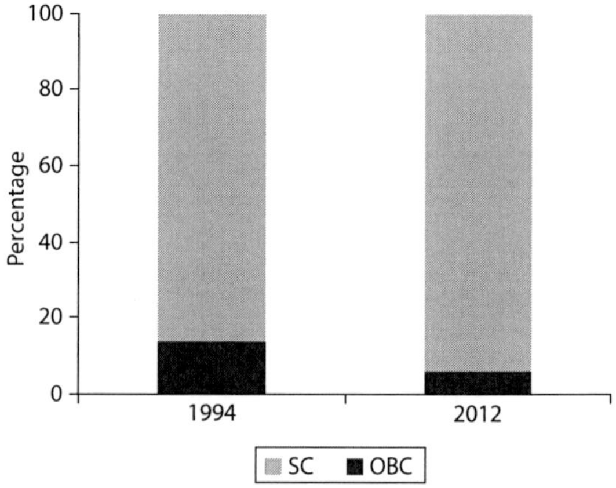

FIGURE 8.4 Distribution of Non-agricultural Wage Labour Days across Social Groups, 2012
Source: Sample Household Survey, Belapur, 2012.

unskilled construction labourers and one as a skilled labourer. In 2012, 15 individuals (14 of them from SC households) from 12 households participated in non-agricultural labour, which included skilled and unskilled construction work, tree/bamboo cutting, and employment generating public works (under MGNREGA).[5]

Local non-agricultural employment is restricted primarily to SC labourers. Even in public works employment, generated under the MGNREGA, most of the labourers were SCs. Discussions with the former pradhan suggests that of the MGNREGA workforce, all except one Brahmin, and two OBC (one Yadav and one Maurya) labourers were from the SC community. This is mainly because of outmigration of non-Dalit men to other destinations. Other backward caste respondents

[5] The National Rural Employment Guarantee Act (NREGA) was legislated by the central government in 2005. It was later named after Mahatma Gandhi. Under the act, workers in rural households can register and seek employment in public works, planned and implemented by rural local bodies, for up to 100 days in a year per household. Wages defrayed by the Centre are as per a Central schedule and were Rs 120 per day (for a standard quantum of work) in 2012.

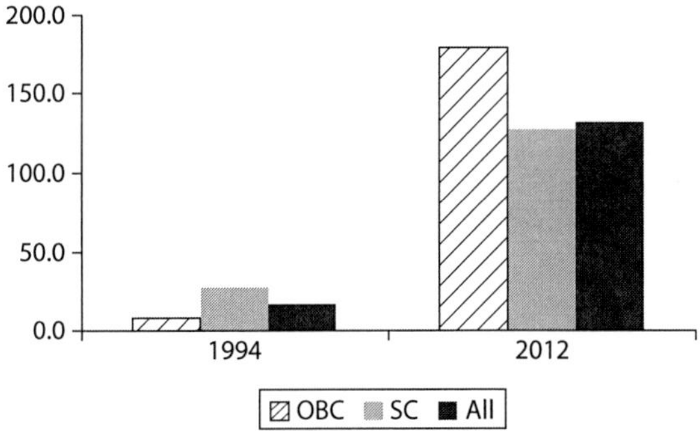

FIGURE 8.5 Employment Days in Non-agricultural Wage Employment, 1994 and 2012

Source: Sample Household Surveys, Belapur, 1994 and 2012.

assert that their 'women do not hire out labour' and that they (the men) 'are ashamed to work as labourers in and around the village and prefer to work outside'.

In the sample households, 85 per cent of employment days in non-agricultural wage employment were taken up by SC labourers while 15 per cent were taken up by OBC labourers. In 2012, the share of SCs in non-agricultural wage employment went up to 91 per cent.

More significantly, employment days rose from only 16 days per labourer in 1994 to 132 days per labourer in 2012 (Figure 8.5).

As has been mentioned, the reference to non-agricultural wage is the wages for unskilled work in the construction sector, currently Rs 150 per day. Workers hired through outside contractors receive a lower wage—about Rs 120 per day. In the reference year, among the sample households, the average wage in non-agricultural employment was Rs 172 per day—Rs 160 for SC labourers and Rs 300 for OBC labourers (for skilled work). About 91.7 per cent of employment was in the construction sector (61.7 per cent in unskilled work) and 6.5 per cent in MGNREGA while 1.8 per cent was in tree-cutting. Construction work is undertaken in the village and in nearby urban locations and markets. Labourers say that the MGNREGA set a reservation wage for unskilled work when it started in 2006 and they used it to bargain for higher wages in construction. In some sense, this continues to be the case. As mentioned earlier, labourers use the MGNREGA wage as a reference floor wage in relation to what is construed to be lighter work intensity, bargaining for higher wages if work intensity is higher. But in actual practice, the employment generated under MGNREGA has been low and prevailing construction sector wages are driven more by demand.

Outmigration

As noted earlier, since the last survey, significant changes have taken place in the employment structure in the village, mainly due to the additional possibilities opened by outmigration. Almost every family among the OBCs and Brahmins has one or more members engaged in an occupation in urban centres (see Table 8.8).

A large number of outmigrants are employed in Mumbai, Surat, and Ahmedabad. Others are employed in Delhi, NOIDA, Kolkata, Hyderabad, Dhanbad, and in other states, or Varanasi, Allahabad, and other cities in UP (89 per cent of the migrants are employed in other states).

The largest number of migrants drive tankers, auto-rickshaws, taxis, or private cars in Mumbai. Other migrants were employed as informal workers in factories in Kolkata, Surat, Hyderabad, NOIDA, or Delhi—in rolling mills, textile printing, power looms, and garment factories, etc. Some others are engaged in petty trade. A few have even become contractors in the real estate industry. These migrants have built upon bridge-heads established a generation ago by some of the pioneering migrants.

As an OBC migrant described to us:

> *My father was one of the first to emigrate to Mumbai and to work as a tanker driver. My uncle joined him some years ago. That opened the way for many of us in the community. Initially, all of us went to Mumbai to drive tankers belonging to the Seths. With electronic metres, pilfering from the tankers has become difficult, and salaries are low and uncertain. So we have gradually switched to driving auto-rickshaws or taxis, but some still continue to drive tankers.*

Government service, which was a major route to upward mobility, has almost dried up. Among the OBCs, there is no one in a government job (a generation ago, two Yadav brothers were in the railways). Among Dalits, two are school teachers. Among the upper castes, a few are in government service, and there are some teachers.

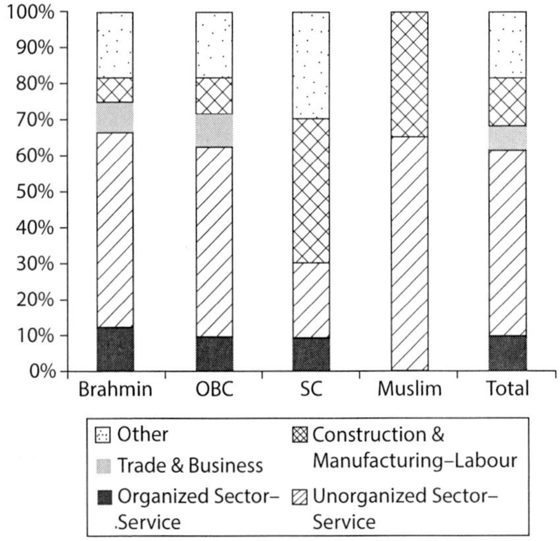

FIGURE 8.6 Per cent Distribution of Migrant Workers by Social Group across Occupations, 2012
Source: Sample Household Survey, Belapur, 2012.

As Figure 8.6 shows, the largest percentage of jobs are in the unorganized service sector. Most of these workers work as drivers of trucks, vans, taxis, three-wheelers, or private cars in Mumbai. SC workers are mostly employed as labourers in the manufacturing or construction sector.

A comparison of the occupational structure of migrant workers in 1994 and 2012, given in Table 8.10, shows that the main increase has taken place precisely in the unorganized service sector where workers are employed as drivers. The percentage of those employed in salaried jobs in the organized sector has declined.

Low-skilled jobs, small businesses, and factory jobs are the major avenues for upward mobility of village households. With migration and cash incomes, money is being ploughed back into agriculture, land purchase, house construction, and education. There is a visible improvement in the living standards of the migrant households. Table 8.11 shows the average incomes and remittances from migration.

Remittances now form a very high proportion of household incomes in Belapur. Table 8.12 presents the average income from each type of

TABLE 8.10 Occupational Distribution of Migrant Workers, 1994 and 2012

Occupation	1994 (%)	2012 (%)
Organized sector–salaried service	17.9	10.1
Unorganized sector service–skilled work	23.1	40.4
Unorganized sector–unskilled work	30.8	11.2
Petty trade, small shop	15.4	5.6
Construction–low skilled	0.0	2.2
Manufacturing–skilled	7.7	4.5
Manufacturing–low skilled	5.1	5.6
Professional	0.0	2.2
Other	0.0	18.0
Total (%)	100.0	100.0
Total (N)	39	89

Source: Sample Household Surveys, Belapur, 1994 and 2012.

activity (except agriculture and livestock). Remittance income constitutes 63.2 per cent of incomes from the designated sources. Among OBC households, remittance constitutes nearly 90 per cent of incomes. Remittance incomes are exceeded by another source (non-agricultural wage income) only for SC households.

Outmigration has still not emerged as a major job avenue for the poorer SC households, although, as shown, some among them have also taken recourse to migration. But *local* occupational diversification has been significant among them. Although wage labour is still

TABLE 8.11 Annual Average Incomes from Migration and Remittance per Household (Rs)

Caste	1994		2012	
	Income from Migration	Remittances	Income from Migration	Remittances
Brahmin	17,377	1,724	130,584	34,937
OBC	15,083	1,917	155,765	67,706
SC	5,764	1,282	36,706	7,765
Muslim	4,000	833	54,000	16,667
Total	12,833	1,602	107,672	35,598

Source: Sample Household Surveys, Belapur, 1994 and 2012.

Table 8.12 Percentage Distribution of Household Income across Sources by Social Group, 2012

Caste	Agricultural Labour	Remittances	Non-agricultural Wage	Farm business income	Net Non-farm Business income	Other Income	Salaries	Total
Brahmin	0.0	54.5	0.0	0.0	11.0	2.1	32.5	100.0
OBC	0.2	89.8	4.2	0.8	1.2	2.2	1.6	100.0
SC	2.1	25.7	56.3	1.6	4.9	0.8	8.7	100.0
Backward Muslim	1.7	49.1	0.0	0.0	49.1	0.0	0.0	100.0
All groups	0.4	63.2	10.0	0.5	7.5	1.9	16.5	100.0

Source: Sample Household Survey, Belapur, 2012.

Table 8.13 Average Characteristics of Households across Classes, 2012

Class	Av. Total Land Owned (acres)	Ag. Wage (Rs)	Non-agric. Wage (Rs)	Migrants' Income (Rs)	Remittances (Rs)	Non-farm Business (Rs)	Salaries (Rs)
Dependent	0.09	1,029	17,418	18,500	6,917	2,083	0
Lower	0.52	188	4,994	91,750	24,875	3,350	1,513
Upper	1.95	0	1,929	151,286	53,821	3,571	2,843
Dominant	6.39	0	0	128,400	36,700	16,000	92,400
All classes		252	5,621	107,672	35,598	4,239	9,275

Source: Sample Household Survey, Belapur, 2012.

the most important activity, male labourers are almost entirely confined to wage occupations *outside* agriculture. Some erstwhile construction labourers have become skilled artisans, team leaders, and even petty contractors. A few SC households are engaged in petty trading. But SC women are still predominantly engaged either in their own cultivation, animal husbandry, or engaged as agricultural wage labour.

Migration has also influenced the demographic structure of households. The joint family structure is still the most common with family branches tending to stay together as one household or under one roof as males migrate, often rotationally. With males outmigrating, women and children stay behind, and farming and family decisions are taken by resident male members—usually old or returnees—or out-migrants who spend some periods at home, by rotation.

Changing Class Configurations

In the preceding sections of this chapter we have analysed changes in socio-economic relations across broad social groups, which, to some extent, have overlapping interests and share common identities But intra-social group differentiation is also an important feature of the rural socio-economic structure; different groups of households also share class interests and exercise different degrees of influence over sociopolitical and economic relations in village life. This leads us to analyse rural change in Belapur in terms of changing class structure, while noting the overlap and relationship between class and caste.

For the earlier study, we had constructed a synthetic index of 'class' extending Bharadwaj's four-fold classification (Bharadwaj 1979) to include diversification and non-agricultural sources. Households had been classified into four classes based on the following criteria:

1. *Dominant*: Households with agricultural surpluses based on systematic hiring in of labour or leasing out of land, or with superior sources of non-agricultural incomes (large business or contractors, superior professions).
2. *Upper Middle*: Households with net hiring in of labour supplementing family labour, small lessors; households with inferior but regular sources of non-agricultural income.

3. *Lower Middle*: Households who are small (net) hirers out of labour, or are skilled casual labourers, are in the main self-employed in agriculture or non-agriculture with petty and generally irregular incomes.
4. *Poor (Dependent)*: Households who are principally hirers out of casual labour or traditional services in agriculture or non-agriculture.

We have applied the same criteria to demarcate the sample households in the recent survey. The growth in sources of urban income and the corresponding diminution in agriculture's importance have increased the order of difficulty with which the above criteria can be applied. Nevertheless we have attempted to do so. In 1994, helped by an extensive census survey, we were able to classify each and every household in the village in the four classes discussed above. Thus we are able to compare the class status of 60 of the 61 sample households (one being an entirely new household) across the two years.

The main average characteristics of the different class categories of households is given in Table 8.13. The average total land (cultivated and non-cultivated) varies from a negligible 0.09 acres for dependent households to 1.95 acres for upper middle households and 6.39 acres for dominant households. The poorest class's dependence on wage income is more than income from other sources (remittances, non-farm business) and there is no salaried income. Remittances are the main source of income for lower middle-income households, although wage income is also important (this category of households also leases in most land).

While upper-middle households own about two acres of land on average, their income from remittances is also quite substantial. Finally, dominant households have more substantial land holdings on average, and the highest average income from salaries (derived locally). Their income from remittances is also quite large, but less than that of the upper-middle income.

Table 8.14 gives the social group-wise distribution of households into classes in 1994 and 2012, whereas Tables 8.15 and 8.16 present the distribution of households within and across social groups in the two years.

In absolute figures, we can see that there is a bulge in the number of households categorized as 'upper middle', their numbers having

TABLE 8.14 Caste and Class, 1994 and 2012

Caste		Class				
		Dominant	Upper	Lower	Dependent	Total
Brahmin	1994	14	6	4	0	24
	2012	5	16	3	0	24
OBC	1994	2	3	8	3	16
	2012	0	10	6	1	17
SC	1994	0	2	1	14	17
	2012	0	2	5	10	17
Muslim	1994	0	0	2	1	3
	2012	0	0	2	1	3
Total	1994	16	11	15	18	60
	2012	5	28	16	12	61

Source: Sample Household Surveys, Belapur, 1994 and 2012.

increased from 11 to 28. There is a corresponding decrease in the number of households categorized as the 'dominant' and the dependent 'classes'.

In 1994, caste and class overlapped quite significantly at the top and bottom ends. Among Brahmins and forward castes, a majority

TABLE 8.15 Social Group-wise Distribution of Households across Classes, 1994 and 2012

Caste		Class				
		Dominant	Upper	Lower	Dependent	Total
Brahmin	1994	58.3	25.0	16.7	0.0	100.0
	2012	20.8	66.7	12.5	0.0	100.0
OBC	1994	12.5	18.8	50.0	18.8	100.0
	2012	0.0	58.8	35.3	5.9	100.0
SC	1994	0.0	11.8	5.9	82.4	100.0
	2012	0.0	11.8	29.4	58.8	100.0
Muslim	1994	0.0	0.0	66.7	33.3	100.0
	2012	0.0	0.0	66.7	33.3	100.0
Total	1994	26.7	18.3	25.0	30.0	100.0
	2012	8.2	45.9	26.2	19.7	100.0

Source: Sample Household Surveys, Belapur, 1994 and 2012.

TABLE 8.16 Class-wise Distribution of Households across Social Groups, 1994 and 2012

		Dominant	Upper	Lower	Dependent	Total
Brahmin	1994	87.5	54.5	26.7	0.0	40.0
	2012	100.0	57.1	18.8	0.0	39.3
OBC	1994	12.5	27.3	53.3	16.7	26.7
	2012	0.0	35.7	37.5	8.3	27.9
SC	1994	0.0	18.2	6.7	77.8	28.3
	2012	0.0	7.1	31.3	83.3	27.9
Muslim	1994	0.0	0.0	13.3	5.6	5.0
	2012	0.0	0.0	12.5	8.3	4.9
Total	1994	100.0	100.0	100.0	100.0	100.0
	2012	100.0	100.0	100.0	100.0	100.0

Source: Sample Household Surveys, Belapur, 1994 and 2012.

were categorized as dominant households with agricultural surpluses derived from hired labour or land rent. Some also had access to salaried jobs. At the other end, a majority of SC households were dependent households, with wage labour or in some cases, with land rented. The OBC households were more differentiated, but most were classified as lower middle.

By 2012, smaller landholdings, changes in labour utilization patterns, and hardly any accretion to salaried jobs moved several upper caste households from the dominant to upper-middle status. At the other end, several 'dependent' SC households moved up the class ladder with greater access to migration-related employment. Among OBCs, while some dominant households lost their class-status due to partitioning, others gained from lower middle to upper middle status due to a substantial increase in migration-related jobs.

The resultant class structure has a greater bulge in the upper-middle segment. The percentage of dominant households declined from 26.7 per cent to 8.2 per cent while at the lower end, the percentage of dependent households declined from 30 per cent to 19.7 per cent (Table 8.15). The percentage of upper-middle households was 18.3 per cent in 1994 but their share increased to 45.9 per cent in 2012. Two-thirds of the upper caste households and nearly three-fifths of the OBC households were upper-middle households.

At the same time, as Table 8.16 shows, dominant households, though fewer, were more concentrated among Brahmins, and similarly SC households constituted a greater percentage of the (fewer) dependent households in 2012.

The contraction of the classes at the two ends of the spectrum, and an increase in the middle segments, implies that features that characterize dominance and dependence might exercise less influence on rural social relations today. This is also confirmed by other evidence discussed elsewhere in this chapter.

Sociopolitical Changes

The focus of this chapter has been on changes and land and labour relationships that have occurred in Belapur in a period spanning roughly two decades. In our previous work, we had made the argument that the sociopolitical changes could not be understood without references to the intended and unintended consequences of the economic changes that had occurred in the village, and which had given the Dalits a measure of autonomy. This autonomy, and the improved economic clout of the OBCs, along with the political changes that had occurred in UP, influenced the course of the struggle and the conflict in Belapur.

The description given in the preceding sections shows that certain types of economic changes had gained momentum over the last two decades. The SC households were even less dependent on the dominant households for their livelihoods. The OBC households had improved their economic position due to incomes earned from migrant occupations, which rose faster than any other group. The Brahmins continued to dominate the rural landscape of Belapur, but with reduced clout.

However, the full import of the changes cannot be understood without reference to the social change that occurred, at a faster rate than the economic, and which impacted on the lives of the SCs even more than the former. This change, the SC respondents attributed directly to the struggles and the conflicts of the early 1990s.

The net outcome was a dramatic reduction in relationships characterized by dominance, social inequality, and exclusion. We have commented on some of the changes while describing the changes in rural labour markets. Their impact went beyond the way economic transactions took place between these groups.

SC respondents pointed out to us how they were treated by the Brahmins as more equal and how they, too, demanded more equality in their treatment. As one of them said:

> *Earlier when there was a wedding in their houses, we went with our families, uninvited, just to feast. We sat separately and ate. Now we go only when we are invited and sit with them and eat. We are no longer treated the way we used to be.*

Why did the upper castes learn to transact social relationships with the SCs on changed terms? There appear to be several reasons for this change. First, even though reduced, the economic inter-dependence between the different groups of households has continued in one form or another. This chapter has analysed this interdependence in land and labour transactions. Second, the changes that have occurred in the last two decades have shifted the control of formal institutions from the Brahmins, and they must now forge alliances to protect or advance their economic interests.

An OBC-SC alliance was in the making when we last surveyed the village in 1994. The panchayat elections were held in 1995, for the first time after the passage of the 93rd Amendment and the pradhan's seat was reserved as a general women's seat. It was contested and won by the wife of a SC (Pasi), a young graduate, who was one of the leaders of the SC 'resistance' against the Brahmins and who had a criminal case registered against him (for 'attempt to murder'). Their supporters were a broad cross-section of SCs and OBCs. In 2000, the seat was reserved as a SC seat and was again won by the same person, and this was repeated in 2005, when the seat became a SC (women) seat, the pradhan put up his wife again as candidate and she won. However, this phase was marked by intra-SC political rivalry and a more conciliatory approach by the winning team towards the Brahmins and the pradhan (husband) was instrumental in striking a legal compromise and withdrawal of criminal cases lodged against the Brahmins.

In 2010, the seat was reserved for OBCs and was won (in a contest between six) by a migrant working as a real estate contractor in Mumbai. Again, alliances were struck with groups of SCs and Brahmins. Brahmins came to terms with the changing local political landscape while at the same time continuing to tout their influence over the regional political leadership as the local MLA has consistently been a Brahmin (from the BJP).

The 1992–2012 period has seen a stepping up of some of the changes witnessed in Belapur in 2012. Customary labour relations, marked by features of dominance and extra-economic coercion, have declined further. Agricultural employment also continues to decline and the smaller-sized agricultural labour market has become more *feminized* and *Daliticized*. Males from upper caste households who earlier only supervised or managed agriculture, now engage directly in agricultural operations to some extent. Brahmins, as a group, own less land than before, which is either-self-cultivated or leased out. The decline in availability of irrigation and electricity has restricted improvements in agriculture. Simultaneously, SC households have increased access to non-agricultural employment, and, overall, households now access employment through urban-ward migration, principally to the informal tertiary sector. While the SC households' options are mainly in informal manufacturing; OBC and upper caste households have accessed semi-skilled jobs in the service sector. Although the level of education is increasing, most migrants are still absorbed in the informal service sector, many as drivers, working, on average, ten hours a day. Access to formal jobs is extremely limited and one notices a narrowing in differences in the types of jobs being accessed by upper caste and OBC migrants.

While the broad correspondence between caste and class remains, both the dominant and dependent classes have become smaller, the middle groups have increased, and some proportion of the SC and OBC households have moved from dependent to lower-middle status and lower-middle to upper-middle status respectively.

All this may suggest that inter-group inequalities may have declined in Belapur over the last two decades. Some of these changes correspond to the inter-group changes at the regional and state level described by us elsewhere (Srivastava 1997, 2004, 2007, 2012). In Srivastava (1997) we have analysed changes in agricultural production, land and labour markets over time in two villages in Eastern and Western UP. Srivastava (2004) had analysed both macro data and field studies to show how various factors including outmigration and employment diversification were impacting on rural labour markets. Srivastava (2012) showed that in UP, between 1993–4 and 2009–10, SC households achieved a higher rate of diversification away from agriculture compared to other groups.

A large part of this was into the construction sector. The average nominal MPCE rose for SCs by a larger percentage than other groups but remained lower than that of other groups. Regular work and employment in higher skilled occupations (NCO groups 0, 1, and 2) rose very marginally both for SCs and others. In education, the gap between SCs, OBCs, and others became much narrower up to the secondary level. The rural Gross Enrolment Rate (GER) for secondary and higher secondary education rose from 29.4, 36.2, 59.5, and 14.2 in 1999–2000 for SCs, OBCs, Other Hindus, and Muslims to 61.6, 68, 81.3, and 36.2 respectively for these groups in 2009–10.

Our findings can also be situated in the debate on growth/development and social inclusion in India in the recent decade, based on macro trends (IAMR, Planning Commission 2012; Jayaraj and Subramanian 2012; Thorat and Dubey 2012). Thorat and Dubey (2012) have discussed the changes in Head-Count Ratios and Gini-coefficient between 1993–4 and 2009–10 at the national level. While poverty is shown to decline at a faster rate in the last quinquennium, there are differences across socio-religious and occupational groups, with SCs showing a lower rate of improvement.

However, our earlier as well as current findings show that the changing configuration between the social groups cannot be relegated purely to growth or development processes and the impact of the latter cannot be understood without reference to social characteristics, inter-group relations, and economic opportunities available locally. Earlier, we had argued that while the intended and unintended consequences of growth processes had given a measure of autonomy to the dependent classes, the changes that could be perceived in social relations were a result of economic changes that were occurring in the condition of the different classes, social mobilization, political changes, and new political alliances in UP. The subsequent changes that we witness are also the result of economic changes, both at local and national levels; and bear the clear imprint of the changes in social relations and sociopolitical alliances that were forged during and after the conflict between SCs and Brahmins in 1993. Among the SCs, groups of households that bypassed participation in the struggles preceding and during 1993, remain in more dependent positions currently.

The gender implications of the changes that we have witnessed in Belapur are quite significant. In contrast to men, women have hardly any access to non-farm jobs, both in proximity to the village, or in urban areas. The MGNREGA has opened up limited opportunities for male labourers in Belapur, but hardly any women are employed in public works. Agricultural female wage employment has also declined, as a result of both supply-side and demand-side factors. Female wages have increased but at a lower rate than male wages and the wage gap has increased. But as far as self-employment in agriculture and animal husbandry is concerned, with the greater participation of upper caste women in these activities, there is almost certainly an increase in the female workforce participation rate in Belapur between 1999–4 and 2011–12. However, at the same time, this participation is also more unlikely to be unrecorded or underestimated in large-scale surveys since upper caste households are less likely to report them for status reasons.

There are some ingredients of our analysis from Belapur, which may be generalizable and some which may not be generalizable, at least to the same extent. In this village, due to the constraints on agriculture and various other constraints, the dominant class households were not able to convert their larger resource base, better networks, and higher education levels into a higher rate of growth and accumulation for themselves, and have, on the contrary, a dwindling, although large, land base. Both they, and the OBCs, have largely accessed similar kinds of income and growth opportunities through urban informal jobs in which networks—in some cases through bridgeheads established by OBCs—have played an important role. The SC households show a greater shift out of agriculture, mainly into construction, or informal jobs in manufacturing, which give them somewhat greater autonomy and possibly also higher incomes. While the last set of changes are probably operative at a fairly general level at this juncture, the other conditions are more particularistic and may not operate at all, or to the same level, in other villages. Again, the caste-class configurations will differ across areas and the social and political factors may not be generalizable to the same extent everywhere.

To conclude: based on this and other field studies, we do believe that traditional relations of dominance and dependence are coming under greater challenge, and that there are economic, and sociopolitical factors that are contributing to this, but we can expect the actual outcomes to vary and the growth process to be mediated very differently by local class structures.

References

IAMR (Institute of Applied Manpower Research), Planning Commission. 2012. *India Human Development Report: Towards Social Inclusion*. New Delhi: Oxford University Press.

Jayaraj, D. and S. Subramanian. 2012. 'On the Interpersonal Inclusiveness of India's Consumption Expenditure Growth', *Economic and Political Weekly*, XLVII (45): 55–66.

Lieten, G.K. 1994. 'On Casteism and Communalism in Uttar Pradesh', *Economic and Political Weekly*, XXIX (14): 777–81.

Lieten, G.K. and Ravi Srivastava. 1999. *Unequal Partners: Power Relations, Devolution and Development in Uttar Pradesh*. New Delhi: SAGE Publications.

Srivastava, Ravi. 1997. 'Change and Resilience in Producer Strategies in Indian Agriculture', in Jan Breman, Peter Kloos, and Ashwani Saith (eds), *The Village in Asia Revisited*, pp. 199–236. New Delhi and Oxford: Oxford University Press.

———. 1999. 'Rural Labour in Uttar Pradesh: Emerging Features of Subsistence, Contradiction and Resistance', *Journal of Peasant Studies*, 26 (2–3): 263–315.

———. 2004. 'Regional Contours of Poverty, Employment, Mobility among Rural Labourers in Uttar Pradesh', in U. Kalpagam, N. Srivastava, and D. M. Diwakar (eds), *Labour and Poverty: Studies on Uttar Pradesh*, pp. 59–95. New Delhi: Segment Books.

———. 2007. 'Economic Change among Social Groups in Uttar Pradesh', in Sudha Pai (ed.), *Political Process in Uttar Pradesh–Identity, Economic Reforms and Governance*, pp. 345–66. Delhi: Pearson/Longman.

———. 2012. 'Economic Change and Social Inclusion in Uttar Pradesh, 1983–2010', *UPEA Journal*, 5 (5): 3–25.

Thorat, Sukhadeo and Amaresh Dubey. 2012. 'Has Growth been Socially Inclusive during 1993–94 to 2009–10', *Economic and Political Weekly*, XLVII (10): 43–54.

9

PRAVEEN JHA
AVANINDRA NATH THAKUR

Thirty Years On

Work and Well-being in Rural Bihar

The focal concern of this chapter is to reflect on a few interconnected themes relating to the work and well-being of rural labour, drawing mainly on repeated field visits to a few villages in Purnia, a relatively backward district situated in the north-eastern corner of the state of Bihar. In this chapter, the term 'rural labour' refers to a person who resides primarily in rural areas and works in 'manual activities', and for whom the sale of labour power for wages—in money, kind, or as a share of output—is a source of livelihood; this, of course, includes anyone who sells his/her labour power for any duration, whether in a sole economic activity or as one among many.

During the mid-1980s, as part of the doctoral work of one of the authors of this chapter (Jha 1997a), a survey of the material conditions of rural labourers was undertaken in a cluster of villages in two Community Development Blocks (CDB) namely, Barhara Kothi and Krityanand Nagar of Purnia district. This survey was the part of a study that attempted to map out the direction of change since Independence, particularly during the 1970s and 1980s, in the major determinants of the economic conditions of rural labour at an all-India level, with particular attention to Bihar.

Of the villages surveyed in the mid-1980s, two villages—Barahari in Barhara Kothi CDB and Majra in Krityanand Nagar CDB—were selected for in-depth studies. Visits to both these villages (in all for about six months), as part of the said doctoral research, was spread over almost four years during the second half of the 1980s. A detailed questionnaire-based survey of 70 labour households undertaken in these villages in 1988–9 was one of the core components of the field work. Subsequently, every two to three years, visits to these villages were made to track the broad directions of change. Another in-depth survey of labour households was done in both the villages in July 1998, that is, almost ten years from the earlier detailed survey, during which 40 households (either original, or segmented from the original, which were now independent) were contacted. Though the canvas of enquiry was more limited than the surveys conducted during the second half of the 1980s, it was sufficient to explore the major trends, during the intervening decade in the living conditions of the poorest occupational category—rural labour—in both the villages. After the 1998 visit, the next visit to both the villages was in December 2001, which was followed by substantive field work in May 2003. Further, brief visits were also conducted in 2005, 2006, 2009, and 2010. Most recently, during March 2012, these villages were again surveyed in detail and 37 households were contacted. The quantitative findings reported here are based on our three in-depth surveys of 1988–9, 1998, and 2012.

During the different rounds of the village surveys, in addition to the respondents from rural labour households, information was gathered from other villagers as well. These discussions covered a wide variety of subjects, including the state of infrastructure, trends in government expenditures, perceptions regarding changes in the larger economic environment, and related opportunities or lack therein, trends in village agriculture, changes in the nature of social institutions, trends and patterns of migration, among other topics. The aim of this chapter is to explore as well as analyse important aspects of continuity and change, with particular focus on the period since the closing years of the 1980s to early 2012, in the socio-economic landscape of rural labourers in the surveyed region, largely based on the aforementioned visits to the two villages.

The structure of the chapter is as follows: the second section provides a brief overview of the dynamics of Bihar's rural economy.

The third section deals with the socio-economic profile of the survey region with a view to contextualize important aspects of its economic transformation with respect to shifts in broader policy regimes. The fourth section focuses on select key indicators reflecting the well-being of the rural masses in general and rural labour in particular. This is followed by brief concluding remarks drawing on the development experiences of these villages over approximately the last three decades.

A Broad-brush Profile of Bihar's Rural Economy

Contemporary Bihar, that is, after the recent division in 2000 when its southern plateau was carved out as a separate state, presently housing about 8 per cent of India's population and constituting about 3 per cent of its geographical area, is among the most backward states in the country. According to the Government of India's Population Census of 2011, this third most populous state of India is the least industrialized/urbanized large state in the country, with an urban population of about 11 per cent. As per official estimates, Bihar also has the lowest per capita income, and the second highest incidence of poverty among the major states of India, and in terms of the so-called human development indicators (such as the literacy rate) does not distinguish itself in any way. The state's per capita income, which was just about 40 per cent of the average for the country in 1993–4 (compared to 60 per cent in 1951, that is, soon after Independence), slipped further down to about 34 per cent in 1997–8. However, during the recent phase of reported high growth rates, this ratio has picked up slightly. Nevertheless, the gap between the average per capita income for the country as a whole and that of Bihar, even after the recent phase of sustained high growth rate, continues to be one of the highest. In short, the surveyed villages are located in a state characterized by a dismal performance in terms of social or economic indicators of development.

As is widely recognized, a number of processes organically linked with the ascendancy of the neo-liberal policy regime (since the early 1990s) in the country have impacted adversely on the well-being of the masses in general. In the case of Bihar, as for the country at large, the period since the early 1990s ought to be characterized as a neo-liberal phase, yet there have been some shifts at specific junctures in the nature of public policies with noticeable changes in economic outcomes in particular sectors. For instance, with respect to government intervention in rural areas, the period from 1991 to 2004–5 was significantly different from 2004–5 to the present. The second period, in contrast to the first, has experienced some increase in public expenditure in the rural as well as the agricultural sectors. The first phase had witnessed a sharp fall in government interventions in the rural areas and particularly in the agricultural sector with clear adverse repercussions for the rural economy in general. For instance, the incidence of rural poverty at the all-India level, and for most states including Bihar, which was declining during the 1980s, seemed to have been reversed in the 1990s despite the unprecedented run of good monsoons from 1988 to 1998; progress on this count remained under considerable pressure till 2004–5. Similarly, the information available from one of the major data sources for agricultural wages (that is, *Agricultural Wages in India*, published annually by the Ministry of Agriculture, Government of India) seemed to suggest that the trend of rising real agricultural wages for the 1980s had come under pressure during the first half of the 1990s, and in fact appeared to have been stalled in a number of states including Bihar (for details, see Jha 1997b). The 1970s and 1980s had witnessed a slow but sure spread of the so-called Green Revolution in major crops (wheat, maize, and paddy), but any further deepening of this revolution ran into rough weather, for a variety of reasons. By all accounts, there had been little increase in the yield per acre of the major crops during the 1990s as also for much of the subsequent decade, which is in sharp contrast to the 1970s and 1980s.

Central to the policy regime that impacted adversely on the rural economy were significant slowing down of public investment in agriculture and rural infrastructure, and a very significant deceleration in the rate of growth of rural credit from government sources. Essentially, one of the key elements of economic reforms since the early 1990s has been fiscal contraction; this has had a very significant adverse impact, in terms of growth and employment, in India's countryside. For instance, to cite just one important trend, the 1990s witnessed a significant decline in the rate of output growth for every single one of the major crop categories compared to the 1980s. In fact, the growth rate of foodgrain production for the country as a whole dropped to 1.75 per cent per annum in the 1990s, compared to more than 3 per cent in the 1980s, and was lower than the average annual population growth rate of 1.9 per cent between 1991 and 2001.

All these trends are well documented and we need not get in to a detailed discussion of relevant facts and figures here.[1] However, it may be useful to comment briefly, on the gravity of some of the problems in Bihar's countryside in the 1990s. The capital expenditure on agriculture and allied activities by the government of Bihar in the 1990s was significantly lower in comparison to that of the 1980s. Taking the average for the triennium ending in 1987–8, the figure was Rs 291.6 million, while the corresponding figure at current prices a decade later (that is, the average for financial years 1995–6, 1996–7, and 1997–8) was less than one-tenth of this figure at Rs 25.2 million.[2] The combined capital expenditure for Bihar and Jharkhand for the triennium ending 2010–11, was Rs 259.63 million which, even at nominal value, happened to be lower than the respective figures for the earlier two decades. In other words, even after a significant rise in the allocation of funds in the rural and the agricultural sector under the new government since 2004–5, the actual capital expenditure on agricultural and allied sectors never reached the level achieved in late 1980s.

Similarly, if we look at the other developmental correlates that have important linkages with the rural economy, such as per capita expenditure on roads, irrigation, and flood control, and the credit–deposit ratio of the banking sector in the 1990s, they emerge in a distinctly poorer light compared to the 1980s. Thus, it is hardly surprising that agriculture in Bihar received a severe setback during the first decade after the initiation of the neo-liberal reforms. However, the improvement in some of these correlates is observed during the second half of the first decade of the 2000s. Consequently, the rate of growth of agricultural output (at constant prices) in the state, which was 1.3 per cent per annum between 1980–1 and 1989–90, and had turned negative for the period 1991–2 to 1999–2000 (it was −1.90 per cent per annum), improved for the period from 2000–1 to 2009–10 to average around

[1] For an excellent survey of the overall economic experience of India during the first decade of the reform period, see Chandrasekhar and Ghosh (2002).

[2] All these numbers come from two annual publications of the Government of Bihar: *Statistical Abstracts* (various years) and *Crops and Seasons Reports* (various years).

1.7 per cent per annum; much of this rise was on account of the relatively higher growth rate after 2005.[3]

Although public expenditure in the rural economy of the state has been on an upswing since 2004–5, particularly in rural roads, school buildings, primary health centres, etc., there is little evidence of any serious engagement with institutional issues (for example, land reforms, financial infrastructure, etc.) as well as a broader coherent macroeconomic framework. It is against this backdrop that we need to comprehend the forces at work that are crucial in shaping the well-being of rural labour in Bihar.

Socio-economic Profile of the Survey Region

State of Infrastructure

As may be evident from the foregoing discussion, the public policy stance towards rural infrastructure in Bihar was one of the indifference if not gross neglect during the 1990s; this was clearly evident in the field work region as well. For instance, during our visit in the late 1990s, we found that the electricity connection for domestic use was still not available in Majra, and it had disappeared from Barahari. Primary health centres in both the villages, which in any case were not in sound condition towards the end of the 1980s, had virtually collapsed. The state of the government-run schools did not seem any better, although in Barahari, the attendance of children from labour households at the primary school had reportedly improved to a certain extent because of the introduction of the government programme of nutritional support for primary education. This programme, launched in 1995, was one under which the families of such children obtained support in terms of rice or wheat entitlements; the programme was implemented quite erratically but definitely seemed to have provided some incentive for several households. The roads from these villages to the block and district headquarters were decidedly much worse than a decade before; in

[3] We may note in passing that there are considerable controversies with respect to official growth figures in Bihar during the recent period (Jha and Singh 2010). Nonetheless, in this chapter we will go, wherever needed, by the official estimates of growth rates.

fact the number of buses plying on these roads had declined during the last couple of decades and had been replaced by smaller commercial vehicles, such as jeeps.

During the recent visit in 2012, it was evident that the prioritization of infrastructure development by the new government has led to significant improvement of rural roads. The connectivity of Majra as well as Barahari from their nearest major town and district headquarters, Purnia, has improved significantly. Moreover, elementary school infrastructure has also received a boost along with sundry other projects. However, the overall approach towards infrastructure has been ad hoc and piecemeal. For instance, the improvement in electricity has little to do with its provision for irrigation purposes; the construction of rural roads is not accompanied by the expansion of cheap public transport to connect these villages to the nearest towns; the improvement in the infrastructure related to school buildings remains largely disconnected from other aspects of provisioning and the issue of the quality of education; the improvement in Primary Health Centre (PHC) buildings is not backed by the confirmed availability of good medical staff and medicines at reasonable costs; and so on.

Thus, one can argue that the recent thrust towards infrastructure development in the region has resulted in some improvement in the day to day life of the rural population in general for these villages; but it continues to be far from adequate with respect to the basic needs of the rural economy and society.

Changing Agrarian Conditions

In the surveyed villages, the aspects of neo-liberal policies that seemed most visible and about which almost all cultivators complained were the drastic reduction in the availability of credit through the public sector banking channels, and the significant increase in fertilizer prices (due to a reduction in subsidies). During the field studies in 1988–9, almost 40 per cent of cultivator respondents (mostly those on the upper rung of the socio-economic ladder) had reported obtaining concessional credit for agricultural purposes from one or other government banking channel; during the 1998 field visits, not a single cultivator respondent was a beneficiary in this respect. In general, the availability of credit seemed to be a graver constraint for local agriculture than was the situation about a decade ago. As regards to fertilizer prices between 1988 and 1998, they had increased by more than twice (as in the case of urea, from Rs 112 to 250 for a 50 kg bag) and even by around four times (as in the case of potash, from Rs 55 to 200 per 50 kg bag). Over the same period, output prices had grown at a rate much lower than that of fertilizer (Table 9A.1). Moreover, cultivator respondents during the 1998 field visit bemoaned the reduced availability of quality seeds and fertilizers from government outlets, unlike in the late 1980s. Further, the agricultural department of the Government of Bihar used to have, in every block, an employee called the Village Level Worker (VLW), who provided a multipurpose Community Development interface between the government and the farmers. This position had been either abolished or had been allowed to remain vacant for some years, and, strangely enough, neither the block nor the district administration had any clear answer as to what actually had happened.

As far as improvement in the agrarian condition is concerned, there is very little to celebrate even during the recent decade of high growth, that is, the decade of the 2000s. The input prices have risen further as cuts in various input subsidies remained prominent on the agenda of the government. The prices of DAP, urea, and potash had almost doubled compared with the prices at the end of the 1990s. Moreover, though the electricity situation for both the villages has improved significantly during the recent period, it was hardly available for irrigation. Approximately, between the mid-1980s and 2012, the cost of the average fertilizer packet had increased by almost twice as much as the increase in price of an average basket of major cereals. Further, the variability of prices of both fertilizers and farm products has risen sharply over the same period. Though some efforts have been made by the government in recent years to strengthen public procurement of the farm products, particularly paddy, the actual benefits of the entire procurement system have remained largely confined to the large farmers and the intermediate business class. The small and marginal farmers are still struggling to get the officially mandated support price for various farm products.

Thus, what clearly emerged from the field visits of 1998 and 2012 was a picture of reduced support and increased apathy from the government towards the agricultural sector, and the significant fallout is that this sector's performance has worsened considerably in comparison to the decade of the 1980s. Some of the processes that led to the improvement in the various indicators of well-being of rural masses in general during the 1980s appear to have been halted, if not reversed since the 1990s, and undoubtedly, this can be traced, to a substantial extent, to the neo-liberal economic reforms in operation.

As far as investment in the farm sector is concerned, to be sure, generally large/better off landowning households, with multiple sources of earning (including government employment, commercial establishments in nearby urban centres, and so on) have not abandoned investment in agriculture. An important indicator of private investment in the farm sector is arguably the purchase of tractors and threshers. In Barahari, the number of tractors and threshers in 1989 were one and two respectively, and by 1998 these numbers had increased to two and four. During the recent visit in 2012, the count of tractors and threshers had gone up to 10 each. In Majra, during the 1990s, the number of tractors had increased from one to two, and that of threshers from three to five; in the 2012 survey, these numbers were 10 and 15 respectively. It is worth emphasizing again that the households owning these implements have large inflows of non-agricultural income. Also, these investments were made in response to a growing reluctance among several better off upper-caste cultivators to have their own livestock (for ploughing, threshing, etc.), reportedly on account of significant cost escalations in maintaining animals, with a resulting growth in demand for a hire-market for these implements in both villages. Further, the rise in the demand for rented tractors is also attributed to the decline in the relative importance of traditional methods of cultivation with bullocks and the rise in the peakedness period for various hybrid crops. We may also note that growing tractorization is also connected with demands in the non-farm economy, such as a rise in construction activities, expansion of brick kiln units, etc. particularly during the recent period. Moreover, the significance of bullock-carts as a mode of transport and carrier of products has reduced considerably; the use of tractors for even these purposes has gained in importance.

With a drastic decline in traditional crops, as well as of traditional methods of cultivation, apart from the shortening of time duration in any particular operations relating to agriculture, the general cost of cultivation has risen very sharply in recent years. In the absence of adequate support from the state, the farmers (particularly small and marginal) including tenants, have been subjected to a significant rise in their cost of cultivation.

With this overview of the broad direction of agriculture in the surveyed villages, it is important to note a few other developments that are significant. According to most of the respondents, the cropping pattern in both the villages had changed to a certain extent, though no increase in cropping intensity was reported. In both the villages, the introduction of banana cultivation from the 1980s had not reaped the expected results. This was for several reasons, including the lamentable state of the infrastructure, and appeared to have become marginal in terms of the share in the total crop acreage. During the 1990s, some cultivators had also experimented with sunflower, but during the visit in December 2001 they were gloomy about its prospects and the crop seemed to be on its way out; it was reported that this crop had not proven to be any more profitable than the other rabi crops and was in fact more risky as it required relatively more care and better management.

A significant change till the end of the decade of 1990, in the cropping pattern, was the near disappearance of jute from Barahari and the decline in its importance in Majra. Increase in the variability of its price over time, linked to global markets, was primarily responsible for damaging its prospects. In small measure, a local factor may have also contributed to the crop becoming insignificant in Barahari: a common facility, adjacent to the village, widely used for retting jute, had been privatized, and the new owner did not permit the use of this water body for free retting of jute anymore. Other changes in cropping patterns include: the near disappearance of the *bhadai* variety of paddy (a variety that ripened and was harvested very early in the kharif season) along with some decline in the *agahani* and increase in *kataki* varieties (both are harvested in the latter part of kharif season); the introduction and some spread of the *garma* variety of paddy (grown in the rabi season), particularly in Majra; a slight increase in the share of area under vegetables, pulses, and oil crops; some switching around within pulses, etc. such as an increase in the proportion of area under *masoor* and decline in that of *moong*; and, finally, a small decline in the share of area under paddy cultivation. However, except for the disappearance of bhadai paddy, and the increase in the kataki variety, none of the other changes appeared significant in either of the two villages. Almost 80 per cent of the cultivator respondents during the 1998 visit reported that they had given up cultivating bhadai as it was no longer attractive because of the rising costs and almost stagnant yield. However, about 50 per cent of our respondents said that the decline in the area under bhadai was made up by the increase in kataki paddy. It may also be noted here that kataki paddy in these villages is among the more attractive high-yielding varieties, but as is the case with such varieties in general, its cultivation is relatively resource-intensive. This also implies that only the relatively better-off cultivators were in a position to undertake cultivation of kataki paddy (Jha 2004).

During the recent visit in 2012, it was clear that the bhadai paddy was completely out of the scene in both the villages. The relative importance of wheat has declined sharply due to a rise in the input costs and the almost stagnant productivity, together with the extremely slow upward trend of its output price over the years. During the more recent period, the cultivation of a new hybrid variety of maize has gained momentum in both the villages. The principal factor responsible for the increasing popularity of maize has been productivity and profitability (Thakur 2013). In one acre, the average yield in Majra and Barahari was found to be around 12 to 15 quintal per acre, which was three to four times that for wheat; at the farm gate prices, the per acre profit for maize was almost thrice that for wheat.[4]

We may also note that the potential yield of maize in this region was above the current average. With proper financial support in terms of subsidy, credit, and market access, etc., maize output in this region can be increased significantly. However, given the existing framework of the agrarian policy of both the central and state governments, it seems rather difficult to achieve any goal of this kind in the near future.

Some Indicators Relating to Work and Well-being of Rural Labour

Access to Land

In case of land ownership as well as operational holdings, a marginal improvement was witnessed in the 1990s, compared with the 1980s, for

[4] It is worth noting that maize cultivation is relatively more resource-intensive, and small resource-poor producers often have to borrow from money lenders. Further, they also get into distress sales due to pressure associated with repayment of loans.

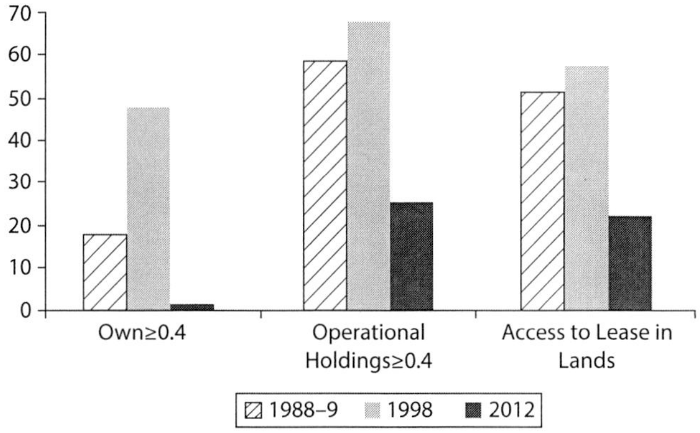

FIGURE **9.1** Access to Land (as percentage of total surveyed Labour Households)
Source: Field Survey.

the surveyed labour households. This was primarily on account of a rise in both leasing-out and sale of land by upper caste landholders, particularly due to a sharp decline in the profit rates in local agriculture.[5] However, the trend was reversed in a substantive manner during the recent decade. In 2012, both ownership holdings and operational holdings for labour households had declined significantly (Figure 9.1). As reported by respondents in 1998, close to 80 per cent of the land leased out by upper caste small and medium cultivators in recent years went to the backward castes, and the rest was rented out to the bigger upper caste landholders. In part, this may have to do with the economies of scale in the latter case, but quite clearly caste consideration was also an important factor. Another significant change related to tenancy worth reporting is that of an increase in the proportion of area under fixed-rent in total tenanted areas, and a substantial decline in the proportion of the traditional 50:50 sharecropping contracts. Towards the end of the 1980s, almost 90 per cent of tenancy contracts were of the traditional sharecropping variety and by the end of the 1990s, this had come

[5] The lessees and tenants are quite a mixed bag, mostly having access to income outside the local farm economy. For reason of space, we stay away from a detailed discussion of these features here.

down to about 50 per cent, and the system of fixed rent tenancy (both in cash and kind) had caught up with it.

During the most recent visit, the relative importance of sharecropping seemed to have declined further. With the spread of the cultivation of maize, sharecropping is now mainly limited to the cultivation of paddy and the terms of sharing has tilted further against the sharecropper. In terms of sharing the cost of cultivation, the proportion borne by the sharecropper has increased significantly during the recent period. For instance, in case of paddy cultivation, the sharable cost for the land owner is only that of fertilizer and irrigation. Other costs, such as seed purchase, ploughing with tractor, labour inputs, and the preparation of fields, etc. are borne by the sharecropper; all these have risen sharply in recent years. As per our recent field-survey, the cost borne by the sharecropper was around 7 to 9 times higher than the cost incurred by the land owner in case of cultivation of paddy.[6]

In all cases of fixed rent tenancy in both the villages, all costs are borne by the lessee and the lessor receives a predetermined cash rent. Such tenancy arrangements are sometimes only for a crop or a season, but typically they are for one agricultural year, and rarely for a longer duration. There are several factors underlying the transition from sharecropping to fixed rate tenancy and from the tenant's point of view, increase in the share of costs is clearly an important one. Second, with the fixed rent system, the land owner is also completely free from any risks as well as the hassles of supervision of cultivation. In fact, most landowners insist that they get their fixed rent right at the beginning of the contract if it is in terms of money.

Further, it is evident from our recent survey that the trend of leasing out by the upper caste landowners has been strengthened and the number of absentee landlords has increased significantly. Transition to fixed rent has made them completely free from staying in the village during the cultivation period. Moreover, in both the villages, cash rent has been gaining popularity over rent in kind in fixed tenancy; most tenants seem to prefer it due to greater freedom with respect to cultivation decisions. We may also note that the yield per unit of

[6] In general, the share of cost incurred by a sharecropper has increased for almost every crop, in varying proportions. In another important crop, namely wheat, this ratio was lower at around 3 to 5 times.

land under the fixed rent system was higher than that for traditional sharecropping contract.[7]

An obvious question to ask is: has the recent trend in land lease transitions benefited the rural labour? It clearly emerges from the survey that labour households have hardly benefited from this transition. If anything, it appears that their access to leased-in land has tended to decline. In our survey of 2012, only 19 per cent of labour respondents reported having access to leased-in land as compared to nearly 49 per cent in 1998 and more than 54 per cent in 1988–9 (Table 9A.7 and Figure 9.1). This could well be because of the rising cost of cultivation, as discussed earlier in the chapter. We may also note here that a major contributory factor to increased rent (or to use the well-known Marxist concept, 'ground rent') has been the ever-expanding number of landless poor and extremely limited possibility of non-farm livelihood options for labour households of the survey region.

Trends of Employment and Wages

One of the most welcome aspects of change with reference to the labour market was that, during the second half of the 1990s, the then stagnant/declining trend in real wages, which had continued for over two decades, seemed to have been halted, and even reversed to some extent. Casual daily wage rates in nominal terms for most operations had, compared to the late 1980s, increased by about three times on average. During the same period the Consumer Price Index for Agricultural Labour in Bihar had increased by a little over two and a half times. This would suggest a small increase in real wages for labourers in these villages, and such a possibility matched the perceptions of all our respondents.

In order to track the movement of real wages over the last three decades, it may be useful to convert the nominal wage to some relevant 'commodity wage'. Since rice has been the staple food of this region, it may be worthwhile to convert the nominal wage over the study period into rice equivalent, to get a sense of the changing

[7] This happens as the tenants, in case of fixed rent, have higher incentive to increase productivity of lands under the given agreement. This is reflected in relatively higher use of inputs per unit of land in case of fixed rent contract than that for traditional sharecropping arrangement.

direction of the material conditions of rural labour in general.[8] As mentioned earlier, the rice wage rate for agricultural operations had not increased much in both the villages in the decade of the 1980s; however, we found in the 1998 survey that there had been a significant jump in the real wage.

In the context of almost stagnant agriculture in the 1990s with respect to net yields in these villages, the small positive development on the wage front during the decade might appear to be a bit surprising, particularly in the absence of any evidence of the tightening of the labour market. In both villages, this change in the wages was brought about by repeated demands for increase in the wages by the labourers. It may be recalled that, during the 1970s and 1980s, there had been no increase in the real wages of agricultural labourers (Table 9A.4), and during the early 1990s, there was a noticeable dip; such a backdrop had made the labourers increasingly restive. Although no instance of workers resorting to any strike was reported from either of these villages, there were repeated clamours for a wage rise and the employers were forced to respond. In part, as mentioned earlier, this could be linked to the increased confidence of the labourers in the wake of new opportunities mentioned earlier. However, for some operations, such as weeding and transplanting, the increase in the wage rate was accompanied by an increase in the length of the working day in both the villages. For instance, during the surveys in the 1980s in both villages, the length of the working day for weeding was generally reported to be six hours, whereas by the late 1990s, it had moved close to eight hours. In the case of transplanting, during the 1980s, a labourer hired on a daily rate basis was required to transplant 16 bundles, and by the time of the 2001 visit, this requirement had gone up to 32 bundles. Those unable to cope with the increased requirement, and typically these were reported to be women, worked 'half-day' (that is, the time taken for 16 bundles) and were entitled to half the daily time-rate for this operation. The other major component of wage incomes in local agriculture, namely the harvest share, had remained the same as was by the end of the 1980s. Thus, in terms of harvest share for major

[8] In passing, it may be interesting to note here that the rice wage rate in Purnia district remained stagnant from the middle of the eighteenth to the last quarter of the twentieth century (Table 9A.4).

crops, such as paddy or wheat, the wage rate continued to be one-twelfth of the crop harvested.

During the 1990s, even though the agricultural labourers in these villages had managed to push for small gains, which were facilitated by the opening of some new opportunities mentioned earlier, the employers were striking back through changes in the length of the working day or shifting from time rate to piece rate and other strategies. The labour market in these villages had become more of a contested domain than ever before. After 1998, there was no increase even in nominal wages for the next several years. It was only after 2005 that the nominal wage rate witnessed a visible rise, more so for male workers as compared to female. This rise was sharper during 2006 to 2012 in both the villages (Tables 9A.2 and 9A.3). From Figures 9.2 and 9.3, it is clear that from 1997–8 to 2005–6, the real wage in the agricultural operations remained almost stagnant in both the villages and it was only after 2006 that there has been an upward movement in the agricultural wage.[9]

We may highlight a few important factors that help us to understand the wage trends during the last five years. First, Purnia was one of the first districts to be included under the MGNREGA programme in 2006. Though the implementation of MGNREGA in these villages has been far from being satisfactory, it has had a significant positive impact on the prevailing floor wage rate in the survey region. Second, prioritization of infrastructural development by the new government in Bihar and the consequent rise in the demand for labour (though the additional demand was not adequate to make the labour market tight enough) played an important role in raising the floor wage rate in rural as well urban areas. Further, the gap between the male and female wage rate has been on the rise during the recent period; this gap has been more

[9] To compare wage rates in agricultural operations, we have included only those activities in which both male and female have traditionally worked together (that is, weeding, transplantation, and harvesting). It does not include any kind of work exclusively done by males, such as ploughing, soil work, etc. for which wage rates were reportedly higher than the former (even during the period 1980–1 to 2004–5). However, in the period post 2004–5, there has been a significant difference in the male and female wage rate even in the common activities. In other words, the wage rate for men has been reported to have gone higher than the wage rate for women for the same work.

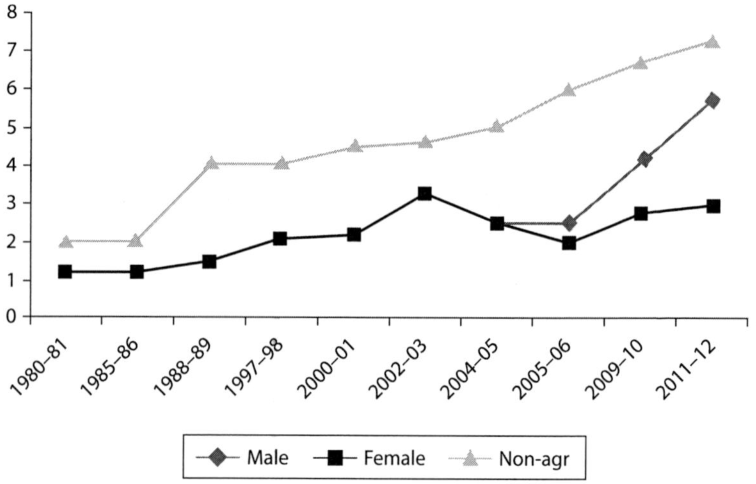

FIGURE 9.2 Rice Wage Rate for Majra (in kg per day)
Source: Field Survey.

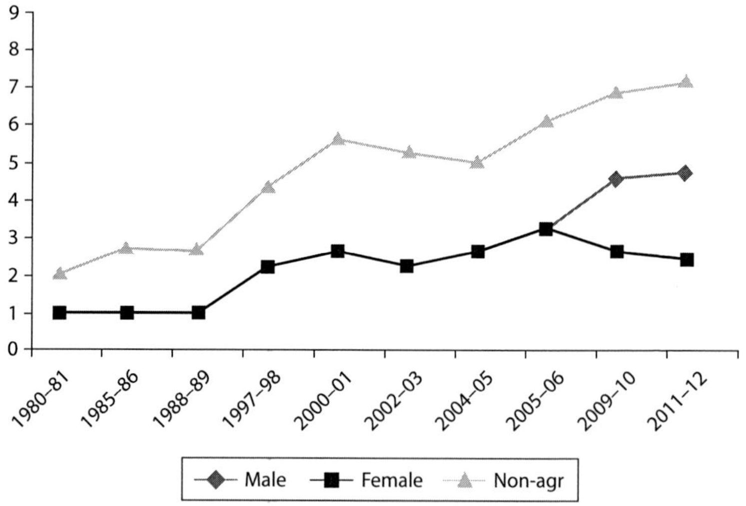

FIGURE 9.3 Rice Wage Rate in Barahari (in kg per day)
Source: Field Survey.

pronounced in Barahari than in Majra. Diversification, as well as segmentation of agricultural work, in general, may be identified to have been at work behind such a rise. In Barahari, it was reported that the majority of erstwhile agricultural workers no longer rely primarily on agricultural work for their livelihood as non-agricultural options have become their main source of income. This has led to a significant feminization of the workforce in the agricultural sector; male workers are hired only for the activities that female workers are unable to do (such as soil work, preparation of fields, etc.). On the other hand, in Majra, where diversification has been relatively low, participation of the male workers in agricultural operations was relatively more pronounced, compared to Barahari.

Given that in recent years, most of the work in agri-operations is done by female workers, it may not be far off the mark to suggest that the wage rate for female workers ought to be considered a proxy for 'agricultural wage rate' in these villages. If we do so, it is evident that, even during the recent phase, the casual impression of rising agricultural wages may be highly exaggerated as there has been near stagnation in the wage rate for female 'agricultural labour'. As regards male rural labour, it has already been noted previously that they reported a strong preference for non-farm employment. Further, it is interesting to note that in recent years the wage rate in agriculture for male workers has tended to converge with wage rates in non-agricultural activities.

As regards employment availability per labourer, the information provided by the respondents during field visits in 1989 and 1998, suggests that there was a marginal improvement in the availability of work in local agriculture during this period, which was mainly due to the increased diversification of crops (such as increased acreage of jute and *makhana,* which required higher labour per acre of land); approximately it was around one-third of the total days in a year at both points. In case of non-agricultural employment, the opening up of a few brick-kiln units in both the villages as well as a few other sundry activities led to some rise in work opportunities during the decade of the 1990s. However, this trend was reversed during the subsequent decade. In the 2012 survey, the average number of days per person in agriculture had come down to less than 95 days and the average number of working days per person in the non-agricultural sector also declined significantly in both the villages (see Figure 9.4 and Table 9A.8).

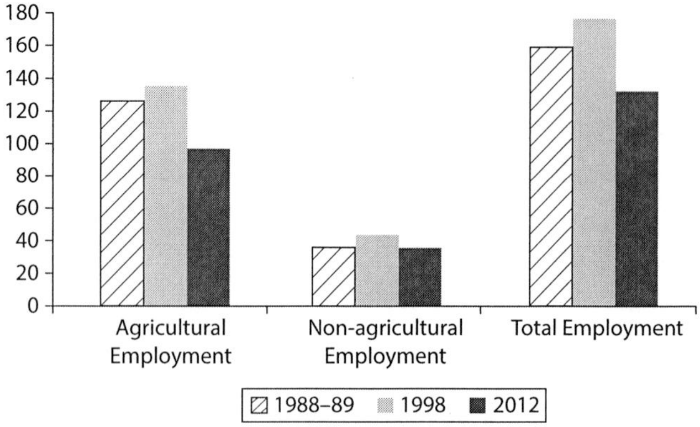

FIGURE 9.4 Total Employment Availability in Local Areas (days per year)
Source: Field Survey.

Thus, the total work opportunities in local areas have shrunk significantly during the most recent decade of our survey period. However, the share of non-agricultural days for male workers in overall working days has gone up significantly during the last decade. It emerged clearly in our field visits that while female labour was generally engaged in various agricultural operations, the majority of male workers gravitated towards non-farm activities whether in local as well as distant areas (for example, through long distance migration). Growing mechanization and use of weedicides have also been important for the sharp decline in the absorption capacity of local agriculture during the recent years.[10]

However, the fluidity across different activities and segments in the labour market, in the surveyed villages, has clearly been on the rise in recent years and signals further significant changes in the foreseeable future. But the odds are still very heavily stacked against rural labourers, given the high incidence of landlessness, growing mechanization, and a whole range of constraints on the rural economy due to neo-liberal policies. Any optimistic projection of the well-being of rural labour at the current juncture, in our judgment, is quite fragile.

[10] However, during the more recent period, increased use of labour-intensive maize cultivation has raised labour demand visibly, though it remained far from being capable of offsetting the decline in the requirement of labour in general due to the above factors in all the other crops in the region.

Incidence of Migration and Its Implications

A marked feature in both the villages appears to be an increase, compared to the 1970s and 1980s, in the incidence of migration from cultivator households, across different castes, including those in the small and medium range of ownership as well as landless labour households.[11] This may be linked, at least in part, to the situation of blocked development in the agricultural sector. Taking into account all the households, in both villages, the proportion of the adult male population going out in search of jobs, which in any case was rising during the 1980s, appeared to have increased further in the 1990s and continued in the 2000s, and this has had a profound social and economic impact.

For a sizeable proportion of rural labour households in this region, income from migration has been a significant component in their total income for almost three decades now. Apart from providing important economic support, the experience of migration has also contributed to their being socially and politically more assertive both in their villages and in their areas of destination. A typical migrant from these households, today, can cope much better, compared to his counterpart in the 1970s and 1980s, with the different aspects of migration.

It is not an overstatement to suggest that increased migration has been among the most important agents of change in the surveyed region during the last three decades. For a number of labour households, it has certainly enhanced the elbow room, not only in the economic, but also in the sociopolitical domain, and has been instrumental in the weakening of the traditional ties of dependency. What probably had begun as a very reluctant supplementary livelihood option in the 1970s gradually came to be viewed by many labour households as an opportunity for economic betterment and an escape route from the stifling hierarchy in their own villages; by the end of the 1980s, at least one male from every third labour household had worked outside the village at some point. By all accounts, the extent

[11] Increasing landlessness, as well as a decline in the availability of land for rent, has pushed up the incidence of migration among labour households in these villages.

of migration from labour households from these villages increased at an accelerated pace during much of the 1990s. In July 1989, there were 14 migrant workers in the sample of 70 labour households in the two surveyed villages. In July 1998, even though the sample was considerably smaller, consisting of only 40 labour households, the number of migrant labourers was substantially higher at 22; in other words, over this period, the number of migrants per labour household had increased from one-fifth to more than half. The incidence of migration has further risen at a significant rate during the recent period as is evident in our survey of 2012. Out of a total of 37 households surveyed during 2012, 28 persons were reputed to be migrant workers (mostly long distance). In other words, the number of migrants per labour household increased from nearly half in 1998 to more than three fourths in 2012 (Figure 9.5).

Another notable change was the significant shift of workers from agriculture to non-agriculture; of a total of 22 migrant workers in the sample in 1998, as many as 17 were engaged in non-agricultural activities, such as construction, small manufacturing industries, the service sector, etc. The work composition of the current migrants, in any given episode of migration has, however, changed significantly in recent years. Now, instead of engaging in any one single activity for the entire period of migration, most of the migrant workers opt for multiple activities within any given migration period. A substantial proportion of workers moving out from these villages go to Punjab for the peak agricultural season and after working for certain days,

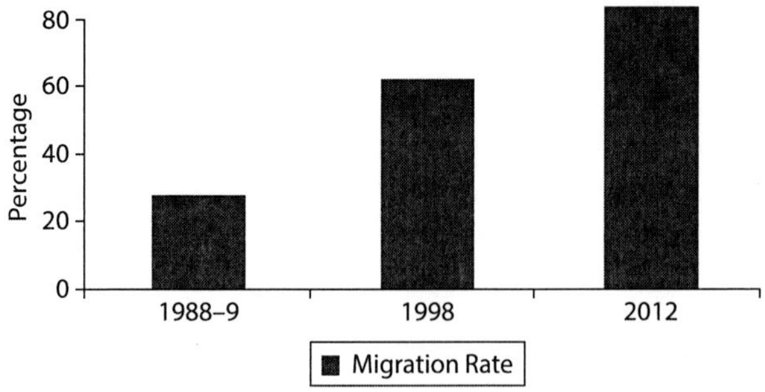

FIGURE 9.5 The Rate of Migration (of households with at least one migrant)
Source: Field Survey.

depending on the availability, they usually move to other kind of casual work related to construction or loading/unloading in the nearest *mandi*. As per our latest survey, out of a total of 28 migrant labourers only four are purely agricultural labour and out of these four, only one worked on a regular basis while all the remaining three were just casual labourers. Fifteen migrant labourers opted for both agricultural work and other casual work, such as construction or any work in the mandi, within a single period of migration. The remaining nine migrant labourers worked entirely in the non-agricultural sector, such as construction and in mandis.

In all the three phases of the survey, 1988–9, 1998, and 2012, not one of these migrants was a female, nor was there any instance of permanent migration. Also, the labour households belonging to the lowest rung in the caste hierarchy, that is, Musahars in Majra and Chamars in Barahari, initially were not in a position to pursue long-distance migration and this trend remained clearly visible till the end of 1990s. For instance, during the 1998 field visit, out of a total 40 labour households from the two villages, ten belonged to these two castes, and out of these ten households only one had a migrant worker. However, in 2012 this relation seems to have weakened considerably. For instance, out of 25 SC and ST households in our sample, 15 reported migration of 18 persons. In case of the OBCs, out of 12 households 9 reported incidence of migration in their families. In terms of percentage in 2012, around 60 per cent of the SC and ST households in both the villages reported at least one migration in their families while the comparable figure for OBC households was 75.

Apart from augmenting the income of a substantial number of labour households in these villages, the most important contribution of migration has been to increase the confidence of labourers and their bargaining power. Quite evidently, in a situation of inadequacies regarding the availability of employment in the region, migration has played an important role in providing additional income to rural labour in general. Those who could migrate at least for some period during a year remained better off in terms of overall livelihood conditions, except for those who have a certain degree of access to cultivable lands. But those who were unable to migrate and do not have access to land are undoubtedly the worst off and the majority of them are heavily indebted.[12] However, it must be emphasized that the increase in migration from labour households should not be construed to imply labour shortage for agricultural operations in the study region; this was reiterated by the cultivator respondents. One may also note that during the 2001, 2003, and 2012 visits to these villages, villagers in general, and particularly those belonging to labour households, had become increasingly pessimistic (compared to the earlier visits) as regards the economic gains from migration and this had reportedly dampened the trend witnessed earlier. It may, therefore, be somewhat early to draw any strong conclusion regarding a significant change in the long-term trend since the 1980s.

Livestock Ownership of the Rural Poor

Another notable change already referred previously, is the fact that the incidence of ownership of livestock by upper-caste households has decreased considerably in recent years (Table 9A.6). Over the last few years, the tilling, furrowing, etc. of land has become increasingly mechanized in the case of better-off households and their reliance on manual ploughing has reduced considerably. Similarly, the harvesting and threshing of crops, such as wheat and paddy, has increasingly become mechanized. In fact, in both the villages, a hire-market for tractors and threshers has acquired more than a foothold. Also, in recent years, as reported earlier, the incidence of leasing-out by upper classes/castes has increased (generally on fixed rent tenancy), and many of them have become absentee landlords. On the supply side, there has been a growing unwillingness on the part of agricultural labourers to provide labour as permanent servants taking care of the livestock in the upper-caste households. A combination of all these factors, both on the

[12] In fact, in some villages in the adjacent district, indebtedness has led to rise of a new disturbing trend. The landless households (for instance, in village Bharri in Katihar district) who are unable to migrate, due to reasons such as illness, lack of threshold cash necessary for moving out etc., are reported to have given their daughters at a price, ostensibly for marriage, through agents coming from western Uttar Pradesh and Haryana. One of the terms in such transactions is that there will be no contact between the girl and her original family henceforth.

demand and the supply side, obviously has reduced the role of livestock for cultivation purposes.

Further, as per our recent survey, yet more twists have been added to the situation pertaining to ownership of livestock. In both the villages, the area under cultivation of maize, which does not produce fodder, has increased significantly, along with a decline of the acreage for paddy as well as wheat. As a result, access to fodder, particularly for households at the lower rung of the economic scale, has become even more difficult. Moreover, the decline in the common grazing lands in the villages, has also contributed to the difficulties in access to adequate fodder in these villages. These factors not only contributed to the shortage of fodder, but also led to a sharp rise in the price of crop-residue, basically straw and husk, which have increasingly come to be used as fodder during the recent times.

Sure enough, under these circumstances, only households with assured access to fodder, which is largely contingent on the size of operational holdings, would be capable of possessing livestock, as was clearly evident in the most recent survey.[13] Moreover, even marginal farmers now use tractors for ploughing and the importance of bullocks in this respect has declined sharply. Therefore, the declining importance of animals in the farming process, the rising cost of fodder, and the declining access to land, inter alia, have been instrumental in marking a shift away from possession of livestock.[14] Only 11 out of 37 of labour households in our 2012 survey reported that they have at least one animal and the remaining 25 households did not possess any livestock (Figure 9.6 and Table 9A.6).

Indebtedness

Contractionary monetary policies during the neo-liberal regime have had clear implications for the rural population at the margin

[13] As the average amount of operational holdings of those households having any livestock was around 1.3 acres while this figure for those households who do not possess any livestock was around 0.1 acres.

[14] The declining trend was not only limited to draught animals but also for milch animals.

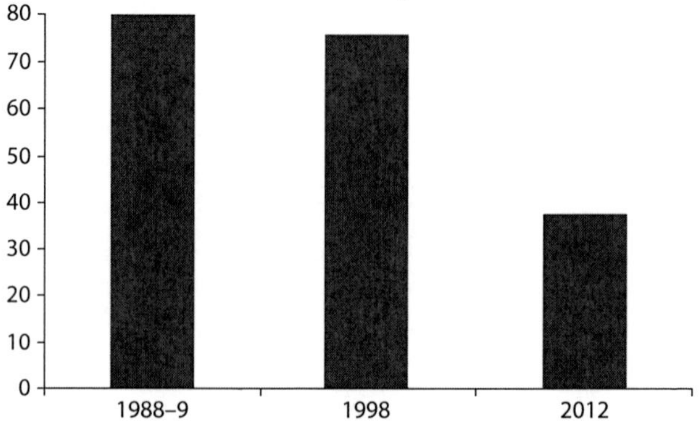

FIGURE 9.6 Percentage of Respondents Reporting Livestock Ownership
Source: Field Survey.

(Figure 9.7). In 1988–9, 40 out of 70 (57.14 per cent) labour households had reported outstanding debt. Out of these 40 households, 6 had access to formal / institutional loans and 3 of them had interest free loans taken either from their relatives or employers. The remaining 31 households had taken loans at rates higher than 50 per cent per annum, of which 13 had incurred loans at the rate of 120 per cent per annum and for one household the rate was as high as 240 per cent per annum. In 2012, however, the situation appeared to have become worse in this regard. Of the total 37 households surveyed, 27 (nearly 73 per cent) had outstanding debt, of which only 4 had institutional loans, and that too from self-help groups with a 24 per cent interest rate. Moreover, almost all the households having access to SHG loans were indebted primarily for short-term consumption purposes (for details, see Table 9A.5).

Thus, in 2012 not only had the incidence of indebtedness risen sharply but the share of formal / institutional loans had come down. Further, in 1988–9 all the institutional loans were taken to purchase livestock under various self-employment schemes, and even loans from informal sources were on account of a mixed bag of productive and immediate consumption needs including medical expenses. As per our 2012 survey, the share of 'unproductive' loans, in particular to meet medical expenditure, had increased significantly.

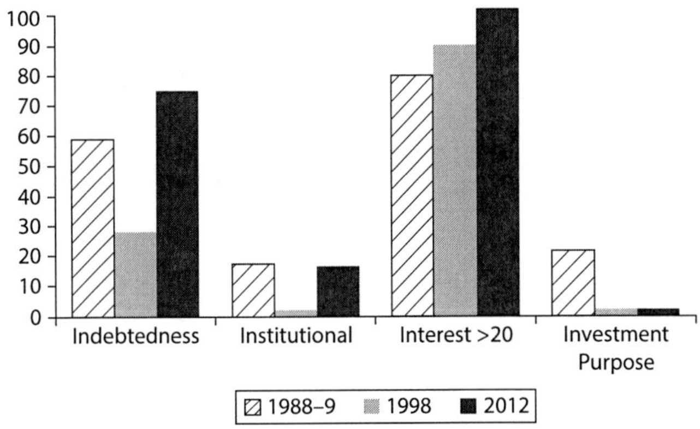

FIGURE 9.7 Indebtedness Indicators in Percentage of Households
Source: Field Survey.

Public Provisioning and the Well-being of the Rural Labour

In spite of limited government support to agriculture even during the recent period of high growth rate, some government initiatives, in particular, such as the Indira Awaas Yojana (IAY) and MGNREGA, have been important in improving the well-being of rural labour in general. One of the positive visible changes in both villages since the 1990s, and more so in Barahari than in Majra, compared to the late 1980s, seemed to be the improved housing for several low income families, including some of the labour households in our panel. This was largely because of the government-sponsored programme, namely, the IAY.[15] However, a beneficiary needs to have access to homestead plots to avail of IAY, which has been a problem for several rural landless households that do not have resources to purchase the required amount of land. In any case, such plots are in short supply in both the villages. Thus, without a programme to ensure availability of some homestead land, the coverage of IAY would not be

[15] The IAY aims at providing dwelling units, free of cost, to the poor families of the SCs, STs, freed bonded labourers, and others below the poverty line in rural areas. The scheme is funded on a cost sharing basis of 75:25 between the Centre and the States. This scheme was initially conceived of as a subscheme of another programme in 1985, but was converted into an independent programme in 1996 with relatively generous financial support.

universal for its intended beneficiaries. This was highlighted by several households during the 2012 survey, most of them belonging to the SC and ST category. Generally they resided either on Bihar government land or on the land of one of their landlords belonging to a higher caste. In both the cases, they were rendered ineligible for getting IAY.

As regards MGNREGA, it is clear from the recent visit that its functioning has been well below its potential. Out of 37 households, only 26 reported having job cards, of which only 20 managed to get employment under this programme. Further, of these 20 households, 15 got just about 10 or fewer days, that is, one-tenth of the provision of 100 days of employment per household as per the Act. Further, the wage paid to the workers was significantly lower than the minimum wage prescribed by the state government, and some of the workers reported non-payment of their wages even after two months from the date of employment. In general, these programmes are riddled with quite a few implementation issues in both the villages, with corruption rampant among the powers that be, and these must be addressed.

Some Qualitative Dimensions of Employment

During the surveys in the 1980s, it was found that a significant proportion of traditional sharecroppers were attached servants, for example permanent ploughmen (*halwaha*). In 1988–9, almost every interviewed landowner in either village, owning more than 10 acres, had one or more permanent ploughmen and some of them also had other kinds of attached servants. Traditionally, small plots of land were leased out to these attached workers on a sharecropping basis. But by 1998, permanent ploughmen had almost disappeared from both the villages and, during the survey in 2012, permanent attached labour of any kind was rarely reported for either of these two villages. Partly, the spread of the hire market for tractors, which had already become visible by as early as the late 1980s, and other changes in agrarian economy have contributed to it. Growing absentee landlordism as a prominent phenomenon since the late 1990s has also meant a decline in the demand for attached workers.

On the supply side, the aversion to traditional forms of attachment, whether as permanent ploughmen or otherwise, has steadily grown over the years. Almost invariably, such attachments had meant that the workers, and often their family members, could be called upon to perform a variety of tasks (for details, see Jha 1997a, ch. 5). In fact, the decline in the share of regular employed including attached labour has been a major phenomenon all over the country (Da Corta and Venkateshwarlu 1997; Djurfeldt et al. 2008; Lindberg 2012; Rodgers 2012; Srivastava 2012). Clearly, the growing resentment over the years as regards almost infinitely elastic work obligations associated with traditional arrangements has led to a situation where there are not many workers willing to enter such arrangements. Thus, a combination of these demand and supply factors has resulted in a drastic decline in traditional forms of labour attachment.

In spite of the fact that attached labour arrangements have become almost insignificant, the informal patron–client relationship continues to be important. The costs and associated obligations, which were characteristic of the attached labour arrangements, rendered the system quite unfavourable to the employers as well as the labourers. In fact, the experience of migration over the years, along with the variety of political processes including the electoral one, have altered the world view of the labourers in fundamental ways, and issues of izzat (dignity), political rights, etc. figure prominently in their aspirations. All this has obviously had an impact on the labour markets in these villages and on the wider social relations between the employers and the labourers.

* * *

On the basis of a point-to-point comparison (based on the 1988–9, 1997–8, and 2011–12 surveys), taking into account the relevant magnitudes, the core concern of this chapter has been to explore whether the situation of labour households have improved, worsened, or remained roughly the same in terms of the various relevant indicators in both the villages over the last three decades. Clearly, with respect to most indicators, there is little to celebrate and the ascendency of neo-liberal macroeconomic policies, since the early 1990s, has not been good news. Of course, village-specific structural features and other dimensions are critical in shaping the overall prospects for labour. For instance, in Majra, the land ownership pattern is much more skewed than in Barahari. Moreover, the availability of non-farm employment in the former is significantly lower as compared to the latter. This is attributed to the fact that the number of brick kiln units in Barahari has been much higher than in Majra. Because of these reasons, the rise in the wage rate in agricultural operations has been higher in Barahari than in Majra. The average wage for male agricultural workers in Barahari was Rs 150 while this figure for Majra was found to be around Rs 100. Further, due to relatively higher availability of non-farm employment in Barahari than in Majra, the rate of outmigration has been lower in the former than the latter.

Much in conformity to most of the country, the households at the bottom of the caste hierarchy (such as Chamars in Barahari or Musahars in Majra) are materially worse off compared to other social categories. In all cases of improvement, access to land (owned or leased in), ownership of livestock, and employment availability outside local agriculture (including migration), or combinations thereof, emerged as critical correlates. It is noteworthy that in quite a few cases of improvement in access to land or ownership of livestock, government programmes were instrumental. The ascendancy of the neo-liberal agenda, has, however, put a question mark over the adequacy of the provisions of such programmes. Any serious illness, death, drought, flood, repair of house, etc. often forces the households concerned to incur debts and in many cases, with disastrous consequences, such as loss of land or livestock. Emergence of sustainable mechanisms, either within the local economy, or through linkages elsewhere, that could lead to significant improvements for the overwhelming majority of labour households, seem to be a distant reality.

Annexure

TABLE 9A.1 Fertilizer and Output Prices (Rs per 50 kg bag) (nominal)

Items	1988–9	1997–8	2011–12	Change between 1988–2012
DAP	100	250 (2.5 times)	900 (3.6 times)	9 times
Urea	112	250 (2.23 times)	500 (2 times)	4.46 times
Potash	55	200 (3.64 times)	600 (3 times)	10.9 times
Average output prices (wheat, maize and paddy)	203	380 (1.87 times)	800 (2.1 times)	3.94 times
Average fertilizer prices (DAP, Urea, Potash)	89	233.33 (2.62 times)	666.67 (2.86 times)	7.49 times

Source: Field Survey.

TABLE 9A.2 Rice Wage Rate for Majra (in kg per day)

Year	Rice wage male (agri.)	Rice wage female (agri.)	Rice wage (non-agri.)
1980–1	1.2	1.2	2
1885–6	1.2	1.2	2
1988–9	1.5	1.5	4
1997–8	2.1	2.1	4
2000–1	2.2	2.2	4.5
2002–3	3.25	3.25	4.6
2004–5	2.5	2.5	5
2005–6	2.5	2	6
2009–10	4.1	2.8	6.7
2011–12	5.75	3	7.25

Source: Field Survey.
Note: Agricultural wages here denote wages given in all agricultural operations for which both males and females work together (such as transplantation, weeding, etc.).

TABLE 9A.3 Rice Wage Rate for Barahari (in kg per day)

Year	Rice wage male (agri.)	Rice wage female (agri.)	Rice wage (non-agri.)
1980–1	1	1	2.25
1885–6	1	1	3.1
1988–9	1	1	3
1997–8	2.5	2.5	5
2000–1	3	3	6.5
2002–3	2.5	2.5	6.1
2004–5	3	3	5.8
2005–6	3.75	3.75	7.1
2009–10	5.3	3	8
2011-12	5.5	2.75	8.3

Source: Field Survey.
Note: Same as Table 9A.2.

TABLE 9A.4 Daily Wage Rate of Unskilled Agricultural Labourers in Purnia

Year	Wage rate in rice (paddy)
1766	2
1810	2.2
1873	3
1877	2.8
1891	2
1900	2.3
1909	2
1953	2.3
1980	2.3*

Source: Jha 1997a, based on Mishra (1979).
Note: * Figure for 1980 is derived from the average rate of rice wage rate for both the villages under survey namely Majra and Barahari based on field report.

TABLE 9A.5 Indebtedness (indicators in percentages of households)

Year	Indebtedness	Institutional	Interest >20	Investment purpose
1988–9	57. 1	15	77.5	20
1998	25.8	0	87.5	0
2012	73	14.8 (SHG)	100	0

Source: Field Survey.

TABLE 9A.6 Livestock Ownership Pattern (percentage of households)

Year	Animal ownership	Owner's average land holdings	Owner's average operational holdings	Non-owner's average holdings	Non-owner's average operational holdings
1988–9	74.67	0.13	0.87	0.03	0.04
1998	71	0.36	1.03	0.18	0.23
2012	30	0.14	1.3	0.03	0.1

Source: Field Survey.

TABLE 9A.7 Access to Land

Year	Average ownership (in acres)	Ownership ≥0.4 (% of households)	Average operational holdings (in acres)	Operational holdings ≥0.4 (% of households)	Access to lease in lands (in acres)
1988–9	0.11	14.28	0.7	55.71	48.57
1998	0.31	45.16	0.8	64.52	54.84
2012	0.06	0.03	0.49	21.62	18.91

Source: Field Survey.

TABLE 9A.8 Employment Availability per Worker in Local Areas (days per year)

Year	Agricultural employment	Non-agricultural employment	Total employment
1988–9	121.7	33.57	155.27
1998	129	41.08	170.08
2012	93.5	32.1	125.61

Source: Field Survey.

References

Chandrasekhar, C.P. and Jayati Ghosh. 2002. *The Market That Failed: A Decade of Neoliberal Economic Reforms in India*. New Delhi: Leftword.

Da Corta, Lucia and Davuluri Venkateshwarlu. 1997. 'Unfree Relations and the Feminization of Agricultural Labour in Andhra Pradesh, 1970–95', in T.J. Byres, Karin Kapadia, and Jens Lerche (eds), *Rural Labour Relations in India*, pp. 71–139. New Delhi: India Research Press.

Djurfeldt, Göran, Venkatesh Athreya, N. Jayakumar, Staffan Lindberg, A. Rajagopal, and R. Vidyasagar. 2008. 'Agrarian Change and Social Mobility in Tamil Nadu', *Economic and Political Weekly*, XLIII (45): 50–61.

Government of Bihar. various years. *Crops and Seasons Report*. Patna: Directorate of Statistics and Evaluation.

Government of Bihar. various years. *Statistical Abstracts*. Patna: Directorate of Statistics and Evaluation.

Jha, Praveen. 1997a. *Agricultural Labour in India*. New Delhi: Vikas Publishing House.

Jha, Praveen. 1997b. 'Devil Take the Hindmost: Economic Reforms and Agricultural Labourers in India', *Economic and Political Weekly*, XXXII (20&21): 1066–8.

———. 2004. 'Continuity and Change: Some Observations on the Landscape of Agricultural Labourers in North Bihar', *Journal of Agrarian Change*, 4 (4): 509–31.

Jha, Praveen and Atul Singh. 2010. 'Deconstructing Bihar's Growth "Miracle"', *Bihar Times*, 12 March.

Lindberg, Staffan. 2012. 'Rural India 1970–2005: An Arduous Transition to What?' *Indian Journal of Labour Economics*, 55 (1): 61–75.

Mishra, Madneshwar. 1979. *Some Aspects of the Land Revenue History of Purnea District: 1765–1950*. Patna: Bharti Bhavan.

Rodgers, Gerry. 2012. 'Four decades of village studies and surveys in Bihar,' paper presented at Conference on Understanding Change in Rural India: Perspective from Longitudinal Village Studies, JNU, New Delhi, 20–2 November.

Srivastava, R. 2012. 'Assessing Change: Land, Labour and Employment in a village in East UP, 1994-2012,' paper presented at Conference on Understanding Change in Rural India: Perspective from Longitudinal Village Studies, Jawaharlal Nehru University, New Delhi, 20–2 November.

Thakur, Avanindra Nath. 2013. 'Economic Well-being of Rural Labour in Contemporary Bihar', PhD thesis, Centre for Economic Studies and Planning, Jawaharlal Nehru University, New Delhi.

10

JOHN HARRISS
J. JEYARANJAN

Rural Tamil Nadu in the Liberalization Era

What Do We Learn from Village Studies?*

A 'Post-agrarian State'

Tamil Nadu has a long and rich tradition of village studies of rural society and economy undertaken by economists and anthropologists, in addition to the 'Slater village' studies that are the subject of Chapter 2 of this volume. In this chapter, we aim to survey the findings of village studies that have been accomplished over the last two decades—the era of economic liberalization—together with those of larger-scale surveys in which households have been studied in a sample of villages from across a small region. A few of the studies involve resurveys of villages, and

* We are grateful to Grace Carswell, Geert De Neve, Barbara Harriss-White, Judith Heyer, and Gerry Rodgers for their comments on drafts of this article. We are also grateful to Isabelle Guerin for permission to quote from the manuscript of her forthcoming, jointly authored paper, and to M. Vijayabaskar for good advice.

there is one case in which the researchers report on a panel study, over a 25-year period, of upwards of 200 households spread across six villages. The studies are quite strongly biased, in terms of their geographical distribution, to the northern, central, and western parts of the state, and there is a relative dearth of material from the southern districts. While we do not intend to generalize, we cannot avoid commenting upon clear commonalities in the findings of the various studies. In general, it seems to us that they tend to support the view that we advanced in our restudy of the Slater village of Gangaikondan in the south of the state (outside the city of Tirunelveli), when we suggested that rural society in Tamil Nadu is in a sense 'post-agrarian' (see Harriss, Jeyaranjan, and Nagaraj 2012). This might be expected in what is India's most highly urbanized state. The share of the population of the state classified as 'urban' in 2011 was 48.45 per cent, and some projections have suggested that the state will be as much as 75 per cent urban by 2026. Several of the recent village studies reviewed in this chapter report rates of population growth lower than the natural rate of growth of population in rural Tamil Nadu, and they supply abundant evidence of migration, often to towns and cities.

The term 'post-agrarian' reflects the general observations that the importance of agriculture in rural livelihoods has declined and that, as in Gangaikondan, far fewer village households than before can sensibly be described as those of 'peasants' (or as those of agricultural petty commodity producers). The diversification of employment, often involving extensive commuting from villages, and resort to migration, both circular and long-term, to towns and cities (in some cases, to other rural sites too—such as in the case of the many people from villages around Villupuram who migrate for long periods for sugar cane cutting) means, too, that the category of 'rural' or 'agrarian labour' now has little meaning. In rural Tamil Nadu we find, in the terminology suggested by Henry Bernstein and, following him, by Jens Lerche (2010), 'classes of labour', rather than peasant classes. As Bernstein has put it: '[c]lasses of labour in the conditions of today's "South" have to pursue their reproduction through insecure and oppressive—and typically increasingly scarce—wage employment and/or a range of likewise precarious small-scale and insecure "informal sector" ("survival") activity, including farming; in effect, various and complex combinations of employment and self-employment'. As we said in our study of the Slater village of Iruvelpattu, this description fits very well 'the increasingly complex, highly diversified ways in which the very mobile people [of this village] secure their livelihoods across a geographically wide range of locations' (this and the preceding quote, Harriss, Jeyaranjan, and Nagaraj 2010: 61). The other village studies that we review here point to the same conclusion. The idea that Tamil rural society is 'post-agrarian' also reflects our view that though Tamil Nadu can no longer adequately be analysed through the categories of peasant studies, the state has still not experienced the full structural transformation of its economy and society. 'Post-agrarian' is intended to indicate a kind of a transitional state of affairs, though one in which the direction of movement is uncertain.

In what follows, we review evidence in particular from an, as yet, unpublished study by N. Arivukkarasi and K. Nagaraj (2009) of agrarian change in three villages of northern Tamil Nadu that have been the subjects of previous studies by several researchers over the last four decades—in the early 1970s, the early 1980s, the early 1990s, and most recently by Arivukkarasi and Nagaraj (2009). Arivukkarasi and Nagaraj take the exhaustive set of studies of these three and of other villages in the old North Arcot District from the early 1990s, edited by Barbara Harriss-White and S. Janakarajan (2004), as a starting point. We also examine the findings of Athreya, Djurfeldt, and Lindberg and their colleagues on trends of agrarian change and social mobility in the region of Tiruchirappalli over the period 1979 to 2004 (Djurfeldt et al. 2008), and consider the observations of Grace Carswell and of Judith Heyer from village studies in the dynamic, industrializing region of Tiruppur, in the west of the state (Carswell 2013; Heyer 2000a, 2000b, 2010, 2012, 2013, 2014, and this volume), and those of Isabelle Guerin and her colleagues from Villupuram and Cuddalore districts (Guerin, Venkatasubramanian, and Michiels 2014). We also refer to our own findings from detailed surveys in the two 'Slater villages' of Iruvelpattu and Gangaikondan, together with our notes from visits to two other of the 'Slater villages', Palakkurichi (in Nagapattinam District), where Jeyaranjan undertook research on agricultural labour relations in 2000, and Dusi (in Tiruvannamalai District), which we visited together early in 2014. We consider, too, findings from a study of rural non-farm employment in the state, carried out by Jeyaranjan for the Planning Commission in 2012, in which surveys were conducted in twelve villages spread across four districts in the southern half of the state, two of them (Tirunelveli and Virudunagar) with a high incidence of rural non-farm employment according to the of Census 2001, and two of them (Thanjavur and Pudukottai) with a low incidence of such activity.[1] Finally, we review some recent village studies of the implementation of the Mahatma Gandhi National Rural Employment Guarantee Scheme (MGNREGS) in Tamil Nadu.

The study by Guerin and her colleagues richly demonstrates the value of studying a number of villages from across a small region. This has led them to recognize the spatial fragmentation of labour, because location—in spite of the relatively high quality transport infrastructure of Tamil Nadu, and improved information circulation given, not least, the ubiquity of the cell phone—still remains a barrier. They distinguish three categories of settlements in their study area: (a) 'migrant settlements', with specialized channels of seasonal migration for brick moulding or sugar cane harvesting, and which may be more or less deserted for many months at a time; (b) 'semi-agrarian settlements', located in 'wet' areas (irrigated tracts) 'with wide scale agriculture and where there is a high level of caste interdependence' (Guerin et al. 2014), though here, too, even the bigger landowners 'increasingly combine agricultural and non-agricultural incomes' (Guerin et al. 2014); (c) 'peri-urban settlements' from which 'most men come and go to nearby towns' (Guerin et al. 2014). The authors show that there are diverse patterns of identities, social hierarchies and social and spatial mobility shaped by these different sorts of locations. The point is an important one—and forcefully reminds us that there are different sorts of villages—though, of course, the particular typology that these authors have developed is not necessarily of general applicability. Amongst the Slater villages both Gangaikondan and Dusi do fit the 'peri-urban' category very well; but Iruvelpattu combines elements of all three settlement types.

[1] We have studied, as well, unpublished resurveys of a number of villages in the state carried out under Jeyaranjan's direction in 2000 as part of the Kerala Research Programme on Local Development, of the Centre for Development Studies in Thiruvananthapuram; and an unpublished resurvey by R. Rukmani of the village of Arkavadi in Villupuram District. This is a village first taken up for study with the Census of 1961 and resurveyed in 2000. Considerations of space have meant that we have referred very little to these surveys in the text, though they provide further evidence that substantiates key points that we make.

All the studies to which we refer also have their own particular foci, and they are not easily compared. But a feature that they do have in common—one that is in line with our suggestion that Tamil Nadu is now 'post-agrarian'—is that few of these recent studies are much concerned with what is going on in agriculture, in sharp contrast with those of Harriss-White and Janakarajan (1997). These two writers, however, in a summary article, also said that '[t]o analyse the technologies and social relations of the agricultural sector alone risks an increasingly incomplete and arbitrary account of the region's development' (Harriss-White and Janakarajan 1997: 1471). In this context, class analysis may have to take account not only of the class relations of the village but also of how rural and urban class relations interlock.[2]

The studies that we review clearly show, indeed, the increasing importance of non-agricultural activity, carried on by village people in urban as well as in rural areas, in a state with one of India's most diversified economies. At the same time, successive state governments in Tamil Nadu have done more than have other state regimes (with the possible exception of Kerala) to improve people's welfare by maintaining a universal PDS—in the face of pressures to introduce targeting; through the consolidation of the long-established noon meals scheme—derided by economists as boding disaster for the state's economy when it was introduced in the early 1980s; more recently, through the relatively successful implementation of the MGNREGA; through establishing a functioning public healthcare system; and by providing better schooling within the public system than is generally available in the country. The combination of a relatively positive employment situation in the Tamil Nadu rural economy, at least for men who are not from the Scheduled Castes (SCs), with the implementation of social policies, has brought about extensive restructuring of rural society, in the context of the neglect of agriculture in public policy through most of the era of economic liberalization—in regard to which Tamil Nadu has shared in a wider national trend.

[2] This is a point that was made strongly by Gerry and Janine Rodgers in the course of their presentation, and subsequent discussions, at the Foundation for Agrarian Studies Tenth Anniversary Conference on Agrarian Issues, Kochi, 9–12 January 2014.

Agriculture and Rural Livelihoods

Harriss-White and Janakarajan sum up on the state of the agricultural economy of their region of northern Tamil Nadu, from their comparison of findings in 1993–4 with those of the studies carried out over the previous two decades, as follows:

> Despite the developmental effort put into agriculture, before, during and since the first generation green revolution, the impact on yields is hardly to be observed, and agricultural production remains extremely vulnerable to its physical environment and its trend is flat (1997: 1473).

Though these remarks refer specifically to the region of the small town of Arni, the picture that they suggest is a fair representation of the state of agriculture across the state as a whole. From about the time of their study, Tamil Nadu, which stands out among the major states as one in which the irrigation potential has been more or less fully realized (see, for example, *Tamil Nadu–An Economic Appraisal* for 2002–3), shared in the stagnation of the agricultural economy of the country as a whole. One marker of this is that yields of paddy—the most important crop in the state—in 2001–2 averaged only 3,196 kg/ha[3] (and in the following year, in circumstances of prolonged drought, they fell to 2,359 kg/ha). More recently, over the period of the Eleventh Five Year Plan, when agricultural growth over the country as a whole took off again, Tamil Nadu's agriculture continued to stagnate. The index of all agricultural production showed no improvement at all in the period from 2007–8 to 2010–11; the yield and production of paddy 'experienced a negative growth of 2.35 per cent and 2.26 per cent respectively'; and all foodgrains a negative growth of 1.40 and 1.49 per cent, respectively, for yield and production (*Tamil Nadu–An Economic Appraisal* for 2010–11: 39). The most recent *Economic Appraisal* (for 2010–11) concludes:

> The performance of the agricultural sector is hobbled by a number of vulnerabilities, such as dwindling supply of irrigation water, over-exploitation of groundwater, climate changes and ozone depletion, fickleness of weather, swelling population, subsistence farming, indebtedness of

[3] This figure is more or less exactly the same as that recorded by Harriss-White and Janakarajan (2004) for the region they studied in northern Tamil Nadu in 1993–4.

farmers, lack of remunerative prices for farm produce, inadequate development of post-harvest technologies, feminization of poverty, seasonal variability, etc.

Plus ça change. Much the same conclusions appear in earlier *Economic Appraisals*, as they did in Harriss-White and Janakarajan's study (2004) from 20 years ago.

The context of the rural economy of Tamil Nadu in the liberalization era is, therefore, one of a more or less moribund agriculture.[4] We noted in our study of the Slater village of Iruvelpattu that the same paddy varieties were being cultivated as in 1981, and we argued that this 'suggests that the wave of innovation of paddy varieties of the 1970s and 1980s ... has passed. Reported yields, too, show little if any increase over 1981' (Harriss et al. 2010: 52). The decline of the agricultural economy of Gangaikondan, where the net sown area has fallen sharply, is very clear (Harriss et al. 2012), as it is also in Dusi. There, proximity to the Dusi-Mamandur tank, one of the largest in the state, has not protected cultivation from the vagaries of rainfall—because the tank no longer receives as much water as it did from the river Palar. The channels from the tank that supplied water to 20 villages have become silted up—an eloquent marker of the neglect of agriculture. In both Gangaikondan and Dusi (and in some others of the villages about which we have studies) there have been extensive sales of farm land for real estate.

Judith Heyer reports on the changing position of the elite cultivators ('*thottam* farmers', as she calls them—cultivators, that is, of large-enough areas of land irrigated by wells as to justify employing permanent labour) in villages in Coimbatore District in the west of the state—the district with the most highly commercialized agriculture in Tamil Nadu—over the period 1981–2 to 1996:

> In 1981–82, agriculture was doing well and thottam farmers looked forward to a bright future despite indications of problems ahead. They were a confident group, powerful in their own local domain [even if they were small operators in the regional economy] ... By 1996, this had changed. Agriculture had declined, and urban and industrial development was

[4] This remark may underestimate modest improvement in some parts of the state in crops other than foodgrains.

> having more influence particularly on labour and on labour costs. In 1996, many thottam farmers had sunk capital into a failing agriculture, and faced a difficult future, without the resources to move into alternatives, not well placed to take advantage of alternative opportunities. (Heyer 2000a: 1)

Heyer shows how these historically powerful farmers were investing in their sons in such a way as to make it possible for them to do well in areas outside agriculture. When she resurveyed the villages in 2008–9, she found that the area cultivated by the dominant landholders from the Gounder community had further declined, and that though Gounders had continued to invest in land, they were now investing more substantially in non-agricultural activities. They had begun, though modestly, to take greater advantage of alternative opportunities, outside agriculture.[5]

While Djurfeldt and his co-authors do not provide directly comparable information, they do say that real farm incomes increased over the period from 1979 to 2005, though much less than did total incomes: 'the overall increase of 42 per cent … implies a modest growth rate of less than 1.5 per cent per year over the period' (Djurfeldt et al. 2008: 56). This, they say, 'appears to have been a respectable rate of growth of farm income'; and they believe that 'agricultural growth may have contributed about as much as local industrialization to growth of real incomes and thus to poverty alleviation' (Djurfeldt et al. 2008: 50). But the published paper supplies too little information about cropping patterns and productivity for it to be clear that the agricultural economy in the region of Tiruchirappalli that they studied bucked the trends of agricultural growth and productivity found across the state as a whole.

In the circumstances of the stagnating agricultural economy of the state, it is not at all surprising that there should be evidence from village studies of the declining importance of agricultural activity as the base of livelihoods. Non-agricultural activity in rural areas is increasingly significant, as is seasonal migration, and there is abundant evidence of pluriactivity (see Carswell and De Neve 2014a). Jeyaranjan's studies

[5] Elsewhere in Tamil Nadu—though not in Heyer's villages—there are reports of men from dominant land-owning, farming communities finding it increasingly difficult to find brides (Sharada Srinivasan, personal communication).

of rural non-farm activity from villages in four districts showed that only 28 per cent of households remained engaged only in agriculture, and that 58 per cent of those in the labour force were working in non-agricultural occupations.

Varying combinations of 'push' and 'pull' factors account for these trends. In the region of Tiruppur, the decline of agriculture is evidently compensated by the industrial development that has taken place and which has set up relatively attractive opportunities outside agriculture for some (much less so for Dalits and for women, see Heyer 2013, and this volume).[6] Elsewhere, as in Dusi, the decline of agriculture has pushed cultivators (for example, the numerous but historically low-ranked Vanniyars, few of whom are more than small cultivators) into activities such as construction labour and work in catering for marriages. Djurfeldt and his co-authors say that 'almost all growth in population has occurred outside the agrarian sector', and they think that that 'in a foreseeable future, the agrarian population will be down to half the total population' (2008: 52–3)—as it is already in others of the villages of which we have studies. They report from their analysis of generational transfer that there has been a net exit from farming (as seems to have been the case in both Carswell's and Heyer's villages, too). They hypothesise that there has been a movement out of agriculture on the parts both of 'underdogs'—primarily the agricultural labourers—because they have been 'more prone to seize new opportunities in the non-agrarian sector than the landed and middling households' (Djurfeldt et al. 2008: 53), and of the 'top dogs'.[7] The top strata of the villages, these authors argue:

> ... tend to exit agriculture, in part due to the constraints on profitability and the scarcity and 'high cost' of labour (high only in relation to an

[6] Jeyaranjan's rural non-farm study reaches the same conclusion: rural non-farm activity employs men rather than women, and members of SCs less than others.

[7] Judith Heyer points out (2010: 234, 236) that in the Coimbatore/Tiruppur villages she has studied, through the 1990s—against what Djurfeldt et al. (2008) have suggested—smaller farmers moved out of agriculture more significantly than either the large farmers or the landless labourers, and that this has changed only slowly, as the larger farmers' investments in their sons' education have started to take effect.

> earlier situation where they could exploit labour at their will and not in terms of any notion of a decent wage) and the increasing difficulties of extracting rent. Perhaps equally or more important is the fact that they may be simultaneously attracted by growing opportunities in the non-agricultural sector. (Djurfeldt et al. 2008: 53)[8]

In the villages they studied around Villupuram and Cuddalore, Guerin and her co-authors (2014) report that only a little over 12 per cent of all households 'live off agriculture alone'—presumably meaning that only a small proportion of village households now depends entirely on cultivation. In the 'peri-urban' village of Gangaikondan, we found that only in about 20 per cent of households was agriculture the principal source of people's livelihoods—though even in this village, agriculture remained the single most important activity. In her two villages in the industrializing belt of Tiruppur, Grace Carswell found that in one of them around 45 per cent of households depended primarily upon cultivation or on agricultural labour, and in the other, now primarily a power loom village, just 22 per cent (Carswell 2013: 329); Heyer found in her two villages in the same region that households whose primary source of income was agriculture declined from 77 per cent in 1981–2 to 64 per cent in 1996 and 54 per cent in 2008–9 (Heyer 2014: 143). There is a great deal of variation, of course, between locations. In Iruvelpattu, we found that, while the proportion of village households depending largely on agricultural activities had certainly declined, such households still accounted for about 60 per cent of the total; while Arivukkarasi and Nagaraj report from the three villages they studied that 'the farm sector continues to be the predominant source of employment' (2009) and that cultivators and agricultural labour together accounted for upwards of 60 per cent of workers in both 1993 and 2009—though over this period the share of cultivators has declined and that of agricultural labourers increased (even in the peri-urban village of Nesal).

Our conclusion from our study of Iruvelpattu that there is a 'continuing dependence of a majority of households on agriculture in spite of the significant diversification of employment that has

[8] The idea that there is a movement right out of agriculture on the part of the 'top dogs'—presumably meaning the largest landowners—did not, however, gain convincing statistical support in the study, probably because of the 'scant statistical basis' (Djurfeldt et al. 2008: 59–60).

taken place, and of apparent stagnation in the agricultural economy…' (Harriss et al. 2010: 48) most certainly cannot be generalized, but it surely is likely to be true of a great many villages outside industrializing belts like that of Tiruppur and peri-urban locations. Guerin and her co-authors make the very good point, too, that '[t]he rise of non-farm labour does not necessarily translate into a willingness to abandon agriculture [altogether]' (Guerin et al. 2014), for cultural and for status reasons. Matters of identity are involved, '[f]or Dalits and middle castes, land and agriculture continue to play a central role, both in terms of occupation—money from non-farm labour is partly invested in the land—and in terms of identity. Being a landowner with access to water is still a strong factor of distinction. Most caste conflicts between Dalits and middle castes [in the region of study, principally Vanniyars] concern in large part land issues' (Guerin et al. 2014). Carswell (personal communication) reports some variation between Gounder landowners in her Tiruppur villages, with some hiring out their land in order to concentrate on their power looms or on businesses in Tiruppur, while others with business interests in town 'spend their Sundays going back to the *tottam* to check up on things'. S. Iyyampillai, however, in a study of two villages in the former Thanjavur district, in the Kaveri delta, goes so far as to argue that there is a process of 'economic Sanskritization' under way, '[w]hile the less privileged have started acquiring lands … the rich ones show signs of shift away from agriculture and eventually merge with urban economy … the poor try to ape the erstwhile rich class, while the latter switch over to the new and more remunerative non-farm sector' (Iyyampillai 2000).

Agricultural Labour

In this context, what has been happening, specifically, with regard to agricultural labour? While the village studies show a great deal of variation between villages and between different groups in the same village, even amongst Dalits, there are some trends that are widely though not invariably observed (and across much of the country, not just in Tamil Nadu). Agricultural labour seems often to have become more than ever dominated by Dalits, probably because they are often excluded from especially the better rewarded non-agricultural labouring jobs. But there is considerable variation between Dalit groups, as between the lower-ranked Matharis, who are still much more heavily dependent upon agricultural wage work, and 'Adi-Dravidas' (higher ranking SCs) in Carswell's Tiruppur villages. Agricultural labour has also often become increasingly the province of women, for whom other opportunities are much more restricted than they are for men. The incidence of permanently attached labour in agriculture is very much lower than it was, and in many cases has disappeared—though relations of neo-bondage may be found outside agriculture, as for example amongst power loom workers in the Tiruppur villages, where attached labour in agriculture has largely disappeared (Carswell and De Neve 2013). There is an increasing incidence of contract labour in cultivation, which has advantages for employers and for some workers too (see Carswell 2013: 330–1; Heyer 2013).

With specific reference to Tamil Nadu, there appear to be other trends as well: there is what cultivators refer to as a 'labour shortage' in agriculture, reflected in the tendency for real wages in agriculture to have increased, because of the availability of other employment opportunities, and perhaps, latterly, because of MGNREGA; and in the unwillingness of labourers to accept the conditions of agricultural employment that once prevailed, when they were at the beck and call of landowners. 'Labour shortage' is also associated with widespread mechanization, of tillage, harvesting, threshing, and even of weeding, in paddy cultivation (see Harriss et al. 2010, 2012). At the same time there are quite frequent reports of the number of days of work in agriculture per labourer as having declined. This, presumably, is because of the increasing availability of non-agricultural work opportunities, which are generally preferred. As Carswell reports from her Tiruppur villages, agricultural work is generally thought to be the least attractive option—even work in power looms, which is pretty gruelling, may be considered to be a step up from agriculture. Non-agricultural work is found attractive not only in terms of wages, but also because of its cultural significance. It means greater 'sophistication'—especially in the case of jobs in the garments industry of Tiruppur, but in other activities too. In Dusi, Vanniyar girls working in a shoe factory in a nearby industrial estate, though their jobs are insecure, find prestige in wearing a uniform and doing 'company work'.

We briefly review key findings from the various studies which bear out these general points. The peri-urban village of Gangaikondan has an exceptionally small share of workers whose primary occupation is agricultural labour (a little over 8 per cent)—and in this case they are *not* disproportionately Dalit (unusually, because of the success of the Pallars—the principal SC group of this part of Tamil Nadu—in gaining both land and education). In Iruvelpattu the share of households that report their primary source of livelihood as agricultural labour is now down to a quarter of the total, and the absolute numbers of those whose primary occupation is agricultural labour are only a few more than they were in the village as long ago as 1937. In this case, almost 70 per cent of agricultural labour households are Dalit (though now only 50 per cent of all Dalit households are so dependent—a considerable reduction from what obtained in the past). Heyer reports from her Tiruppur villages a decline in the proportion of households depending on agricultural labour from 43 per cent in 1981–2 to 36 per cent in 2008–9 (2014: 144, 147), with the decline having been much less among Dalits. She finds significant improvements in real wages (Heyer 2012: 100). In our studies of both Gangaikondan and Iruvelpattu, we advanced evidence of increased real wages in agriculture though the number of days of agricultural employment per worker have declined, especially for men, given the mechanization of most farm operations.

Djurfeldt and his co-authors find that, over the 25-year-period they have studied in their sample of Tiruchirappalli villages, 'average households have increased their allocation of household labourers to non-farm activities by more than 100 per cent' (2008: 53). They too find that the average number of days of employment in agriculture has generally gone down, except for men in the 'dry' villages they studied, where the decline of the total labour force has brought about an increase in employment for those men who continue to work as agricultural labourers (though the total number of days is still only 91, on average, through the year). Unsurprisingly, agricultural labour incomes have stagnated, especially in the wet/irrigated villages, though we may infer from their account that real wages have increased, as they have elsewhere.

Guerin and her co-authors (2014) find that '[n]on-farm employment is now a fundamental part of rural household income while being a male preserve, agricultural labour being in large part female', and Carswell's findings are very much the same. She, too, says that 'most coolie workers were women' (Carswell 2013: 335). Unusually, Heyer finds in her Tiruppur villages that agricultural labour, though heavily the province of Dalits, has become increasingly male in its composition. Here too, however, women find little opportunity for employment outside agriculture, but have rather withdrawn from the labour force altogether—as has also happened in Thanjavur (Jeyaranjan 2011).[9] Arivukkarasi and Nagaraj find in the three villages of their study that 85 per cent of women workers are still in the farm sector, and that this proportion has registered a marginal increase over time. The loss of employment in silk weaving in these villages (as also in Dusi, which is no longer the weaving village that it had become by 1983) has apparently thrown women workers back into the farm sector. The villages studied by Arivukkarasi and Nagaraj are exceptional, among the village studies we are reviewing here, in that in them it seems that the share of agricultural labour in all employment has been increasing, even if only to a small extent, because of the decline of owner-cultivation and of employment, both in the livestock sector and in silk-weaving. But it is still the case that almost 40 per cent of male workers are engaged in construction and in other activities outside agriculture—and in the peri-urban village of Nesal, this share is almost as high as 60 per cent.

Guerin and Carswell both draw attention to the extent of labour market segmentation on caste lines, and the disabilities, especially of Dalits. As Guerin and her co-authors (2014) say 'old hierarchies persist in the midst of the changes that India has undergone over the past decades'—though as Carswell concludes '[i]t is not simply that Dalits are excluded from urban jobs. Rather, some Dalits, from some villages, have less access to urban jobs than others ... labour market segmentation works differently in localities just a few miles apart' (Carswell 2013: 335; and see Carswell and De Neve 2014). The point is also brought out strongly by Heyer (2000b, 2010).

Land, Class, and Caste Relations

The *Tamil Nadu Economic Appraisal 2010–11* draws attention to the skewed distribution of landholdings in the state, and suggests that it is one of the causes of low productivity (though the basis for this suggestion is not stated). It is said that

[9] Heyer argues that this is a clear sign of increasing well-being in Dalit households.

> The marginal and small farmers who constituted a higher proportion of 91 per cent of the total farmers held a lesser extent of land holdings (59 per cent), whereas medium and big farmers [by which is meant those holding upwards of 4 hectare, or about ten acres] who formed 2.3 per cent of total farmers possessed a larger chunk of 20 per cent of land holdings. (*Tamil Nadu Economic Appraisal* 2010–11: 37–8)

This is even after a small decline in the numbers of medium and big farmers and in the extent of their holdings between 2000–1 and 2005–6.

Several of the recent village studies, given their thematic focus on labour, include only general observations on landholding. There are indications from others, however, of the increased incidence of landlessness, which might be taken as an indicator that the classic process of differentiation with the development of capitalism in agriculture is taking place, with increasing proletarianization and polarization between rural classes. Increased landlessness is shown in the study by Arivukkarasi and Nagaraj who find in their three villages in northern Tamil Nadu that landlessness has increased sharply (between 1993 and 2009) from 46 per cent to 60 per cent of households (and among Dalits from 71 per cent to 80 per cent). In the peri-urban village, Nesal, nearly three-quarters of households (73 per cent) are now landless, including even 62 per cent of the households of the Agamudaiyan Mudaliars, who were clearly the dominant landholding caste of the village in the early 1970s, and were still so in the 1980s (see Harriss 1982). These are striking findings given the conclusions from mobility studies conducted in the same villages in 1983 that showed net reduction in landlessness and entry into agriculture (Harriss 1991), exactly as Djurfeldt and his co-workers also found in their comparable studies in 1979. A similar picture to that from the three northern Tamil Nadu villages comes from Iruvelpattu, where the proportion of landless households increased from 29 per cent in 1981 to 49 per cent in 2008. In Heyer's Tiruppur villages landlessness increased from 40 per cent in 1981–82 to 51 per cent in 2008–9 (Heyer 2014: 140, 142). In the area studied by Djurfeldt et al., on the other hand, it appears that the share of landless households in the wet villages remained more or less constant over the 25-year period from 1979, and that it actually *decreased* quite sharply in the dry ones. The authors find, too, that inequality in the distribution of the operated area in their study region has gone down, as has inequality in the distribution of household income for all agrarian households. They hypothesize that the decline in overall inequality is the outcome of the increased significance in most households of non-farm income.

Djurfeldt and his co-authors specifically address what they refer to as 'the proletarianization and polarization theses' (2008: 55). Clearly, in the region they have studied, as in others, there is evidence of increased proletarianization, given the increasing dependence on various forms of wage labour outside agriculture. But their findings on trends of inequality call into question the idea of 'polarization'. Their view is that what has gone on over the 25 years to 2004 has seen rather the reinforcement of family farming, with increasing reliance on household labour,[10] as both (the erstwhile) poor peasants and landless labourers, and some of the bigger landowners have moved out of agriculture (the latter at least in the sense that their interests are increasingly outside agriculture)—rather than 'polarization'—even though they were not finally able to demonstrate this conclusively through their regression modelling. Heyer's observations on what has happened to the Gounders of her Tiruppur villages (in Chapter 12 of this volume) point to a similar conclusion; and we believe that much the same is probably true of trends in landholding in Dusi, where the remaining large Brahmin landlord-owned holdings that were still present in 1983 have been broken up (though with some sales of land for real estate developers). The focus on 'the differentiation of peasant classes' in much earlier research on agrarian change begins to seem misplaced.

But what of agrarian power, and of landlordism? We have shown the continuing presence of one big Reddiar landlord in Iruvelpattu, even though his power is much more constrained than it was. From the same part of Tamil Nadu, Guerin and her co-authors (2014) report as follows, with regard to the 'semi-agrarian settlements': '[m]ost big landowners, all of whom are high caste, increasingly combine agricultural and non-agricultural incomes, but still farm land and live in the village, such that some vestiges of the old attached labour system remain. They go on to describe two big landowners, each

[10] In other words, they are suggesting that the 'middle peasantry'—as this category was understood in the classical literature on peasant societies—has been gaining ground. This goes against the expectation that these societies will eventually be transformed by a process of 'differentiation' so as to see a class of capitalist farmers on the one hand, and a rural proletariat on the other.

of them owning 70 to 100 acres of land, one of them now living in the US who employs a manager to look after his lands, and the other still resident in the village who has five attached Dalit families, 'two of them from far away who live in the cow shed' (Guerin et al. 2014). We may presume that the situation in the region near Tiruchirappalli that Djurfeldt and his co-workers studied is comparable with this, and these authors note from their studies of inter-generational mobility that it is still the 'big farmers' who face the least risk of downward mobility. Carswell notes of her Tiruppur villages that 'the land-owning Gounders make up the dominant caste in terms of economic wealth and political power ... they own most of the land, wells and bore wells. They are also dominant within the urban and rural parts of the textile industry' (2013: 328). Heyer described the continuing power of the thottam farmers (predominantly Gounders) from her Tiruppur villages at least up to 1996. In spite of their weakened economic position, she wrote, 'these thottam farmers still [as of 1996] had a surprisingly strong hold over labourers and others at the bottom of the hierarchy' (Heyer 2000a: 1). She showed that the Matharis (or Chakkiliyans) in the villages, the most numerous but also lowest status SC group, remained tied to agricultural employment:

> This was partly because they were still getting a *relatively* attractive agricultural employment package in 1996, partly because they were in such a weak position in relation to alternative opportunities ... (and) ... Moreover, housing and increased indebtedness in the villages resulted in the Chakkiliyans being tied in some ways more strongly to agricultural employment in 1996 than 1981–82. Other low caste labourers were getting urban and industrial opportunities that were likely to give them better prospects in the longer term. Chakkiliyans were not. (Heyer 2000b: 1, emphasis added)[11]

Her more recent studies in the same villages, however, show that while Dalits generally remain tied to agricultural employment, their conditions of employment have greatly improved (Heyer, this volume). The power of the Gounders is not what it was (Heyer, personal

[11] Heyer's points here draw attention to the segmentation in labour markets that is the subject of Carswell's article (2013), and that is also discussed by Guerin and her co-authors (2014).

communication). The same is true of the Naidus of Palakkurichi. They are still the largest landowners but their control over the village, in 2000, was much less than it had been before (Manimohan and Jeyaranjan 2000). Agrarian power persists, therefore—very significant disparities in land ownership remain, and larger landowners are still commonly also moneylenders[12]—but it is less significant than it was, and the classic landlordism of the past has certainly declined (see Harriss 2013a). In Gangaikondan, we know of a number of big landowners, even after the departure of the Brahmins, who controlled virtually all of the land of the village a century ago, and of most of the Forward Caste Pillais. But the big landowners include SC Pallars, as well as others from historically low ranking castes, and we were unable to find indications of the persistence here of landlord power. This is a reflection of relative equality of social and economic status between the Pallars in this village, at least, and the otherwise most numerous caste community, the Thevars, and of the political power of the Pallars. In the northern Tamil Nadu villages studied by Arivukkarasi and Nagaraj there is evidence—as we noted above—that the formerly dominant landowners, the Agamudaiyan Mudaliars are leaving the land, possibly to the advantage of the Yadhavas, who resemble much more the 'family farmers', relying extensively on household labour, whose position is described by Djurfeldt and his co-authors in their study.

All the studies we are considering record the near disappearance of Forward Castes from the villages, as is the case of the Reddiars of Iruvelpattu, and of Brahmins and Pillais from Gangaikondan, and of Brahmins from Dusi. Djurfeldt et al. say of their wet villages that 'Brahmins used to own the lands farmed by Dalit tenants (but) today most of the lands have been taken over by middle and Dalit castes' (2008: 52). Guerin and her co-authors, note that 'the upper castes have mostly moved away from the villages in recent decades to nearby towns, adopting urban jobs and lifestyles' (2014), as is the case of the Agamudaiyan Mudaliars further north. In Iruvelpattu and Gangaikondan, certainly, Dalits are becoming relatively more numerous in relation to other

[12] Carswell tells us that people in the villages she has studied usually prefer to borrow from the ex-landlords, rather than from roaming moneylenders who charge higher rates on interest.

communities, and the caste structure is becoming increasingly simplified. There is a smaller range of caste groups in the villages than was the case in the past, as many of the specialist castes have moved away. Over much of northern Tamil Nadu, Vanniyars and Paraiyars are the two major population groups in the villages, and increasingly confront each other. As Guering and her co-authors note 'Vanniyars are a farming caste with a low ritual rank, classified as Most Backward Classes' (Guering et al. 2014), though they are here the locally dominant caste community, according to the way this idea has been used by anthropologists. Conflict often breaks out between them and the Paraiyars (as is the case in Iruvelpattu). Much the same is true of Thevars and Pallars in the southern districts, as we recount in our study of Gangaikondan.

Though residues of landed power persist, the major landowning castes no longer enjoy the same extensive powers over others that the village landlords once had.[13] As Djurfeldt and his co-authors put it 'opening of opportunities in the off-farm sector and policy interventions including affirmative action of various sorts have made it possible to an increasing extent for the Dalits to escape the indignity and degradation of village society' (Djurfeldt et al. 2008; and see Carswell and De Neve 2014a). This may mean that 'deprived of a cheap source of labour, the old patrons opt out of agriculture', as has certainly happened in the case of the Reddiars of Iruvelpattu (Djurfeldt et al. 2008: 52). The research by Djurfeldt et al. (2008), by Guerin and her co-authors (2014), and by Heyer (2012), as well as our own studies in Iruvelpattu and Gangaikondan, show improvements in the living standards of many Dalits in rural Tamil Nadu.

Djurfeldt et al. make the point rather too strongly, however, when they say 'being a Dalit is no longer as big a handicap in economic terms' (2008: 59) because we have to note the strong evidence in these village studies of labour market segmentation and of the disabilities confronted by Dalits in general and by the lowest ranked Dalit groups in particular. Such groups, like the Matharis/Chakkiliyans of Heyer's Coimbatore

[13] There is some irony in the fact that the one village of which the recent study reports the persistence of labour attachment, records an incident in which a landowner tied a Dalit labourer to a tree and subjected him to a public flogging, is a village dominated by Vanniyars, considered a 'Most Backward Class'. See Rukmani (2000).

villages, must often find it difficult to stand up against those who are locally powerful, and where they are bound by indebtedness (on which see the studies both by Carswell [2013] and by Guerin and her co-authors [2014]). Heyer concludes a recent essay with the words '[n]either the modernization of agriculture, nor urbanization and industrialization, has led to significant changes in the *relative* position of SCs. SCs still face greater barriers to progress than others among the working poor' (2010: 241, emphasis added).[14] And though many of the Dalits of rural Tamil Nadu, like those Iruvelpattu, may have loosened ties of dependence, they still exercise little leverage over the political space.

Social Policy Interventions

A key question is, then, whether the recent raft of legislation that has created a new social welfare architecture for India—legislation that includes the MGNREGA of 2005, the Right to Education Act of 2009, and the Food Security of Act of 2013—has the potential to transform the state of ill-being especially of Dalits, and of women, all of whom as the studies we have reviewed clearly show, are discriminated against in labour markets. It is too soon for us to be able to reach firm conclusions, but there are certainly indications of the positive impact of these new measures. It has come to be recognized fairly widely that Tamil Nadu has done, relatively, much better than most other states in regard to human development—indeed, probably better than all other states with the exception of Kerala. All the studies we have considered make some reference to the significance of social welfare interventions, such as the public distribution system (PDS), which has never been targeted in Tamil Nadu, and has a much better record for its efficiency than in other states (Himanshu and Sen 2011); the noon meals scheme and the Integrated Child Development Scheme. The public healthcare system, too, generally works better in the state than elsewhere. Heyer provides an overview of the significance of social welfare interventions in the villages she has studied, reporting that

[14] The point is confirmed in Jeyaranjan's rural non-farm study. Members of 'Other Castes'—neither Scheduled nor Backward—are much more likely to get into the better paid jobs in manufacturing.

Dalit labourers talk 'about not having to work as much, or as hard, because of the PDS (etc.)' (2012: 102), and showing that '[b]y 2008–9 it was clear that (state social welfare policy) was making a major contribution to labourers' standards of living, something that it had not been doing either in 1996, or in 1981–82' (Heyer 2012: 106). Our own conclusions, from our study of Iruvelpattu in particular, are similar to Heyer's. But village studies, so far, tell us relatively little about how and why these schemes function, as it seems, better than elsewhere in the country, or about their outcomes—except in general terms. A partial exception is that there are now village studies of the implementation of the MGNREGS.

Grace Carswell, with Geert De Neve, has recently completed a study of the implementation of MGNREGA in the two Tiruppur villages in which she had previously done the research on which we have commented in this chapter (Carswell and De Neve 2014b). In 2011, the two researchers conducted a survey of 109 MGNREGA workers, carried on ethnographic research in the villages and at worksites, and interviewed site organizers and officials at different levels. They set out to interrogate different meanings of 'success' in regard to the programme, but they focus on 'localized understandings of success and ... explore how success is understood and expressed by different social actors' (2014b: 3). Jeyaranjan (2011) conducted similar research in a village in Thanjavur, coming up with broadly similar findings, for the period after 2010 when the work schedule in the programme was relaxed and wages increased, which resulted in 'a tenfold increase in the number who sought work' (Jeyaranjan 2011: 66). Jeyaranjan is, however, perhaps less optimistic about the transformative potential of MGNREGA than are Carswell and De Neve.

According to these studies, MGNREGA in Tamil Nadu can be considered to be a success from several different points of view. The evidence, according to Carswell and De Neve (2014b: 19):

> ... shows that MGNREGA reaches the poorest and most vulnerable sections of the rural population, including the old, infirm and widowed, and that Dalits and women are the primary beneficiaries ... in terms of providing a degree of social security, MGNREGA is undoubtedly a success in Tamil Nadu. It is also clear that the workers themselves perceive the scheme as valuable to their livelihoods and to the maintaining of minimum levels of consumption.

Jeyaranjan, too, finds that the reworked MGNREGA, with other social interventions, has led 'to a new kind of diversification … towards a better livelihood for the poor' (2011: 73). As Carswell and De Neve say, however, the question of whether the scheme has brought about empowerment through rights-based law is harder to assess. They found 'clear evidence of empowerment both through increased wage levels in agriculture and a strengthened bargaining power of rural wage labourers' (Carswell and De Neve 2014b: 19)—which has been particularly significant for low-caste women. On the other hand, there is little evidence of the realization of the governance reform through the scheme that some observers have thought possible because of the clause in the act requiring the conduct of social audits (Harriss 2013b, referring to arguments put by Rob Jenkins). Carswell and De Neve (2014b) concluded that 'while the scheme appeared to be implemented in an efficient and transparent way [being driven by a bureaucracy, tightly supervised from the chief minister's office, "that is at least to some extent independent from local village elites" (p. 581)], there was no evidence that it established a new form of governance based on grassroots democracy' (p. 19). Such socially transformative potential as the scheme has, therefore, does not extend to rural people's relationships with the state.

⋆ ⋆ ⋆

Commenting on findings from the Report No. 554 of the NSSO, on the 2011–12 round of studies on employment, the *Sunday Times* (for 9 February 2014) argued that 'the jobs scenario has been decidedly grim for more than a decade', and that this is a key issue for the 2014 general election. The phenomenon of 'jobless growth' has been widely commented upon. Nationally, the *Sunday Times* says, agricultural employment 'the mainstay for over two-thirds of the people, has practically not grown (in the thirteen years from 1999–2000)'. The sectors in which employment has grown are construction, which is now the second biggest employer in rural areas after agriculture, trade, and hotels and restaurants ('which includes all petty shopkeepers, hawkers, roadside food-sellers etc.'), and 'other services' (including personal services 'like cooks, maids, guards, washer men, and so on'), As the *Sunday Times* goes on to say 'the booming sectors that are drawing people away from failing agriculture are very low-paying. Also, these jobs are often seasonal, mostly contractual and with very minimalist facilities or benefits (offering only basic subsistence)'.

These national trends, over the more recent decade or so of the era of India's economic liberalization when there has been sustained economic growth, are observed in Tamil Nadu as well, as the village studies on which we have commented here broadly show. Indeed, the village studies show that agricultural employment in the state, both in own account cultivation, and in agricultural wage work, has declined significantly, and more than in the country as a whole. Agriculture still remains the most important single sector for employment, but in many villages it now provides the main source of income for less than half the households. Construction probably is the next most important source of employment, but there is also a good deal of employment in manufacturing, in what is one of India's most industrialized states with a relatively highly diversified economy. According to the *Annual Survey of Industries* (ASI) data for 2005–6, Tamil Nadu then held the first position in terms of the number of factories and total number of persons engaged in various industrial processes across the country. Tamil Nadu is also, as we said at the outset, India's most highly urbanized state, with significant numbers of smaller towns and cities, and a high level of connectivity. This has facilitated the movement of labour, both in daily commuting (which was the case of 45 per cent of the workers in Jeyaranjan's sample of twelve villages in his rural non-farm study), and in longer term circular migration, whether to brickfields and construction sites, for sugar cane cutting (as from the villages studied by Guerin et al. 2014), or for other activities.

Whereas it is quite often argued that workers are being pushed out of agriculture into 'distress' employment in other sectors (which may be the implication of the report in the *Sunday Times* from which we have quoted) there is little indication of this in the village studies from Tamil Nadu. Rather, these studies generally show up the tightening of rural labour markets, and increasing real wages, and (with less certainty) incomes, both in agriculture and outside it. There is probably less reliance on poorly remunerated self-employment in the state ('reluctant entrepreneurship') than is the case elsewhere in the country. These trends have been enhanced latterly by the extent of welfare provisioning in the state, as Judith Heyer, in particular, has argued from her village studies. The availability of cheap, and now free, foodgrains through the PDS, and of employment through MGNREGA have further weakened the historic hold of landowners over rural labour. Though it is certainly too soon to speak of the disappearance of agrarian power, based on the continuing inequality in land ownership in the state, the village studies all tell of its decline. The phenomenon of landlordism, whereby a small number of larger landowners, usually from higher castes, exerted their sway over rural labour and society, through land-leasing and labour attachment on onerous terms, often combined with money-lending and speculative trading, has very largely disappeared from rural Tamil Nadu. Though there is evidence of increased landlessness from a number of the village studies, there is little or no evidence that this has meant the consolidation of larger landholdings. Rather, in some cases, small-scale 'family farming' (term introduced by Djurfeldt et al. 2014), relying substantially on household labour, may well have been strengthened.

Yet we do not mean to paint a Panglossian picture. The village studies we have been able to study bear out Heyer's (2012: 106) conclusions:

> Improved terms and conditions of employment and expanded state social welfare policy have combined to produce ... substantially improved standards of living for the labourer population between 1981–82 and 2008–09. It is only in comparison with what were very poor standards in 1981–82 [or, we can add, 1991–92] that this looks impressive though. Labourers were still working hard for long hours for low pay. There were still few opportunities to move into employment other than low-skilled manual labour. State social policies may have improved the conditions of manual labourers, but they were not equipping many to move out of manual labour. These were policies supporting an economy relying on large quantities of relatively unskilled labour still.

We also note the strong evidence from the village studies of the continuing exclusion of Dalits, and of women, from better-paying non-agricultural activities. Tamil Nadu still has a ways to go in the achievement of greater social justice.

References

Arivukkarasi, N. and K. Nagaraj. 2009. 'Some aspects of socio-economic change in rural Arani with special reference to the silk weaving industry', unpublished manuscript, Madras Institute of Development Studies, Chennai.

Carswell, G. 2013. 'Dalits and Local Labour Markets in Rural India: Experiences from the Tiruppur Textile Region in Tamil Nadu', *Transactions of the Institute of British Geographers*, 38: 325–38.

Carswell, G. and G. De Neve. 2013. 'From Field to Factory: Tracing Transformations in Bonded Labour in the Tiruppur Region, Tamil Nadu', *Economy and Society*, 42 (3): 430–54.

———. 2014a. 'T-Shirts and Tumblers: Caste, Dependency and Work under Neo-Liberalism in South India', *Contributions to Indian Sociology*, 48 (1): 103–31.

———. 2014b. 'MGNREGA in Tamil Nadu: A Story of Success and Transformation', *Journal of Agrarian Change*, 14 (4): 564–85.

Department of Evaluation and Applied Research, Government of Tamil Nadu. various years. *Tamil Nadu—An Economic Appraisal.*

Djurfeldt, G., V. Athreya, N. Jayakumar, S. Lindberg, A. Rajagopal and R. Vidyasagar. 2008. 'Agrarian Change and Social Mobility in Tamil Nadu', *Economic and Political Weekly*, XLIII (45): 50–61.

Guerin, I., G. Venkatasubramanian, and S. Michiels. 2014. 'Labour in Contemporary South India', in J. Heyer and B. Harriss-White (eds), *Capitalism in Development*. London: Routledge.

Harriss, J. 1982. *Capitalism and Peasant Farming: Agrarian Structure and Ideology in Northern Tamil Nadu*. Bombay: Oxford University Press.

———. 1991. 'The Green Revolution in North Arcot: Economic Trends, Household Mobility and the Politics of an "Awkward Class"', in P. Hazell and C. Ramasamy (eds), *The Green Revolution Reconsidered: The Impact of HYVs in South India*, pp. 57–84. Baltimore and London: Johns Hopkins University Press.

———. 2013a. 'Does "Landlordism" Still Matter? Reflections on Agrarian Change in India', *Journal of Agrarian Change*, 13 (3): 351–64.

———. 2013b. 'Audacious Reforms? India's New Rights Agenda: An Introduction', *Pacific Affairs*, 86 (3) 561–8.

Harriss, J., J. Jeyaranjan, and K. Nagaraj. 2010. 'Land, Labour and Caste Politics in Rural Tamil Nadu in the 20th Century: Iruvelpattu (1916–2008)', *Economic and Political Weekly*, XLV (31): 47–61.

———. 2012. 'Rural Urbanism in Tamil Nadu: Notes on a "Slater" Village, Gangaikondan, 1916–2012', *Review of Agrarian Studies*, 2 (2).

Harriss-White, B. and S. Janakarajan. 1997. 'From Green Revolution to Rural Industrial Revolution in South India', *Economic and Political Weekly*, XXII (25): 1469–77.

———. 2004. *Rural India Facing the 21st Century: Essays on Long Term Village Change and Recent Development Policy*. London: Anthem Press.

Heyer, J. 2000a. 'The Changing Position of Thottam Farmers in Villages in Rural Coimbatore, Tamil Nadu, between 1981/2 and 1996', Working Paper No. 59, Queen Elizabeth House, University of Oxford, Oxford.

Heyer, J. 2000b. 'The Changing Position of Agricultural Labourers in Villages in Rural Coimbatore, Tamil Nadu, between 1981/2 and 1996', Working Paper No. 57, Queen Elizabeth House, University of Oxford, Oxford.

———. 2010. 'The Marginalization of Dalits in a Modernizing Economy', in B. Harriss-White and J. Heyer (eds), *The Comparative Political Economy of Development, Africa and South Asia*, pp. 252–74. London: Routledge.

———. 2012. 'Labour Standards and Social Policy: A South Indian Case Study', *Global Labour Journal*, 3 (1): 91–117.

———. 2013. 'Integration Into a Global Production Network: Impacts on Labour in Tiruppur's Hinterlands', *Oxford Development Studies*, 41 (3): 307–21.

———. 2014. 'Dalits in Industrializing Villages near Coimbatore and Tiruppur: 1981/2, 1996, and 2008/9', in V.K. Ramachandran and M. Swaminathan (eds), *Dalit Households in Village Economies*. New Delhi: Tulika.

Himanshu and A. Sen. 2011. 'Why Not a Universal Food Security Legislation?' *Economic and Political Weekly*, XLVI (12): 38–47.

Iyyampillai, S. 2000. 'Changing Trends and Implications of Landholding Patterns in Thanjavur', manuscript, Dynamics of Rural Transformation in Tamil Nadu—Study Series, Institute of Development Alternatives, Chennai.

Jeyaranjan, J. 2011. 'Women and Pro-Poor Policies in Rural Tamil Nadu: An Examination of Practices and Responses', *Economic and Political Weekly*, XLVI (43): 64–74.

———. 2012. 'A Study on the Rural Non-farm Employment in Tamil Nadu', manuscript, Institute of Development Alternatives, Chennai.

Lerche, J. 2010. 'From "Rural Labour" to "Classes of Labour": Class Fragmentation, Caste and Class Struggle at the Bottom of the Indian Labour Hierarchy', in B. Harriss-White and J. Heyer (eds), *The Comparative Political Economy of Development, Africa and South Asia*, pp. 64–85. London: Routledge.

Manimohan, R. and J. Jeyaranjan. 2000. 'Resurvey of Palakkurichi (Slater) Village', manuscript, Dynamics of Rural Transformation in Tamil Nadu—Study Series, Institute for Development Alternatives, Chennai.

Rukmani, R. 2000. 'Socio-economic Changes in the Village of Arkavadi', manuscript, Dynamics of Rural Transformation in Tamil Nadu—Study Series, Institute for Development Alternatives, Chennai.

HIMANSHU
PETER LANJOUW
RINKU MURGAI
NICHOLAS STERN

Non-farm Diversification, Inequality, and Mobility in Palanpur*

One of the important objectives of the Palanpur survey has been to track the evolution of incomes and the drivers of change over time.[1] While inextricably linked to the way agriculture has been organized in the village, the evolution of incomes in the village has been a

* This chapter arises out of an ongoing project to resurvey the village of Palanpur in 2008–10 funded by the UK Department for International Development (DFID). The Palanpur project is a collaborative effort based at the Asia Research Centre (ARC), London School of Economics (LSE), and at the Centre de Sciences Humaines (CSH), Delhi. We acknowledge the excellent research assistance by Maria Mini Jose and Vaishnavi Surendra. We are grateful for comments received at the conference on 'Longitudinal Village Surveys' at Jawaharlal Nehru University (JNU), New Delhi, 2012. The views in this article are those of the authors and should not be interpreted as those of the World Bank, JNU, or LSE. All errors are our own.

[1] However, tracking household incomes over a long period is not straightforward, notwithstanding the close attention to the quality of data collected.

focal point of the earlier analysis. Data from the recent round, however, suggests that agriculture now plays a less important role in the village economy than in the years of the previous surveys. With the expansion of outside jobs and migration, employment and income sources have diversified; even within the village, a household's well-being is no longer dependent on income from agriculture. While the non-farm sector has emerged as a major driver of change in the village, access to this sector and its impact on income inequality and mobility are not so clear. In Palanpur, poor people were historically sharply disadvantaged in terms of access to a non-farm sector that started to become significant for the village economy in the 1970s. Given that one of the important findings from the previous surveys has been the role of outside jobs as a driver of change (Lanjouw and Stern 1998), it is important to understand the impact of the growth of non-farm employment and income not just on village economy but on income inequality and mobility, particularly for those at the bottom of income and caste hierarchy.

The expansion of non-farm employment has also brought in widespread prosperity in the village, as seen through many of the indicators of well-being. But a puzzling feature of this increased prosperity is the sharp increase in income inequality, despite the evidence of the broadening of access to non-farm incomes and employment for the poorer sections of the village. The analysis of the preliminary evidence, however, suggests that such an outcome may not be entirely surprising, given the nature of economic opportunities that the non-farm sector presents. Unlike the evidence in earlier surveys of networks, social status, and other factors instrumental in defining access to non-farm jobs, these factors appear less relevant to low-productivity informal sector jobs where most of the non-farm expansion has occurred.[2] What is also obvious

---

Some of the problems are methodological but some of them are also because of the inherent inability of surveys to capture aspects of income and mobility that can have only very limited quantification. However, since Palanpur offers the unique advantage of having very detailed longitudinal data for a single village, where measures of income, occupation, and related covariates are available for a fairly long period of time, it presents an important opportunity to analyse the factors that have contributed to the growth of the village economy.

[2] However, high paying regular jobs and capital intensive non-farm self-employment opportunities are still being rationed out of the reach of poorer households.

is that the economic opportunities opened up by the non-farm sector remain universally accessible mainly at the bottom end of wage rates and activities. This process is not dissimilar to the story of inter-sectoral transfer described by Arthur Lewis (1954), in which growth takes place against a background of labour transfer out of traditional subsistence cultivation and agricultural wage labour toward a modern sector. This is also consistent with observations of Fields (1980, 2000) that such a process is able to generate the well-known 'inverted U-curve' of first rising and then falling inequality, first described by Kuznets (1955, 1963). Indeed, this is very much what Kuznets himself had in mind. What is interesting to observe from the Palanpur context is that this process can occur *within* a village, as well as in the links to activities outside the village, as a result of the modern economy entering into the village economy via non-agricultural activities.

Clearly changing activities within the village economy does not involve migration; but in addition, and importantly, many of the jobs outside the village involve commuting, not migration—it is the latter in the more conventionally used narratives describing the Lewis (1954) process.

The trend towards non-farm diversification in Palanpur also resonates with the broader trend in India, which has seen an acceleration in non-farm employment in the last decade. For the first time since Independence, the period from 2004–5 onwards has shown an absolute decline in the number of workers in agriculture. While the period since 2004–5 is also the period of slowest growth in employment, the fact that this low growth in employment is seen largely as a result of decline in agricultural employment, with non-farm employment creation accelerating during the same period, is also consistent with rising prosperity in rural areas. Along with a faster rate of growth of agriculture during 2004–5 to 2011–12, the decline in the absolute number of workers in agriculture also implies a narrowing down of the gap between the per worker productivity in agriculture vis-à-vis the non-farm sector. The analysis also shows that the growth of the non-farm sector has also been accompanied by the declining 'quality' of non-farm jobs, notably in the direction of increased casualization of non-farm employment, away from regular, salaried employment. Nonetheless, this trend appears consistent with the evidence of falling rural poverty. Preliminary analysis also suggests that the increase in non-farm employment opportunities has also translated into improved access for the historically disadvantaged segments of rural society to non-farm employment. Given that returns from casual non-farm employment are still higher than from agricultural labour (though markedly lower than from regular non-farm employment), the growing participation of disadvantaged groups in this (sub) sector is likely to have been a positive force for poverty reduction. We find a similar process underway in Palanpur, although the extent of poverty reduction may have been lower and improvement in other indicators of well-being do not suggest an acceleration in the rate of improvement.

The chapter begins by examining National Sample Survey Office (NSSO) survey data to look at the transformation of India's countryside currently underway. We examine in detail the evidence covering the period between 1983 and 2011–12, documenting a process of diversification out of agriculture that is slow but accelerating. Subsequently, we describe the process of non-farm diversification in Palanpur and its implications for inequality and mobility, particularly of disadvantaged groups.

Economic Diversification and Rural Poverty: All-India Trends

After a long period during which the share of agriculture in the Indian labour force remained constant, its share started declining in the mid-1970s, a trend that continues to this day. The share of the rural non-farm sector (all rural employment activities other than agriculture and its associated enterprises) has been increasing ever since (see Figure 11.1).[3]

In fits and starts (with a slowdown immediately following the reforms in the early 1990s), the pace of diversification away from agriculture further speeded up in the 1993–2004 decade, especially after 1999.[4] Over the first period, 1983 to 1993–4, the average annual growth in non-farm jobs was just over 2 per cent. Between 1993–4 and 1999–2000, this increased

[3] Unless mentioned otherwise, the NSSO-based employment data presented in this chapter refer to the Usual Principal and Subsidiary workers ('usual status') definition of employment.

[4] Eswaran et al. 2009; Himanshu 2008; Lanjouw and Murgai 2009. Sen and Jha (2005) contend that there was no acceleration in the first half of the nineties due to a decline in public expenditure in large parts of rural India in the post-reforms period. Accelerated diversification of the rural workforce towards non-farm activities is due to recovery in the sector since 1999–2000 as well as a shift of workers out of agriculture due to a series of droughts in the early 2000s that placed a great deal of pressure on agricultural incomes (Himanshu 2011).

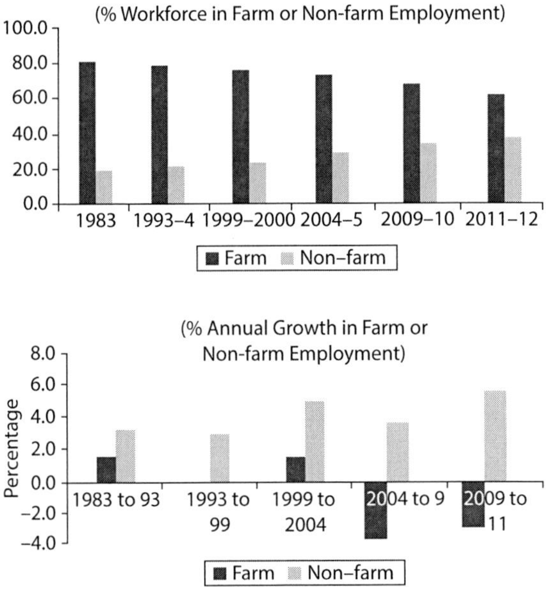

FIGURE 11.1 The Rural Non-farm Sector is Expanding, at a Pace that Exceeds that of Agriculture

Sources: Estimates based on 'Employment and Unemployment Survey' (EUS) of respective NSSO rounds of 1983, 1993–4, 1999–2000, 2004–5, 2009–10, and 2011–12.

Notes: Employment defined on the basis of principal-cum-subsidiary ('usual') status. Farm versus non-farm assignment is based on workers' reported industry, occupation, and employment status. Numbers of farm and non-farm workers are calculated using (a) estimated proportions from unit level data, and (b) total rural workforce as in Sundaram (2007).

to 3 per cent, and from 1999 to 2004–5, this increased again to 4 per cent, and has continued to increase further with non-farm jobs increasing by 5.6 per cent per annum between 2009–10 and 2011–12. In the eighties, of the nearly 40 million additional rural jobs generated, the majority (6 out of every 10) were in the farm sector. Subsequently, between 1993 and 2004, non-farm employment growth outstripped agricultural employment: of the 56 million new rural jobs created over this period, 6 out of every 10 were in the non-farm sector (Figure 11.2). After 2004–5 these trends become more dramatic as there was a significant net decline of employment in the farm sector, and the non-farm sector thus accounted for the entirety of new employment in rural areas.

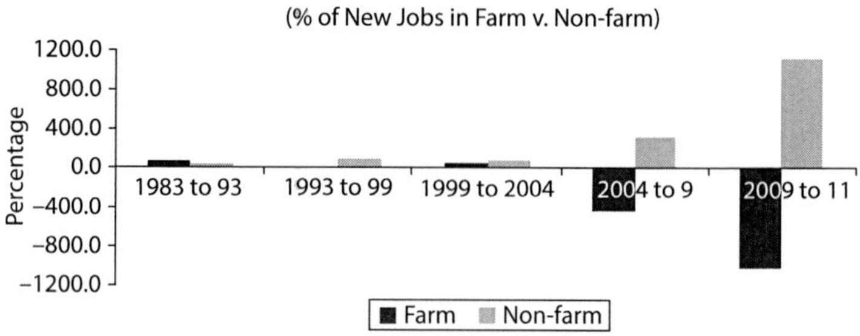

FIGURE 11.2 The Non-farm Sector is the Source of Most New Jobs
Sources: Estimates based on 'Employment and Unemployment Survey' (EUS) of respective NSSO rounds for 1983, 1993–4, 1999–2000, 2004–5, 2009–10, and 2011–12.
Notes: Employment defined on the basis of principal-cum-subsidiary ('usual') status. Farm versus non-farm assignment is based on workers' reported industry, occupation, and employment status. Numbers of farm and non-farm workers are calculated using (a) estimated proportions from unit level data, and (b) total rural workforce as in Sundaram (2007).

Nationally representative data on rural non-farm income is not available over time. But, according to the 2004 NCAER-University of Maryland India Human Development Survey (Dubey 2008), nearly one-half (48 per cent) of the income of the average rural household came from non-farm earnings in the early 2000s (Dubey 2008). This is true also of farming households for whom the share of their income from non-agricultural activities (46 per cent) matches the contribution of agricultural incomes (Cai, de Janvry, and Sadoulet 2008).

The rural non-farm sector displays enormous heterogeneity, both in terms of sectors, and in terms of type of employment. The evidence points to a growing, but increasingly casualized, rural non-farm sector. The casualization of non-farm work is evident in the types of sectors where jobs are being created and the types of jobs generated.

While manufacturing activities are often the first that come to mind when discussing the non-farm sector, by 2011–12 services (transport, trade, communications, and social services) provided employment for nearly two-fifths of rural non-farm workers (Figure 11.3). Less than a quarter was in manufacturing; the remaining 30 per cent in construction. These shares have changed significantly over time. In particular, note the rapid rise of construction since the early 1990s: from only 11 per cent of

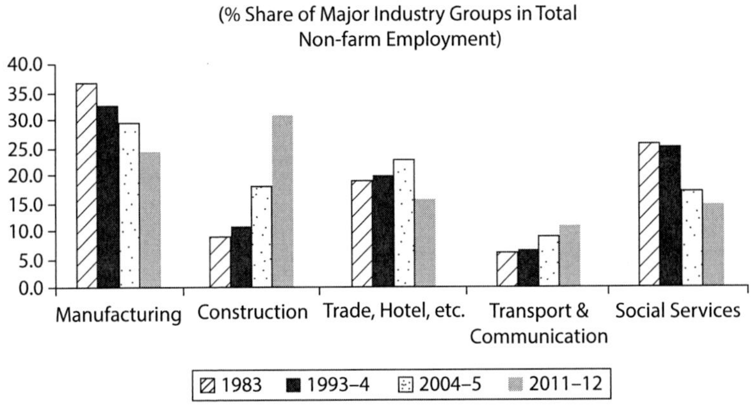

FIGURE 11.3 Construction is the Major Employer in Non-farm Sector

Sources: Estimates based on 'Employment and Unemployment Survey' (EUS) of respective NSSO rounds for 1983, 1993–4, 1999–2000, 2004–5, 2009–10, and 2011–12.

Note: (a) Social services include public administration, defence, education, health, community, and other personal or household services.

rural non-farm employment in 1993 to 31 per cent in 2011–12. The share of social services (which includes public administration and community services, as well as health and education) shows a corresponding decline over the same period: from 26 per cent to 15 per cent.

Non-farm activities can be crudely divided into three sub-sectors representing very different types of employment: *regular, salaried employment* where the worker has a long-term contract that does not require daily, weekly, or monthly renewal; *casual wage labour* that entails a daily or periodic renewal of work contract; and *self-employment* where the worker operates her own business.

Regular non-farm employment is typically highly sought after and most clearly associated with relatively high and stable incomes. But only 22 per cent of the non-farm workforce held regular salaried jobs in 2011–12. Of the rural non-farm workforce, 37 per cent was employed as casual labourers. While it is generally thought to be less demeaning to a worker than agricultural wage labour, and it pays better, casual non-farm work may be both physically demanding as well as hazardous (construction, rickshaw pulling, industrial workshops, etc.). In 2011–12, the remaining two fifths of the non-farm rural workforce was involved in self-employment. Non-farm self-employment activities can be residual, last-resort options (for example, unpaid family labour and wage work concealed as self-employment under different forms of contracting out tasks) as well as high return activities. Whether they are of the former or latter variant generally depends on the skills and capital available for deployment.

The growth of casual employment accelerated between 1983 and 2011–12, dramatically so between 2004–5 and 2009–10 (Figure 11.4). Between 2004–5 and 2011–12, growth in regular non-farm employment tapered off, and self-employment growth halted altogether. The share of the self-employed fell to just over 40 per cent, while that of casual employment grew from 24 per cent in 1983 to 29 per cent in 2004 and continued to rise to just under 40 per cent in 2009–10. The share of regular employment fell slowly but consistently from 24 per cent to 22 per cent.

The declining share of regular employment between 1983 and 2009–10 is surprising since, in the normal course of development, one would expect the share of regular jobs to increase. The slower growth of jobs in the regular sector since 1993 would seem to be linked to the absence of growth in social services employment, in which regular jobs would be more common, and the very rapid growth of construction and other services, in which casual jobs would predominate.

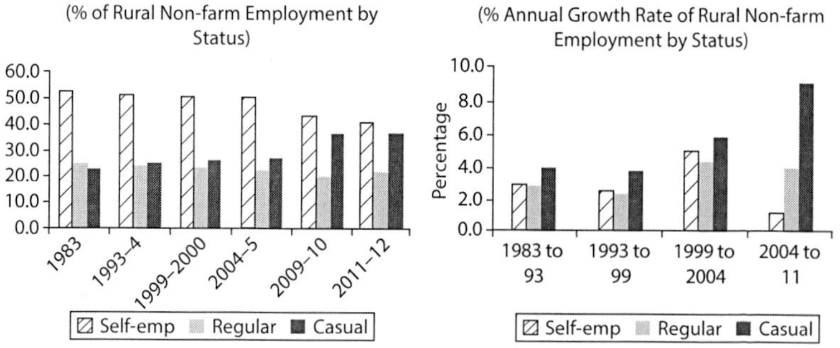

FIGURE 11. 4 Growth of All Three Types of Non-farm Jobs, 1983 to 2009–10
Sources: Estimates based on 'Employment and Unemployment Survey' (EUS) of respective NSSO rounds of 1983, 1993–4, 1999–2000, 2004–5, 2009–10, and 2011–12.
Notes: Self-emp – Self-employment, Regular – Regular Salaried/Wage Employee.

Indeed, the puzzle becomes why the number of regular jobs has gone up at all after 2009–10, rather than down. The contraction of jobs in the public sector, which has historically been the primary source of salaried work in rural areas, has been offset by a growth in private sector jobs. Public sector jobs are highly coveted for the job security and the wage premium they provide over private sector jobs. Private sector jobs share few of these characteristics.[5] Unfortunately, the NSSO does not collect data on income from self-employment. Since the self-employed make up more than 40 per cent of the rural non-farm workforce, this makes it impossible to analyse changes in the income of the non-farm workforce. Our discussion is perforce restricted to the *employed* non-farm workforce.

Against the background of a growing rural non-farm sector, poverty in rural India has been falling. A complicating factor in tracking the evolution of poverty from the early 1980s to 2009–10, is that official poverty lines have changed. The World Bank (2011) documents poverty trends between 1983 and 2004–5 as having declined from 46.5 per cent of the population in 1983, to 36.8 per cent in 1993–4 and declining further to 28.1 per cent in 2004–5. These estimates are based on the report published by the 1993 Planning Commission Expert Group on Estimation of the Proportion of the Poor. In 2012, the Planning Commission published new official poverty lines for 2009–10 in its Press Note on Poverty Estimates. These new poverty lines address a number of concerns that had been raised with respect to the earlier series, but it has not been possible so far, to back date these poverty lines all the way to 1983. Based on the new poverty lines, poverty in rural India declined from 50.1 per cent in 1993–4 to 41.8 per cent in 2004–5 to 33.8 per cent in 2009–10 and 25.7 per cent in 2011–12. Both sets of poverty lines document a steady decline in rural poverty, although the new lines

[5] Using the ARIS-REDS panel data set (1969–99), Foster and Rosenzweig (2003 and 2004) report very rapid growth in rural factory employment. In their data, rural factory employment increased tenfold between 1980 and 1999; about half the villages in their sample were located near a factory, and in those villages, 10 per cent of the male labour was employed in a factory. NSSO data over the same period do not show any such growth although they do confirm the importance of manufacturing as the next most important source of salaried jobs after the public sector.

indicate that, even at the end of the 2000s, more than a third of the population in rural India remains below the poverty line. This conclusion also resonates with estimates published by the World Bank on poverty in rural India based on an internationally comparable poverty line of $1.25 in Purchasing power parity (PPP) terms. Indeed, the World Bank series can be scrutinized for trends all the way back to 1983, and documents that in terms of both percentage points, and percent declines, poverty has fallen at an increasing pace over time (Table 11.1).

In an article, Himanshu et al. (2013) document that the expansion of non-farm employment in rural India has increasingly been drawing from ranks of the socially disadvantaged. This is in large part due to the fact that the sub-sector that has seen the most rapid growth in recent years has been casual rural non-farm employment. This is the segment that has the highest participation by the socially disadvantaged (lower caste) and the illiterate. Given that casual non-farm employment, though worth considerably less than regular employment, still pays considerably better than agriculture (the wage premium is around 40–50 per cent in 2011–12) the direct impact of non-farm growth on rural poverty in India has thus been positive. Himanshu et al. (2013) also point out that direct effects are likely to be reinforced by indirect effects. Notably, they find evidence from regression analysis based on a region-level panel covering the period 1983 to 2004–5 that expansion of the non-farm sector is accompanied by general labour market tightening. This has the effect

TABLE 11.1 The Incidence of Poverty in Rural India: 1983–2009/10 (Per cent of Population Poor)

	1993 Expert Group Poverty Lines	2012 Expert Group Poverty Lines	Global Poverty Line (PPP $1.25 per day)
1983	46.5	*NA*	57.8
1993–4	36.8	50.1	52.3
2004–5	28.1	41.8	43.8
2009–10	*NA*	33.8	34.3
2011–12	*NA*	25.7	*NA*

Source: Quinquennial rounds of the NSSO Consumption surveys 1983–2009/10. *PovCalNet* calculations for the global poverty line estimates.
Note: NA – Not Available.

of raising wages among agricultural labourers—typically the poorest of the rural poor—and thereby contributing to poverty alleviation even among those who are not directly employed in the non-farm sector.

But other than the poverty-reducing impact of non-farm employment, recent data also suggest a structural change in the occupational pattern in rural India. While the non-farm employment growth has accelerated, although mildly, it is also accompanied by a reduction in workforce in agriculture since 2004–5. This is the first time that the farm sector has seen a reduction in workforce—this has been accompanied by a better than average rate of agricultural output growth at more than 3.5 per cent per annum. The implication of this on per worker productivity in agriculture vis-à-vis the non-farm sector does point to better outcomes on poverty in rural areas, even though most of the non-farm jobs created since 2004–5 are casual. Also worth noticing is that most of the incremental employment in the case of non-farm employment has been in construction with low productivity and inferior working conditions than the manufacturing and services sector. Nonetheless, the fact remains that this process of casual employment in construction and elsewhere may not be the best way out of poverty, but is certainly helping the rural poor move out of the low-productivity farm sector and is also helping to reduce the burden on agriculture. These could be seen as early signs of a Lewis transformation with workers moving out of agriculture. But the sustainability of this may be questionable: Lewis had constant wages, in this story they are rising.

[6] Palanpur was first surveyed by the Agricultural Economics Research Centre (AERC) of the University of Delhi in 1957–8. The AERC resurveyed the village in 1962–3. These initial studies were part of the continuous village survey programme of the AERC, and Palanpur in particular was chosen to study the impact of integrated cooperative marketing schemes. In 1974–5 Christopher Bliss and Nicholas Stern selected Palanpur as a village in which to study the functioning of rural markets and the behaviour of farmers. Given their research agenda, the survey that they conducted in 1974–5 thus focused primarily on agriculture. A fourth survey of Palanpur took place in 1983–4 when Jean Drèze and Naresh Sharma, assisted by V.K. Sharma and S.S. Tyagi Jr lived in the village for 15 months, once again collecting data for the entire village population and liaising closely with Stern. A further resurvey of

Expansion of Non-farm Employment in Palanpur

We now move to Palanpur, a small village in Moradabad district in west Uttar Pradesh (UP), which has been the subject of study since 1957–8.[6] Chapters 5 and 15 in this volume describe in detail the population composition as well as movement of incomes in the village over time.[7] However, for contextual purposes, we reiterate a few developments in the village that have a bearing on the evolution of incomes in the village as well as on non-farm employment.

The population of Palanpur has grown at a rate similar to that of the population of India as a whole. The rate of population growth for Palanpur was slightly above that for India in the 1950s and 1960s and was substantially below the national rate in the last 25 years. The proportion of Hindus and Muslims in the total population, and the relative numbers of the main castes, has remained fairly stable since the start of the Palanpur surveys in the late 1950s. The Thakurs (a sub-group of the Kshatriya caste or a 'warrior' group) are generally ranked highest in the caste hierarchy of the village, while the Muraos (a sub-group of the Sudra caste or a cultivator group) are ranked next. The Telis and Dhobis in the village are Muslims. Of all the caste groups, the Passis appear to have reduced in share most drastically, primarily due to outmigration. All other population shares have increased with the increase for the Telis and Dhobis among Muslims being noteworthy.

Incomes in Palanpur have doubled in real terms during the last 25 years, representing an average annual rate of growth of 2.5 to 3 per cent. While this may not be the highest rate of growth that

---

the village, once again by Drèze and Sharma, was conducted in 1993. In the period between May 2008 and April 2010, Himanshu of Jawaharlal Nehru University in Delhi led a team of researchers to survey Palanpur for a sixth time. The fieldwork was organized in close consultation with Nicholas Stern, Jean Drèze, Peter Lanjouw, and Naresh Sharma and was structured and carried out in such a way as to maximize comparability with the earlier waves of data collection.

[7] For the sake of brevity we avoid any description of the village economy in this chapter. However, interested readers may look at Chapters 5 and 15 in this volume on details of caste composition, agricultural performance, and tenancy, as well as the changes in the village in terms of social and human development indicators.

Palanpur has seen between the surveys, this was 5 per cent per annum between 1962 and 1975 immediately in the wake of increased agricultural productivity due to the green revolution; these are comparable to the average rate of growth of incomes in rural areas seen between 1983 and 2008 from the national accounts. At the same time, it is also obvious that the growth of incomes is not driven largely by increases in yields that have grown sluggishly, compared to all the previous such periods. Increase in wheat yields, which is the dominant crop in Palanpur at 1.4 per cent per annum, contributes only in a small way to the increase in overall incomes. However, the growth rate of wages does suggest that the income of wage earners has continued to increase, although at a slower rate than in the 1970s and 1980s. While the growth has continued, it is also worth noticing that it has also been accompanied by increasing inequality in the village. While this is true with regard to comparable income inequalities, even the consumption inequality is higher than the respective income inequality in 1974–5 and 1983.

While the decline in inequality in the 1960s can be attributed to land reforms, in particular, the abolition of the zamindari system, the low inequality trend continued until 1974–75. This could partly be due to the rise of irrigation and cropping intensity which benefited virtually all households in the village, coupled with the fact that 1974–5 was a good agricultural year. Along with increased yields as a result of the green revolution and increase in wages, 1974–5 continued to have low inequality in incomes. However, inequalities rise sharply after the 1983 survey year and are the highest in 2008–9. This again is consistent with the overall story emerging from secondary data, which shows increasing inequality since the 1990s.

Throughout the survey period, the economy of Palanpur has essentially been one of small farmers. The proportion of landless households is relatively small by Indian standards and there are no clearly outstanding large farmers. The bulk of economic activity is in agriculture; since the late 1950s, the village has seen agricultural practices transformed in connection with the spread of irrigation, the introduction of new seed varieties, fertilizers and pesticides, the emergence of rental markets for agricultural equipment, and the introduction of new crops. Nonetheless, in the face of ongoing population growth and roughly constant village land availability (village lands cover about 400 acres), a growing share of village income comes from non-agricultural wage employment outside the village. The economy is by and large a market economy with few restrictions on production and exchange. However, the village's economy does differ from standard textbook models of market economies due to factors, such as incomplete markets, imperfect information, transactions costs, and extra-economic coercion (see Lanjouw and Stern 1998).

In their account of Palanpur's growing interconnectedness with the wider economy of Uttar Pradesh, Lanjouw and Stern (1998) documented a process of expanding non-agricultural wage employment amongst villagers. In the period up to 1993, much of this took the form of regular or semi-regular employment outside the village (distinguished from 'casual' daily wage employment by a modicum of employment security, and usually involving weekly or monthly, as opposed to daily, wage payments). Between 1957–8 and 1993, the number of villagers with regular or semi-regular employment outside of agriculture rose from 11 to 49.[8] Most of these jobs occurred outside the village, within commuting distance for Palanpur's inhabitants. The range of activities gradually expanded over time, but one clear pattern was that employment opportunities tended to cluster around well-defined locations and socio-economic groups. Employers that accounted for a significant number of jobs included the railways, a cloth mill in the nearby city of Moradabad, bakeries in the neighbouring town of Chandausi, a liquor bottling plant, various marble and steel polishing shops in Moradabad, and brick kilns in the surrounding areas. Lanjouw and Stern (1998) noted that the growth of non-farm jobs in Palanpur was associated with some household members commuting out of the village and a shift in the balance of activities in the household.

Data on employment patterns in Palanpur over the period between 1993 and 2008–9 have recently been subjected to detailed scrutiny in Mukhopadhyay (2011). Between 1993 and 2008, the number of non-farm jobs (primary and secondary combined) continued to grow significantly (Table 11.2). In 2008–9, 200 non-farm jobs were held by villagers, up from 107 in 1993 (and 125 in 1983–4), while the population of the village grew only from 1,133 in 1993 to 1,270 in 2008–9. An important change in employment trends, however, and one that

[8] The number of outside jobs in 1993 was somewhat lower than in 1983–4 due to the closure of some local cloth mills.

TABLE 11.2 Occupation Status in Palanpur 1957–8 to 2008–9 (male 15+)

	1957		1983		1993		2008	
	Primary	Secondary	Primary	Secondary	Primary	Secondary	Primary	Secondary
Cultivation and Livestock	141 (81)	12	141 (50)	32	187 (55)	13	184 (48)	122
Self-employment (Non-farm)	6 (3)	2	17 (6)	6	16 (5)	7	45 (12)	26
Skilled Self-employed	6	2	5	3	9	5	13	3
Unskilled Self-employed			12	3	7	2	32	23
Wage Employment (Regular/Semi Regular)	5 (3)	6	72 (26)	2	46 (14)	3	43 (11)	8
Regular (Skilled)	1		7	1	7		13	
Regular (Unskilled)	4	4	48		21	1	17	
Semi-regular (Skilled)			1		1		6	3
Semi-regular (Unskilled)		2	16	1	17	2	7	5
Wage Employment (Casual)	22 (13)	24	23 (9)	36	34 (10)	34	36 (9)	74
Agriculture Labour	22	7	10	21	16	17	2	30
Non-farm Casual Labour	0	17	13	15	18	17	34	44
Study	0 (0)		9 (3)		28 (8)		46 (12)	
Other	0 (0)		5 (2)	2	4 (1)		9 (2)	1
None	1 (1)	131	17 (6)	206	25 (7)	280	24 (6)	156
Total	175 (100)	175	284 (100)	284	340 (100)	340	387	387

Source: Mukhopadhyay (2011).

Note: Figures in parenthesis are the percentage distribution of persons in various activities. Primary activity refers to the activity of the person done for majority time in a year. Secondary activity refers to activity engaged by the person for a shorter period of time or intermittently.

echoes the NSSO-based findings discussed above, is that non-farm employment expansion between 1993 and 2008 occurred mainly as a result of the expansion of self-employment activities and casual wage labour outside of agriculture. The number of self-employment activities tripled (from 23 to 71), and casual wage jobs more than doubled (from 35 to 78). But regular (and semi-regular) jobs increased marginally from only 49 to 51. Mukhopadhyay points to two explanations for the slow growth of regular non-farm employment. First, it appears that the closure of the cloth mills in the vicinity of Palanpur in the late 1980s was not reversed in the years after 1993. The existence of small and medium enterprises was a major source of non-farm employment in the 1980s. Thirty-nine persons were employed in the cloth mill, biscuit, and brass factories in 1983. The closure of these factories in later years meant that very few employment opportunities were available in nearby factories. By 2009, only one person was working in the neighbouring paper mill. The decline of small and medium enterprises in small and medium towns has been documented in several studies; we do not discuss the reasons of it but suffice to say that this certainly seems to have had an impact in the village economy with non-farm regular jobs declining after 1983.

Second, his analysis reveals that an important number of households and individuals that reported regular non-farm employment in 1983–4 were no longer residing in the village by 2008–9. Regular employment in the 1980s had been concentrated among villagers belonging to the Passi caste in the earlier survey years. By 2008–9, as a result of selective migration, no Passi villagers reported any regular non-farm employment, and indeed, the size of the Passi community had declined significantly as well. While the exact trajectories of those who migrated out of the village are yet to be explored in detail, it does appear that exposure to outside job markets did enable the households with regular employment in 1983 to migrate out. A small but important consequence of this is also that the percentage of individuals reporting themselves as non-farm workers by primary status appears to be lower than would have been the case had these persons/households stayed inside the village.

These two points are important for any understanding of the changes in occupational patterns in the village. The high participation in non-farm employment in the village in 1983 was largely due to participation in factory employment. However, the subsequent expansion in non-farm employment in the village is primarily driven by increase in self-employed non-farm work and casual employment. However, unlike regular factory employment, which is a full-time employment outside agriculture, most of the individuals who work as self-employed and casual workers in non-farm jobs do so along with some involvement in agriculture. Some of this is also seasonal, which is also reflected in a much larger increase in secondary non-farm employment, compared to primary non-farm employment between 1983 and 2008–9.

Further, the range and radius of non-farm jobs has also continued to increase. While there has been continued involvement in the usual activities, such as regular employment in railways and as casual wage workers in nearby urban areas, the increase is particularly marked in case of casual wage employment and self-employment in non-farm activities. Among the dominant activities, Palanpur villagers' involvement in the labour market of Moradabad has been noted from earlier surveys (Lanjouw and Stern 1998). However, there has also been a substantial increase in the involvement of Palanpur residents in brick kiln work and marble polishing. A preliminary analysis of the labour market in these three dominant activities suggests expanding access for a larger number of households to such non-farm jobs, particularly poorer households. However, it also confirms the existence and importance of social networks noted earlier (Lanjouw and Stern 1998). In what follows, we provide some detail on the nature of employment and characteristics of the labour market in these three activities during the survey years (2008–9).

The Moradabad Railway Yard has been an old site for wage work by Palanpur residents. It currently provides employment to anywhere between 10–50 villagers, with the number fluctuating in accordance with the labour requirements of the agricultural cycle, and the availability of other non-farm jobs. Villagers join groups of labourers that unload rakes[9] of cement and fertilizer bags, receiving payment on a per-sack-unloaded basis. The work is generally carried out through contractors, who are licensed by the railways. Most of the sacks unloaded contain cement and fertilizers and the contractors have a direct contract

[9] Rakes are railway wagons used to carry freight.

with the companies for unloading the rakes. There are five main contractors at the Moradabad Railway Yard. The contractors are paid anywhere between 70 paise to Re 1 on a sack of 50 kg. The labourers on the other hand are paid a fixed amount of 50 paise for unloading each sack. The contractors are required to clear the rakes as soon as possible. Failure to do so invites penal action from the railways which charges Rs 100 per hour of delay per rake if the rakes stand loaded for more than nine hours on the track.

The workers in groups (usually 10) are required to unload the rake and carry the sacks on their head to the godowns located at one end of the platform. The dominant group among the group of labourers would usually occupy the rake closest to the godowns since it involves least effort in carrying the sacks. Political factors as well as the physical strength of groups matter in deciding which group gets the coveted rake.[10] The Palanpur villagers, under Udayveer Thakur generally get rakes quite far from the godowns.

After claiming the rakes, the headman breaks the seal of the rake in the presence of the contractor and deposits it at the railway office, from where he gets a receipt. After that, the unloading starts; at the end of the day, the headman gets payment for the rakes at the rate of Rs 0.50 per sack. The money earned is distributed equally among the group. Influential headmen don't take part in the unloading process, but lay a claim on the final payment. For example, in a group of 10 labourers, only 9 labourers unload, but the final payment given by the contractor on the whole rake is distributed in 10 parts. This is called *patti chalna*. However, in the Palanpur group, the headman is not influential and also takes part in the unloading process just like any other labourer. On an average day, the earnings for the members come to Rs 200 each. However, there is a variation in the daily earnings depending on the availability of rakes. It also depends on the number of groups available. Although most of the Palanpur residents work in a group, some of them also join other groups.

However, given that the money is divided equally among the labourers, inducting a new labourer reduces the income for each labourer.

[10] Two of the dominant groups are of Hamid and Aftab, both not belonging to Palanpur. Both of them are close to the contractors and are generally among the groups to lay claim to the rakes closest to the godowns.

Therefore, it is very difficult for a new labourer to get a job immediately at the warehouse. If the number of people in the group is low, or the rakes in claim are higher than the capacity of the group members, then the new worker may get an easy entry for the day. Personal relations and the number of labourers in a group are important considerations when inducting a new labourer in the group. But the worker's physical capacity and ability to work in a team are also taken into consideration. Workers who shirk or are slow are less likely to be included in a group.

In terms of effort, the work is very difficult, tiring, and requires physical stamina to do it on a regular basis. Most workers take a break for a day or two in a week. There have also been instances when the workers do not get work either because the rakes have not arrived or because they have been pushed out by the dominant groups. It is important for the workers to remain in the good books of the contractors. Lately, the workers also reported that contractors would often telephone the headman or labourers from Moradabad if there is heavy requirement for workers. The relationship also worked the other way round when labourers called up the contractors to find about the possible arrival of rakes. Despite the physical demand, most workers prefer to work at the railway yard because they find it much more rewarding than agricultural labour in the village. On an average day, earnings for the members of the group come to around Rs 200 each, much more rewarding than agricultural labour (where the daily wage in 2008 was Rs 100); more important, the work is considered to be much less demeaning than working as an agricultural labourer.

Follow-up visits to the village after 2010 suggest a process of expansion of the radius of locations for manual labour on the railways. Palanpur residents now go to Aligarh, which is more than 100 km from Palanpur. While the job requirements are similar to the one at Moradabad, what attracts the workers is the high demand for labour in Aligarh compared to Moradabad.[11]

[11] This process of going to Aligarh started because one of the contractors who used to work at Moradabad shifted base to Aligarh. It is interesting that one of the key middlemen who supply labour from Palanpur is a Jatab from Palanpur. He gets information on the demand for labour on his mobile phone and it is his responsibility to arrange for workers who then go to Aligarh for the work and return after 2–3 days.

The other major activity that has seen an expansion is the work at the brick kilns. Palanpur residents used to work at the brick kilns earlier but in smaller numbers. By the last survey, while there was an increase in households who reported working at the brick kiln, it was still largely restricted to the Jatabs. The work is primarily seasonal, with most of the work taking place between October and June. Workers work in a team, mostly comprised family members. While some go seasonally and are based at the brick kiln during the season, some families also commute daily. Each team has a wooden frame for making bricks called a *saancha*. One team makes about 1,500 to 2,000 bricks daily. The work is mainly piece rate with the rate fixed at Rs 170 for making 1,000 bricks. But not all of the money is paid during the season. The brick kiln owners retain Rs 50 out of the Rs 170 that they earn for making bricks. This sum is paid at the end of the season. This is mainly to keep the workers tied to the work throughout the season.

Apart from the daily commuters, some families also migrate seasonally. These households are provided dormitory accommodation at the worksite. For seasonal migrants, the daily working hours are generally from dawn to dusk. Since the payment is piece rated, most families try and put in as many hours as possible. Payment is usually made after 15 days but only Rs 100 is paid during the season, with Rs 70 retained by the owners, to be paid at the end of the season. Most Jatab families are indebted to the brick kiln owners. The owners usually provide an advance during the rainy season with the promise by workers to repay it by working in the season. In this sense, the brick kiln work also represents a classic debt-bondage relationship. Labourers are generally organizsed and managed by the contractors. The contractor for Palanpur is a resident there. The contractor is given a commission of Rs 5 per 1,000 bricks for managing and organizing the work. There are 10–12 families who work on the brick kilns regularly. Almost all of the families who work on brick kilns are Jatab families.

While manual labour in the railway yard and working at the brick kilns have been traditionally popular among casual workers, the village has also witnessed an expansion of non-farm self-employment. This has taken the form of small-time repair shops, *kirana* (general shop selling local merchandise) shops, as well as mechanics and marble polishers. Compared to 1983, there is significant expansion of marble polishing in the neighbouring towns. While some Palanpur residents are working as casual labourers, there are some who have their own marble polishing machine and are now self-employed. Most of the self-employed started as casual labourers but acquired a marble polishing machine over time. The work is done on a piece rate basis with rates determined on a per square foot basis. However, the labourer is paid daily. The work is less strenuous since it is generally within houses but is dependent on the availability of electricity. Since electricity is only available for a few hours a day, the work of marble polishing takes place as and when the electricity is available. Although there are no middlemen with marble machine owners themselves negotiating the deal, they do keep in touch with other construction contractors for information on the availability of work.

Some of the Palanpur residents are also working as machine repairers and a few have also started their own repair shops. They generally repair cycles and motorcycles in the neighbouring areas. In most cases, the training for repairing motorcycles as well as marble polishing has been acquired on the job. Interestingly, unlike the work at the railway yard or at the brick kiln, both of which are primarily accessed by Jatabs and poorer households, marble polishing and repair shops involve households with some access to capital; this is primarily a result of the choice by households to diversify their income sources in this way. Since both these also involve some kind of skill and training, the investment in acquiring these skills make it more likely by the households which are relatively better off.

Income from Non-farm Employment

Alongside the expansion of non-farm jobs has come a significant increase in the contribution of non-farm income to village income (Table 11.3). The non-farm income sources have been further broken down in Table 11.3 into casual non-farm, regular non-farm, and self-employed non-farm income.

In 1958, most households derived their income from agriculture with the Thakurs and Muraos, who had access to land, deriving their income almost entirely from cultivation. Dhimars, Gadariyas, and Passis were the only caste groups that had significant exposure to non-farm sources of income. Most of these derived their income from regular non-farm income (primarily railways). On the other hand, Jatabs derived one-fourth of their income from casual manual labour. In the next

TABLE 11.3 Share of Various Income Sources by Caste

	Farm	Casual Labour	Regular Employment	Self-employment	Other Non-farm
			1958		
Thakur	96.9	0.0	0.8	0.0	2.3
Murao	95.5	0.6	1.6	2.3	0.0
Dhimar	38.6	40.7	19.0	1.7	0.0
Gadariya	71.3	0.0	28.7	0.0	0.0
Dhobi	82.2	0.0	0.0	17.8	0.0
Teli	53.0	43.4	0.0	3.6	0.0
Passi	52.5	9.6	16.8	9.3	11.7
Jatab	76.7	23.3	0.0	0.0	0.0
Others	5.0	0.0	44.4	50.6	0.0
			1983		
Thakur	72.0	4.2	18.1	5.7	0.0
Murao	82.0	1.2	10.1	6.6	0.0
Dhimar	51.1	4.1	42.4	2.4	0.0
Gadariya	63.1	7.9	27.4	0.4	1.2
Dhobi	66.7	2.0	1.3	22.9	7.1
Teli	59.3	15.8	22.8	1.8	0.3
Passi	17.9	35.6	35.2	10.8	0.5
Jatab	65.6	26.1	6.7	1.6	0.0
Others	9.1	5.9	52.7	32.3	0.0
			2009		
Thakur	45.1	4.6	23.6	22.8	3.8
Murao	54.5	4.8	2.3	31.8	6.6
Dhimar	14.6	7.8	47.9	29.4	0.3
Gadariya	47.6	5.3	10.6	34.6	1.9
Dhobi	50.6	4.7	0.0	44.6	0.2
Teli	21.6	3.3	23.6	51.1	0.5
Passi	40.8	8.2	16.3	17.2	17.6
Jatab	52.9	29.2	7.7	10.2	0.2
Others	9.7	0.0	11.4	48.7	30.2

Source: Authors' calculation based on survey data of Palanpur.

Note: Other non-farm incomes include remittances, pensions, and other transfers, and also includes rental incomes.

25 years, with the advent of the green revolution, the employment profile had changed with many more persons working in non-farm jobs. But the increased agricultural productivity associated with the green revolution also meant that agriculture continued to dominate the sources of income, particularly for those who had access to land. By 1983, other than the three castes who had access to regular jobs, Thakur households had also moved into regular employment along with some Teli households. The existence of a cloth mill during 1983 was a significant factor explaining the increase in regular employment in the village. The expansion of non-farm income in the village in 1983 has been described in detail in Lanjouw and Stern (1998). However, it is the next 25 years after 1983 which suggest a marked departure from the existing dominance of agriculture as the primary source of income in the village. Not only did farm incomes account for less than half of the total income of the majority of households, the only exception being Muraos and Jatabs, it also witnessed non-farm self-employment emerge as an important category of employment. While self-employment in non-farm work was the dominant income source for Telis, it was also significant for other caste groups except the Jatabs who continued to rely on casual non-farm work as the primary channel for accessing non-farm jobs.

While most castes saw an increase in the share of non-farm income sources in total income, the route varied across castes. Since regular non-farm jobs as well as self-employed non-farm jobs still depend on the access to networks and the availability of physical and human capital, the better-off castes have been able to diversify their income through these channels. Further details on the nature of non-farm diversification is available by looking the share of different sources of income by quintiles of income (Table 11.4).

The share of farm income has been declining across all quintiles. In the first 25 years (1958–83), the decline in farm income share was accompanied by increasing share of regular employment with a clear pattern of increasing contribution of regular non-farm income as one moved upwards in the income quintiles. On the other hand, casual employment and self-employment were easily accessible to the households at the lower end of the spectrum. However, higher non-farm dependence of the lower quintiles than the higher remained until 1983. This was largely a result of the access to land; those households better endowed with land continue to take special interest in the agriculture.

TABLE 11.4 Share of Various Income Sources by Income Classes

	Farm	Casual Labour	Regular Employment	Self-Employment	Other Non-farm
			1958		
Lowest	50.8	24.2	14.0	11.0	0.0
Q2	47.3	38.7	2.0	7.1	4.9
Q3	78.3	14.7	0.0	1.4	5.6
Q4	80.6	4.4	13.5	1.6	0.0
Highest	87.0	0.0	7.6	3.9	1.5
			1983		
Lowest	36.9	29.2	14.0	14.3	5.6
Q2	51.5	21.3	15.6	10.4	1.3
Q3	61.2	8.5	19.8	10.1	0.5
Q4	59.2	5.4	30.6	4.7	0.0
Highest	71.3	6.3	17.0	5.4	0.0
			2009		
Lowest	52.3	27.2	3.7	8.1	8.8
Q2	58.3	14.1	8.8	14.2	4.7
Q3	45.6	20.0	12.4	19.6	2.3
Q4	53.2	5.3	7.7	26.1	7.7
Highest	31.3	2.2	23.1	40.5	2.9

Source: Authors' calculation based on survey data of Palanpur.

The green revolution contributed to this trend with Muraos as well as Thakurs less likely to diversify.

The next 25 years saw this pattern reverse with the share of non-farm income growing much faster among higher quintiles than those at the bottom. The primary reason for this appears to be the increase in self-employed non-farm income sources, which accounted for as much as two-fifth of all income for the highest quintile. One can also observe a pattern of the increasing share of self-employment non-farm income as we move from the lowest quintile to the highest quintile. In fact, an opposite trend of this is seen in the case of casual non-farm income sources, which continue to be important for those at the bottom of income distribution. The pattern in case of regular employment is not so clear but does suggest better access for richer households.

While detailed analysis on the nature of discrimination in the access to better quality non-farm jobs is still being processed, some conjectures based on the analysis of the labour market, as well as extensive discussions with workers suggest the role of networks, skills, and access to capital may still be important. But this has also resulted in increasing inequality in incomes with better-off households managing to take advantage of these opportunities more than those at the bottom. Nonetheless, even the poorer households have benefited from the availability and accessibility of these jobs, which has resulted in many poor households—including many among the Jatabs—moving up the income ladder in the last 25 years.

Income Mobility

We turn now to a further examination of the improving circumstances of the Jatabs. In Tables 11.5–11.8 we divide the village population, in turn in 1983–4 and 2008–9, into fractiles of economic well-being, and consider how over time Jatabs have lifted themselves out of the lowest margins of the welfare distribution. We proceed in two steps. We first revisit a concept of 'observed means'[12] described in Lanjouw and Stern (1991, 1998) whereby Palanpur households are ranked on the basis of their 'apparent prosperity' by the field investigators directly involved in the intensive fieldwork for each respective year. The point of departure here is that the affluence of a household in a small Indian village is, to some extent, a matter of common knowledge in the sense that its asset position and purchasing power is widely known. For the 1983–4 data, Jean Drèze and Naresh Sharma, first classified households into seven 'groups' of increasing prosperity labelled 'Very Poor', 'Poor', 'Modest', 'Secure', 'Prosperous', 'Rich', and 'Very Rich'. The investigators classified households in this way independently, without consultation. It is of some comfort that Drèze and Sharma agreed to a considerable extent in their ranking of households, confirming the view that the relative position of households in the scale of economic affluence is in many cases fairly clear to informed observers. A final stage of classification consisted of reclassifying the households into

[12] The word 'means' here is a crude indication of assets, lifestyle, and command over resources.

five quintiles of roughly equal size, designated 'Very Poor', 'Poor', 'Secure', 'Prosperous', and 'Rich'.

This exercise was repeated in 2008–9, this time by four investigators involved in the detailed fieldwork covering a period of nearly two years. While the same five fractile headings were employed, it was decided not to impose the requirement that the village population be divided evenly into each group. In this sense, there was some attempt to allow the investigator's assessment to also accommodate an overall improvement in living standards.

Tables 11.5 and 11.6 present the results of the 'observed means' classification for 1983–4 and 2008–9, respectively. Table 11.5 indicates that in 1983–4, 90 per cent of Jatab households had been classified by Jean Drèze and Naresh Sharma as being either 'Very Poor' or 'Poor'. There was not a single Jatab household that could be categorized as 'Prosperous' or 'Rich' in this year. By 2008–9 this assessment had changed somewhat (Table 11.6). Although half of the Jatab households were still being assessed as 'Very Poor' or 'Poor' in that year, the other half of Jatab households were being judged as either 'Secure' or 'Prosperous' in that year. On the basis of this subjective assessment of well-being,

TABLE 11.5 Observed Means Classification of Palanpur Households by Caste in 1983–4

	Very Poor	Poor	Secure	Prosperous	Rich	No. of hhs (%)
Thakur	0.0	0.267	0.233	0.267	0.233	1.00 (30)
Murao	0.0	0	0.222	0.370	0.407	1.00 (27)
Dhimar	0.154	0.462	0.308	0.077	0.0	1.00 (13)
Gadariya	0.0	0.250	0.25	0.167	0.333	1.00 (12)
Dhobi	0.250	0.250	0.250	0.0	0.250	1.00 (4)
Teli	0.375	0.313	0.188	0.063	0.063	1.00 (16)
Passi	0.400	0.067	0.133	0.200	0.200	1.00 (14)
Jatab	0.737	0.158	0.105	0.0	0.0	1.00 (19)
Other	0.286	0.143	0.0	0.429	0.143	1.00 (8)
% of households	22	19	20	19	20	(143) 100

Source: Authors' calculation based on survey data of Palanpur.
Note: For definition of 'observed means', see text.

TABLE 11.6 Observed Means Classification of Palanpur Households by Caste in 2008–9

	Very Poor	Poor	Secure	Prosperous	Rich	No. of hhs (%)
Thakur	0.052	0.121	0.345	0.259	0.224	1.00 (56)
Murao	0.036	0.200	0.400	0.182	0.182	1.00 (58)
Dhimar	0.136	0.364	0.273	0.091	0.136	1.00 (18)
Gadariya	0.0	0.133	0.533	0.267	0.067	1.00 (16)
Dhobi	0.250	0.250	0.250	0.250	0.00	1.00 (8)
Teli	0.273	0.182	0.273	0.136	0.136	1.00 (21)
Passi	0.0	0.167	0.667	0.0	0.167	1.00 (6)
Jatab	0.077	0.436	0.410	0.077	0.0	1.00 (38)
Other	0.182	0.182	0.182	0.455	0.0	1.00 (9)
% of households	8	23	37	19	13	(230) 100

Source: Authors' calculation based on survey data of Palanpur.
Note: For definition of 'observed means', see text.

the evidence points to a strong improvement in the relative position of Jatabs by 2008–9: almost half of them were secure or prosperous in 2008–9, but only around 10 per cent in 1983–4.

We turn next to a repeat of this exercise using per capita income, rather than 'observed means', as our indicator of economic status. Table 11.7 reveals that, on the basis of an income criterion, as was seen with the 'observed means' classification, roughly 90 per cent of Jatab households in 1983–4 were counted in the bottom two quintiles of the per capita income distribution. Again, this picture had evolved markedly by 2008–9 (Table 11.8). Although 60 per cent of Jatab households were still counted among the bottom two quintiles of the per capita income distribution, the other 40 per cent were now at less risk. The percentage of Jatabs in the lowest quintile has halved with 12 per cent of Jatab households in 2008 counted among the richest quintile in per capita income terms.

The evidence for Palanpur thus points to a striking improvement in the relative position of what has historically been a particularly vulnerable and disadvantaged group of households. These households are also, for the first time, actively engaged in the non-farm sector,

TABLE 11.7 Per Capita Income Classification of Palanpur Households by Caste in 1983–4

	Very Poor	Poor	Secure	Prosperous	Rich	No. of hhs (%)
Thakur	0.067	0.233	0.267	0.233	0.200	1.00 (30)
Murao	0.037	0.222	0.111	0.333	0.296	1.00 (27)
Dhimar	0.231	0.231	0.154	0.231	0.154	1.00 (13)
Gadariya	0.083	0.250	0.333	0.083	0.250	1.00 (12)
Dhobi	0.250	0.0	0.500	0.250	0.0	1.00 (4)
Teli	0.375	0.063	0.250	0.250	0.063	1.00 (16)
Passi	0.267	0.133	0.067	0.067	0.467	1.00 (14)
Jatab	0.632	0.263	0.105	0.00	0.00	1.00 (19)
Other	0.143	0.143	0.286	0.286	0.143	1.00 (8)
% of households	22	19	20	19	20	(143) 100

Source: Authors' calculation based on survey data of Palanpur.

earning roughly as much from non-farm sources (as a percentage of total income) as the other castes. The picture is one of an expanding non-farm sector generating returns that appear to exceed those from

TABLE 11.8 Per Capita Income Classification of Palanpur Households by Caste in 2008–9

	Very Poor	Poor	Secure	Prosperous	Rich	No. of hhs (%)
Thakur	0.088	0.140	0.246	0.281	0.246	1.00 (56)
Murao	0.109	0.309	0.218	0.182	0.182	1.00 (58)
Dhimar	0.409	0.091	0.182	0.091	0.227	1.00 (18)
Gadariya	0.067	0.200	0.067	0.400	0.267	1.00 (16)
Dhobi	0.625	0.125	0.125	0.125	0.000	1.00 (8)
Teli	0.190	0.095	0.190	0.190	0.333	1.00 (21)
Passi	0.000	0.333	0.500	0.167	0.000	1.00 (6)
Jatab	0.308	0.282	0.154	0.154	0.103	1.00 (38)
Other	0.500	0.100	0.100	0.100	0.200	1.00 (9)
% of households	20	20	20	20	20	(230) 100

Source: Authors' calculation based on survey data of Palanpur.

agriculture, slowly becoming less exclusively the preserve of the well-off, and therefore representing an increasingly important engine of rural poverty reduction.

Income Inequality

While rising incomes, falling poverty, and increased mobility of the historically disadvantaged Jatabs all represent genuinely encouraging distributional trends in Palanpur, an accompanying development has been a marked increase in income inequality. Table 11.9 documents that between 1983–4 and 2008–9, income inequality as captured by the Gini coefficient increased from 0.307 to 0.427. Although absolute values of the Gini coefficient cannot be easily interpreted, such an increase is not commonly observed and would generally be viewed as a very strong increase in inequality. An alternative measure, such as the Theil L, which is particularly sensitive to changes in incomes amongst poor people, also records a dramatic increase—indicating that the assessment of rising inequality is not an artefact of the use of a specific measure such as the Gini coefficient.

Analyses of inequality in rural India commonly focus on social stratification—particularly differences between castes—as an important source of income inequality. Caste-based inequality is considered notoriously durable and has been the subject of a lot of work across the social sciences (for example, Deshpande 2000; Dumont 1966). In light

TABLE 11.9 Income Inequality has Risen Sharply in Palanpur

	Theil L Measure	Gini Coefficient
1957–8	0.188	0.336
1962–3	0.282	0.390
1974–5	0.169	0.253
1983–4	0.174	0.307
2008–9	0.336	0.427

Source: Authors' calculation based on survey data of Palanpur.

[13] Following Bourguignon (1979), Cowell (1980), and Shorrocks (1980) inequality by population sub-groups is a basic tool of inequality analysis, permitting the quantification of the 'contribution' to overall inequality of differences in average incomes across a given set of population sub-groups.

of the evidence presented above pointing to a noticeable increase in social mobility amongst Jatab households since 1983, one might expect that that a decomposition of inequality in Palanpur by caste, would reveal that between-caste differences have come to account for a significantly lower share of overall inequality in 2008–9, relative to earlier years.[13] Some support is given to this contention in Table 11.10, where it can be seen that the contribution to total inequality of between-caste differences is 17 per cent in 2008–9, down from 29 per cent in 1983–4. However, decomposition analyses have indicated that differences between castes in Palanpur have never appeared to be the dominant determinant of inequality in Palanpur: even in 1983–4, more than 70 per cent of income inequality can be attributed to within-caste differences between individuals. This might appear in tension with a strongly caste-based narrative (as sketched above) to explain both the organization of economic activity in Palanpur and the evolution of living standards over time across different groups in the village.

There has long been some dissatisfaction with inequality decompositions based on the conventionally applied decomposition methodology.[14] Elbers, Lanjouw, Mistiaen, and Özler (2008) point out that the standard procedure for decomposing inequality into a between- and a within-group component fails to capture a particular feature of group differences that might be highly relevant to an assessment of their importance. Standard decomposition procedures assess the extent to which group divisions contribute to inequality by giving everyone

TABLE 11.10 The Contribution to Inequality of Caste Differences has Changed Little

	Theil L Measure	Within-caste Contribution (in %)	Between-caste Contribution (in %)
1957–8	0.188	77	23
1962–3	0.282	82	18
1974–5	0.169	69	31
1983–4	0.174	71	29
2008–9	0.336	83	17

Source: Authors' calculation based on survey data of Palanpur.

[14] See, for example, Kanbur (2000).

within a group the average income of the group and then asking how much of overall inequality can be attributed to the inequality accounted for by the inequality in these group-average income levels. By comparing group-average income inequality against total inequality, the procedure in effect compares observed group differences against the extreme benchmark where each individual in the data is treated as a separate group. As a result, the proportion of between-group inequality is always rather low, in comparison with the benchmark. Furthermore, standard measures have the mathematical property that between-group inequality will increase (or more precisely, never decrease) with a greater number of groups.

Elbers et al. (2008) propose a relatively minor adaptation of the conventional procedure to produce an alternative statistic that overcomes some of these issues. Suppose that a given population is divided into two groups. The approach proposed by Elbers et al. (2008) compares the extent of between-group inequality against a new benchmark, namely the extent to which these two groups are completely 'separate' from each other in income terms; that is, whether the richest person of the poorer group is poorer than the poorest person in the richer group. The standard decomposition procedure is entirely silent on this question. Yet, from the perspective of assessing the importance of, say, caste differences in a village such as Palanpur, the Elbers et al. (2008) index is arguably quite relevant. If two population groups divide the income distribution into two entirely non-overlapping partitions, but there exists a high level of inequality within each of the two groups, overall between-group inequality—conventionally calculated—would be relatively low. Yet a fairly strong statement about the relevance of the contribution of groups to inequality would remain unstated; namely, that the two groups 'stand apart' in income terms—they are somehow economically 'excluded' from one another.[15]

[15] Elbers et al. (2008) illustrate this point with reference to South Africa. They show that when inequality is decomposed by racial group defined in terms of a 'white/non-white' classification, the conventional decomposition suggests that only about 27 per cent of inequality is attributable to between-group differences. Their alternative statistic, on the other hand, shows that two groups are 80 per cent of the way towards a completely partitioned South African income distribution.

Lanjouw and Rao (2010) compared the Elbers et al. (2008) statistic with standard inequality decomposition measures to study the dynamics of caste inequality in Palanpur, drawing on data covering the survey period up to 1983–4. They found that when Jatabs are compared to the rest of the village population taken as a single group, the Elbers et al. (2008) statistic reveals that Jatabs in 1983–4 were 50 per cent on the way of standing fully apart from the rest of the village, up from 39 per cent in 1974–5 and even lower in the earlier survey years. There was clear evidence, consistent with the narrative offered above, that over the decades since the 1950s, Jatabs as a group were steadily falling further behind the rest of the village in terms of their living standards—even though within the Jatab community, there existed differences across individuals and households. The analysis in Lanjouw and Rao (2010) thus found strong support for the perception that caste-based inequality in Palanpur was strong and durable.[16]

Table 11.11 revisits the calculation undertaken in Lanjouw and Rao (2010) and updates the analysis to include the 2008–9 data. The evidence points to a clear turnaround with the Elbers et al. (2008) statistic

TABLE 11.11 Growing 'Isolation' of Jatabs has Reversed Since 1983–4

Jatabs versus the rest of the village	Overall Theil L Measure of Inequality	Elbers et al. (2008) partitioning index (in %)	Inequality Contribution from 'Classic' Decomposition (in %)
1957–8	0.188	7	3
1962–3	0.282	10	4
1974–5	0.169	39	9
1983–4	0.174	50	22
2008–9	0.336	2	12

Source: Authors' calculation based on survey data of Palanpur.

[16] Lanjouw and Rao (2010) also documented that while caste-based inequality in Palanpur was significant, preliminary analysis based on other criteria for group differentiation—education of household head, and household landownership—failed to reveal sizeable between group differences, whether based on the Elbers et al. (2008) statistic or the standard between group decomposition.

registering a significant decline between 1983–4 and 2008–9, from 50 per cent to 29 per cent. Whereas in the survey rounds leading up to 1983–4, the picture is one of the Jatabs as a group falling ever further behind the rest of the population to the point where even the richest Jatabs have lower incomes than the poorest non-Jatab households, the 2008–9 data indicates a substantial attenuation of this pattern. The evidence from this decomposition exercise thus accords well with the story offered earlier in this chapter, of the Jatabs registering significant upward mobility since 1983–4, the result of markedly improved access to non-farm earning opportunities for at least a subset of Jatab households.

Contribution of Non-farm Income to Overall Inequality

The analysis above confirms that widening group differences are unlikely to explain the strong increase in income inequality between 1983–4 and 2008–9. Much more plausible is the impact of the expansion of, and growth in, incomes from non-farm sources in the village. This conjecture can be investigated on the basis of an inequality decomposition by income sources. Following Shorrocks (1982) the Gini coefficient G, can be obtained as a weighted 'average of 'pseudo Gini' coefficients Gi^* for each component, where the weights are given by the share *k* of component income in total income:

$$G = \alpha_1 G_1^* + \cdots + \alpha_k G_k^* + \alpha_n G_n^*$$

The 'pseudo Gini' coefficient for an income component is similar to the Gini coefficient for that component but with the modification that individuals are ranked in terms of their total income rather than component income. In general, the change in the overall income inequality brought about by an increase or a reduction of income from a given source will be smaller the closer the pseudo-Gini coefficient for that source is to the overall Gini (Elbers and Lanjouw 2000; Lanjouw and Stern 1998).

Table 11.12 shows that, in Palanpur, the contribution of non-agricultural income inequality to overall inequality in 2008–9 is 67 per cent, compared to 28 per cent for farm income. Based on this statistic, more than two-thirds of overall inequality is attributable to the distribution

TABLE 11.12 The Growing Contribution of Non-farm Incomes to Inequality

	Gini Coefficient	Contribution from Non-farm Income (in %)	Contribution from Agricultural Income (in %)	Contribution from Other Income Sources (in %)
1957–8	0.336	8	92	0
1962–3	0.390	13	81	6
1974–5	0.253	4	105	-9
1983–4	0.307	49	53	-3
2008–9	0.427	67	28	5

Source: Authors' calculation based on survey data of Palanpur.

of non-farm incomes, a significant increase over the preceding survey year, mirroring the significant increase in total income inequality. It thus seems clear that the expansion of non-farm income sources into the village is associated not only with falling poverty and increased income mobility, but also with rising overall income inequality.

* * *

This chapter has analysed data for the village of Palanpur in UP, to document the growing importance, and influence, of the non-farm sector in the rural economy. The acceleration in the pace of non-farm diversification mirrors in many ways the processes underway in rural India. The analysis of NSSO data however, also suggests that there is a lot of heterogeneity in the non-farm sector and the shift of rural workers, its timing, whom it affects and how it happens, from farm to non-farm, may have distributional consequences. A significant feature of the non-farm diversification of rural India is the increasing importance of construction as a driver of non-farm growth. This is both a reflection of the increasing prosperity in rural areas and the consequent demand for construction workers; the fact that the majority of these workers are in the informal sector with uncertain and vulnerable working conditions, implies a mixed result for the sustainability of the non-farm diversification. This process is similar to the process of non-farm diversification in Palanpur where poorer people still access the majority of the casual jobs linked to the construction sector (unloading cement in railway yard, working at the brick kiln, and so on) but with associated uncertainty. The presence of contractors, networks, and debt bondage reflect the vulnerability of these groups. However, Palanpur also offers evidence of the richer households diversifying to non-farm jobs taking advantage of the growing consumer base in neighbouring urban areas. The relative importance of physical and human capital for the regular and self-employed jobs also implies an uneven distribution of gains from non-farm diversification. Nonetheless, even the limited opportunity offered by the non-farm sector has contributed to increasing prosperity among the poorer households, including the Jatabs. While higher wages in the non-farm sector has definitely contributed, the fact that the non-farm sector acts as an insurance against vagaries of agricultural production and employment along with an additional source of income, has also contributed to the improvement in the well-being of the poorer households.

Nonetheless, the preliminary conclusion from the Palanpur data is of a slow process of non-farm diversification, where the distributional incidence, on the margin, is increasingly pro-poor. The rich insights offered by the village study suggest that the non-farm sector is not only increasing incomes and reducing poverty, but also appears to be breaking down long-standing barriers to mobility among the poorest segments of rural society. Efforts by the Government of India to accelerate the process of diversification could thus yield significant returns in terms of declining poverty and increased income mobility. It is important to recognize, however that rising income inequality could, at least initially, accompany the declining poverty and expanding social mobility. At the all-India level this process may not be as apparent as rising rural incomes; such incomes, even if they are associated with increases in village-level inequality, could contribute to a narrowing of the gap between rural and urban areas, and thus lead to a reduction in inequality at the all-India level (see Elbers and Lanjouw 2000). What this paper has documented, however, is that, at the level of the village, non-farm diversification could well be associated with significantly higher income inequality. This may be an inherent part of the mobility processes for transformation in rural India.

Rising village-level inequality can be of potential concern as a growing body of evidence shows that inequality can shape the fabric of village society, the way in which village institutions function and evolve, and the scope for collective action at the village level (Mansuri and Rao, 2012, provide an extensive review). Going forward, it will be important to monitor distributional outcomes at the local level, and there may be a need to adopt measures to counter the more adverse impacts on local-level inequality. The concern is that failure to keep such inequalities in check could threaten the pro-poor impacts that we currently see from the ongoing process of structural transformation under way in rural India.

References

Bourguignon, F. 1979. 'Decomposable Income Inequality Measures', *Econometrica,* 47 (4): 901–20.

Cai, J., A. de Janvry, and E. Sadoulet. 2008. 'Rural Households in India: Sources of Income and Incidence of Burden of Rising Prices', Background paper prepared for India Poverty Assessment Report, World Bank, Washington, DC, USA.

Cowell, F. 1980. 'On the Structure of Additive Inequality Measures', *Review of Economic Studies*, 47 (3): 521–31.

Deshpande, A. 2000. 'Does Caste Still Define Disparity? A Look at Inequality in Kerala, India', *American Economic Review, Papers and Proceedings of the 112th Annual Meeting of the American Economics Association*, Boston, United States, May: 322–5.

Dubey, A. 2008. 'Consumption, Income, and Inequality in India', Background paper prepared for India Poverty Assessment Report, World Bank, Washington, DC, USA.

Dumont, L. 1966. *Homo Heirarchicus: The Caste System and Its Implications.* Chicago: University of Chicago Press.

Elbers, C. and P. Lanjouw. 2000. 'Intersectoral Transfer, Growth, and Inequality in Rural Ecuador', *World Development,* 29 (3): 481–96

Elbers, C., P. Lanjouw, J. Mistiaen, and B. Ozler. 2008. 'Re-Interpreting Sub-Group Inequality Decompositions', *Journal of Economic Inequality,* 6 (3): 1569–721.

Eswaran, M., A. Kotwal, B. Ramaswami, and W. Wadhwa. 2009. 'Sectoral Labour Flows and Agricultural Wages in India, 1983–2004: Has Growth Trickled Down?' *Economic and Political Weekly*, XLIV (2): 46–55.

Fields, G. 1980. *Poverty, Inequality, and Development.* Cambridge: Cambridge University Press.

Fields, G. 2000. *Distribution and Development: A New Look at the Developing World*. New York City and Cambridge MA: Russell Sage Foundation and MIT Press.

Foster, A. and M. Rosenzweig. 2003. 'Agricultural Development, Industrialization, and Rural Inequality', mimeo, Brown University and Harvard University, Providence and Cambridge.

Foster, A. and M. Rosenzweig. 2004. 'Agricultural Productivity Growth, Rural Economic Diversity, and Economic Reforms: India, 1970–2000', *Economic Development and Cultural Changes*, 52: 509–42.

Himanshu. 2008. 'Agriculture and Non-farm employment: Exploring the inter-linkages in Rural India', Background paper prepared for India Poverty Assessment Report, World Bank, Washington DC.

———. 2011. 'Employment Trends in India: A Re-examination', *Economic and Political Weekly*, XLVI (37): 43–59.

Himanshu, P. Lanjouw, Rinku Murgai, and Nicholas Stern. 2013. 'Nonfarm Diversification, Poverty, Economic Mobility, and Income Inequality: A Case Study in Village India', *Agricultural Economics*, 44 (4–5): 461–73.

Kanbur, R. 2000. 'Income Distribution and Development', in A.B. Atkinson and F. Bourguignon (eds), *Handbook of Income Distribution*, pp. 791–841. North Holland: Elsevier Science Publishers.

Kuznets, S. 1955. 'Economic Growth and Income Inequality', *American Economic Review*, 45 (1): 1–28.

———. 1963. 'Quantitative Aspects of the Economic Growth of Nations: VIII, Distribution of Income by Size', *Economic Development and Cultural Change*, January, Part 2: 1–80.

Lanjouw. P, and R. Murgai. 2009. 'Poverty Decline, Agricultural Wages, and Non-farm Employment in India: 1983–2004', Policy Research Working Paper, No.4858, World Bank, Washington, DC, USA.

Lanjouw, P. and V. Rao, 2010. 'Revisiting Between-Group Inequality Measurement: An Application to the Dynamics of Caste Inequality in Two Indian Villages' *World Development*, 39 (2): 174–87.

Lanjouw, P. and N. Stern. 1991. 'Poverty in Palanpur', *World Bank Economic Review*, January, 5 (1): 20–60.

Lanjouw, P. and N.H. Stern (eds). 1998. *Economic Development in Palanpur Over Five Decades*. New Delhi and Oxford: Oxford University Press.

Lewis, W.A. 1954. 'Economic Development with Unlimited Supplies of Labour', *The Manchester School*, 28 (2): 139–91.

Mansuri, G. and V. Rao. 2012. *Localizing Development: Does Participation Work?* Washington DC: World Bank.

Mukhopadhyay, A. 2011. 'Stepping Out of Palanpur: Employment Outside Palanpur, from Short Visits to Long Term Migration and how they are Linked', mimeo, Planning Unit, Indian Statistical Institute and Institute of Economic Growth, Delhi.

Sen, A. and P. Jha. 2005. 'Rural Employment: Patterns and Trends from National Sample Survey', in Rohini Nayyar and A.N. Sharma (eds), *Rural Transformation in India–The Role of Non-farm Sector*, pp. 57–74. New Delhi: Institute for Human Development.

Shorrocks A. 1980. 'The Class of Additively Decomposable Inequality Measures', *Econometrica*, 48 (3): 613–25.

———. 1982. 'Inequality Decomposition by Factor Components', *Econometrica*, 50 (1): 193–211.

Sundaram, K. 2007. 'Employment and Poverty in India: 2000–2005', *Economic and Political Weekly*, XLII (30): 3121–31.

World Bank. 2011. *Perspectives on Poverty in India: Stylized Facts from Survey Data*. Washington, DC and New Delhi: World Bank and Oxford University Press India.

JUDITH HEYER

Rural Gounders on the Move in Western Tamil Nadu

1981–2 to 2008–9*

Gounders are well known for playing a leading role in the development of the dynamic industrial economy of the Coimbatore–Tiruppur region in western Tamil Nadu. This chapter uses village-level data to look at the changing character of Gounder communities in multi-caste villages in the vicinity of Coimbatore and Tiruppur over

* The research on which this chapter is based was funded by the UK Department of International Development (DFID, formerly ODA), the Oxford University Webb Medley Fund, the Leverhulme Trust, and the Queen Elizabeth House Oppenheimer Fund, at various stages. The 2008–9 research was part of a project on the effects of the expansion of the knitwear industry in the Tiruppur region funded by a DFID–ESRC Research Award (RES-167-25-0296), a project in which Grace Carswell, Geert De Neve, and M. Vijayabaskar were also involved. The research could not have been done without the support of Dr V. Mohanasundaram, my interpreter and co-researcher for most of the fieldwork since 1981–2, and without the contributions of M.V. Srinivasan, Paul Pandian, Selva Murugan, Arul Maran, Gowri Shankar, and S. Saravanan who acted as research assistants at different stages in the field. The research has also benefited from discussions, particularly with K. Nagaraj, J. Jeyaranjan, Karin Kapadia, and Barbara Harriss-White.

the past 30 years or so, focusing on villages that were until recently relatively remote and predominantly agricultural. The chapter documents the integration of these village Gounders into the wider regional economy. Reductions in fertility and increased participation in higher education play important parts in the story, as do changes in gender relations. Gender relations were less unequal in 2008–9 than in 1981–2.

The Coimbatore–Tiruppur region has a history of strong agricultural and industrial development. Agriculture was already relatively commercialized in the late nineteenth century and relatively capital-intensive at that stage too (Baker 1984; Harriss-White 1996). The region was known later on for its early adoption of purchased agricultural inputs, in the late 1950s. It was also the foremost industrial region of Tamil Nadu for most of the twentieth century, with an emphasis on textiles and engineering products. It was the site of a dynamic pattern of small-scale industrialization spreading into the rural areas in the 1980s, 1990s, and 2000s, a period when agriculture was doing less well.

The villages on which this chapter is based are 20–30 km from Tiruppur and 40–60 km from Coimbatore. They were relatively remote in 1981–2, as the transport system was still poor. Coimbatore was already a major industrial centre. Tiruppur grew rapidly after 1981–2. There were a number of smaller urban centres near the study villages that grew after 1981–2 as well.

The chapter is based on fieldwork that began with a two-month period in 1980 looking at the Small Farmer Development Agency (SFDA) and Marginal Farmer and Agricultural Labourer Development Agency (MFALDA), which promoted and subsidized the acquisition of productive assets by poorer households. The villages were selected for their relatively strong agriculture and their relatively high levels of uptake of SFDA and MFALDA loans. Further fieldwork was undertaken in 1981–2, in 1996, and in 2008–9, and for shorter periods in several years in the 2000s as well. The focus was on long-term household strategies. The 1981–2 fieldwork involved a systematic survey of 20 per cent of the households in seven hamlets in two revenue villages, supplemented by in-depth interviews. Data were collected on household composition; land ownership and acquisition; wells, pumpsets, and other irrigation equipment; buildings, farm equipment, and livestock, in a community that was predominantly agricultural. There were questions on marriage and dowries, which were seen as central components of household investment and accumulation strategies.[1] I conducted the majority of 230 survey interviews, and a number of in-depth interviews, with a research assistant acting as an interpreter. The remainder of the survey interviews were conducted by V. Mohanasundaram, one of my research assistants at that time, on his own. The 1980 and 1981–2 fieldwork produced a substantial body of data much of which is only now being written up.

I returned in 1996 to do a survey of the descendants of the 1981–2 sample households still resident in the villages. Some information was also obtained on the 15 per cent or so that had left. There had been dramatic changes. Agriculture had suffered serious setbacks due at least in part to the declining water table. Non-agricultural activities had expanded. There was now a significant amount of commuting associated with these. Transport and communications had developed. The villages were much more integrated into the surrounding regional economy than they had been in 1981–2. The 1996 survey focused on similar issues to those covered in 1981–2. Some of the 1996 data have been written up in comparisons of the position of labourers, Dalit labourers in particular, in 1996 and 1981–2 (Heyer 2000, 2010).

I conducted a third systematic survey in 2008–9 as part of a larger project on the impact of the expansion of the knitwear sector in Tiruppur. This survey was based on a new 20 per cent sample, and a questionnaire very similar to those used in 1996 and 1981–2. The fact that the focus had been on longer-term strategies proved to be a good basis for exploring questions that remained relevant over time. It would have been better not to have used a completely new sample though. An augmented sample retaining descendants of 1981–2 sample households would have provided more information on important aspects of household trajectories and on migration associated with these. I did short bouts of fieldwork in 2003, 2004, 2010, 2011, 2012, and 2013, updating some of the information as well as focusing on particular issues. Some of the 2008–9 and other material collected in the 2000s has been written up in analyses focusing on Dalits and labour again (Heyer 2012, 2013, 2014a, and 2014b).

[1] 'Investment' is a term that is used in this chapter to denote expenditures associated with returns broadly construed. Marriages and dowries thus feature as 'investment', as does housing expenditure.

Long-term village studies are centred on residents in villages whose population change over time. In this case, the villages changed from agricultural communities in which inmigration and outmigration was driven by the availability of land and housing associated with the pursuit of agriculture in 1981–2; to communities in which there were also commuters depending on non-agricultural activities and there was outmigration to urban and industrial areas, in 1996; to villages in which there was less commuting, a few industries which had set up in the villages, and there were middle-aged people who had come back to agriculture after working elsewhere, as well as old-age dependents of people working elsewhere. Migration was picked up to the extent that it was directly linked to people resident in the villages. It is not easy in long-term village studies to document migration at all thoroughly.

Village studies in general, and long-term village studies in particular, make important contributions to the discussion of issues of broad contemporary relevance. I have used the data that I have collected to analyse and write on Dalit oppression and exclusion (Heyer 2010, 2013, and 2014a), the impact on Dalits of Tamil Nadu social policy (Heyer 2012), and declining female labour participation among Dalits (Heyer 2014b), for example. These contributions focus on issues best analysed at the household rather than the individual-level, and best viewed over the longer term. Social policy, for example, has an impact on whole households, and its impact is long- as well as short-term. What the village case study shows about the effects that social policy can have is a matter of general interest at a time when social policy is a continuing subject of debate at the national level. Another example, the analysis of declining female labour participation among Dalits (Heyer 2014b), is also best conducted at the household level. It has ramifications for gender relations within the household, which are played out over the longer term. The analysis raises issues that merit more attention than they have as yet received in discussions of declining female labour participation rates in the country as a whole.

The study villages were multi-caste villages in which caste played an important role. The major landowning groups were Naidus, Gounders, and Chettiars, Gounders being the most numerous of the three. Dalit agricultural labourers made up 30 per cent of the population in 1981–2, the majority landless. The clearest caste divide was between Dalits and non-Dalits. There were important distinctions between non-Dalit castes as well.

My previous work on the village data has focused on Dalits. This chapter focuses on Gounders. Gounders were a cohesive Other Backward Class (OBC) landowning group with distinctive kin and caste relationships and a reputation as successful entrepreneurs both in the agricultural and in the industrial sectors in the Coimbatore–Tiruppur region (Chari 2004; Damodaran 2008). They also had a reputation for being frugal and hardworking, and were known for working in the fields alongside their labourers. Smaller numbers of Naidus played similar roles. Gounders came through strongly in the Dalit account as an oppressive elite (Cederlof 1997; Heyer 2000, 2010). However there were also significant numbers of Gounder small farmers and labourers who were poor.

Gounders have been prominent in the development of the Tiruppur knitwear industry, rural Gounders included (cf. Chari 2000, 2004; Damodaran 2008; Vijayabaskar 2005). Gounders who migrated earlier to Tiruppur and settled there were heavily involved in the development of the industry. This chapter focuses on the large numbers of rural Gounders who were not part of the early development of Tiruppur. Gounders from the study villages came into the Tiruppur story late, by which time it had become much more difficult to enter successfully. The focus of this chapter is thus on small-time Gounders, pursuing small-scale agriculture and business, with at most a low-level college education leading to modest employment or self-employment acquired only in the past decade or so. The majority had been able to keep going on slow upward trajectories, reproducing themselves at progressively higher standards of living over time. Those at the bottom had made progress through long periods of hard work in low-skilled jobs. It is noteworthy that the Gounders from the study villages have not done better than this, given that they have been operating in a region that has been the site of dynamic industrial development and relatively successful agriculture for so long. They are typical of the large majority of Gounders in the region nevertheless (cf. Carswell and De Neve 2013, 2014, 2015; for example, though the villages on which they focus were in the power loom belt where Gounders are more dominant still).

The chapter shows the reduced role that agriculture played in Gounder livelihoods, the decline in fertility and rise of higher education, and changes in family and kin relations and marriage strategies, which played crucial roles in the long-term strategies of these households. Changes in gender relations are an important part of the story. The fact that the study focused on households and families enabled gender relations to be brought out. It was also important that the study was long-term. Many of the processes involved were inter-generational.

The chapter proceeds with sections on 1981–2, 1996, and 2008–9. The final section contains a summary of the overall findings.

1981–2

In 1981–2, the Gounder community in these villages consisted of small agriculturalists with livestock, together with agricultural labourers, some leasing in land. Many Gounders were part of the village landowning elite, but there were also many who were poor.

Table 12.1 compares the position of Gounders with that of other caste groups, by the occupations of their household heads. Sixty-three per cent of Gounder household heads were agriculturalists, 20 per cent agricultural labourers, and 11 per cent had non-agricultural occupations. The other members of the village landowning elite were Naidus and Chettiars. A slightly larger percentage of Naidus than Gounders were agriculturalists, some combining agriculture with trade and business. There were also significant numbers of Chettiar agriculturalists, and trader agriculturalists, as well as significant numbers of Chettiar agricultural labourers. The other large groups in the village population were the two Dalit labourer groups: Arunthathiyars and Pannadis. Virtually all of the households in these Dalit groups were headed by agricultural labourers in 1981–2.

The occupational mix in Gounder households is shown in Table 12.2. In 49 per cent of the Gounder households in the sample, all members were engaged in own account agriculture in 1981–2; in 25 per cent, some members worked as hired agricultural labourers and in some of these cases, some members also worked their own land but none worked outside agriculture; in 25 per cent, some members were engaged in non-agricultural occupations and others in agricultural (Table 12.2). Only 1 per cent of Gounder households had no members engaged in agricultural activities in 1981–2. Table 12.3a gives a breakdown of the non-agricultural occupations of individual male members of Gounder

Table 12.1 Occupations of Household Heads by Caste in 1981–2

1981–2: Household heads (%)	Gounders	Naidus	Chettiars	Other Non-Dalit	Pannadis	Arunthathiyars	All
Agriculture and livestock	63	57	34	6			32
Agricultural labourer	20	14	26	6	96	95	42
Construction, borewell mechanic, wood	1		3	3		2	2
Shops, trade, transport	8	14	34	10			10
Government, Coop, Electricity, et al.	2		3	13	4	2	4
Other Services				55			7
Knitwear, mills, workshops, powerlooms							
Dependents	5	14		6			3
All	100	100	100	100	100	100	100
Nos	84	14	35	31	27	43	234

Source: Village Surveys.

households in 1981–2, complementing the household figures. There were no female members of Gounder households in the villages engaged in non-agricultural occupations at the time.

Relatively small numbers of Gounders had been moving in and out of the villages in 1981–2, to and from other rural areas. Women migrated much more than men, in association with marriage, though some Gounder women married within the villages. Households sometimes moved to the villages of maternal kin to take advantage of the availability of land, housing, or employment, as also in times of adversity. Movements involving men as well as women were the exceptions though. The large majority of Gounder men lived where their fathers and grandfathers, and often great-grandfathers, had lived before.

The largest landholdings in the villages were just under 30 acres in 1981–2. Most were much smaller than this. Gounders were the largest group of landholders, with an average of 5.4 acres (Table 12.4). The wealthier Gounders were a sophisticated group of agriculturalists with profitable, commercialized, and relatively capital-intensive holdings. Nearly half (48 per cent) of their cultivated land was *thottam* land, that is land irrigated by wells, many of which were shared and nearly all powered by electric pumpsets. There was very little mechanization of field operations. There were only one or two tractors in the villages in 1981–2. The most important irrigated crops were cotton, turmeric, and sugar cane. There was a range of minor irrigated crops including fruit and vegetables. Groundnuts and *cholam* (sorghum) were grown on dry land, interplanted with a variety of other pulses and oilseeds. The

TABLE 12.2 Distributions of Occupations of Gounder Households

Households (%)	1981–2	1966	2008–9
Agriculture only	74	52	45
of which no hh members AL	49	32	39
of which at least 1 hh member AL	25	20	6
Agriculture and Non-Agriculture	25	42	42
Non-Agriculture only	1	2	8
Dependents	0	4	5
All	100	100	100
Nos	84	91	78

Source: Village Surveys

Note: hh–Household.

region as a whole was known in the early 1980s for the unusually high and sometimes excessive levels of purchased inputs used. Most Gounder households kept livestock, as draught animals, and for milk, and small stock for meat. The majority of agricultural labourers were Dalits. Arunthathiyars were the main source of tied labour, under employment conditions that were harsh (cf. Heyer 2000, 2010). Non-Dalits, including poorer Gounders, worked as casual or contract labourers.

The state had a strong presence in agriculture in the study villages in 1981–2, epitomized by the role of the Tamil Nadu Agricultural University (TNAU). Agriculturalists looked to the TNAU for new crop varieties, new agronomic practices, and solutions to pest and disease problems. Livestock owners were also well-served by veterinary services. Subsidized credit was available from the Village Community Agricultural Cooperative Society (VCACS), and from other agencies and banks. The SFDA and MFALDA had been actively involved in supplying bullocks, cows, implements, and equipment to small and marginal farmers, many of them Gounders. There was a strong farmers' association, the Tamil Nadu Agriculturalists' Association (TNAA) in which Gounders were active in 1981–2.

The main investments in Gounder households in the decades before 1981–2 had been in land, wells, and houses. Forty per cent of sample households had purchased land in the 1970s. Many had also invested in wells. Electric pumpsets replaced the *kavalai* system powered by bullocks in the 1960s and 1970s, allowing water to be lifted from greater depths. The wells were open, up to 100 ft deep, with bores that often went down another 100 ft, in 1981–2. The costs of digging new wells were in the tens of thousands of rupees.[2] Wells also had to be deepened every so often to reach the declining water table.

Houses also represented substantial investments in Gounder households in the decade preceding 1981–2. They made significant contributions to well-being. They were also major status symbols and played important roles in connection with daughters' marriages in particular. Twenty-four per cent of the households in the sample had bought or built houses in the 1970s, some of the expenditures concerned

[2] I have been wary of using monetary values in this study. Those that I have used are rough. Deflators are problematic. Moreover, the dates at which investments had been undertaken were not always easy to pin down.

amounting to as much as Rs 20,000–40,000. This was a time when the top price paid for an acre of good thottam land was Rs 20,000.

The primary motivation behind investment and the generation of surpluses was to provide for the next generation. For daughters, the key considerations were the need to provide dowries and to build up the asset position of their natal households to enhance their marriage prospects. For sons, the main concern in 1981–2 was the build-up of assets that would form the basis of their future in agriculture.

The average number of surviving children in Gounder families had been decreasing, as had the range. The mean amongst those who had started families in the 1950s was 3.4, and in the 1960s it was 3.0. By the 1970s, the mean had fallen to 2.2. There were significant numbers of families started in the 1950s and the 1960s that had four or five children or more. It was these children that had reached adulthood in the early 1980s, which was when their marriages and inheritances were coming up.

The need to make adequate provision for 1–2 sons or more had become an increasingly pressing issue as the cost of land rose, and as more capital was needed to work the land as well. The cost of getting daughters married had been increasing too.

The decrease in numbers of children per couple generally increases the problems associated with son preference which has been a major issue in Tamil Nadu as elsewhere (cf. Srinivasan and Bedi 2011, for example). With no sex selection, the probability of having no sons increases quite dramatically as the number of children per couple falls. While the child sex ratio became increasingly masculine in the 1970s suggesting that some sex selection was already taking place the number of daughter-only households also rose (Heyer 1992, Forthcoming). The proportion of households with no sons was much lower in the 1950s and 1960s when the total numbers of children per couple were higher and the range around the mean was much higher too.

The cost of educating children was not a major factor in decisions about family size in 1981–2. All Gounder children who went to school were in government schools in the villages that were free. Large numbers of boys, and some girls, had been getting some primary schooling for some time. There had been a gradual increase in the numbers getting at least some secondary schooling too. By 1981–2, the large majority of 5<15 year-old boys in the sample were in school and on track to complete secondary school. Very few in the sample had continued with post-secondary education however (Figure 12.1). The completion or near completion of secondary school was all that was considered important for a career in agriculture, which was what the majority of Gounders in the villages aspired to for their sons in 1981–2.

Women and girls had been getting less education than men and boys. The large majority of 5<15 year-old girls were in school in 1981–2, but high levels of enrolment for girls were very recent. Seventy per cent of 15<25 year-old women and girls had no formal education at all (Figure 12.1). It was still considered a problem for girls to have too much education as far as marriage was concerned. Women with too much education were considered a threat to their husbands and their in-laws, not likely to play subordinate roles. The low female participation rates in education in the decades preceding 1981–2 reflected this fact.

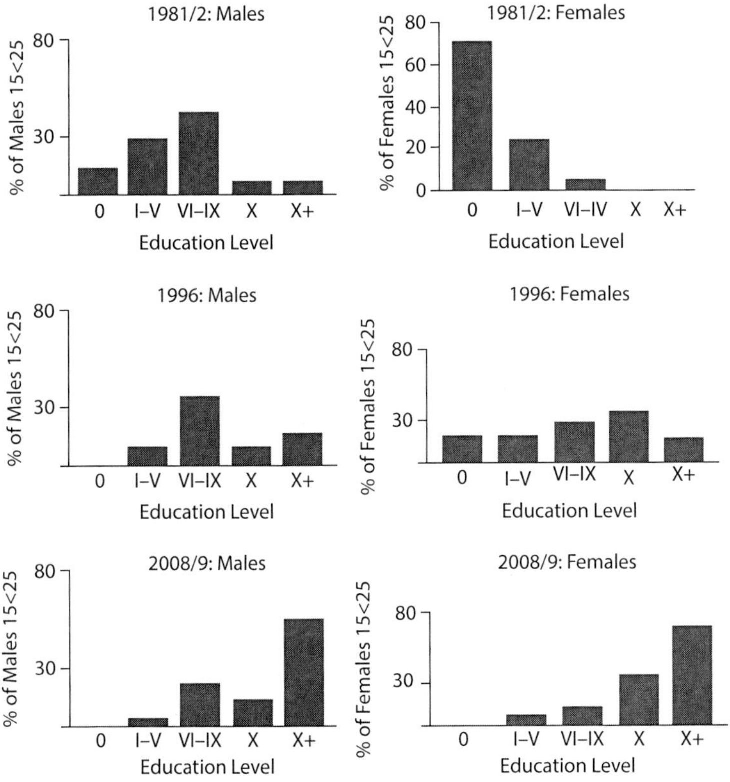

FIGURE 12.1 Education Levels of Males and Females Aged 15<25, in 1981–2, 1996, and 2008–9

Source: Village Surveys.

Daughters' marriages featured strongly in discussions of investment strategies in Gounder households in 1981–2. They made important statements about status. They could form the basis of economic alliances as well. This was a community in which there was relatively easy continuing social contact with daughters' families after marriage and in which it was not uncommon to find business alliances between brothers-in-law.

The payment of dowry was widespread in 1981–2 although bride price had been the norm among Gounders until the 1930s or the 1940s. In 1981–2, dowries were seen both as daughters' inheritances, and as the means whereby daughters could be well-settled. Daughters could inherit land, and had always done so in the relatively small number of households in which there were no sons in the past. Otherwise their inheritance took the form of dowry gold. Daughters being well-settled was an important consideration. There were significant numbers of instances in the sample of daughters returning to live with their parents after their marriages had broken down. There was almost no chance of remarriage in such cases, as the blame for failure fell on daughters and not on their husbands. Their husbands nearly always married again.

The dowries paid by Gounder households in the sample averaged 16–17 sovereigns in the 1960s and 1970s with no discernible upward trend.[3] The price of gold increased though, from Rs 300 per sovereign in 1970 to Rs 1,100 in 1980. The cost of daughters' marriages averaged more than Rs 20,000 in 1981–2, including expenses. Many households also incurred the cost of buying, building, or improving houses ahead of daughters' marriages. Daughters were nearly always married before sons, regardless of sons' ages. Outgoing dowries thus preceded incoming, making them and other expenses incurred difficult to finance.

Sons' marriages did not appear to be nearly as much of an issue as daughters' marriages were. Incoming dowries were valuable though, and used to finance the purchase of land, and houses, as well as for 'family expenses' in times of difficulty. The dowries that came with sons' marriages were linked both to the success of their sisters' marriages, if they had sisters, and to the value of their inheritances once any sisters' marriages had been accounted for.

Marriage and kin relationships played an important part in the resilience of the Gounder community and its reputation for withstanding

[3] Contrary to the upward trend for caste Hindus in general which was dominated by Naidus and Chettiars (Heyer 1992).

high levels of risk (Chari 2004; De Neve 2011). A good deal of time and money went into nurturing these relationships. Ceremonies associated with life-cycle events, such as ear-piercing, and puberty, could be lavish, though not as lavish as those associated with marriage. There was also a good deal of everyday visiting between kin. Women played an especially important role in maintaining and nurturing family and kin relationships. It was a burden for men as well. Daughters being married nearby was an important consideration in the maintenance of these relationships. It was also important, if sons moved, that they did not move too far away.

Women in Gounder households with land supervised female agricultural labourers, sometimes working alongside them in the fields, and looked after livestock (Heyer 2016). They also did all the domestic work, including cooking for labourers, who were provided with meals. It was very seldom that anyone was employed to help with any of this. In households with less land, women worked in the fields with other members of the household, looked after livestock, and often worked as agricultural labourers as well. In most landless households, women worked as agricultural labourers, earning considerably less than men in doing so.

Women in agrarian households in the Gounder community were in a stronger position than women in communities in which women married further away and once married did not visit their natal households, and communities in which there were strict embargos on women's work outside the house. There were many respects in which Gounder women remained very subordinated nevertheless.

1996

By 1996, the villages were no longer as exclusively agricultural. They had become part of a growing process of rural industrialization in which the expansion of the knitwear industry in Tiruppur was the driving force. Transport and communications had developed considerably and this had a major impact, making Tiruppur and other urban centres much more accessible than they had been in 1981–2. It was not only knitwear but metalworking and engineering workshops, other textile operations and other light industries, and all the activities associated with the development of these industries, which were opening up opportunities. Larger numbers from the villages were now working in mills, factories, and workshops, substantial numbers commuting as much as one and a half hours at either end of the day to do so. The population of the villages had changed from a population that was occupied predominantly in agriculture and agriculture-related activities in the villages in 1981–2, to a population in which there were substantial numbers of commuters and others working outside the villages in addition to those still working in the villages in 1996. Gounders were very much part of all this.

Sixteen per cent of the Gounder households in the 1981–2 sample were no longer represented in the villages in 1996, and in another 18 per cent, at least one of the subdivided households descended from a 1981–2 sample household had moved out. Nearly all of this outmigration was to urban centres and associated with non-agricultural opportunities. The majority of the outmigrants between 1981–2 and 1996 were small farmers and agricultural labourers, most of them going into low-skilled non-agricultural employment, which did not pay much more than agricultural labour. The pay for agricultural labour had increased substantially though (see Heyer 2010, 2012).

The total number of Gounders in the study villages had barely changed between 1981–2 and 1996. The natural increase in the population had almost exactly offset the outmigration in households in the sample.[4] The number of households in the sample increased however (from 80 in 1981–2 to 92 in 1996) as subdivisions created smaller households overall. In 32 per cent of these households all members were engaged in own account agriculture; and 20 per cent consisted of members who were agricultural labourers as well as members working their own land in some cases (Table 12.2). Forty-two per cent had members engaged in non-agricultural activities as well as agricultural, and 2 per cent members engaged in non-agricultural activities alone. Four per cent of the households were made up only of dependents, a category that had emerged since 1981–2. The numbers of individuals working in mills, factories, and workshops had nearly tripled since 1981–2 (Table 12.3b). There were still very few Gounder women in the villages in non-agricultural occupations though.

[4] The descendants of the 1981–2 sample do not constitute a 20 per cent sample of those resident in the villages in 1996. This has to be borne in mind in comparisons based on the two samples.

TABLE 12.3A Distributions of Occupations of Gounder Male Individuals Aged 5 Years or More (percentages of total males)

Male Individual Occupations (%)	1981–2	1996	2008–9
Agriculture and livestock	52	33	36
Agricultural labourer	13	10	4
Construction, borewell mechanic, wood		1	1
Shops, trade, transport	5	8	6
Government, Coop, Electricity, etc.	4	2	1
Knitwear, mills, workshops, powerlooms	6	19	18
In school or college	16	19	31
Unemployed: looking for work	2	2	
Dependent	2	8	3
All	100	100	100
Numbers	193	181	158

Despite the fall in numbers engaged in agriculture, the total area of land owned by the Gounders had increased between 1981–2 and 1996, more land having been purchased by Gounder households than sold. Mean landholdings per household were very similar in 1996 to those in 1981–2, however, with the increase in the number of Gounder households (Table 12.4). There had been a substantial increase in holdings between 2.5 and 7.5 acres, and a decrease in larger holdings, and a small decrease in the number who were landless. The Gounder land distribution was less polarised than it had been in 1981–2.

TABLE 12.3B Distributions of Occupations of Gounder Male Individuals Aged 5 Years or More (percentages of males in the workforce)

Male Individual Occupations (%)	1981–2	1996	2008–9
Agriculture and livestock	66	46	55
Agricultural labourer	16	14	6
Construction, borewell mechanic, wood		1	2
Shops, trade, transport	6	11	9
Government, Coop, Electricity, etc.	5	2	1
Knitwear, mills, workshops, powerlooms	8	26	28
All	100	100	100
Numbers	154	129	104

Source: Village Surveys.

TABLE 12.4 Landholding Size Distributions, Gounder Households

Acres	0	>0<2.5	2.5<5	5<7.5	7.5<10	10+	All	Total and Av. Per Household Areas
				1981–2				
nos.	12	16	15	18	7	16	84	455 ac
row %	13	19	18	21	8	19	100	av. 5.4 ac
				1996				
nos.	9	18	26	20	3	15	91	482 ac
row %	10	20	29	22	3	16	100	av. 5.3 ac
				2008-9				
nos.	12	19	23	10	4	10	78	336 ac
row %	15	24	29	13	5	13	100	av. 4.3 ac

Source: Village Surveys.

Agriculture was not doing as well in 1996 as it had been in 1981–2. Although there had been talk in 1981–2 about the continuing decline in the water table, few in the villages appeared to have foreseen the severity of the problem, which came to a head in the drought of 1984. Large open wells had been replaced by bore wells with powerful compressor and submersible pumps drawing water from as much as 600 ft in 1996. Despite substantial continuing investment in irrigation however, less land was irrigated and what was irrigated was irrigated less intensively than it had been in 1981–2. The cost of labour had also increased as non-agricultural employment competed with agricultural (Heyer 2010, 2012). Agriculturalists had not responded at all fully to this changed environment by 1996, although they were now growing substantial quantities of bananas alongside cotton, sugar cane, and turmeric on irrigated land. More cholam and fewer groundnuts were being grown on rain-fed land. There were fewer minor crops as well. Livestock numbers had fallen. Bullocks were no longer used as widely for transport, though they were still used for nearly all field operations. There were still only 4–5 tractors in the villages in 1996. The numbers of animals kept for milk and meat had fallen too. Fodder shortages were a factor here.

In 1996, investments in non-agricultural activities featured among major investment categories in addition to investments in land, wells, and houses. There had been roughly similar numbers of land purchases among Gounders residing in the villages in the 1980s and early 1990s as there had been in the 1970s, but unlike in the 1970s, there had also been substantial numbers of land sales. These occurred both as households got into difficulty, and as household members moved out of agriculture.

There had been more investments in non-agricultural activities in the 1980s and early 1990s than in the 1970s, mainly in trade and agri-processing, and in one or two power loom units. Some households with large landholdings were combining agriculture with moneylending, trade of various kinds, and groundnut oil crushing. Someone who was a fertilizer sales representative in 1981–2 had a fertilizer shop in a nearby urban centre in 1996. A young man had set up a Tiruppur knitwear unit in 1991, which had failed after a couple of years. He had then set up a micro-dairy, which he was running alongside a business selling saris in 1996. Someone else had established a power loom unit that he was leasing out in 1996. One or two Gounders had small retail shops. Another Gounder had obtained a Life Insurance Corporation (LIC) agency. None of this amounted to very much though. It represented early attempts to diversify out of agriculture in a period in which agriculture was doing less well.

Fewer new houses were built, bought, and renovated in the 1980s than in the 1970s. The numbers had picked up again in the early 1990s though. Many of the houses were better and cost more than those of the 1970s, the most expensive amounting to Rs 1.5 lakhs. This was about twice the price that was paid for an acre of good thottam land in the early 1990s. Another notable change was that 30 per cent of the households in the sample now had motorcycles as opposed to only 8 per cent in 1981–2. Motorcycles were becoming a major form of transport. They were a very visible presence on the roads around the villages in 1996. The community was clearly wealthier than it had been in 1981–2.

The numbers of children in Gounder households were beginning to stabilize at two per couple with less variation around the norm than earlier. A norm of two-child families was firmly established over the 1970s and the 1980s and more daughters-only households accompanied this.[5] While the child sex ratio was becoming more masculine it was

[5] The child sex ratio had continued to become more male though.

also clear that many couples starting families in the 1970s and 1980s had accepted that they would not have sons (Heyer Forthcoming).

Gounders were investing more in education in 1996 than they had been in 1981–2. Boys were now being sent to private schools, a number of which were within 5–10 km of the villages. The alternative was to go further away, staying in hostels, which cost more. One or two were staying with maternal grandparents in order to go to good schools in or near Coimbatore. More men and boys aged 15<25 were continuing in education in 1996 than in 1981–2 (Figure 12.1). One or two of those who had completed post-secondary qualifications in 1981–2 had made further progress too. A BSc clerk of 1981–2 had become a Coimbatore mill supervisor, and there was the BA fertilizer representative of 1981–2 who now had a shop. One or two more had completed post-secondary education after 1981–2 and had embarked on trajectories that might lead to some upward mobility in the future. Most of them who had post-secondary education were not doing anything different from those with less education, however.

There had been a considerable increase in the numbers of women and girls aged 15<25 who had completed secondary education (Figure 12.1). Significant numbers were continuing with post-secondary education in 1996 too (Figure 12.1). Most women and girls only went as far as class XI or class XII however, unlike men and boys, many of whom went on to do degrees. A young woman who had completed XII had a position on the staff of an engineering company on the outskirts of Coimbatore. The other women who had completed XI or XII were married, or destined to be married, and housewives. It was a sign of progress that it was now easier to find husbands for educated girls. In 1996, education could even be an advantage in the marriage market as far as girls were concerned. This was a big improvement over the situation in 1981–2.

Daughters' marriages were still a major preoccupation in 1996. There was no discernible upward trend in numbers of sovereigns given as dowries, but the price of gold had continued to rise. There were now more households with no adult daughters, and most of those with adult daughters had fewer than before, reflecting the fall in fertility in families started in the 1960s and 1970s. There were also more households with no adult sons. One of the ways of accommodating the fact that a household had no sons was to get a son-in-law to come and live in his wife's natal home, effectively taking the place of a son (see Srinivasan 2005, on this among Gounders in villages near Salem too). There were a number of such examples in sample households in 1996. There were other examples of elderly parents being supported by daughters living elsewhere (see Heyer [Forthcoming] for more on this). The support of elderly parents whose children had moved elsewhere was more of an issue in 1996 than it had been in 1981–2. The fact that there was more migration than in 1981–2 meant that parents could no longer always expect to have children and grandchildren living with them when they were old and needed care.

2008–9 et seq.

By 2008–9 the process of rural industrialization in which the villages were involved was further advanced. There had been further expansion of industrial activities in small urban centres and the countryside as well as in Tiruppur and Coimbatore. There were now two knitwear units in the study villages. A major development of a very different kind was the establishment of steel mills at either end of the study villages in 2009 but they had few linkages with the villages. There were several housing layouts in and near the villages too. These were unrelated to the steel mills, which provided their own accommodation for their workers, nearly all of whom came from far away. The housing layouts were established in anticipation of an increased demand for housing in the region as a whole, a demand to which they would be able to cater as industrialization spread further towards the villages and as transport and communications continued to improve. There had been considerable developments in transport and communications already between 1996 and 2008–9. Mobile phones had entered the scene by 2008–9 too.

There had been a significant decrease in the population of Gounders living in the villages between 1996 and 2008–9. There were only 314 in the 2008–9 sample, compared with 359 in 1996. There were still large numbers of Gounder commuters in the villages but not as many as there had been in 1996. By 2008–9, many who in 1996 would have been commuting had moved out. On the other hand, there were Gounders who had gone to work elsewhere and returned in their 40s and 50s. There were Gounder dependents as well.

The proportion of Gounder households in the villages, all of whose members were engaged in own account agriculture had increased slightly between 1996 and 2008–9, from 32 to 39 per cent (Table 12.2). The proportion of households made up of agricultural labourers as well as in some cases members working their own land had fallen substantially though. The proportion with members engaged in non-agricultural activities had increased. The numbers of males in the working population had fallen both because of outmigration and because significantly more young people were continuing for longer in school and college. The largest decrease was for agricultural labourers. The number of male individuals who were agriculturalists had fallen slightly and the number working in mills, factories, workshops, and power loom units had barely changed. There were still very few Gounder women in the villages engaged in non-agricultural occupations in 2008–9.

Despite the fact that the number of agriculturalists had increased, the total area of land owned by Gounders still living in the villages had fallen substantially as non-residents had been buying village land. The mean holding of Gounders still living in the villages was now 4.4 acres (Table 12.4). There was a larger proportion with holdings of less than 2.5 acres, and a smaller proportion with holdings of 5 acres and above. Some who previously had more than 5 acres had subdivided and not bought more, as they had gone into non-agricultural business or employment.

There had been a significant fall in land under cultivation too. Drip irrigation had been introduced in 2006, initially for bananas. By 2008–9, it was being used for other crops as well. It was being promoted by private companies selling equipment subsidized by the state, as state extension services had been run down. Agricultural officers were much less in evidence than they had been in 1996 and they were in much less demand when they did appear. The main crops being grown on irrigated land were now bananas, turmeric, and sugar cane. Cotton had almost entirely disappeared. The main dryland crops were cholam and groundnuts still, but the balance had shifted further towards cholam and away from groundnuts. There were fewer minor crops both on irrigated and on rain-fed land.

Most field operations were now mechanized. There were very few bullocks left. The numbers of milch animals had also fallen by

40 per cent since 1981–2; and, most of those were now cows rather than buffaloes. The number of sheeps and goats owned by Gounders had fallen by half. The livestock economy was playing a much less important role in Gounder households than it had been in 1981–2 or 1996. There were more tractors, trucks, and other motor vehicles in the villages. One of the households in the sample owned a car, and another had a number of trucks. The proportion of households with motorcycles had more than doubled, to 70 per cent.

Gounders were continuing to invest in agriculture, but there had been more investment in non-agricultural activities by 2008–9, some of it financed by the sale of land. There were more land sales than land purchases by sample households in the 2000s, the total area sold greatly exceeding the total area bought. The 2000s was the decade in which the sale of land for real estate came to dominate the sale for agriculture, and land prices lost their link with agricultural productivity. What was now crucial was the location of the land in relation to roads and transport routes.[6] The first agriculturalists to sell for real estate had seen their land sold on for several times the price that they themselves received. Later sellers were wiser to this.

The deepest wells were now 1,200 ft, and the cost of sinking a successful bore well and fitting it with a pumpset and pipes was Rs 2–2.5 lakhs. Continuing investment in irrigation was necessary for success in agriculture. The 10–15 per cent continuing so to invest were doing well.

There had been a wide range of non-agricultural investments in the late 1990s and the 2000s and these included almost as many that failed as were successful. There were investments in shops and in trade, most of which were successful, and continuing; likewise investments in the LIC agency, a finance company, and in moneylending. There were successful and unsuccessful investments in knitwear units, in power loom units, and in units making elastic for the knitwear sector. The two investments of well over Rs 1 crore in sample households were in a spinning mill and in a transport business. Both resulted in

[6] The highest price recorded in the 1990s was Rs 1 lakh per acre. By 2012 the price was Rs 10 lakhs per acre if the land was on the main road, and Rs 7 lakhs if it was not. See Rajshekar (2013) on the rise in rural land prices in the 2000s being an all-India phenomenon, which suggests that there were more general factors at work here.

heavy losses for the households and families concerned. There were 'investments' in politics, one of which led to a lucrative business in contracting, and one of which failed to produce a return. Members of extended families usually contributed to the financing of investments, bearing substantial losses when they did not go well. There were impressive accounts of recovery from failure, heavy losses followed by new starts, often several new starts, before success was eventually achieved. The ability to bounce back from failure was something for which the Gounder community was renowned. The narrative emphasized the value of experience and the value of a fresh start without outside finance. What should also be added is the value of kin and caste relationships, which allowed the losses to be dissipated and the new starts to be financed.

There had been a substantial increase in investment in houses in the 2000s when as many as 40 per cent of the households in the sample had built, or bought and renovated, houses, many in connection with daughters' marriages. Whereas in the 1990s, most of the expenditures amounted to less than Rs 1 lakh, and the highest was Rs 3 lakhs, in the 2000s most of the expenditures were between Rs 1 and 5 lakhs, and the highest by a household in the sample was Rs 13 lakhs. (Someone outside the sample had built a new house for Rs 20 lakhs in 2012.) Many of the houses being built in the 2000s were of higher quality than those built earlier, with glass windows and steel frames, tiled floors, elaborate fittings, and inside bathrooms and toilets. These investments were indicative of increasing wealth, agricultural as well as non-agricultural, among Gounders in the villages. The majority had been financed out of the proceeds of agriculture alone.

The numbers of children in Gounder households had now stabilized at two per couple with very little variation around the norm.

There was more investment in higher education, as Gounders aspired to have their children move out of agriculture (Figure 12.1). Among households in the sample that had children old enough for it to be possible to tell if they were investing in higher education or not, half were investing or had invested in some post-X education though there were also significant numbers of men and boys who had less than X. Those investing in post-XII education either had 5 acres or more land or enough outside income (including income from many years of low-skilled work in knitwear units) to supplement what they were getting from agriculture. The majority *not* investing in higher education were small farmers, labourers, petty traders, and so on.

Nearly all of the men and boys continuing in or completing higher education in 2008–9 had been to private English-medium schools for all or part of their education. Moreover, whereas in the 1980s and 1990s, those who went into higher education did BA and B.Com degrees, in the 2000s there was a heavy emphasis on engineering. Costs ranged from Rs 1 to 5 lakhs for a degree, depending on the subject, the quality of the institution, and whether it involved a hostel or commuting.

It is significant that most households found it difficult to fund more than one child through higher education well. Several households had taken bank education loans, ranging from Rs 1 to 4.5 lakhs, most finding them difficult to repay. There were only a few cases in which land had been sold to finance education, but several households continued to live in modest houses, because they were spending on education instead. Maternal grandparents helped in some cases too.

It was too early to see much pay off from higher education, because most of it was so recent. Isolated individuals had made it through higher education and into good jobs earlier. One or two had done well through part-time education while working, and/or through being sent by an employer to work far away. The majority worked within the region and were under strong pressure from families to do so. The expectation of the majority in 2013 was that young men who had completed degrees would get low-level administrative and/or engineering jobs that would pay Rs 10,000–12,000 per month or less initially, rising to Rs 25,000–30,000 with experience. There were the odd one or two getting into jobs with starting salaries of Rs 15,000–20,000 per month in the IT sector. These were the exception though. This contrasts with the UP situation described by Jeffrey, Jeffery, and Jeffery (2008) in which young men continued taking courses, and/or remained unemployed, right into their 30s. That was not an option in the study villages. There was too much pressure from families to get employment, even low-paying employment, once young men had completed one, or at most two, college degrees. It may be a factor that there is no shortage of employment in the region. More important appeared to be the pressure put on young men to repay a family that had found it difficult to finance the education in the first place though.

Few in the current generation with higher education were expecting to set up their own businesses, though they might do so after they had had some employment experience. The young man with an MBA who had set up the spinning mill that failed was an exception. He was distributing diesel generators in Coimbatore in 2012 and had ambitions to be a businessman of substance in the future. He came from one of the wealthier extended families and members of this family appeared willing and able to continue to provide him with support. Few with higher education were planning to be agriculturalists, though some might well end up as such.[7]

A similar proportion of women and girls had post-X education to men and boys in 2008–9 (Figure 12.1). Very few of them had been to private schools however, and the colleges to which they went, and the degrees for which they studied, were less costly and less prestigious than those of men and boys. One of two exceptions was the older of two daughters who had completed a Bachelors degree in International Business followed by an MA. The other was a young woman who had completed a Bachelors degree in Zoology followed by a B.Ed and an MSc. Both went on to do degrees in MPhil.

Whereas men and boys were being educated for careers, the majority of women and girls were being educated for marriage. In 2008–9, Gounder households were looking for educated brides, sometimes to compensate for relatively poorly educated bridegrooms, more often to complement bridegrooms who were well-educated themselves. Brides with higher education were not being sought primarily as good mothers who would be able to support their children's education. Nor were they expected to continue with their education or careers. They were being sought to strengthen their husbands' activities. The exceptions included the International Business graduate who was married to someone who supported her continuing studies and aspirations for a career as a college lecturer, and the Zoology graduate, married in 2012, who was hoping to be a teacher.

Being more educated might have been expected to give women more status within the households into which they married, whether

[7] Some individuals with higher education who were looking for non-agricultural employment in 1996 had ended up in agriculture in which they were doing relatively well in 2008–9.

they were allowed to continue with their education and/or careers or not. There had been some improvement, but not as much as many of the women with higher education would have liked (Heyer Forthcoming). Their parents' control over their marriages, and their husbands' control after that, was something that most still had to accept. A few were trying to persuade their parents to find husbands who would allow them to continue with their studies. Others were disappointed that they had not been allowed to study further but appeared resigned to this.[8]

Daughters' marriages were still a major preoccupation in 2008–9. In households in which there were no sons, 20 per cent in the 2008–9 sample,[9] land and other property went to daughters, on the understanding that sons-in-law would manage it. Many of these sons-in-law brought their own inherited property to the marriage as well. Some resided in daughters' natal households where they continued as agriculturalists. However, most moved out of agriculture and away from the villages. What was then important was that they took responsibility for looking after the property of their in-laws, and that they took responsibility for looking after their parents-in-law in old age. This all took place in what was in many ways still a very patriarchal society. Daughters might inherit property but it was their husbands who controlled it. Daughters might take responsibility for their aging parents but they depended on support from their husbands to do so. What was crucial was that parents could rely on daughters as well as sons to look after them as they aged. This was one of the factors that made it possible for couples to accept the fact that they had no sons.

There had been no significant change in the average numbers of sovereigns being given as dowries in the 1990s and 2000s, as compared with the 1970s and 1980s, and there were very few instances of perks, such as motorcycles or cars, being given in addition to gold. More daughters

[8] Guerin, Kumar, and Agier (2013) give a good account in the context of microfinance of the deference that more outgoing women feel they have to show in the household context. Others have drawn attention to similar situations in other contexts too.

[9] Many of the daughters being married in the 2000s would have been born around the time of the first survey in 1981–2.

were inheriting property though. This is very different from the situation being described by Srinivasan (2005) in Salem villages in which both dowry gold and perks had been increasing quite substantially in the 1980s and the 1990s. One of the factors responsible for the relative stagnation in dowries here may have been the increasing shortage of women. Another may have been that investment in education replaced dowries at least to some extent.

There was no longer an expectation that sons would necessarily continue to reside on parental holdings. They were now expected to move out of agriculture and this often meant moving out of the villages. However, sons were expected to take responsibility for parents and for the family land. They and their families often visited at weekends, and grandchildren stayed in school holidays as well. This was possible because sons did not move too far away.

It was more difficult to get sons married in 2008–9 than earlier. A distinct shortage of brides had developed in the region as a whole, a result at least partly of increasingly male sex ratios in the Gounder population (Heyer Forthcoming). A number of sons in poorer Gounder households in the villages had remained unmarried well into their 40s with no obvious prospect of getting married at all.

⋆ ⋆ ⋆

This chapter has documented the gradual transformation of Gounder communities in a particular set of villages in the Coimbatore–Tiruppur region over the 1980s, 1990s, and 2000s. These Gounder communities changed from communities of agriculturalists and agricultural labourers with a few people engaged in petty trade and so on in 1981–2, to smaller communities of older agriculturalists with married sons and daughters living elsewhere, substantial numbers of commuters, small numbers of agricultural labourers, small numbers of businessmen, and some dependents, in 2008–9. These are the sorts of changes one would expect as the role of agriculture declines, and rural populations become involved in industrial and related non-agricultural activities. More specifically, in 1981–2 the villages in which the Gounder communities on which this chapter has focused, lived, were far enough away from urban and industrial centres to be predominantly rural and agricultural, and by 2008–9 the urban and industrial economy had expanded, transport and communications had developed, and large numbers of these Gounders had become involved in the nearby urban and industrial economy. One of the things that is distinctive here is that these Gounders had not had to migrate outside the region, which was a major importer of labour, not an exporter. What is also distinctive is the family, kin, and caste relationships underpinning their economic activities, which were unusually strong, and which provided important support in the risky economic environment in which they found themselves. Also important is the fact that the period under review was a period in which the results of a significant decline in fertility fed into the adult population with noteworthy consequences for gender relations and household organization. Increased participation in higher education for girls as well as boys had a major impact as well.

The main findings elaborated in this chapter can be summarized as follows:

1. Increasing numbers of Gounder men and boys living in the villages entered industrial and other non-agricultural activities from the mid-1980s on, some but not all migrating to do so. However, virtually all Gounder women remaining in the villages continued in agriculture. It was only women in households that migrated that left agriculture.
2. The numbers of Gounders in the village population stabilized between 1981–2 and 1996, and then declined between 1996 and 2008–9. Commuting kept substantial numbers in the villages, more so in the former than in the latter period though.
3. The composition of the Gounder population in the villages changed over the period under review as younger people left, and older people stayed, and/or returned from working elsewhere.
4. There was very little change in the amount of land owned by Gounders in the villages between 1981–2 and 1996, but there was a substantial reduction between 1996 and 2008–9 as land was bought by outsiders, most of it for real estate. There was considerably less land under cultivation in 2008–9 than there had been in 1981–2 or 1996.
5. There was a general increase in income and wealth in these Gounder communities between 1981–2 and 1996, and between 1996 and 2008–9. This was reflected in better standards of housing, and in such things as increased ownership of motorcycles. There was rather

less change in standards of food consumption or expenditure on household consumer durables.

6. The levels of education increased between 1981–2 and 1996, particularly for girls. They reached substantially higher levels between 1996 and 2008–9 as both boys and girls went to college in significant numbers.
7. There was a decline in fertility among Gounders in the 1970s and 1980s when a two-child norm was firmly established. There had been some acceptance of the increase in daughter-only households associated with this. The child sex ratio became increasingly male though. This was creating problems for sons' marriages, particularly in poorer households in 2008–9.
8. The decline in fertility on the one hand, and the increased rates of outmigration on the other, had marked effects both on family and kin relations, and on gender relations, that were evident in 1996 and 2008–9. Increased participation in higher education also played a role. It is significant that the value attached to daughters both within their natal and within their marital households increased over the period under review. There is still a long way further to go to achieve anything approaching equality between Gounder women and Gounder men in these villages though.

References

Baker, C.J. 1984. *An Indian Rural Economy 1880–1995, The Tamilnad Countryside*. Oxford: Clarendon Press.

Carswell, G. and G. De Neve. 2013. 'From Field to Factory: Tracing Transformations in Bonded Labour in the Tiruppur Region, Tamil Nadu', *Economy and Society*, 42 (3): 430–53.

———. 2014. 'T-shirts and Tumblers: Caste, Politics and Industrial Work in Tiruppur's Textile Belt, Tamil Nadu', *Contributions to Indian Sociology*, 48 (1): 103–32.

———. 2015. 'Litigation against Political Organisation? The Politics of Dalit Mobilization in Tamil Nadu, India', *Development and Change*, 46 (5): 1106–32.

Cederlof, G. 1997. *Bonds Lost: Subordination, Conflict and Mobilisation in Rural South India c. 1900–1970*. New Delhi: Manohar.

Chari, S. 2000. 'The Agrarian Origins of the Knitwear Industrial Cluster in Tiruppur, India', *World Development*, 28 (3): 579–99.

Chari, S. 2004. *Fraternal Capital, Peasant-Workers, Self-Made Men, and Globalization in Provincial India*. New Delhi: Permanent Black.

Damodaran, H. 2008. *India's New Capitalists, Caste, Business, and Industry in a Modern Nation*. New Delhi: Permanent Black.

De Neve, G. 2011. 'Keeping it in the Family: Work, Education and Gender Hierarchies among Tiruppur's Urban Industrialists', in H. Donner and G. De Neve (eds), *Being Middle Class in India, A Way of Life*, pp. 73–99. Abingdon: Routledge.

Guerin, I., S. Kumar, and I. Agier. 2013. 'Women's Empowerment: Power to Act or Power Over Other Women? Lessons from Indian Microfinance', *Oxford Development Studies*, 41 (Supplement): S76–94.

Harriss-White, B. 1996. *A Political Economy of Agricultural Markets in South India, Masters of the Countryside*. New Delhi and London: SAGE.

Heyer, J. 1992. 'The Role of Dowries and Daughters' Marriages in the Accumulation and Distribution of Capital in a South Indian Community', *Journal of International Development*, 4 (4): 419–36.

———. 2000. 'The Changing Position of Agricultural Labourers in Villages in Rural Coimbatore, Tamil Nadu Between 1981–2 and 1996,' Queen Elizabeth House Oxford, Working Paper Series, No. 57.

———. 2010. 'The Marginalisation of Dalits in a Modernising Economy', in B. Harriss-White and J. Heyer (eds), *The Comparative Political Economy of Development, Africa and South Asia*, pp. 252–74. London: Routledge.

———. 2012. 'Labour Standards and Social Policy: A South Indian Case Study', *Global Labour Journal*, 3 (1): 5–29.

———. 2013. 'Integration into a Global Production Network: Impacts on labour in Tiruppur's rural hinterlands', *Oxford Development Studies*, 41 (3): 307–21.

———. 2014a. 'Dalit Households in Industrializing Villages in Coimbatore and Tiruppur, Tamil Nadu: A Comparison across 3 Decades', in V.K. Ramachandran and Madhura Swaminathan (eds), *Dalit Households in Village Economies*, pp. 133–69. New Delhi: Tulika.

———. 2014b. 'Dalit Women Becoming "Housewives": Lessons from the Tiruppur Region, 1981–2 to 2008–9', in Clarinda Still (ed.), *Mobility or Marginalization: Dalits in Neo-Liberal India*, pp. 208–35. New Delhi: Routledge.

———. 2016. 'Loosening the Ties of Patriarchy with Agrarian Transition in Coimbatore Villages: 1981/2–2008/9', in Bibhuti Mohanty (ed.), *Critical Perspectives in Agrarian Transition: India in the Global Debate*. New Delhi: Routledge.

———. Forthcoming. 'The impact of bride shortages in South India: Vellala Gounders in Villages in Western Tamil Nadu', in Sharada Srinivasan and

Shuzhuo Li (eds), *'Scarce' Women and 'Surplus' Men in Communities of Asia: Macro Demographics versus Local Dynamics*. New Delhi: Springer.

Jeffrey, C., P. Jeffery, and R. Jeffery. 2008. *Degrees without Freedom, Education, Masculinities, and Unemployment in North India*. Stanford CA: Stanford University Press.

Rajshekar, M. 2013. 'The Great Rural Land Rush', *Economic Times*, New Delhi, 12 November.

Srinivasan, S. 2005. 'Daughters or Dowries? The Changing Nature of Dowry Practices in South India', *World Development*, 33 (4): 593–615.

Srinivasan, S. and A.S. Bedi. 2011. 'Ensuring Daughter Survival in Tamil Nadu India', *Oxford Development Studies*, 39 (3): 253–84.

Vijayabaskar, M. 2005. 'Labour and Flexible Accumulation: The Case of Tiruppur Knitwear Cluster', in K. Das (ed.), *Industrial Clusters, Cases and Perspectives*, pp. 37–54. Aldershot: Ashgate.

13

JANINE RODGERS

Changes in Rural Labour Markets in Bihar

1981–2011

Up to the 1980s, Bihar's rural labour markets functioned along semi-feudal principles characterized by a highly unequal distribution of land, and the exploitation of labour through indebtedness, tenancy, and labour bondage (Prasad 1979, 1987). By 2009–10 most attributes of semi-feudalism had disappeared and market mechanisms prevailed, though some remnants of the old order, such as the payment of harvest wages on a share basis, survived. The chapter examines the changes that occurred in labour force participation, occupations, employment statuses, wage systems, and real wages over the 30-year period under consideration.

Every year, millions of men leave Bihar and go to work in other states for shorter or longer periods while their spouses and children remain in their villages of origin. More recently, the growth of Bihar's economy has accelerated, opening up new employment opportunities closer to home. Migration and commuting for work have brought major changes in rural life. They have had consequences for the individuals and families concerned, the labour market, gender relations, and agricultural development (Rodgers et al. 2012).

The findings presented in this chapter are based on surveys of the same 36 villages of Bihar,[1] at three points in time: 1981–3, 1998–9, and 2009–11. The first survey was a joint venture of researchers from the A.N. Sinha Institute, Patna, and the International Labour Office (Prasad et al. 1988). The last two were carried out under the auspices of the Institute for Human Development, New Delhi (IHD 2004, 2011; Sharma et al. 2001). Twelve villages, selected to reflect the principal characteristics of the different regions of the state were subjected to a more in-depth study.[2]

Changes in Labour Force Participation

Table 13.1 presents the labour force participation rates of men and women aged 15–59 in the 12 core villages covered by the three surveys.[3] The comparison is based on the combined primary and secondary economic activities performed under the statuses of employer, own account worker / self-employed, regular wage / salaried worker, attached labourer, casual wage worker, or unpaid family worker. Household (domestic) work is excluded, as are other statuses such as student, pensioner / too old to work, rentier, and disabled.

TABLE 13.1 Changes in Labour Force Participation, Primary and Secondary Activity Combined 1981–3, 1998–9, and 2009–10 (per cent)

	1981–3	1999–8	2009–10
Men	94	93	94
Women	56	58	67

Source: Sharma et al. (2001); Bihar Project, Household Survey 2009.

[1] The 36 villages were originally drawn from a cluster analysis of the districts of the plains of Bihar, which resulted in the identification of six distinctive groups. One district was selected in each group and six villages in each district.

[2] The 12 villages are: Alapur Bishunpur and Rupaspur Salempur in Gaya district; Dewan Parsa and Paharpur Deyal in Gopalganj; Khangaon and Mahisham in Madhubani; Chandkura and Mohiuddinpur in Nalanda; Belabadan in Purnia; Jitwarpur in Araria; Amarhi and Samhauti Buzurg in Rohtas.

[3] The household sample from those villages covered 554 households in 1981–3, 891 in 1998–9, and 974 in 2009–11.

The male labour force participation rate remained stable at the same high level over time (93–4 per cent). But the female labour force participation (FLFP) rose from 56 per cent to 58 per cent in 1998–9 and then 67 per cent in 2009–10. This means that it increased by 11 percentage points, corresponding to an almost 20 per cent increase over the thirty-year period. The bulk of the change occurred after 1998–9.

How can this increase in FLFP be explained? The determination of women's participation in the labour market is complex as many factors interact, some tend to increase FLFP while others tend to decrease it (see for example Bardhan 1979; Dasgupta and Goldar 2005: Srivastava and Srivastava 2009). The relative importance of the various forces at play varies with the characteristics of individual households and villages. Factors that tend to increase the demand for female labour include a shortage of male labour (for example, due to migration), an increase in agricultural productivity (for example, due to an increase in yields and cropping intensity), the introduction of new labour-intensive crops (for example, vegetables), or an increase in animal husbandry. Other factors tend to increase the supply of female labour such as survival needs and an increase in poverty, a reduction in the gender wage differential (it may be an incentive for women to enter the labour market), and changes in social norms. A third category of factors may decrease women's labour force participation: life cycle factors (child bearing and care responsibilities); an income effect (derived from an increase in the household's disposable income due to remittances from migrants, for example) as FLFP tends to follow a U-shaped curve in relation to household income.

An additional factor that may affect labour force participation over time is a change in the age structure of the population as participation rates differ across age-groups (Rodgers 2012). The main factors that tend to alter labour force participation in relation to age are: changes in the age of marriage, fertility rates, and life expectancy, and the spread of education. We observe that the structure of the overall working-age population has remained fairly stable over the 30-year period, though the relative proportion of women in the 15–24 age group has decreased by 3.8 percentage points.

In Bihar villages, all the determinants of female labour force participation listed above are at play to a lesser or greater extent but two seem to have had a more significant impact: a) the high incidence of

TABLE 13.2 Caste Distribution of Workers in 1998 and 2009

	Caste Distribution of All Households	1998		2009	
		Male Workers	Female Workers	Male Workers	Female Workers
Forward castes	29.7	29.1	1.8	30.0	5.4
OBC-I	17.0	18.3	21.4	17.4	34.1
OBC-II	20.7	20.1	29.9	20.3	17.1
SC	22.0	23.1	35.9	22.2	31.5
ST	0.5	0.3	0.0	0.6	0.0
Muslim (upper)	2.6	2.9	2.6	2.9	2.9
Muslim (backward)	7.4	6.0	8.5	6.5	9.0
Total	100.0	100.0	100.0	100	100.0

Source: IHD databases, 1998–9 and 2009–10 Bihar surveys.

male migration (women have had to assume more responsibilities, partly substitute for male labour while men are away, and to increase their mobility), and b) a change in social norms (it has become more acceptable for some women to work outside their home).

It is interesting to look at the relationship between caste and labour force participation over time as it can partly (although not exclusively) reflect changes in social norms. In a previous chapter, it was found that caste was a strong determinant of female labour force participation, while class had a stronger effect on employment status (Rodgers 2012). Table 13.2 presents the distribution of male and female workers by caste in 1998 and 2009. In both years, the distribution of male workers mirrors more or less the caste distribution among the sampled households. The picture is somewhat different for female workers. In 1998 Scheduled Caste (SC) and Other Backward Castes (OBC) II women were over-represented among female workers and Forward Caste women much under-represented. In 2009, the two most striking changes were the increase in the shares of OBC-I and Forward Caste women among female workers. The majority of OBC-I households belong to the agricultural labouring or small peasant classes; the incidence of migration among OBC-I men aged 15–59 increased by 60 per cent between 1998 and 2009, which induced women into entering the labour force. While 76 per cent of OBC-I women declared domestic work as their main occupation in 1998, the proportion had dropped to 48 per cent in 2009. The higher participation of Forward Caste women is explained by the availability of 'acceptable' jobs with the extension of education and healthcare programmes.

Occupational Change

The analysis of change in occupations over time is somewhat hampered by the fact that definitions and concepts have changed from one survey to another but comparisons can be made across broad categories. Though Bihar's rural economy remains heavily dependent on agriculture, with little diversification, a surprisingly large variety of occupations and economic activities are reported by villagers nowadays. The change in class structure observed between the 1981 and 2009 surveys (Rodgers et al. 2012) shows only a modest increase in the proportion of households exclusively dependent on non-agricultural work (from 6 to 13 per cent) but does not reflect adequately the change in occupations within the whole labour force. The types of non-agricultural work have changed, the sources of income have diversified, and many more households report some non-agricultural income sources.

Table 13.3 shows the distribution of workers by sector of economic activity. In 1981, the structure was quite undifferentiated. Almost 80 per cent of workers reported agriculture, livestock, or fishing as their principal occupation; some 8 per cent were in services, including many caste occupations; and 3 to 4 per cent were to be found in each category of industry, trade/transport, and white collar or government jobs. Secondary occupations were even less differentiated, with 94 per cent in agriculture and allied activities.

By 2009, a substantial change had occurred. Only 44 per cent of principal occupations were in agriculture and allied activities. Outside agriculture there was a fairly balanced occupational structure. Some 9 to 11 per cent of total workers were found in each of four categories—skilled workers, traditional artisans, industrial workers, and professional workers, with 16 per cent in unskilled physical work (of which 15 per cent were in construction). A detailed breakdown of these

TABLE 13.3 Occupations of Workers Aged 15–59, 1981–2, and 2009–10 (per cent distribution)

	1981–2			2009–10	
	Principal occupation	Secondary occupation		Principal occupation	Secondary occupation
Agriculture, livestock, fishing	80	94	Agriculture, livestock, fishing	44	88
Construction	< 1	< 1	Traditional village-based trade, service, artisan	10	2
Small industry	3	< 1	Skilled technical	11	<1
Large industry	< 1	< 1	Unskilled physical	16	8
Service	8	< 1	Industry	10	<1
Trade/transport	4	< 1	Modern services and professional	9	<1
Govt/white collar	4	< 1	Other	<1	0
Other	< 1	0	Total	100	100
Total	100	100			

Source: Prasad et al. (1988); IHD databases, 1998–9 and 2009–10 Bihar surveys.

broad categories into 28 occupations[4] shows that workers were scattered among a diversity of occupations. In contrast, the change had been much smaller for secondary occupations. Sixty-one per cent of the respondents declared a secondary economic activity and these occupations were heavily dominated by agriculture, livestock, and fishing (88 per cent of all secondary activities) and to a lesser extent construction work. In practice, the difference with principal occupation is largely due to animal husbandry (included with agriculture), which accounts for 37 per cent of secondary occupations.

However, aggregate figures represent poorly the actual situation because occupations are highly differentiated by sex. Women who report an economic activity as principal occupation overwhelmingly work in agriculture and only 19 per cent work outside agriculture (that is less than 4 per cent of all women aged 15–59). Men, on the other hand, show a diversified occupational pattern, with only 37 per cent declaring agriculture as their primary activity and the others working in a wide variety of non-agricultural occupations. There is less difference between men and women in secondary occupations, though the concentration in agriculture and related activities is still stronger for women.

The detailed breakdown of occupations by sex show that women are a majority in only two occupations out of 28—animal husbandry and modern health services. In half of the occupations, they account for less than 10 per cent of workers. Only in agriculture, brick making, teaching, traditional health services, and political representation do they cross 20 per cent (the last of these no doubt the result of reservation policies).

[4] Occupation mapping: *Agriculture, livestock, fishing* = cultivation annual crop, cultivation perennial crop, animal husbandry, fisheries. *Traditional village based trade, service, artisan* = traditional artisans, religious function (Brahmin, nai), personal services, traditional health services, sales worker. *Skilled technical* = skilled artisans, repair mechanic, transport worker, agriculture equipment operator. *Unskilled physical* = construction, brick making, coolie, mining/quarrying. *Industry* = agro-processing, small/household industry. *Modern services and professional* = hotel/ dhaba/ restaurant/ tea-stall, teaching, lower-level administrative work, higher professional and technical services, modern health services, financial and legal services, security workers, political representatives. *Others* = None of the above.

How is the considerable shift in occupation among men in view of the limited local development in the villages concerned to be explained? It can be traced primarily to migration and commuting. The decline in the importance of agriculture as an occupation could already be observed between 1981 and 1999, when the share of agriculture declined from 81 per cent to 74 per cent;[5] but it has clearly accelerated since the beginning of the century. Though migration had already grown significantly by 1999 and provided sizeable additional incomes to households, it had not yet had a substantial impact on the occupational structure. Much migration had been for agricultural work and for short periods; but by 2009, the nature of migration had evolved: the majority of migrants headed towards urban areas, stayed for longer periods at a time, and looked for more regular work in industry and services. At the same time, during the 2000s, the Bihar economy picked up, the pace of growth accelerated, and new non-agricultural employment opportunities were created within commuting distance from some villages. New occupations have emerged through migration or commuting—security guard, driver, plumber, hotel or factory work, etc.—for which training is acquired on the job and not passed on from father to son.

There are significant differences in the types of economic activities performed by migrant and non-migrant workers. Twenty-five per cent of migrants work as unskilled workers in construction, brick kilns, or as coolies; 21 per cent are industrial workers in small or large scale industrial firms, and 18 per cent are skilled artisans, repair mechanics, transport workers, etc. On the other hand, 60 per cent of non-migrant workers work in agriculture, 13 per cent in village-based activities (trade, services, or as traditional artisans), and another 10 per cent do some unskilled physical work.

The diversification of occupations within the villages themselves has remained fairly limited. In many villages, traditional artisanal and service occupations have declined and the jajmani system tends to disappear. Where those occupations have survived, their content has often changed. For example, at the beginning of the 1980s, a village carpenter mainly made or repaired wooden agricultural appliances, but nowadays he mostly makes furniture. Furthermore, in some service occupations,

[5] Figures from the IHD NABARD report (IHD 2004).

women have replaced their absent migrant husbands, as was observed among some Dhobi communities, for example. On the other hand, new occupations have emerged—tailor, plumber, electrician, etc.—for which training was often acquired on the job during migration.

Over the last 30 years, rural incomes in Bihar have increased significantly due to a growth in agricultural wages (real wages increased between two and three times since 1981) and remittances sent or brought back by migrants. As a consequence, consumption has increased and village grocery shops, tea-stalls, repair shops, etc. have spread. A few agro-processing facilities, such as rice and flour mills, have expanded in the agriculturally more advanced villages; but overall the level of employment created locally has remained very limited. The recent acceleration of growth of the Bihar economy has created an embryo of local development within the reach of some villages but not of those more remote.

Changes in Employment Status

The analysis of change in the employment status structure is based on the occupations of men and women aged 15–59 with either a primary or secondary economic activity. Workers are classified into three main categories: self-employment (including the economic activities performed by unpaid family workers), wage/salaried regular work (including tied labour), and casual work.

As Figure 13.1 shows the employment structure of men and women has not followed the same evolution. The two striking features are: (a) the steady fall in the incidence of self-employment among men and its increase among women, and (b) the share of regular employment that has made significant progress among men but has had little dent among women.

Between 1982 and 1999, the trend in regular employment among men was the result of two tendencies that offset each other: the decline in attached labour and the growth in regular jobs secured by skilled and semi-skilled migrants and the better educated. At the same time a casualization of the male labour force occurred due to both the gradual disappearance of tied labour and the increasing incidence of migration among unskilled labour. Between 1999 and 2010, the increase in the share of regular employment continued. Now it represents 26 per cent of the male labour force (28 per cent if considering only principal occupation).

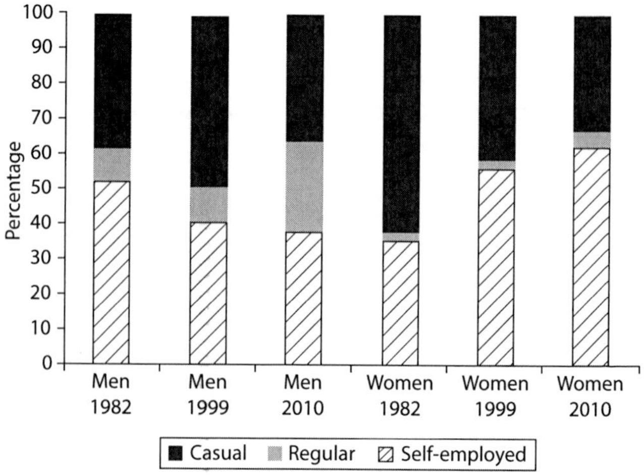

FIGURE 13.1 Status of Economically Active Men and Women Aged 15–59
Source: A.N. Sinha/ILO project 1981–3; IHD Bihar Surveys 1998–9 and 2009–10.

The marked increase in female self-employment is due to their growing involvement in agriculture and animal husbandry and to their status as unpaid family workers (which represents two thirds of women's 'self-employment'). There is a positive and significant correlation between women's labour force participation and the proportion of migrants within a village (Rodgers 2012) which supports the hypothesis that the work-load of women left behind increases when men migrate (Datta and Rustagi 2012). It reflects a feminization of agriculture.

The share of women's regular employment has progressed little (from 1 per cent in 1982 to 3 per cent in 2010) because women's mobility is restricted and employment opportunities outside agriculture within villages are limited. The decrease in the relative importance of casual labour can be partly explained by an income effect. As migrants from the poorest households access more regular and better-paid jobs, their spouses may withdraw their participation in the labour force.

How are these shifts in employment status distributed over different categories of households? Table 13.4 shows the percentage of

TABLE 13.4 Percentage of Households Where One Member had a Principal Occupation in Non-agricultural Work (by work status in that occupation and class of the household), 2009–10

Class	Non-agricultural self-employment/ employer	Non-agricultural regular wage employment	Non-agricultural casual wage employment
Agric. Lab. Landless	7.2	16.8	46.3
Agric. Lab. Cultivating	7.7	18.6	35.3
Small Peasant	21.2	31.9	39.4
Medium Peasant	19.4	32.3	26.5
Large Peasant	20.1	42.4	15.9
Landlord/Supervision	27.2	65.1	6.2
Non-agric. Wage Employment	10.9	51.2	33.6
Non-agric. Self-Employment	89.0	24.9	14.4
Total	15.5	28.5	34.0

Source: IHD Bihar Survey, 2009–10, Household sample.

households where, in 2009–10, at least one member had his principal occupation in a non-agricultural sector, as self-employed/employer, regular wage worker, or casual wage worker, by (agrarian) class. It can be seen that non-agricultural principal occupations were very common in all classes. They were found in 68 per cent of households altogether, a considerable change compared with 1981, when, as seen above, 80 per cent of principal (economic) occupations were in agriculture.

However, the pattern of this work was strongly related to agrarian class. Only 7 per cent of agricultural labour households reported self-employment in non-agricultural work, against 20 per cent or more among the cultivating or landlord classes. Even more striking, the proportion of households with regular non-agricultural wage work rose steadily from 17 per cent among landless labourers to 65 per cent among landlords; while for casual non-agricultural work the reverse was true, declining steadily from 46 per cent for landless labour to 6 per cent for landlords. So the old class hierarchy clearly carries over to the new economic environment.

What role does education play in determining employment status? Table 13.5 presents the distribution of the educational attainment of

TABLE 13.5 Employment Status by Level of Education, 1998–9 and 2009–10 (per cent)

	1998–9						2009–10					
	Self-employment		Regular employment		Casual		Self-employment		Regular employment		Casual	
	Men	Women	Men	Women	Men	Women	Men	Women	Men	Women	Men	Women
Illiterate	29	85	19	20	67	94	21	79	14	19	43	89
Up to primary completed	20	7	15		13	6	11	8	11	4	24	7
Middle	18	4	17		11	–	11	7	14	8	15	1
Matriculation	19	4	22	30	7	–	35	3	31	19	14	2
Pre-University	7	–	10	20	2	–	13	3	10	27	3	1
Above	7	–	16	30	1	–	9	–	21	23	1	–
	100	100	100	100	100	100	100	100	100	100	100	100

Source: IHD Bihar surveys 1998–9 and 2009–10.

workers within each category of status for 1998–9 and 2009–10. As expected, the incidence of illiteracy and low level of education is higher among casual workers, and more so among women than among men. The more even representation of different levels of education within self-employment and regular employment attests to the heterogeneity of the jobs within those two statuses. We also note that though the general level of education has improved between the two surveys, the education pattern within and across statuses has not changed much. Education is certainly a lever to access better quality employment but it is by no mean sufficient. Family and social networks play an important role.

In the previous sections, migration was identified as the main driver of occupational diversification; how is it reflected in employment status? The incidence of migration is high in rural Bihar. It varies from village to village but overall, during the year prior to the 2009–10 survey, half the men aged 15–59 migrated for a shorter or longer duration: 6 per cent went away for less than 3 months, 43 per cent between 3 and

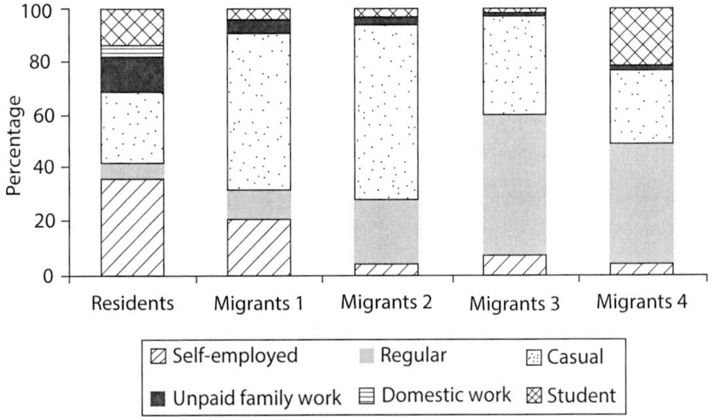

FIGURE 13.2 Work Status and Migration, 2009–10 (men aged 15–59, primary activity)

Source: IHD Bihar Survey, Household sample, 2009–10.

Notes: Migrants 1 = away less than 3 months, Migrants 2 = away between 3 and 8 months, Migrants 3 = away more than 8 months but spouse and children living in the village, Migrants 4 = away more than 8 months and unmarried.

8 months, 28 per cent for more than 8 months but their spouse and children remained in the village, 14 per cent for more than 8 months and were unmarried, among them 23 per cent are students. Also, 9 per cent of migrants left for more than 8 months but the spouses were not living in the village.

Over time, migration has not only increased but its profile has changed. The majority of migrants are now heading towards urban areas and the duration of migration has lengthened. Figure 13.2 shows that work status differs between residents and migrants and that the length of migration is associated with different patterns of employment.

The proportion of self-employed is higher among residents and, to a lesser extent, among short-term migrants. Those two categories correspond mainly to households that operate landholdings either as owners or sharecroppers. Short-term migrants are circular migrants who come back regularly and contribute to the economic activities of their villages, in particular at peak agricultural seasons. Casual work is undertaken by both residents and migrants. Its incidence varies between 30 per cent and 70 per cent. It is most prominent among short- and medium-term migrants; construction is a big employer of casual labour. The incidence of regular employment increases with the duration of migration. In the group of migrants away for more than 8 months and unmarried, 22 per cent are students and 44 per cent are regular workers.

Changes in Wages

Wage structures in rural Bihar are complex. In the 1970s and 1980s there was usually a single dominant daily agricultural wage within a village (or rather two wages, one for men and one for women), alongside a fixed share of the crop at harvest time. Today wages are more diverse and fluctuating, they are not always paid on a daily basis (contract work is expanding)[6] and the wider range of crops and activities undertaken implies a correspondingly wider range of wage levels.

[6] In 19 villages out of 36, some agricultural operations are performed under the contract system.

Despite the monetization of the economy, in one-third of the villages the most common daily wage (in addition to the harvest wage) is still paid entirely in kind, and in all wages there is a kind component consisting of a *nashta* (breakfast) or a meal, or both. The variability of wages in function of crops and operations and the difficulty of measuring village-level averages make the evaluation of change in wages over time a challenge. The detailed information from the three surveys is given in the Annexure I. A fairly complex manipulation was required to convert the various elements of the wage to first cash terms,[7] and then correct for price changes.[8] The results are given in Table 13.6 by district.

Wages are mean daily wages. The last three columns, in constant prices, show that the increases in real wages have been large. Between 1981–2 and 1998–9, wages doubled in Gaya, Nalanda, and Purnia, and rose less but nevertheless quite substantially in Madhubani, Gopalganj, and Rohtas. These last three districts had the highest recorded wages

[7] Nashta and meals have been converted into rupee equivalents using the average valuation by cultivators and agricultural workers (nashta = Rs 9.55; meal = Rs 17.9). Wages paid entirely in kind, including harvest share, have been converted into approximate cash equivalents, using average retail prices prevalent in the villages at the time of the survey (Per kilo: rice = Rs 15.5; paddy and marua = Rs 10; wheat and atta = Rs 11.5; pulses = Rs 60; onions = Rs 18; potatoes = Rs 12; sattu = Rs 20).

[8] Conversion to rupees at 2010–11 prices: In 1981, the price of rice was Rs 2.58 in Monghyr market, wheat Rs 2.05 per kg. This has been used as a reference. 'Grain', which may include inferior grains, has been evaluated at Rs 2 per kg. The nashta is estimated at Rs 0.75 and the meal at Rs 1.25, on the basis that the latter could be substituted by 0.5 kg of rice. For 1998–9 or 1999–2000 wages were converted to rupees in the IHD NABARD report, and that figure has been used. The same report indicates that the consumer price index for agricultural labourers for October 1999 to April 2000 stood at 387 (1981 = 100). This has been used to correct for price changes between the first two surveys. In September 2010–March 2011 the average price index was 533 (1986–7 = 100); and on the same scale the average for the period October 1998 to March 1999 was 282. This has been used to correct for price changes between the second and third survey. The data reported in Table 13.3 refers to the kharif season 2010 and rabi 2011. Estimates for the nashta, the meal, and the price of foodgrains are noted in the above footnotes.

in 1981–2, so there was some homogenization across districts in this period. From 1998–9 to 2010–11, there was again a substantial increase, varying from 34 per cent in Rohtas to 91 per cent in Gopalganj. The highest increases occurred in Gopalganj (91 per cent), Madhubani (77 per cent), and Purnia (64 per cent), and these are the three districts with the highest incidence of migration.

This trend in real wages is consistent with earlier findings from detailed enquiries in two villages in another part of Purnia district (Rodgers and Rodgers 2011). That study found that, between 1981 and 1999, real wages doubled for casual agricultural work, and between 1999 and 2009, they rose again by another 50 per cent; these estimates are very close to those for Purnia in Table 13.6. That study also found that male-female wage differentials had declined.

The trends in real wages in Table 13.6 refer only to male casual daily wages, and the harvest share can show a different pattern. The institution of the harvest share is persistent, but the level of the share is not. This is not surprising. As real casual daily wages rose, the harvest share should also have risen to maintain parity. It is true that yields have risen, and that makes it possible to harvest more per day, raising the returns to a day's labour. But the effort needed also increases and the daily gain from that source is certainly less than the rise in productivity.

Table 13.7 shows that, between 1981–2 and 1998–9, when real casual wages doubled or almost so, the harvest share also rose almost

TABLE **13.6** Changes in Casual Wages (male, full day) from 1981 to 2011, rupee equivalents, at current and constant (2010–11) prices

Districts	1981–2	1998–9	1981–2	1998–9	2010–11
	In current Rs		In 2010–11 Rs		
Gaya	4.58	36	34	68	91*
Gopalganj	5.25	29	38	55	105
Madhubani	5.75	30	42	57	101
Nalanda	4.12	35	30	66	99
Purnia	3.75	29	27	55	90
Rohtas	7.00	43	51	81	110

Sources: Prasad et al. (1988); Sharma et al. (2001); IHD database, 2011 Bihar survey.
Note: * 2 villages were surveyed in each district but for 2010–11 only one village is taken into account because of conflicting estimates for the second village.

TABLE 13.7 Harvest Shares (Paddy) over Time

District	Village	1981–2	1998–9	2011
Gaya	Alapur Bishunpur	1/16	1/11	1/11
	Rupaspur Salempur	1/16	1/11	1/12
Gopalganj	Dewan Parsa	1/20	1/10	1/10
	Paharpur Deyal	1/20	1/10	1/8
Madhubani	Khangaon	1/15	1/12	1/12
	Mahisham	1/15	1/12	1/12
Nalanda	Chandkura	1/16	1/14	1/14
	Mohiuddinpur	n.a.	1/14	1/10
Purnia/	Belabadan	1/9	1/8	1/9
Araria	Jitwarpur	1/8	1/8	1/8
Rohtas	Amarhi	n.a.	1/13	1/12
	Samhauti Buzurg	n.a.	1/12	1/12

Source: Village schedule, round 2, 2011, Bihar Project on Inclusive Development, IHD; Sharma et al. 2001; Prasad et al. 1988; reprocessed data, village schedule, 1981.

everywhere—but the extent of the change varied widely, from little or no change in Purnia to a doubling of the share (from 5 per cent to 10 per cent) in Gopalganj. There was a clear tendency for the share to rise most where it had been lowest before (as in the case of daily wages, there was some homogenization). But between 1999 and 2011, this trend came to a halt, and the harvest share stabilized, although daily wages continued to rise. The wage for harvesting has therefore declined in relation to the wage for other operations, although of course its real value has been maintained since it is paid in kind, and has probably increased somewhat because of the productivity point made above.

Contrasting the Process of Change in Wages in Two Villages

There are considerable differences among Bihar villages in terms of size, caste and class composition, land distribution, level of agricultural development, literacy rate, infrastructure, economic structure, incidence of migration, etc. Some of these differences reflect regional characteristics, but there are also different types of village within the same region. A comparative advantage of the Bihar study is to enable us to identify and contrast different development paths among the survey villages. This has not yet been fully analysed but a case study of two villages was conducted at the beginning of 2012 (Datta et al. 2014) and will allow us to refine the analysis of wages.

In 1981, Chandkura, a Kurmi-dominated village in Nalanda district, was described as a relatively prosperous village of medium peasants typical of South Bihar while Mahisham, a village dominated by Brahmins and a few Muslim landlords in Madhubani district, was described as a backward village typical of North Bihar.[9] In 1981, wages were paid in kind in both places but the rates were quite far apart. The most common daily wage in Chandkura was in the range of 1.2 to 1.7 kg of grain compared with 2.2 to 2.5 kg in Mahisham. At first sight, it may seem surprising to find lower wages in the agriculturally advanced village and higher wages in the more backward village. But daily wages do not take into account the amount of work available the whole year round nor the overall earnings of the labouring households. In Mahisham, crop diversification was very limited, production and yields were much lower than in Chandkura, so employment levels were lower and therefore higher wages had to be paid for the maintenance and reproduction of the labour force.

By 2011 wages were still paid in kind in Chandkura but had been monetized in Mahisham and the wage differential between the two villages had disappeared. For example, half a day weeding was remunerated with 2 kg of rice plus nashta in Chandkura and Rs 30 plus nashta in Mahisham. At the time of the survey, the average retail price of rice in Chandkura was Rs 14–16 per kg, which would bring the wage rate to Rs 28–32 plus a nashta, more or less equivalent to that in Mahisham. It seems that the wage increase accelerated in Chandkura over the last five years.

How far have wages risen over the whole 30-year period? Because of the complexity of the wage system—partly cash payment, partly payment in kind, varying with the agricultural operations, the crop, etc.—the estimation is not simple. In Chandkura, it is estimated that the rise may lie between 90 and 230 per cent and in Mahisham between 60 and 110 per cent (for a detailed calculation, see Annexure II).

[9] See Prasad et al. (1988).

In 1981, both Chandkura and Mahisham were labour-surplus villages. In 2011, farmers in both places complained about the difficulty of hiring labour, but the labour shortage process has evolved differently in the two villages. The pressure on land and a poorly performing agriculture in Mahisham pushed labourers to look for sources of earning outside the village. Development in North Bihar being sluggish, they migrated further afield, to other states in Western India. In the case of Chandkura, a more dynamic agriculture offered work opportunities in the village until the rate of growth of agricultural production slowed down. By that time the growth of the Bihar economy had picked up and work opportunities were being created within the commuting belt of Chandkura (from Hilsa to Patna). Non-agricultural wage work being more remunerative than agricultural activities, competition for labour inside the village drove agricultural wages up.

A gender dimension needs to be added to the analysis. Only men are migrating or commuting to find jobs outside the villages, resulting in shortages of male labour for agricultural work. But in Mahisham, the unabated increase in population, the sluggishness of agricultural production, and the lack of alternative job opportunities for women within the village have slowed down the progression of female wages. Though female labour force participation has increased, agricultural employment has to be shared among an increasing female labour force and half-day work seems to have become a generalized pattern. On the other hand, in Chandkura crop diversification and the expansion of labour-intensive crops, such as vegetables, requiring weeding, spraying, and other labour-intensive operations, has increased the demand for female labour and hence pushed the wage up in a tight labour market where female labour force participation has not been expanding. Over the years, wage rates have become more differentiated according to the agricultural operation, the sex of the labourer, and the peaks of demand for labour. Men tend to restrict their agricultural work inside the village to the most remunerative operations and periods. But women are less mobile; they remain confined to the village and have to take what is on offer. This differentiation in employment opportunities clearly helps to segment the wage system in the village.

It can be concluded that, in 1981, agricultural wages were determined by internal factors such as the size of the village labour force and the agrarian structure. Nutritionally-based wage determination prevailed (Rodgers 1975). Thirty years later, external factors have gained importance; part of the male labour force is increasingly employed both outside agriculture and outside the village. Village labour markets are now integrated into regional and national labour markets and rural wage determination responds to market forces. This has changed the balance of power to negotiate increase in wages.

Summing Up Changes in the Labour Market

Villages in Bihar have not all developed at the same pace or followed the same path but a broad picture of changes in the rural labour markets emerges from the three surveys on which this chapter is based. Migration and more recently, commuting, have been the main drivers of change. Through migration and commuting, men have been able to diversify their occupations while women's activities have remained rooted in the villages, overwhelmingly restricted to agriculture and allied activities, except for a few openings in social services. The shortage of male labour for agricultural operations has led to an increase in female labour force participation and a feminization of agriculture.

Changes in employment status have been greater for men than for women. Twenty-eight per cent of the male labour force aged 15–59 are now regular wage or salaried workers. Diversification has brought new occupations and new skills, often acquired on the job during migration. But it should be pointed out that though regular employment may confer a certain degree of security, it is no guarantee of decent working conditions. Migrants often work long hours in insalubrious environments. Over 60 per cent of women are self-employed (two-third being unpaid family workers); the lack of employment opportunities outside agriculture within the villages hampers their participation in the labour force.

Wage determination has evolved from an efficiency-based nutritional floor to a determination based on market mechanisms. Migration and commuting have induced a tightening of the village labour markets and put some upward pressure on wages and in some villages, the gender pay gap has narrowed. Through migration and commuting, the Bihar labour market is now integrated with the national and state markets. There has been a convergence of wages within the state and what happens to Delhi wages has some knock-on effect in Bihar villages. Agricultural real wages have been multiplied by a factor of 2 to 3.

Annexure I

TABLE 13A.1 Casual Agricultural Wage Rates, full day, non-harvest, 1981–2011

	1981–2			1998–9			2010–11		
	Cash (Rs)	Meal	Kind	Cash (Rs)	Meal	Kind	Cash (Rs)	Meal	Kind
GAYA									
Alapur Bishunpur		1.0	2 kg paddy		1.5	2.5 kg	.	1.5	4 kg rice
Rupaspur Salempur		1.5	1 kg rice		1.5	2.5 kg		1.5	4 kg rice
GOPALGANJ									
Dewan Parsa		0.5	4 Rs or 2.5 kg grain	35	1		90	1	
Paharpur Deyal		0.5	4 Rs or 2.5 kg grain		0.5	5 kg wheat	100	1	
MADHUBANI									
Khangaon		0.5	2.5 kg grain		1	3 kg	100	0.5	
Mahisham		0.5	2.5 kg grain	20	1		60	1.5	
NALANDA									
Chandkura		1.5	1 pucca seer rice	0	1.5	2		1.5	4 kg wheat
Mohiuddinpur		1	1kg rice	0	1	2		1	4 kg rice
PURNIA/ARARIA									
Belabadan	2	1.5		15		0.5 kg	?	?	
Jitwarpur	1.5	1.5		20	1.5		80		1 kg rice
ROHTAS									
Amarhi	5	1.5		40	0.5		87.5	1.5	
Samhauti Buzurg	5	1.5		40	1.5		100	1.5	

Source: Prasad et al. (1988); IHD; Sharma et al. (2001); IHD Bihar survey 2011 (2nd round), Village schedule.

Annexure II: Increase in Wages in Chandkura and Mahisham

In Chandkura, we can compare the 1981 wage of 1 pucca seer of rice plus a nashta and sometimes a meal with the minimum wage in 2011 of 2.5 kg plus a nashta plus a meal. In 1981, a meal was generally considered the equivalent of half a kilo of rice or roti, and a nashta 250 grams.[10] So we can compare a total wage of 1.2 to 1.7 kg of rice in 1981 with at least 3.25 kg in 2011, a rise of between 90 and 170 per cent. This is a minimum because of the increase in the wage at peak seasons in 2011. If instead, we take the 3.5 kg plus meal per day reported for transplanting paddy, so about 4 kg in total, the rise is of the order of 135 to 230 per cent. In Mahisham, the comparison is more difficult because of the switch from wages in kind to cash. One way is to convert the cash wage in 2011 into grain, for comparability with Chandkura. If we take the full-day wage of Rs 60 to 70 plus nashta reported for some operations in 2011, this comes to the equivalent of 3.75 to 4 kg of rice at local retail prices. Compared with the 1.9 to 2.3 kg per day reported in 1981, this is an increase in the range 63 to 110 per cent, much less than in Chandkura.[11]

References

Bardhan, Pranab K. 1979. 'Labour Supply Functions in a Poor Agrarian Economy,' *American Economic Review*, 69 (1): 73–83.

Dasgupta, Purnamita and Bishwanath Goldar. 2005. 'Female Labour Supply in Rural India–An Econometric Analysis', Working Paper Series No. E/265/2005, Institute of Economic Growth, Delhi.

Datta, Amrita and Preet Rustagi. 2012. *Status of Women in Bihar: Exploring Transformation in Work and Gender Relations*. New Delhi: Institute for Human Development.

Datta, Amrita, Gerry Rodgers, Janine Rodgers, and B.K.N. Singh. 2014. 'Contrasts in Development in Bihar: A Tale of Two Villages,' *Journal of Development Studies*, 50 (9): 1197–208.

[10] See Rodgers (1975).

[11] Comparing wages in grain equivalents is in principle less accurate than using a full price index. However grain still constitutes the largest component of consumption of agricultural workers, and applying a normal price index also faces a variety of methodological difficulties in situations where wages are paid in a mix of cash and kind, so in practice this may be the best first approximation.

IHD (Institute for Human Development). 2004. 'Dynamics of Poverty, Employment and Human Development in Bihar', Report of project sponsored by National Bank for Agricultural and Rural Development (NABARD), Institute for Human Development, New Delhi.

———. 2011. 'The Pattern of Rural Development and Growth in Bihar and the Emerging Policy Framework', Report to UNDP, Institute for Human Development, New Delhi.

Prasad, Pradhan H. 1979. 'Caste and Class in Bihar', *Economic and Political Weekly*, XIV (7/8): 481–4.

———. 1987. 'Towards a Theory of Transformation of Semi-Feudal Agriculture', *Economic and Political Weekly*, XXII (31): 1287–90.

Prasad, Pradhan H., Gerry Rodgers, Shaibal Gupta, Bachchoo Sharma, and Alakh N. Sharma. 1988. *The Dynamics of Employment and Poverty in Bihar*. Patna: A.N. Sinha Institute of Social Studies.

Rodgers, Gerry. 1975. 'Nutritionally-Based Wage Determination in the Low-Income Labour Market', *Oxford Economic Papers*, 27(1): 61–81.

Rodgers, Gerry, Amrita Datta, Janine Rodgers, Sunil K. Mishra, and Alakh N. Sharma. 2012. *The Challenge of Inclusive Development in Rural Bihar*. New Delhi: Manak Publications and Institute for Human Development.

Rodgers, Gerry and Janine Rodgers. 2011. 'Inclusive Development? Migration, Governance, and Social Change in Rural Bihar', *Economic and Political Weekly*, XLVI (23): 43–50.

Rodgers, Janine. 2012. Labour Force Participation in Rural Bihar: A Thirty-Year Perspective Based on Village Surveys, IHD Working Paper 04/2012, Institute for Human Development, New Delhi.

Sharma, A.N., A.K. Karan, V. Gayathri, and Pushpendra. 2001. 'Dynamics of Poverty, Employment and Human Development in Bihar', report to ACTIONAID India, Institute for Human Development, New Delhi.

Srivastava, Nisha and Ravi Srivastava. 2009. 'Women, Work, and Employment Outcomes in Rural India', Paper presented at the FAO-IFAD-ILO Workshop on Gaps, trends and current research in gender dimensions of agricultural and rural employment: Differentiated pathways out of poverty, Rome, 31 March–2 April 2009. Available at http://www.fao-ilo.org/fileadmin/user_upload/fao_ilo/pdf/Papers/17_March/Srivastava_Final.pdf (last accessed 3 September 2015).

AMRITA DATTA

Migration from Rural Bihar

Insights from a Longitudinal Study (1981–2011)*

This chapter is on the story of migration from Bihar. It is based on a longitudinal study that collected data at three points in time—in 1981–3, 1998–9, and 2009–13 in 36 representative villages in the state. The focus of the first study in the early 1980s was on agricultural production, work and employment, poverty and living standards, and demographic change in the rural areas (see Prasad et al. [1988] for details). The second study in the same villages in the late 1990s concentrated on much of the same issues and examined changes in the villages after the first survey (see Sharma et al. [2001] for details). By the time of the third study, almost 3 years had passed after the first, and extensive social and economic changes had taken place in rural Bihar (see Rodgers et al. [2013] for details). Labour mobility emerged as significant in all the three studies, but there had been a substantial rise in its incidence over time. Migration has become an increasingly important aspect of rural life and plays a significant role in the story of long-term change. We examine

* Thanks are due to Rekha Gupta, Arjan de Haan, Gerry Rodgers, Janine Rodgers, and Shivani Satija for their comments on an earlier version of this chapter.

migration from the lens of this longitudinal study in rural Bihar, and present a perspective of its area of origin.

This chapter is organized in four parts. In the second part of the chapter, we rely on three methods to narrate this story. First, household and community surveys conducted at all three time points of the longitudinal survey are used to present the core of the story of migration—its incidence, its key characteristics, the role of remittances, and the increasing dependence on migration as a livelihood strategy in the rural areas, among others. Second, surveys of the second and the third studies cover the same households in twelve core villages, so this is a panel, and there is scope to engage with household trajectories over time. While the first method helps us assess overall changes, the second enables us to study the dynamics of this change. Third, insights from case studies conducted in 2012 enable an engagement with processes of long-term change, how respondents perceive some of these changes, and where migration is located therein. One finding that emerges from this work is that while aggregate data are important to understand migration, different villages, communities, and regions have different development paths, and experience migration differently (Datta et al. 2014).

So, with diverse methods we are able to study different aspects of the same phenomenon. While no method is superior to another, this article relies extensively on the first as it provides much of the information and is common to all the three surveys. Initial results are presented from the second method, for the matching of households across surveys and the construction of panel data has been underway and is only partially complete. The third method may appear limited in scope compared to the others, but gives some fascinating insights, and together, through these three methods, we see that migration is an integral part of the story of social and economic change in rural Bihar in the last three decades.

The third part of the chapter tries to locate the findings of our study within the broader literature on this topic. We conclude with some reflections on methods, on 'village' longitudinal studies, and rural–urban migration, and the possibilities of future research on migration in the Bihar studies.

Before we begin, a caveat is in order. While we present the story of migration from Bihar, we are aware that there is no *one* story of migration. Every individual, household, community, and region engages with migration in myriad ways, and in that sense there are *many* stories of migration. In the course of this chapter, an attempt is made to capture some of these. Having said that, we move to the next part, which is based on key findings from different research methods.

Migration Observed from Different Longitudinal Sources

From Household and Community Surveys

Household and community surveys have been the primary method of data collection in the study. This section is based on cross-section data from household census surveys in 1981 and 1998, several rounds of sample surveys in 1981, 1998, and 2009, and village surveys in 1981 and 2009. We use these sources to build a story of migration, and this is further developed with information from other sources (panel data and case studies) in successive sections.

1981

Migration was already important in 1981. Some 10 per cent of the adult males were away for work for a significant period of time; a majority of them for more than 6 months in the year. The multi-locational household model was under way, with the adult male member(s) of the family, often the household head, away from the village, returning only for festivals, while the wife and children stayed behind. Households with migrant members had a relatively old household head, thus lending support to the hypothesis that migration was a family strategy.[1]

There were two main streams of migration at this time—a relatively short distance migration within Bihar and longer distance migration outside the state. The latter, predominantly from north Bihar (from the study districts of Gopalganj, Madhubani, and Purnia) was more dominant among the two, and was characterized by agricultural work at the destination. Other studies in this period have also reported the migration of men to north-western India in the states of Punjab and Haryana, where the green revolution had led to a high demand for casual labour in agriculture

[1] Other studies have also argued that migration from Bihar, and in fact, from many parts of rural India around this time was a part of household strategies (Connell et al. 1976; de Haan 1997). See the section entitled 'Towards a Synthesis With the Literature' for more details.

(Singh 1995); this is where a large proportion of migrants went. On the other hand, we find that migration *within* Bihar was considerably lower, and dominated by non-agricultural work. It is interesting, thus, to note that shorter distance streams of migration tended to be associated with non-agricultural work, while long-distance ones, were associated with agricultural work at this time.

1998

By 1998, about 45 per cent of households had at least one member who had migrated for work. Around 40 per cent of the adult males were migrating for work, for shorter or longer periods (while only 1.5 per cent among women reported doing so). In addition, less than 4 per cent women migrated with male members of their family, but did not work at destination; the remainder stayed behind. As earlier, most of the migration continued to be outside the state, but now, the most dominant form of migration was to the urban areas, be it long-term (91 per cent) or short-term migration (70 per cent).[2]

Higher wages and better job opportunities were the two most important reasons for migration cited by the respondents. More than 90 per cent of the migrant workers sent remittances, and these are estimated to be about 22 per cent of the total household income (including that of non-migrant households) in the village during this time.

Remittances were used for a variety of reasons, but most importantly, a majority of migrants reported that they used them for everyday consumption expenses, and a substantial proportion of migrants used them for medical expenses. At the same time, remittance use varied by types of migration; for instance, more short-term migrants were dependent on remittance income for expenses related to the marriage of a female member in the family, than long-term migrants. They were almost

[2] One of the ways in which the surveys classify migrants is by the duration of migration. Long-term migrants are defined as those who migrated for more than 8 months in the year preceding the survey, while short-term migrants migrated for less than 8 months. The cut-off point of 8 months is useful as it enables us to distinguish between the two aforementioned streams of migration. In the former, migrants tend to work *only* in labour markets outside the village, while in the latter stream, they are likely to have worked within and outside the village, that is, in both source and destination locations.

twice as much likely than long-term migrants to use remittances for the repayment of debt, while the latter were more than four times as likely to spend remittances on consumer durables compared to the former. Similarly, the higher incomes of long-term migrants enabled them to spend remittances on items beyond their everyday needs, such as house repairs and construction. A very small proportion reported to have used remittances to purchase land.

Social networks were important in organizing migration, particularly among short-term migrants who were more likely to be involved in casual work. In 1998, less than 1 per cent of such migrants had a pre-arranged job. They most commonly found work through relatives and friends (45 per cent) or by organizing themselves in a group; often workers from the same village sought employment together (36 per cent). Also important was migrants' own agency; 12 per cent of them reported that they had found employment using information and knowledge they had gathered themselves. The role of intermediaries was not substantial (about 6 per cent of the migrants had migrated via intermediaries), but they were important in organizing a particular stream of migration–agricultural work in north-western India. For instance, middlemen in Madhubani district, locally known as *sardars*, recruited workers from villages in Bihar, organized them in groups, and took them to the farms in north-western India, where they worked for multiple landlords, typically at the onset of the kharif season. The sardars often took an advance from the landlord and gave workers some advance payment, which would later be deducted from their wages. They also took a commission from both the landlords in the destination areas and the workers in the source areas.

It is interesting to note that almost 75 per cent of the short-term migrants felt that the behaviour of their employer in the destination, often in distant labour markets, was better than that of the local employer.[3] This is important, for in many villages, caste hostilities and aversion, particularly among the youth to work for the same employers that their parents and older generations did, 'pushed.' them out in search of work outside the village. Distant labour markets and diverse employ-

[3] In the neighbouring state of Uttar Pradesh, Srivastava (1999) finds non-discriminatory wage payments at destinations as a reason for migration among the labouring classes.

ers in many ways offered migrants anonymity and a route to break away from the rigid social hierarchies in the village. Migrant workers were able to tap in on opportunities provided by labour markets elsewhere in the country, and thus, it is not surprising that an overwhelming proportion (96 per cent) of short-term migrants felt that migration was beneficial for them.

2009

By 2009, migration, measured in a variety of ways, continued to increase. About 60 per cent of households in rural Bihar had at least one migrant worker; the proportion of adult males migrating from the village had risen to 43 per cent.[4] For adult women, this number remained less than two per cent. Among better off migrants, some chose to take their wives and other family members with them. About 6 per cent of the adult females now accompanied male members of their families to the destination, but did not work there. So, in all, more than 90 per cent of adult women continued to stay back in the village, of which women workers were concentrated in agriculture and related activities. This skewed sex-distribution of the population in the source areas is a persistent feature of migration, and has become more pervasive over time with the increase in the incidence of migration. Migrant workers predominantly worked in urban centres across the country—in the north, in Delhi, Punjab, and Haryana; in Gujarat and Maharashtra, and further south in Andhra Pradesh, Karnataka, Tamil Nadu, and Kerala. Earlier streams of migration to Calcutta, to the tea gardens of Assam and agricultural work in north-western India were marked by their decline. There was still a small stream of migrants (from Purnia and Madhubani, as earlier) that went to north-western India for agricultural work, but their numbers had substantially declined by 1998, and this trend has continued.

In tandem with the aforementioned, the proportion of short-term migrants among migrant workers has declined, and that of long-term migrants increased; in other words, migration streams across the state have shifted from short towards relatively longer durations. At the

[4] This migration has continued to increase, as indicated by surveys undertaken in 2011 and in 2013 in the 12 core villages of the study.

same time, the number of households with short-term or temporary migration also increased substantially. Disaggregated by region, the proportion of migrants in regular wage work is higher in the south Bihar districts; this is reflected in their diverse occupational profile characterized by non-agricultural work. However, in north Bihar, the pattern is converse; Purnia district in particular has a predominance of casual workers, and not surprisingly, a majority of them work in just two occupations—construction and agricultural labour.[5]

Migrants were not a homogenous category. We have already seen that some migrated for shorter durations while others did so for longer durations. Another way of distinguishing between migrants is on the basis of whether a migrant reported a secondary activity back in the village, for this tells us about his participation (or the lack of it) in the labour market in the source areas. About half of all male migrants did not report a secondary occupation. In other words, migration was their sole source of employment, and they did not work elsewhere, particularly in the village. They were more likely to be salaried workers in urban areas who had families back in the village.[6] They sent remittances and visited the village regularly. Migrants worked in a variety of occupations that included construction, artisans, textile and garment manufacturing, factory work, in hotels and restaurants, as transport workers, and as security guards and salesmen. A small minority of those who did not report any secondary work were in better-paid occupations, such as professional and technical services. In fact, the incidence of migration was highest among the most educated, lending support to the hypothesis that pull factors are at work.

The remaining half of the migrants reported a secondary activity. They worked, both, in the village as well as in distant labour markets. Unlike their primary activity, their secondary activity was likely to be in agriculture; about 70 per cent of them reported this. Thus, while outside the village, they worked in distant urban labour markets; within

[5] For details on the pattern of migration by district, caste, class, and other variables in 2009, see Rodgers et al. 2013.

[6] 'Salaried workers' here refers to those workers who obtain a monthly salary (as opposed a daily wage). It does not imply working in the formal or organized sector, but salaried work has connotations, more or less, of some stability and continuity of work.

the village, they continued to work in agriculture and were directly a part of the labour force and involved in agricultural production in the village. These migrants traversed the village and the city, the rural and the urban, agricultural and non-agricultural work several times in the course of a year. This back and forth from one geography to the other, these rural–urban and urban–rural interactions and experiences, are a way of life for a substantial proportion of adult men in rural Bihar.

Both types of migrants sent or brought back remittances to the village. By 2011, remittances were estimated to be about 29 per cent of the total income in the village. In households which had migrant members, they comprised more than half of total incomes. While migrants in upper castes and classes sent more remittances in absolute amounts, the share of remittances in total income was higher for households of lower castes and classes, and landless households; this indicates not only the importance of remittances, but also their overwhelming dependence in source households, particularly those in the lowest rung of social and economic hierarchy.

To sum, the story of migration from Bihar is one of both change and continuity. In 1981, while mobility was important in rural Bihar, its persistence was much lower compared to 1998 and 2009. Over time, migration has intensified; more people go out now than ever before (and there appear to be no signs of reversal of this trend in our survey villages). Over time, migration destinations have changed from rural to urban, and new destinations, across India, and even abroad have been brought into the fore. Migrant occupations have diversified owing to the demand for labour in a variety of sectors in urban India. Contractors and intermediaries, once important in organizing migration to the agricultural fields of north-western India, now have little role to play—in long distance migration.[7] Better transport and communication, aided by mobile phones, enable migrants to undertake long journeys to distant locations and remain in touch with their family members while

[7] The presence of contractors and middlemen, however, is found in somewhat precarious streams of migration—shorter-distance family migrations to brick kilns and longer-distance migration of children to urban areas. Overall, while these two distinct streams comprise a very small proportion of the total migration from the state, they seem to be growing, the former, particularly due to the construction boom in the state.

they are away. They remain connected, and contribute to the local economy; the share of remittances in village incomes has substantially increased with time.

Elements of continuity remain. Migration remains male-dominated; men go out for work and women, children, and the elderly stay behind in the village. Migration continues to be a family strategy, where the main motivation to migrate is for higher earnings, much of which are remitted to the village. Migration continues to be circular; most men work outside the village for most of their productive lives only to return back eventually. One thing that is increasingly becoming clearer with time is that while mobility is very high, and continues to increase, permanent migration, of the kind that entails relocation of the entire household from the village is very limited.[8] This is important, for it is clearly related to the nature of the labour market in urban areas, which is characterized by work in the informal economy, with little or no social protection, or housing for workers, let alone their families. Thus, increasingly, it is the pattern of economic growth and development in urban India that not only drives, but also defines the nature of migration from rural Bihar.

From Panel Data

In this section, we look at some initial findings from the panel data, which has been constructed based on studies of 904 households in the 12 core villages. These households, surveyed in 2009 and 2011, are the same as, or successors, of households studied in 1998 and 1999.

The panel enables us to study the dynamics of change; we are able to move beyond cross-section analysis and it is possible to examine how households fare over time. We classify household typologies by migration status in 1999 and 2011. The four categories of households are:

i) Continuing migrant households—those that had migrant members in 1999, and continue to have them in 2011.
ii) Continuing non-migrant households—those that did not have migrant members in 1999, and don't have any in 2011.

[8] Thirty-eight households, or about 4 per cent of the total sample permanently out-migrated from the village between 1998 and 2011.

TABLE 14.1 Migration Status of Panel Households: 1999 and 2011

Migration status of household in 2011 (%)	Migration status of household in 1999 (%)	
	Migrating households	Non-migrating households
Migrating households	36.9	24.4
Non-migrating households	12.3	26.3

Source: Household survey, 1999, 2011, Institute for Human Development.
Note: N = 904

iii) New migrants households—that have migrant members in 2011, but did not in 1999.
iv) Erstwhile migrant households—those that had migrant members in 1999 and don't have any in 2011.

We have already seen that households with migrants increased substantially between 1999 and 2011. A look at household trajectories reveal the shifts from migration to non-migration (and vice-versa); about 12 per cent of the survey households in 2011 were erstwhile migrants; they had shifted from being migrant households to non-migrant households in this period. It emerges that almost 24 per cent of the households were new migrant households, and this is quite a large number. In other words, together, more than 70 per cent of the total households had experienced migration in one survey or the other (see Table 14.1).[9]

We now examine the characteristics of the four categories of households mentioned earlier. In all, about 37 per cent of the households were continuing migrant households. These were more likely to belong to upper castes, Other Backward Classes (OBC) I, and Muslims, where migration was higher than average in 1999 and continued to be so in 2011; and, less likely to belong to OBC-II households, many of which are traditionally cultivating castes that practice agriculture and are less inclined to move out of the village.

[9] We have not factored in household splits that may have occurred from 1998 to 2009–11.

What about the continuing non-migrants? Again, these are more likely to belong to the peasant classes and OBC-II. The continuing non-migrants are also over-represented in the lowest income quintile categories, in both 1999 and 2011. In fact, the incidence of migration is substantially lower in households in the lowest income quintile compared to those in other quintiles. This suggests that extreme poverty may not have been a determinant of migration in rural Bihar in the last decade and a half.

Who are the new migrants? The new migrants, that is, households that have migrant members in 2011, but not in 1998, are disproportionately higher among the Scheduled Castes (SCs), and lower among OBC-II, the traditional peasant castes. They are more likely to belong to the labouring classes and landless households. By and large, it is the new migrants who have responded to the growing demand for casual and low-skilled labour in urban areas across India. New migrant households are also more likely to belong to the higher income quintiles, but we have to factor in the role of remittances here, for remittances enable these households to have a higher income in the first place. In fact, the mean income of this group drops by almost 30 per cent if remittances are not included.

What about the erstwhile migrant households? It is not a large sample; initial results suggest that about 12 per cent of all households slipped into non-migration. Households that slipped into non-migration were spread across various castes, but, were less likely to belong to upper castes and more likely to belong to SCs. These households were also more likely to belong to the peasant classes, where migration has always been low. However, whether or not this decline in migration in these groups can be attributed to better prospects in Bihar agriculture is a matter of further study.[10]

In the movement of migration to non-migration and non-migration to migration, there is little variation in trends across districts. Further analysis will allow us to explore in-depth the role of caste, class, and land, of assets and living standards, of education status and

[10] Ghosh and Sharma (1995), in a study of three districts in Bihar (Saran, Samastipur, and Purnia), have found that villages with better agriculture have low incidence of migration, while those with poor agriculture have high migration.

health of individuals, among others, in household trajectories, and in the movement of households from non-migration to migration and vice versa.

From Case Studies

This section is based on case studies, some 20 of which were conducted in 2 of the 12 core villages to study village development paths.[11] These case studies provide many insights on migration and complement findings from the surveys.

Since the panel data is of surveys done at two points in time (1998 and 2009–11), what has transpired in the intermediate period is a story that is often not known. The case study method offers possibilities to engage with and study in-depth a particular phenomenon—migration in this case—and can significantly add to the analyses of the large-scale surveys. They can be an important tool in studying the various processes that are at play. The retrospective household case studies offer some interesting facts and perspectives about the phenomenon of migration and how it has changed. One revealing insight is the sheer scale of mobility an individual experiences over time; the same person had worked at many destinations, in diverse occupations, and with several employers in the course of migration. They also throw some light on the nature of labour circulation, how migrants remained connected with their families, and integrated with their villages. Here are two examples from the case studies that highlight some of the aforementioned issues.

Traversing the Rural and Urban

Take the case of BM from Madhubani. As a teenager, BM started migrating to Punjab and Haryana with his three brothers and fellow-villagers due to lack of work in the village, and to be able to earn more money. After that, they started going to Bhadohi (a hub of carpet production in the region), in Uttar Pradesh, where they worked in the carpet industry

[11] Fieldwork was undertaken with Gerry Rodgers, Janine Rodgers, and B.K.N. Singh in February–March, 2012. For details, see Datta et al. (2012, 2014).

for 10–12 years, where BM became a labour contractor after working as a labourer for a few years. He came back to the village when the carpet factory that employed him shut down, and did not migrate for about 5 years. For the last one year, he has been going to Panipat in Haryana, where he works, again, in a carpet factory. His son KM also migrates with him to Panipat and works in a towel factory. BM returns to the village about 3–4 times in a year (while KM does not; he does not like to work in agriculture); from October to December for the harvesting of the paddy crop and the sowing of wheat; and again in April for the harvesting of wheat. He saves money and brings it back to the village in each of his visits. He has been able to buy some land (184 square metres in area) about 6–7 years ago with regular remittance income. He also leases in land, which he cultivates with his family.

So, clearly, BM traverses the village and the outside world, and has made gains in income—in agriculture (in the village) and from migration outside, in a variety of occupations in multiple locations—and this is something that his son continues to do. Over the last 30 years, he sees some improvement in his family's lives; 'Earlier, we had to count and eat grains, now we don't have to count anymore.' (*Pehle anaaj gin kar khana padta tha, ab ginana nahin padta*).

A 'Permanent' Job elsewhere, but Home in the Village

CJ belongs to Madhubani district. In 1977 he landed a 'permanent' job with the Bihar Police, and has been a migrant since. He has worked and lived in many parts of the state, while his wife and children live in the village. He prefers not to take his family with him as he feels that their lives in the village offer stability, which is not possible in his job as it involves transfer from one location to another at regular intervals. He visits the village once every month and is actively involved in the everyday cultivation decisions and management of the family farm, which his brother actually cultivates. Through the mobile phone, they discuss matters related to crops grown, inputs used, irrigation, and sale of crops. When asked why he comes so often in spite of having a full-time job elsewhere, '*khet aur ghar ki dekhrekh karne chale aate hai*' ('I come back to take care of the farm and the family,' he says).

We discuss two more important insights from the case studies—first, the impact of migration on household structures, in particular the joint family.[12] De Haan (1997) in the case of circular male-labour migration, particularly from, and, in the (cultural) context of Bihar and eastern Uttar Pradesh has argued, '... the process of rural–urban migration, has not dissolved "traditional" family ties. On the contrary, there are indications that families of migrants may be more "joint", albeit in a slightly different sense, than families without migrants.... the existence of the joint family and this form of migration reinforce each other.'

In rural Bihar, the average household size is greater for households with migrant members than in households with no migrant members. Having said that, we find that the notions of 'joint' and 'nuclear' family are not mutually exclusive; often households exhibit features which vary across the spectrum from 'joint' to 'nuclear'. Even if we were to go by the apparently simple definition of household characterized by the 'common kitchen', often, to gauge whether a source household with migrants has a common kitchen (or not) is fraught with difficulties. For, remittances offer the possibility of more *chūlhās* (it is not uncommon for women to prefer separate chūlhās), and migration, thus, triggers the splitting of households. So remittances, in some ways, facilitate the splitting up of households; yet, the transition of joint to nuclear is neither linear nor irreversible. Migration often deepens intra-household inequality; members who control and use remittances are able to exercise more power within the household. They tend to have a superior consumption pattern (Datta et al. 2012).

Second, it is interesting to note how women experience migration. It was found that remittances often reached women in the family who had stayed back in the village and they exercised considerable autonomy in the use of remittances. Though they seldom migrated, one case that

[12] It is interesting to note that the (official) definition of household (and family) are not static. From 1971, the Census of India defines the household as 'a group of persons who commonly live together and would take their meals from a common kitchen unless the exigencies of work prevented any of them from doing so'. But this has not always been so. The household or family was first defined in 1872 as comprising those who lived together and ordinarily cooked at the same hearth. From 1891 to 1941, the term 'family' was used; from 1951, the 'household' was back in use, and has since been so (Census of India, 2010–11, available at http://censusindia.gov.in/Data_Products/Library/Indian_perceptive_link/Census_Terms_link/censusterms.html [last accessed 20 September 2015]).

we came across deserves special mention. HJ's husband FJ worked in a printing firm in Delhi. She visited Delhi in the previous year for medical attention, which required a surgery and stayed there for 2–3 months. A resident of Madhubani district, for HJ the nearby hospital in Darbhanga district, 50 km away was very expensive and she therefore preferred to go to Delhi (her first ever trip so far!), a thousand kilometres away, where, she told us, public hospitals cost much less.

To sum up, the case studies are able to provide rich information which supplement the information of the surveys and offer deep insights on many aspects of migration overtime.

Towards a Synthesis with the Literature

We now attempt to locate the findings of the Bihar longitudinal research in the broader literature on migration in the region. An engagement with the historical roots of migration helps locate contemporary migration and migratory trends overtime. De Haan (2002) has argued that circular migration of men from the region has existed for more than a hundred years. Labour mobility has thus been an integral part of rural life for a long time.

As far as migration trends are concerned, two well-known longitudinal studies in India report findings similar to what we see in Bihar; outmigration for work has increased, and the pattern of migration has changed. In Palanpur village in Uttar Pradesh, the number of households with migrants doubled from 21 per cent to 42 per cent in the period between 1993 and 2008. Here too, the most common form of migration was one where some members of the family migrated, while others stayed behind in the village (Mukhopadhyay 2011). The ICRISAT studies in Maharashtra and Andhra Pradesh also find that outmigration has increased, but over time, what is different here is that migratory flows have changed from predominantly permanent movements (in the earlier surveys of 1975 to 1984) to temporary movements (in the period 1992 to 2004–5) (Badiani 2007).

As other researchers have noted, it is difficult to categorize this migration into either push or pull categories, for they interact with one another, and are not mutually exclusive. Connell et al. (1976), based on village studies undertaken in many parts of the developing world, argue that,

> Migrants 'pushed' out of the village are attracted to more satisfactory earning opportunities outside, while migrants 'pulled' to a city job are induced out by the failure of the rural area to supply adequate income or status. We need to understand the interaction between the rural (village) environment, a series of wider economic networks (town, region, country), and the perception and position of the migrant in that system.

In the case of migration from Bihar, De Haan (1997) has argued that migration needs to be understood in terms of both economic and cultural factors. Cultural restrictions do not allow women to migrate—this clearly emerges in our study villages too. Those who do not migrate and are left behind experience the ramifications of migration in a myriad of ways. They may not have gone there, but are familiar with distant lands. For children, migration is an inevitable and very real part of the future. For the women, living without their husbands has become a way of life in rural Bihar (see Datta and Mishra 2011 for details).

Mobility has also been located in the history of feudal exploitation and caste tensions, and violence and strife in some parts of the state in the recent decades. There is an aversion among the lower castes to work in the village. In the late 1990s, Sharma (2005) notes the increase in commuters to nearby villages and towns. Many commuters were also seasonal migrants; they preferred to work outside the village. Increased migration is thus an important agent of change in rural Bihar (Sharma 2005), and has provided a route to 'work with dignity and freedom' (Deshingkar et al. 2006).

The findings here, in the case of Bihar, in relation to impact in source areas are similar to other studies in the region. For instance, in the neighbouring state of West Bengal, Rogaly and Coppard (2003) see a change in seasonal migrants; they argue that although there is (always) a compulsion to earn a wage, but, (earlier) 'they used to go to eat, now they go to earn' (Rogaly and Coppard 2003). Although their work is arduous, seasonal migrants are not powerless; they are able to make choices in the labour market; they are able to send back remittances (Rogaly et al. 2001). This migration can also be seen as what Deshingkar and Grimm (2005) call 'accumulative kinds of migration'—migration that contributes to economic development and poverty reduction (Deshingkar and Grimm 2005). But, like other studies in the state we find that remittances are excessively used for consumption; little goes into production (IIPA 2010; Rodgers and Rodgers 2011).

The circularity of labour migration in Bihar needs to be emphasized. Men go out to work and ultimately return to their village. It has clearly emerged from successive visits to the field that permanent migration of the kind that involves relocation of households from the village is very limited. Other village studies in Bihar corroborate this (Jha 2004; Rodgers and Rodgers 2011). Given that most of this migration is to urban labour markets across various locations in India, we have argued elsewhere that, since the rural areas bear the cost of the production, maintenance, and reproduction of the labour force, they are subsidizing economic growth and development in the urban areas (Datta et al. 2014).

We have not looked at state policies on migration, for they are conspicuous by their absence. In Bihar, the discourse that migration has been in decline since the state has assumed a high growth trajectory in recent years does not find resonance in the villages of our study. To the contrary, in *all* the villages, there are indications that migration has continued to remain at the same (high) levels or increased in the last few years. Others have argued that it is naïve to assume that migration can be easily controlled (IIPA 2010), and that uneven levels of urbanization and employment opportunities will continue to drive migration from Bihar (Singh and Stern 2013). In fact, the state's (in this case, the state at source, that is, in Bihar) perspective that migration is declining is a denial of the extent of migration, which results in the invisibility of migrant workers (Datta 2013).

Reflections on the Future on Methods: On 'Village' Longitudinal Studies and Rural–Urban Migration

This section reflects on methods that have been used to study migration in 'village' longitudinal studies, the implications of these methods, and raises some questions that have emerged in the course of this study. With the changing nature of migration, and the overwhelming significance of migration in village life, we feel that there is a now a need to collect information on migration in urban areas. We end with some experiences of the author in the course of fieldwork in rural Bihar.

Longitudinal village studies offer a unique perspective to study migration. Through these studies in Bihar, it has been possible to trace the evolution of migration since the 1980s, and its broad pattern of change over time. We are able to see ramifications of migration on work, employment, occupations and incomes, and the crucial role of migration in changing rural landscapes.

At the same time, this perspective on migration is one from a rural lens. Household and community surveys collect data from the village, and we thus have information from source locations. Often, information about migrant members of the household is collected in their absence; information on destinations, mostly cities, collected in the village. This is a crucial missing link, and there is a need for data collection and engagement with migrant workers in their destination locations for a fuller understanding of rural–urban migration. So, for future research, particularly on migration, the next step is to collect information about migration from migrants, and expand the geography of research to the urban areas, to be able to synthesize 'rural' and 'urban' perspectives. So, to understand village India, we need to go to the city; engaging with the urban will give us a fuller and more nuanced understanding of the rural, for, in a sense, the rural and the urban are not simply physical spaces, geographical entities, but also ways of life. As Fox (cited in Connell et al. 1976) has noted: 'Migrant labour takes and returns people each year—the same people—and they return changed—and culture changes with them. New ideas, needs, values and artifacts are fed back into the culture yearly, and yearly it changes...'

A pertinent question that emerges is whether (and for how long) will migration from Bihar continue to remain circular? De Haan (2002) has argued that for more than a century such migration has remained circular, and based on his fieldwork in the early 1990s, he finds that migrants aspire to return back to their villages after their working life.

Is this still the case? Research elsewhere in India sheds interesting insights. In the ICRISAT villages, temporary migrants in 1992 have a much higher rate of permanent migration after 2000; in other words, temporary migration is part of a longer-term strategy of permanent migration (Badiani 2007). In rural Bihar, such a transition from temporary to permanent migration is uncommon; for, a necessary condition of such migration would be that wage levels in the destination location are high enough to cover the living and housing cost of families. However, this is simply not the case; on an average, Bihari migrants' earnings, which contribute significantly to household income in source areas by way of remittances, are far from what is required for the sustenance of the same household in the city. Of course, other factors, such as job security at the destination, the family's willingness to migrate etc., also play an important role in the decision to permanently migrate.

How and when does circular migration change to permanent migration? For this, it is worthwhile to engage with households that have left the village. While permanent migration remains low, it is present, nonetheless. And this is where the change is happening—at the margins. We must engage with migrants who have left the rural areas completely—for they are an important element in the story of change, in the transformation (or the lack of it) of Bihar.

In the course of fieldwork, I have had the opportunity to meet many migrants in the village. What is striking about these interactions with migrants, across caste and class, and across different categories of migrants—young men who have started migrating recently, older men who have been going out for several years, or migrants who are now back in the village is that more often than not it is possible to distinguish those who migrate from those who don't. For those who have regularly been going outside the village, be it for longer or shorter durations, have a sense of confidence, and a greater awareness of the world around them, and these are reflected in their mannerisms. The younger migrants also appear different for they often wear western clothes and accessories. Many narrate migration and urban experiences with a sense of adventure and novelty.

At another time,[13] we had a chance to interact with young boys and girls in a government school in one of the remotest villages of our study in north Bihar. We asked a rather conventional question to the sixty students present in class 9 that day—what they wanted to do when they grew up. The children reported a variety of occupations—driver, conductor, teacher, doctor, nurse, and so on. All the answers had to do with work outside the village; they also had little to do with agriculture. Typically, class IX students are 14 years old. In another year, if not in education, they are likely (more boys than girls) to join the labour force in a context where agriculture is the mainstay of village life in Purnia. What is striking, thus, is that mobility is such an integral part of the children's lives, their imagination of the future.

[13] In November 2009, in the high school in Belabadan village, Purnia district.

References

Badiani, R. 2007. *Temporary and Permanent Migration in Six Villages in the Semi-Arid Tropics*. Andhra Pradesh: International Crops Research Institute for the Semi-Arid Tropics.

Connell, J., B. Dasgupta, R. Laishley, and M. Lipton. 1976. *Migration from Rural Areas: The Evidence from Village Studies*. New Delhi: Oxford University Press.

Datta, Amrita. 2013. 'Migration from Contemporary Bihar', Paper presented at the Conference on Internal Migration in Contemporary India, Rajiv Gandhi Institute for Contemporary Studies, New Delhi, 22–3 February.

Datta, Amrita and Sunil Kumar Mishra. 2011. 'Glimpses of Women's Lives in Rural Bihar: Impact of Male Migration', *The Indian Journal of Labour Economics*, 54 (3): 457–77.

Datta, A., G. Rodgers, J. Rodgers, and B.K.N. Singh, 2012. 'A Tale of Two Villages: Contrasts in Development in Bihar', Working paper no. 5, IHD Working Paper Series, Institute for Human Development, New Delhi.

———. 2014. 'Contrasts in Development in Bihar: A Tale of Two Villages', *Journal of Development Studies*, 50 (9): 1197–208.

de Haan, Arjan. 1997. 'Migration as Family Strategy: Rural-Urban Labour Migration in India During the Twentieth Century', *The History of the Family*, 2 (4): 481–505.

———. 2002. 'Migration and Livelihoods in Historical Perspective: A Case Study of Bihar, India', *Journal of Development Studies*, 38 (5): 115–42.

Deshingkar, P. and S. Grimm. 2005. *Internal Migration and Development: A Global Perspective*. Geneva: International Organization for Migration.

Deshingkar, P., S. Kumar, H.K. Chobey, and D. Kumar. 2006. *The Role of Migration and Remittances in Promoting Livelihoods in Bihar*. London: Overseas Development Institute.

Ghosh, P.P. and A.N. Sharma. 1995. 'Seasonal Migration of Rural Labour in Bihar', *Labour and Development*, 1 (1): 118–35.

IIPA (Indian Institute of Public Administration). 2010. *A Study of Bihari Migrant Labourers: Incidence, Causes and Remedies*. New Delhi: Indian Institute of Public Administration.

Jha, Praveen. 2004. 'Continuity and Change: Some Observations on the Landscape of Agricultural Labourers in North Bihar', *Journal of Agrarian Change*, 4 (4): 509–31.

Mukhopadhyay, A. 2011. *Stepping Out of Palanpur: Employment Outside Palanpur*. London: Asia Research Centre, London School of Economics and Political Science.

Prasad, P.H., G. Rodgers, A.N. Sharma, S. Gupta, and B. Sharma. 1988. *The Dynamics of Employment and Poverty in Bihar*. Patna and Geneva: A.N. Sinha Institute of Social Studies and International Labour Organization.

Rodgers, G., A. Datta, J. Rodgers, S.K. Mishra, and A.N. Sharma. 2013. *The Challenge of Inclusive Development in Rural Bihar.* New Delhi: Institute for Human Development and Manak Publications.

Rodgers, G. and J. Rodgers. 2011. 'Inclusive Development? Migration, Governance and Social Change in Rural Bihar', *Economic and Political Weekly*, 46 (23): 43–50.

Rogaly, Ben and Daniel Coppard. 2003. '"They Used to Go to Eat, Now They Go to Earn": The Changing Meanings of Seasonal Migration from Puruliya District in West Bengal, India', *Journal of Agrarian Change*, 3 (3): 395–433.

Rogaly, Ben, Jhuma Biswas, Daniel Coppard, Abdur Rafique, Kumar Rana, and Amrita Sengupta. 2001. 'Seasonal Migration, Social Change and Migrants' Rights: Lessons from West Bengal', *Economic and Political Weekly*, 36 (49): 4547–59.

Sharma, A.N., S. Sarkar, A.K. Karan, V. Gayathri, and Pushpendra. 2001. 'Poverty and Livelihoods in Rural Bihar', Report of project sponsored by Action Aid, Institute for Human Development, New Delhi.

Sharma, Alakh. N. 2005. 'Agrarian Relations and Socio-economic Change in Bihar', *Economic and Political Weekly*, 40 (10): 960–72.

Singh, Manjit. 1995. *Uneven Development in Agriculture and Labour Migration: A Case of Bihar and Punjab*. Shimla: Indian Institute of Advanced Study.

Singh, N.K. and Nicholas Stern. 2013. *The New Bihar, Rekindling Governance and Development*. New Delhi: HarperCollins Publishers.

Srivastava, Ravi. 1999. 'Rural Labour in Uttar Pradesh: Emerging Features of Subsistence, Contradiction and Resistance', *Journal of Peasant Studies*, 26 (2–3): 263–315.

15

DIPA SINHA
DINESH KUMAR TIWARI
RUCHIRA BHATTACHARYA
RUTH KATTUMURI

Public Services, Social Relations, Politics, and Gender

Tales from a North Indian Village*

Palanpur village in the Moradabad district of western Uttar Pradesh (UP) has been studied through a series of surveys beginning from the 1950s onwards. While we cannot claim that Palanpur is in any way 'representative' of rural UP or even Moradabad district, it is not an outlier either. The sixth round of survey in Palanpur was conducted in 2008–10. The primary focus of the previous rounds of the survey was to understand how the economy of the village functioned and how it was

* This work is based on a programme of work in Palanpur, a village in the Moradabad district of Uttar Pradesh. There are now six surveys of the village, one for every decade since Independence, the most recent being 2008–10. We are very grateful to Nicholas Stern, Himanshu, Peter Lanjouw, Jean Drèze, and the entire team of research assistants and interns at Centre de Sciences Humaines (CSH), Delhi for their guidance, advice, and support. The work is supported by a grant from The Department for International Development (DFID), to whom we are very grateful.

changing, especially in relation to the agrarian economy, farming practices, rural markets, outside opportunities, and population growth.[1]

In each round of the survey, the areas of investigation were expanded to include newer topics, including various social and economic aspects of life in Palanpur. In this chapter, we focus on poor human development indicators and their relationship with the failure of public services and the absence of collective action (and effective demand) in the village for the same. Earlier rounds of surveys, especially the one conducted in 1983–4, documented valuable qualitative information on various aspects of village life, including women's lives, caste relations, and health and education practices, based on informal discussions, a few interviews, and observations. In addition, this time systematic data in greater detail were collected in relation to women's status, public services, child labour, and health expenditure.

Human development indicators, as well as the performance of public services in UP, are among the poorest in the country (Drèze and Gazdar 1997; Drèze and Sen 2013; IAMR 2011; Parker and Kozel 2003; Sinha 2013). There are multiple factors that contribute to human development outcomes, as well as failure of public services, including poverty, poor status of women, inadequate provision of services, income inequality, political priorities, and so on. Many of these are not village-level factors and are influenced by larger political, social, and economic developments. The analysis in this chapter, however, is mainly focused on village-level issues.

During our stay in the village, we were puzzled by the absence of any public pressure towards improving public services, such as education and health, in spite of the failure of existing services to meet people's needs. Although in individual conversations, people expressed dissatisfaction over the way things were, this was not a topic of discussion in any collective forum in the village, nor was there any instance where people took up the issue of poor functioning of public services at higher levels, such as the block or district administration. This observation on the poor state of public services in the village and also the absence of collective action in the village has also been discussed in detail by Drèze

[1] For details on earlier surveys and findings, see Lanjouw and Stern (1998). Chapters 5 and 11 in this book also related to the Palanpur village survey.

and Sharma (1998) based on the previous round of surveys. They argue that the limited reach of collective action in Palanpur is responsible for some of the failures of its development experience. They further reason that it is the highly fragmented nature of the village society that offers few rallying points for collective action. In this article, we revisit the issue of failure of public services, lack of collective action, and its relation to social fragmentation (based on gender and caste) and conclude that the high level of social inequality in the village continues to be a reality contributing to a failure of collective action as found by earlier researchers.

Economic Changes and Human Development in Palanpur[2]

There has been substantial improvement in the economic conditions in the village during the survey period (1957 to 2009), especially since 1983–4. Real incomes have risen substantially across all castes. The data from various rounds of surveys show that the per capita income in the village has more than doubled since the first survey in 1957–8, with most of this increase being seen in the second half of the period, between 1983–4 and 2008–9. The real wages of casual labourers, which were almost stagnant from 1958 to the late 1980s, have begun to rise, especially in the last decade. The real wages (of casual labourers) increased almost two times between 1983 and 2008 (Himanshu and Stern 2011).

It is evident from the longitudinal data that while agriculture continues to be a major source of income and employment for most of the households in the village, there is an increasing share of non-farm income and employment. There has also been a tremendous rise in the assets that people own, with the number of productive assets, such as tractors, tube wells, pumpsets, etc., going up. While there were two motorcycles and three televisions (per 1,000 population) in 1993, this increased to respectively 14 and 64 in 2008. There are now two cars in the village. The number of small shops in the village has grown. These

[2] For more details on economic changes in the village, see Chapters 5 and 11 that are related to the Palanpur village study, in this book.

shops now sell a wide range of products, including basic groceries, candies, and cosmetics. There are no kachcha houses in the village anymore and all the houses now have pakka walls and roofs. These are all clear signs of change in the village and data show that a large part of this change occurred after 1983–4.

While there has been such significant change in the village, some fundamental problems are still to be overcome. The village streets are still narrow and dirty, drainage systems non-existent, the school is functioning poorly, many children look unhealthy, and there are severe restrictions on women's mobility. The only public transport reaching the village continues to be the train service twice a day. This situation has recently seen some improvement with the approach road to the village and some of the internal roads being re-laid.[3]

In terms of human development indicators, it is seen that while there is tremendous improvement, particularly after the 1983 survey, Palanpur still lags behind the rest of the country and state quite significantly. The literacy rate[4] (of persons aged 7 and above) in Palanpur increased from 25 per cent in 1984 to 50 per cent in 2009; however, this is still much lower than the literacy rate for UP as a whole (69.7 per cent, according to Census 2011) or even Moradabad district (58.7 per cent). Age-wise literacy rates for the 15–19 age group, which presents a picture of the recent trends in literacy, show considerable gains with 85 per cent of the boys and 44 per cent of girls in this age group in Palanpur being literate.[5]

It is more difficult to comment on health outcomes in Palanpur because of sample size issues to estimate mortality indicators. Further, we do not have morbidity indicators from the earlier rounds of the survey to make comparisons. However, using data on birth histories some estimates have been made of the infant mortality rate (IMR) in the village. The estimated IMR in 1993 was 160 deaths per 1,000 live births (Drèze and Sharma 1998) and for 2009 the estimated IMR is

[3] These developments were noticed during recent visits to the village (in 2014).

[4] The Census of India treats a person aged 7 and above who can both read and write with understanding, in any language, as literate. The same definition has been used here.

[5] See Kattumuri and Tiwari (2011) for more data on literacy in Palanpur.

93 deaths per 1,000 live births.[6] In both years, this estimated IMR is considerably higher than the IMR for rural UP (139 in 1991 and 66 in 2009).[7] While the ratio of IMR for Palanpur to that for UP was 1.15 in 1993, it increased to 1.4 in 2009. What it does show once again is that Palanpur is making significant progress but is still far behind the rest of the state and does not seem to be catching up.

The story of Palanpur, like the story of UP in general and that of rural India to some extent, is therefore one of impressive economic growth with improvements in human development not commensurate with the economic possibilities (Drèze and Sen 2013). While we leave the analysis of different factors explaining slow changes in human development for later, in this chapter we delve into the poor state of public services and the high levels of social inequality in the village as an explanation for lack of collective action towards improving them.

Poor State of Public Services

Government School

Palanpur has had a government primary school right from the beginning of the survey period.[8] This school has been upgraded to the elementary

[6] The earlier IMR estimates were computed using the 'children ever born, children surviving' method (Drèze and Sharma 1998). The latest estimates of IMR are calculated using World Bank's Child Survival Rate (Pierre 2011). The formula is:

$$S_j = \prod_{k=1}^{j} \frac{n_k - d_k}{n_k - \frac{c_k}{2}}$$

Using the children born in the last 10 years, the data is aggregated into semester intervals j (1, 2 ... j) where n_k is number of children at risk during a particular interval, d_k is number of children dead in that interval, and those who were born within the semester interval, that is, c_k and therefore, are not fully exposed to risk are censored children. Still births or miscarriages are not taken into account while calculating IMR. Survival Rate is first calculated from the life table using the formula. Then (1-Survival Rate) gives the mortality rate.

[7] The IMR of rural UP and Palanpur for 1991 are from Lanjouw and Stern (1998). IMR data for 2009 is from GoI (2011).

[8] The village survey of Palanpur started in 1957 with the latest being 2008–10. The term 'survey period' here refers to the entire '1957–2010' interval with six rounds of surveys at an average ten years interval.

level in 2012 (up to class 8). For high school, the nearest government school is in Akrauli village about 3 km away. For university education, the nearest institutions are located in Chandausi (13 km away, the nearest town and former block headquarter) and Moradabad (31 km away, the district headquarters).

Until 1974–5, Palanpur's government primary school was functioning well. At one point, it had five teachers and one headmaster but after 1974–5, the number of teachers reduced, apparently due to the adoption of a policy of spreading teaching posts more evenly between villages. By late 1992, the school had only one teacher. In 1993, a new directive from the UP government required that local teachers cannot teach in primary schools resulting in the transfer of the local teacher and recruitment of two teachers from outside the village. The survey team then felt that this led to an improvement in the attendance of students; but still the performance of the school remained poor. The government school in Akrauli had better infrastructure and staff, and some parents sent their children there (girls were not going to Akrauli) (Drèze, Lanjouw, and Sharma 1998).

> The expansion of basic education in Palanpur has been considerably slowed down by the poor functioning of the village school. In fact, around the end of the survey period, the village school remained virtually non-functional for more than ten years, due to systematic absenteeism and shirking on the part of the local teacher. The most extraordinary aspect of this situation is that there has been no concerted effort to do anything about it. Admittedly, the scope for putting pressure on the village teacher has been somewhat reduced by the fact that, for much of the relevant period, he was the son of the village headman. (Drèze and Sharma 1998: 73)

Children in Palanpur also access a few private schools, but none of them are currently within the village. Education in the government schools is almost free, while on an average the fee in private schools was Rs 650 per child per year as per data collected in 2009 (Bersier 2009). Up to 2005, there was a small private school running in Palanpur village itself. The reports of earlier survey teams and villagers suggest that this school used to function fairly regularly. However, this school closed down because the two teachers running it got jobs in government primary schools.

Almost 30 per cent of school-aged children from the village attend private schools in nearby villages, while the rest are enrolled in government schools. Therefore, the government school is still the main source of education in the village. However, the state of the government school is very poor. Although there is a considerable increase in the number of children attending school in the village (234 children are enrolled there), the quality of education is a cause for concern.[9]

When we began the survey in 2008, there were four teachers in the school. Two of them were regular teachers and lived outside the village, while the other two were *Shiksha Mitras* from the same village. The two permanent teachers were very irregular and used to come once in a while. They have now been transferred elsewhere. One of the Shiksha Mitras also left once she got married. By the end of the survey (2010) there was only one teacher, although five teachers' posts have been sanctioned by the government for the school. This teacher was also a Shiksha Mitra[10] (para teacher) and not a fully qualified permanent teacher. Data for 2009–10 show that 38.4 per cent of all government teachers in UP are para teachers and of them only 33.4 per cent in UP have received professional training (DISE 2011).

In terms of infrastructure, the school has seen major improvements since the previous survey in 1993. There are separate toilets for boys and girls (often non-functional), a kitchen for midday meals and four rooms for classes. Many of the rooms are kept locked and different classes are merged together with only two rooms being opened.

There was no supervision visit by any senior official from the education department during our stay, nor was there any attempt by the community to demand accountability from the school, although parents were dissatisfied that the teachers did not come regularly. The only time any government officer came to the school was to distribute scholarships and that was also a time when many parents visited to collect the money. But during these visits, there was no discussion on the quality or regularity of the teaching in the school. When the teachers were present in the school, they complained that there were not enough teachers and so it was not possible for them to teach the different classes.

[9] Since the private schools are outside Palanpur, we did not get an opportunity to observe them as intensively.

[10] The Shiksha Mitra scheme was started in UP to provide para teachers for primary schools as a part of the Basic Education Project in 1993 to compensate for the lack of adequate teachers.

A year after we began this round of the survey in the village, the midday meal in the school was restored. This was one of the changes brought in by the new panchayat pradhan.[11] Although the children started attending the school more regularly, they would often be found playing outside waiting for meal time.

Therefore, although in theory, most children are enrolled in the school, the teaching itself is inadequate in the government school in Palanpur. As most of the children going to the government school are first generation literates, they are unable to get much help at home either (more details on which children go to private schools in the later sections). While there is a latent desire amongst parents in all the castes to send their children to school, there is however no proactive action being taken by them to seek and secure improvements in the functioning of the school.

Health Services

There is no government sub-centre or Primary Health Centre (PHC) in the village, but it has a designated Auxiliary Nurse Midwife (ANM), who is supposed to visit the village regularly to provide immunization, ante- and post-natal care, child health services, and some primary healthcare. The ANM is supposed to come to the village at least twice a month. The ANM in Palanpur usually came once a month as part of the Pulse Polio campaign held monthly in the entire state. The general complaint in the village was that she did not provide any services except for the polio vaccine; at other times, even if she came to the village, people were not informed, and she would just spend her time sitting in one place, talking to some influential people and leave. This is also reflected in the data on immunization, which shows that while 99 per cent of all children under six in 2009 had received at least one dose of polio drops, only 38 per cent had received at least one dose of DPT vaccine (they are supposed to get three). Less than 40 per cent of the children had immunization cards. Over 90 per cent of the women delivered at home. While we do not have exact data for the previous years, based on the survey in 1984, Drèze

[11] The head of the panchayat (elected local body) is called the pradhan. In 2009, a new pradhan was elected in the village following the impeachment of the previous pradhan.

and Sharma (1998) write, '[f]amily planning practices are quite limited in Palanpur leading to high fertility rates and short birth spacing ... A delivery almost invariably takes place at home with the help of a local daˉıˉ (midwife) with no formal training ... No publicly-provided maternal health services are conveniently available' (pp. 53–4).

In 2009, an Accredited Social Health Activist (ASHA), or voluntary health worker, was appointed in the village to play the role of a link worker with the health services. Her main tasks are to motivate people to access immunization services and to encourage women to go for institutional deliveries. The ASHA worker was from a Thakur family, chosen mainly because her husband knew some people in the health department. She had been appointed towards the end of the survey period, and we did not get much of an opportunity to observe her. In the initial months, she was still not sure of her role and was trying to understand what she was supposed to do in the absence of any guidance from the ANM.

There is an anganwadi centre (AWC)[12] in the village, to provide for the health, nutrition, and education needs of children less than six years of age. The anganwadi worker and helper are both from the same family and have been working here for over twenty years. The AWC functioned even more poorly than the school. It did not have a building of its own and was technically supposed to be functioning out of the home of the anganwadi worker (AWW). However, since there was not enough space there, she operated out of the school. The anganwadi worker sometimes was seen taking classes for the older children who were enrolled in the school.

Of all the women with children under six years of age in the village, only about 9 per cent said that their children were given any supplementary nutrition from the anganwadi centre ever and less than 5 per cent reported their children having ever been weighed at the AWC. The ICDS is supposed to provide six services for children under six including supplementary nutrition and growth monitoring. In 1993, the anganwadi centre was functioning out of the worker's home. 'None of

[12] An anganwadi (courtyard) centre is a government-sponsored child and mother-care centre in India for children in the 0–6 age group. It started in 1975 as a part of the Integrated Child Development Scheme (ICDS) of the central government.

the six services mentioned above are actually supplied at the anganwadi except sporadic doses of nutritional support. In 1993, many Palanpur residents were not even aware of the fact that an anganwadi has been set up in one of the Kayastha homes' (Drèze and Sharma 1998: 189).

The AWW complained of irregular supply, poor quality, and the system of 'cuts' to higher authorities. The take-home rations that were supposed to come to the AWC were always less than what was recorded because it was siphoned off at different levels. She claimed, verified by the AWW in the neighbouring village as well, that they also had to give a fixed proportion of their salary every month to their superiors. Since they are 'honorary' workers and have no job security, they felt very vulnerable and did not question this practice openly.

For primary healthcare, residents of Palanpur mostly go to (unqualified) medical practitioners in the village. Both of them (one lives in Palanpur and the other comes from the neighbouring village of Pipli) have not been formally trained but prescribe a range of medicines from painkillers to antibiotics. There are also others in the village who do not have a 'clinic' but are called doctors and prescribe medicines for common illnesses. For further care, people go to private practitioners in nearby towns, such as Bilari and Chandausi.[13] A lot of money is spent on healthcare, but the quality of healthcare received is poor and there is no faith in the public health system.

A survey on health expenditures in 2009 showed that the share of out-of-pocket expenditure[14] to total consumption expenditure in Palanpur is 5.9 per cent, which is slightly higher than the share for all India (5.1 per cent according to NSSO 2004–5). Twenty-one per cent of the people reported suffering from any ailment in the 15 days before the survey.[15] Of these, 90 per cent sought treatment; among those who sought treatment, 92 per cent went to a private source. Similarly 5 per cent

[13] Bilari and Chandausi are nearby towns approximately 3 km and 13 km south of Palanpur respectively.

[14] Out of pocket expenditure includes medicines, fees for doctors, and other extra charges of treatment for non-institutionalized medical care. It doesn't include hospitalization and related costs.

[15] This is very high compared to rural UP (10 per cent in 2004–5 based on NSSO data). However, this is possibly because of the familiarity of the respondents with the investigators resulting in better reporting.

of persons reported hospitalization in the last 365 days of whom 86 per cent were in a private hospital. The expenditure on treatment was much higher in private institutions (average Rs 6,259 per hospitalization case) compared to the public (Rs 839), in spite of which people preferred private care. When asked why they did not prefer public hospitals, 72 per cent of the respondents said that they were not satisfied with the quality of care in a government hospital. The other reasons given were that the health centre was too far and that there was a long waiting period before getting any care (Pierre 2011). These data are not very different from the earlier rounds of surveys, where it was found that: '... public facilities, however, are rarely used by Palanpur residents. The main reasons for this seem to be that they have little faith in the quality of the services provided. They resent the brusque behaviour of the health staff and expect to be asked to pay for services that are supposed to be free.' (Drèze and Sharma 1998: 189–90)

Very soon after the survey was completed a PHC was opened in a nearby village (Akrauli, 3 km away).[16] While this PHC had excellent infrastructure in terms of the building and the space it occupied, a recent visit (in 2013) showed that it was understaffed (only one homeopathic doctor, one lab technician, and one pharmacist), had limited supplies, and the operation theatre and labour room had neither any staff nor furniture in them. It is therefore seen that the health services available in the neighbourhood of Palanpur remain very poor.

Other Services

The state of other public services in Palanpur is also similarly poor. MGNREGA[17] was started in 2008, but as of 2009, only 22 out of 233 households in the village had job cards. The opening of works was irregular and there were reports of wrong entries in the muster rolls by

[16] During the survey in 1983–4 there was a government health centre in Akrauli but it was not very functional even then (this was probably a sub-centre). When we did the survey in 2008–10, nobody mentioned a health centre in Akrauli. It was only after we completed the survey that a new building was constructed and a PHC inaugurated here.

[17] MGNREGA or the Mahatma Gandhi National Rural Employment Guarantee Act started in 2005 in a limited number of districts and expanded later. It

the pradhan and *rozgar-sevak*.[18] However, after the initial hitches, there seems to have been improvements in its implementation.

The ration shop under the Public Distribution System (PDS)[19] that used to operate in 1984 was closed down in 1991. The villagers were assigned to a neighbouring PDS store in Pipli for some time. Before 2008, the Palanpur PDS shop was shifted from one village to another many times. After the 2009 panchayat elections, the dealership for the fair price shop (FPS) was given to a resident of Palanpur. In a subsequent visit after the survey, villagers complained of corruption, alleging that PDS items were sold in the open market and that the ration dealer had connections with the food supply inspector. On the other hand, the ration shop owner complained of a loss as the villagers were not buying from him due to the bad quality of grains and that he had to spend his own money to go to the godown in Bilari and get the grains.

As for the coverage of this scheme, there are only 16 households in the village (out of 233 households) that come under the Below Poverty Line (BPL) or Antyodaya Anna Yojana (AAY) schemes. Two hundred households have Above Poverty Line (APL) cards, on which (for most of the survey period) they could only buy kerosene. Data on consumption

---

is a job guarantee scheme for the rural population providing 100 days of work per household at not less than minimum wages based on demand from the beneficiaries; failing which they are eligible for monetary compensation. Every rural household is eligible to get a 'job card' under this scheme, which registers demand for work, work provided, and wages given, and so on.

[18] The rozgar-sevak is the frontline worker for the administration of the MGNREGA. For implementation of the act (MGNREGA), the State Government recruits rozgar-sevaks on contract through Block Development Officers (BDOs) in agreement with the pradhan. They help the technical person to strengthen the MGNREGA works and also other official works related to MGNREGA.

[19] Under the PDS, foodgrains and kerosene are provided at subsidized prices to targeted consumers. The number of eligible beneficiaries is identified using a cut-off of the poverty line. Those below poverty line (BPL) receive grains at very low prices (procurement, handling, and distribution are paid by the government) and those above poverty line (APL) at about double the BPL prices. There is another special category of households marked as the poorest of the poor who are provided foodgrains at subsidized cost by the Antyodaya Anna Yojana (AAY).

expenditure was collected from the village, enabling us to identify households below the poverty line, using the same methodology as the Planning Commission, based on the state poverty line for UP.[20] Among the 88 households that were found to be below the poverty line (that is, a poverty ratio of 38 per cent) on the basis of their consumption expenditure, 5 households had BPL cards and 2 had AAY cards, while 77 had APL cards, and 4 had no cards. Further, among those who had BPL or AAY cards, 8 were above the poverty line. While the problem of inclusion and exclusion errors in identification is widespread across the country, Palanpur is no different. Moreover, the PDS in Palanpur is not a very effective scheme, particularly because of the low number of BPL cards. In general, the supply of kerosene was regular, although there was always confusion on whether the quota was 3 litres per household per month or 2 litres per household per month. The supply of grains, especially for the APL beneficiaries, was very irregular and unpredictable.

In other schemes too, coverage was low. In the period of 12 months prior to the latest round of surveys, one out of 14 eligible households got the benefit under the Indira Awaas Yojana[21] (IAY), 2 out of 4 the incentive for institutional delivery; 1 out of 37 elderly, 1 out of 22 widows, and 2 out of 17 disabled persons got the pensions they were eligible for.

Inequality and Collective Action

As seen above, the state of public services in Palanpur, as in the rest of UP, is very poor. What is perplexing is the almost complete absence of any collective action by the people of the village towards demanding better services. Drèze and Sharma (1998) based on the previous round of the survey, had stated a few opportunities for obvious collective action that could have helped to improve the quality of life for all, such as improving the drainage system and coordinating the sowing time. During this round of the survey, we observed further failures of public services, such as the stopping of the midday meal in the school, the irregularity of the nurse coming to the village, and the other failures of public services listed above, as situations evidently waiting for active

[20] See Himanshu, Bakshi, and Dufour (2011) for details

[21] A housing scheme for the rural poor.

engagement by the people. With strong collective action, the village could see improvements in their public service provisions. Another example of lack of collective action related to the 'monkey menace'.[22] While residing in the village for our field work, we observed major disruptions being faced by people in the village due to the hundreds of monkeys running wild in the village, causing destruction of crops in the fields and stealing and spoiling food in the homes, etc. As residents of the village undertaking field work, we were also affected by this menace and wondered why the community was not getting together to do something to find a solution.

Drèze and Sharma (1998) as well as Drèze and Gazdar (1997) postulate that one of the reasons for the lack of collective action in Palanpur is because of the social stratification in the village, which does not allow people to come together. Some quotes from previous writings by Drèze and Sharma (1988) are presented below to give an idea of the arguments made earlier.

> ... Class (however defined) is only loosely related to other important bases of social division, such as caste and gender. This does not necessarily affect the notional division of society into classes, but it can blur this division for concerned parties, obscure any consciousness of class interests, and reduce the scope for collective action along class lines. (p. 38).
>
> By now, it should be clear that the society of Palanpur is a highly divided one ... it is not just that economic and social inequalities are quite large ... there are many different bases of social division (caste, class, gender, kinship, ownership, occupation, education etc.), leading to multiple solidarities and oppositions ... the village society in short is highly fragmented with few solid rallying points for collective action, whether of a 'cooperative' or 'adversarial' type. (p. 67)
>
> The failure of collective action in Palanpur has far-reaching implications. Indeed, the effectiveness of a whole range of local public services can be greatly enhanced through skilful use of local channels of information and accountability. (p. 75)

In the following sections we present the situation of caste and gender inequality in the village and make some observations on the possible pathways through which inequality hinders collective action in Palanpur.

[22] As will be seen below, this later became an example for the success of collective action.

Social Inequality—Caste

In Palanpur, as in the rest of the country, the role of caste in determining social and economic opportunities has become less perceptible in the course of the survey period, particularly since 1984. However, it still operates in subtle ways, resulting in large inequalities in human development outcomes. There are principally eight castes represented within the village: Thakur, Murao, Dhimar, Gadariya, Dhobi, Teli, Passi, and Jatab. Since 1957, in terms of population the three largest castes in Palanpur have always been Thakurs, Muraos, and Jatabs (Table 15.1). Thakur, a warrior caste, is the top-most in hierarchy among the castes present in the village. Just below the Thakurs is a cultivating caste, the Muraos, who are the largest group within the population of the village. Muraos are traditional cultivators who have continued to specialize in agriculture. They are known to be very hard-working and have seen a rapid rise in their wealth and socio-economic status in the village. Today, Muraos even tend to be more prosperous than the Thakurs and challenge the previously unquestioned political and economic dominance of the Thakurs. At the bottom of the caste hierarchy are the Valmikis and Jatabs, both Scheduled Castes (SCs). While there only a few Valmiki households, the Jatabs accounted for around 17 per cent of the population in 2009. Traditionally 'untouchable' leather workers, Jatabs are now primarily engaged in agricultural wage labour. They own little or no land, have low education levels, and have little access to non-farm employment outside the village. They live at the edge of the village and have visibly smaller houses and poorer living conditions. Muslims (Dhobis and Telis by caste) accounted for nearly 13 per cent of the Palanpur population in 2009. The differences in culture and lifestyle between the two communities (Hindu and Muslim) are slight. In terms of the social hierarchy in the village, the Muslims are considered inferior to the Thakurs and Muraos but above the Jatabs.[23]

Strict untouchability, which was practiced earlier, is no longer practiced. For example, the Jatabs, who were considered untouchables and were not permitted to have food in the houses of any other caste, are now allowed to take food from Muraos. However, Thakurs still openly support untouchability. None of the castes still accept food cooked by Jatabs.

[23] See Drèze and Sharma (1998) for more details.

TABLE 15.1 Proportion of Caste Groups in Palanpur: 1958–2009[24]

% of Households	1958	1964	1974	1983	1993	2009
Thakur	17	17.9	22.3	20.9	24.9	24.5
Murao	21	23.6	25	18.2	22.8	23.6
Dhimar	10	8.5	7.1	10.1	7.2	8.1
Gadariya	9	8.6	8.9	8.1	7.2	6.4
Dhobi	2	0.9	2.7	2.7	2.6	3.4
Teli	8	8.6	10.7	11.5	10.4	9.0
Passi	12	15.1	7.1	10.1	7.8	2.6
Jatab	16	12.3	12.5	12.8	12.4	16.7
Others	5	4.7	3.6	5.4	4.7	5.6
Total	100	100	100	100	100	100

Source: Calculated using field survey data.

On social occasions like a wedding in a Jatab family, people from upper castes do attend and eat as long as the cooking has not been done by a Jatab. While these are the broad features, there are also sub-groups within each caste the details of which we do not get into presently.

Interestingly the data show that the inter-caste inequality in income has decreased with many Jatabs doing well. However, at the same time, the inter-household inequality in the village has risen in this period. Although there has been a decline in inequality amongst the different castes in terms of per capita incomes, there is still a wide gap in the absolute income level of the Thakurs and Muraos on the one hand and the Jatabs, Dhobis, and Telis on the other (see Chapter 11 in this book for details).

Inequality in Literacy—Caste and Gender

With regard to literacy rates, it is seen there has been a tremendous increase in literacy rates among all castes, especially after 1983–4. The literacy rate has increased for all castes in Palanpur (Figure 15.1); however, the level of literacy is much lower for the lower castes and more so for women. Although women of the upper castes, especially the Thakurs, show a considerable increase in literacy rates, the women

[24] The proportion of the number of households to total households.

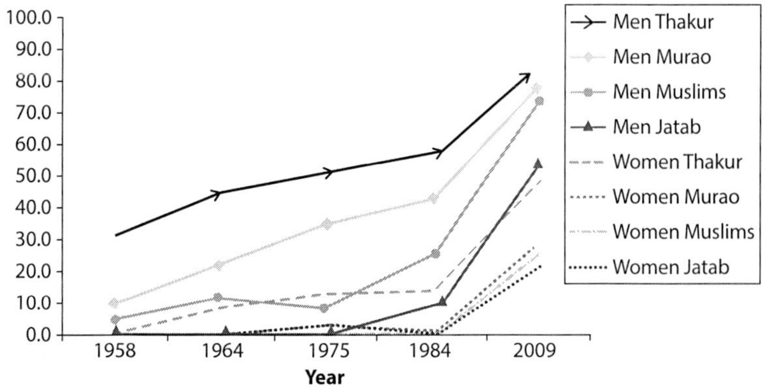

FIGURE 15.1 Change in Literacy Rates for Major Castes in Palanpur: 1958–2009

Source: Graph created by authors using field survey data of Palanpur (1958–2009).

from other castes are far behind. The literacy rate is lowest for Jatab women, which shows a visible improvement from 1993 to 2009 but is still much lower when compared to all other categories—even lower than the literacy rate for Thakur men in 1958.

By looking at a simple percentage change in literacy rates, the biggest improvements are among Jatabs in comparison with all other castes. But this is because the Jatabs have improved from a very low base. It is well known that the scope for improving human development indicators is narrower and becomes more and more difficult at higher levels of human development, and therefore percentage change is not a good measure. Other indices, such as the Sen 'improvement index', have therefore been proposed to take account of the initial level of the outcome indicator and measure the change in relation to that (Chakraborty 2011; Sen 1981). This improvement index is based on the formula

$$(X_2 - X_1)/(X_{max} - X_1),$$

where X_1 and X_2 are the indicator values in the initial year and the final year, respectively, and X_{max} is the chosen upper bound (100 per cent in the case of literacy rate). This is based on Sen (1981) where he takes the absolute shortfall of literacy from some chosen upper bound and then examines the percentage decline of this shortfall. The improvement index of the literacy rate for each caste between 1984 and 2009 is shown in Table 15.2. It shows that, among the major castes, the improvement is fastest for the Thakurs, followed by the Muraos with the Jatabs being way behind—much lower than the average improvement level of the village. What this shows is that although the literacy rates are improving for all the castes, the rate at which the literacy rates for Jatabs is increasing has to be much higher if they are to catch up with the higher castes.

Looking at the access to private and public schools by caste and gender (Table 15.3) it is seen that a much higher percentage of boys and girls from the Thakur and Murao caste attend private schools compared to Jatabs. The gender bias also becomes clear when the attendance of children is classified between private and public school attendance. There is a clear pattern that shows that within each caste, parents send their male child to a private fee-paying school while girl children are sent to free government education institutions. Thirty per cent and 20 per cent of all girls among Thakurs and Muraos respectively are going to private schools but none among Jatabs. Among boys 39 per cent Thakur children, 32 per cent among the Muraos, and 25 per cent among the Jatabs are sent to private schools. This reflects the

TABLE 15.2 Improvement in Literacy Rates, 1984–2009

Caste	Literacy Rate (Men)		Literacy Rate (Women)		Sen's Improvement Index 1984–2009	
	1984	2009	1984	2009	Men	Women
Thakur	56.7	82.6	15.1	48.3	81.34	48.10
Murao	43.2	78.9	1.3	28.3	78.10	28.32
Dhimar	26.5	74.0	0.0	35.7	73.64	35.71
Gadariya	36.7	70.3	13.2	31.7	69.69	31.56
Dhobi	12.5	60.0	0.0	0.0	59.86	0.00
Teli	27.9	78.6	0.0	32.2	78.18	32.20
Passi	47.2	75.0	9.1	36.4	74.11	36.26
Jatab	7.5	51.3	0.0	21.7	51.17	21.74
Other	38.9	82.4	47.4	33.3	81.72	32.43
Total	37.6	73.6	8.7	33.1	73.03	32.97

Source: Calculated using field survey data.

TABLE 15.3 Percentage of Children Going to Public and Private Institutions by Sex, 2009

Caste	Boys		Girls	
	Private	Public	Private	Public
Thakur	39.0	61.0	30.8	69.2
Murao	32.4	67.6	20.0	80.0
Dhimar	21.4	78.6	0.0	100.0
Gadariya	53.8	46.2	20.0	80.0
Dhobi	0.0	100.0	0.0	0.0
Teli	50.0	50.0	9.1	90.9
Passi	0.0	100.0	0.0	100.0
Jatab	25.0	75.0	0.0	100.0
Other	16.7	83.3	50.0	50.0
Total	32.7	67.3	18.4	81.6

Source: Calculated using field survey data.

caste and the gender differentials in relation to education—it shows that parents give greater priority to boys' education and therefore a higher number of boys are sent to private schools, which are perceived to be of better quality.

Further, it also shows that with the poor functioning of the government school, the better-off are shifting towards private schools. The people who can afford it are exercising their choice of what is perceived as better quality education even if they have to pay for it. This is one of the ways by which families are dealing independently with the lack of good quality government education service in the village.

The Sopher's index in literacy rate throws further light on the gender and caste inequality in education. The higher the value of the Sopher's index, the greater the inequality (in case of perfect equality the value is zero). Table 15.4 on the modified Sopher's Inequality index[25] shows the trends in gender inequality between male and female literacy from 1958 to 2009 for all ages and also for the 7–15 age group. The inequality in the 7–15 age group reflects the status of

[25] Modified David Sopher's Index (Kundu and Rao 1983) of inequality shows the inequality between men's and women's literacy rates. The formula used is

TABLE 15.4 Values of Sopher's Index for Literacy Rates between Men and Women: 1958–2009

Caste	Age group	1958	1964	1974	1984	1993	2009
Thakurs	7–15		0.4	0.4	0.6	0.5	*(–0.2)*
	all ages		0.8	0.7	0.7	0.8	0.3
Muraos	7–15			1.0	1.1	2.3	0.5
	all ages			1.1	1.6	2.8	1.4
Jatabs	7–15						0.2
	all ages			0.47	1.35		0.5
All Castes	7–15		0.5	0.6	0.5	1.3	0.1
	all ages	1.3	0.9	0.8	0.7	1.4	0.5

Source: Created by authors using field survey data of Palanpur (1958–2009).
Note: The blank cells are years where women's literacy was nil and hence inequality was 100 per cent.

gender discrimination in education in Palanpur village more clearly, since this age group does not have any women from other villages who are married into the village.

For all castes, the gender gap has gone down from 1.3 in 1958 to 0.5 in 2009. For the 7–15 age group, the gap is fairly low being just 0.1. Thakurs and Muraos have done considerably well from no women

$$D_s = \log\frac{X_2}{X_1} + \log[\frac{200 - X_1}{200 - X_2}]$$

where X_1 is the literacy rate of the usually deprived group—in this case women's literacy–and X_2 is the literacy rate of dominant group—in this case men. The index is 0 when the literacy rate is the same for both groups and increases as inequality increases. It is appropriate to observe changes in inequality levels over time as the index satisfies both the additive monotonicity axiom (addition of any constant to the series should reduce inequality) and more importantly the multiplicative monotonicity axiom – which means if the indicators in question increase with their ratio intact, the inequality should not go down. For example, if time 1 has 10 per cent women and 20 per cent men literates and time 2 has 30 per cent and 60 per cent women and men literates the inequality should not be lower in time 2. Sopher's Index satisfies this axiom and is therefore suitable for a trend analysis. In this paper Sopher's Index is calculated between men and women's literacy rates separately for each caste for all ages and the 7–15 age group.

literate in 1958 to a smaller gender gap of 0.3 and 1.4 currently.[26] Jatabs too show some improvement in the gender gap in literacy between 1984 and 2009. Overall, it is seen that while the gender inequality in education is going down within each caste, across castes the inequality is higher as we go down the caste hierarchy among the 7–15 years old. It must also be noted that among Jatabs, 7–15 years old girls have started reporting education only in the latest round. This divergence between castes in social indicators is one of the factors that could explain the lack of collective action by the villagers.

Different Aspects of Gender Inequality[27]

After the initial visits to Palanpur, the impression was that there was nothing likely to be particularly surprising about women's lives in the village. The writings based on earlier surveys also suggested that women's status in the village was very slow to improve. In the context of discussing change in gender relations over the survey period, Drèze, Lanjouw and Sharma (1998) write: 'These perceived changes in gender relations, however, are small in relation to the persistent inequalities. And the basic framework has remained remarkably stable over the survey period ... boy preference continues unabated.... Similarly there has been no change in women's roles in the family and society, or in their freedom of movement and action' (p. 222).

There are still few women seen out on the streets, there is an obvious boy preference, *purdah* is still practiced, and very few worked outside the home for a wage, and so on. However, there were subtle changes that we slowly observed. For instance, there was a woman who had completed her postgraduate studies and was working as a teacher in the government school. There was another woman in Palanpur who was widowed and living with her parents and fighting a legal battle

[26] The negative sign in 7–15 group of Thakurs is due to a small sample; although in absolute numbers, boys are more literate than girls, percentage terms show greater female literacy in that age group for Thakurs.

[27] This section is based on the analysis presented in Sinha and Coppoletta (2011).

with her husband's family[28] for her share in the property. There was another woman whose husband was working in the army and posted in Kashmir, who was handling all the affairs of agriculture and the land they owned herself. Many older women talked about how (in the old days) they could not even sit down or speak if their fathers-in-law were anywhere around. But now younger women, in spite of continuing to practice purdah, could sometimes give their opinion on household issues.

Apart from education, a very important aspect of social life is the nature of occupation and the division of labour between men and women. In this chapter we present the broad findings on women's work, while further work on this is planned. Based on data collected at the household level it is seen that there are very few women (above 15 years of age) reported as participating in the labour force. The primary occupation of most of the women is domestic work. While the primary occupation of more than 95 per cent women in 1984 and 1993 was reported as being domestic work, this decreased to 88 per cent in 2009. However, rather than due to an increase in labour force participation, this was because of the increase in the number of women for whom no occupation was reported in 2009. These were either women who were unmarried or older than 60.

In 2009, the primary occupations for a slightly higher number of women were reported as being cultivation. However, in 1984 cultivation was the secondary occupation for 21 women (7 in 1993 and 18 in 2009). There are two women in government service in 1993 and three in 2009. These are the anganwadi worker, anganwadi helper (both existed in 1993 as well), and shiksha mitra. After the survey in 2009, one woman was appointed as the ASHA worker.

While information on the main and subsidiary occupations of all members of the family was collected along with the general information for the household, which was usually provided by an adult male, during the 'women's round', all women in the reproductive age were also asked about whether they did any work outside the home. These

[28] This woman's natal village is Palanpur, whereas her marital village is a slight distance away in the same district. While she went to live with her husband's family post-marriage, after his death she moved back to Palanpur.

TABLE 15.5 Women's Occupation in Palanpur: 1984 to 2009

Women's Occupation (all women aged 15 and above)	Primary Occupation			Secondary Occupation		
	1984	1993	2009	1984	1993	2009
Domestic Work	245	301	327	2	5	11
Cultivation	1	0	7	21	7	18
Agriculture labour	1	2	2	0	0	3
Non-agriculture labour	1	0	2	0	0	0
Non-agriculture Self-employed (Tailor/Shopkeeper)	0	1	0	5	1	4
Government Service	0	2	3	0	0	0
Jajmani/village sweeper	1	1	0	0	1	0
None	9	6	32	230	299	337
Total women	258	313	373	258	313	373

Source: Calculated from field survey data.

interviews were conducted by women where the respondents were also women themselves. In these interviews, more time was spent on the different work women do. The findings based on this data show more number of women working, although the labour force participation is still very low.

Of the 224 women in the reproductive age who were interviewed, only 42 said that they were engaged in any kind of paid work in the last one year. Of these 25 did work for which they were paid in kind and the remaining 16 were paid in cash. Therefore, about 19 per cent of the women were engaged in paid work.[29]

Among women who did any paid work, the highest were among Jatabs (15), followed by Muraos (10). Only two Thakur women reported ever having done any paid work. Of which, one was the village health worker (ASHA) appointed under the government's National Rural Health Mission and the other was working as a teacher (shiksha-mitra) in the school. Two Kayastha women were employed as the anganwadi

[29] Further information on the exact nature of work that women were engaged can be got from the detailed diaries that were maintained for a sample of the households. These data are yet to be analysed.

worker and the anganwadi helper. The Jatab and Murao women were mainly involved in agriculture labour, while some Jatab women also went along with their families for a few months in a year to work in the brick kilns.

Age at Marriage

The age at marriage, especially for women, is still quite low in India and in UP. According to the NFHS-3 data, 53 per cent of all women aged 18–29 in rural India (59 per cent in UP) were married by the age of 18 (IIPS 2007). Age at marriage has an impact on fertility and also women's autonomy. Standard marriage practices, such as caste endogamy, village exogamy, hypergamy, and patrilocality[30] remain in Palanpur as in most parts of rural North India. While the parents still made the decision on who their daughter should marry, in some cases women did mention that their parents would ask them for their consent before finalizing the match. However, this does not yet mean that the girl and boy get to meet and talk before the marriage. One change that people did mention was that now there was a greater 'demand' for 'educated' girls, especially among Thakurs, and this was one of the reasons why parents felt it was important to send their daughters to school.

Many factors influence age at marriage (dowry, number of siblings and rank, network, schooling, etc.). Although the average age of marriage is still low, it is slowly increasing in Palanpur. Even though the age at marriage was not directly asked in the 1984 and 1993 surveys, the marital status of all village inhabitants was reported. Figure 15.2 indicates that there is a change in the age of marriage between 1984 and 2009. In 1984, 44 per cent of the girls aged 15–17 in the village were married; this came down to 18 per cent in 1993, whereas none of the girls in this age group was married in 2009. Such a difference is also seen in the 18–20 and 21–23 age groups. Ninety-one per cent of girls aged 18–20 were married in 1984 compared to 73 per cent in 1993

[30] A young woman is married to a boy of the same caste (caste endogamy), in another village (village exogamy), preferably to a family of somewhat higher status (hypergamy) and after marriage, she leaves her parental village and is incorporated in her husband's family (patrilocality). In Palanpur, these practices apply to all castes (with some exceptional cases) (Drèze and Sharma 1998).

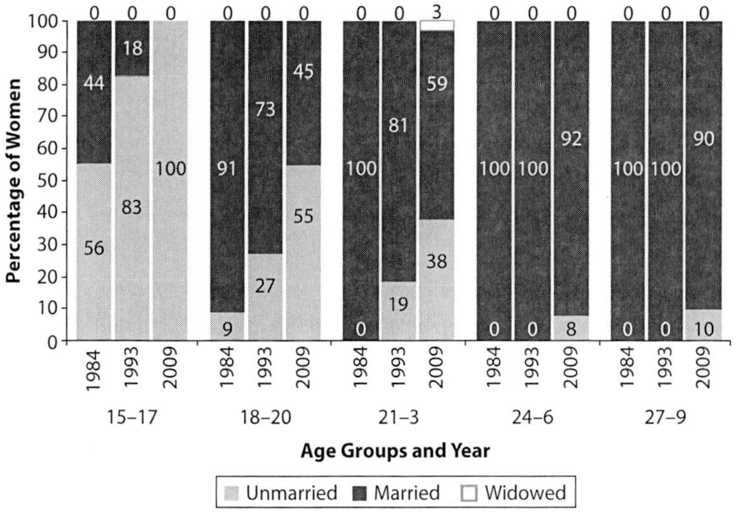

FIGURE 15.2 Age Group-wise Marital Status in Palanpur: 1984 to 2009
Source: Graph created by authors using field survey data of Palanpur (1958–2009).

and 45 per cent in 2009. There were no unmarried girls in the village in the age group of 21–23 in 1984; in 1993, 81 per cent of girls aged 21–23 were married, compared to 59 per cent in 2008. In the higher age groups, up to 29 years, there are still a few unmarried women in 2009 whereas all women of this age group were married women in 1984 and 1993. All women above 30 years of age were either married or widowed in all three survey years reported here. The fertility rate in Palanpur has also decreased over time from 0.87 in 1984 to 0.72 in 2009 (Watine 2008).

Women's Autonomy

Defining and measuring 'autonomy' or 'empowerment' is a complicated issue. It is however important to keep in mind that talking about the status of women is not always appropriate as it is a multidimensional concept spanning the social, economic, political, and psychological sectors (Jejeebhoy 2000; Kabeer 2001; Mason 1986, 2005). We present the different indicators on which data were collected, separately without trying to construct one indicator of women's autonomy.

TABLE 15.6 Indicators of Autonomy among Women in Palanpur: 2008

Indicator	Per cent of Women (of 217)
Economic Decision-Making:	
Have a say in spending	74
Have cash in hand for expenses	88
Have land in own name	8
Have a bank/post office account in own name	18
Mobility (can go the following places alone)	
Local market	31
Village doctor	62
Fields outside the village	53
Relative's house	61
Village temple	70
Nearby shrine	21
Parents' house	49
Health centre	33
Exposure to Media (Ever)	
Read newspapers	6
Listens to radio	26
Watches TV	34
Ever gone to cinema	11
Participation to civic life	
Been to government office (outside or in Palanpur)	14
Voted in last elections	78

Source: Calculated using field survey data.

An important aspect of women's autonomy is whether they have control over how the household resources are spent. As seen in Table 15.6, whereas 3 out of 4 women say they have a say in household expenditures and 88 per cent get cash in hand, only 8 per cent have any land in their name, and only 18 per cent have a bank account. We asked women whether they could go alone to a list of commonly visited places. The place where women can most often go alone is the village temple (70 per cent), followed by the village doctor (62 per cent), relatives or friends in the village (61 per cent) and the fields outside the village (53 per cent).[31] One woman out of two can go alone to visit her parents (49 per cent). The places where fewer women can go alone are the health centre outside the village (33 per cent), the local market in the village (31 per cent), and the shrine or market outside the village (21 per cent).

Mobility varies a lot depending on what caste women belong to. Jatab women are most free to go where they want to in almost every category and Thakurs are at the bottom of the list in terms of mobility. The practice of purdah is also most stringent amongst the Thakurs and least among Jatabs.

Women were asked whether they read a newspaper or magazine, listen to the radio, or watch television and if they did, how frequently they did so. Fourteen women (6 per cent) said that they read the newspaper, of which one does it every day and three at least once a week. 57 women (26 per cent) listen to the radio, most of them (40 women) almost every day. 74 women (34 per cent) watch television, half of them almost every day, 16 of them at least once a week, and 21 less than once a week. We also asked women whether they had ever gone to a cinema hall or theatre to see a movie and only 24 women (11 per cent) said they did. On TV, women mostly watched daily serials ('soaps') or Hindi films, and on radio listened to songs from Hindi films. Although they did not watch 'news' or other informational programmes, watching TV gave them an exposure to the 'outside world'. Some women also told us that they got to know about immunization, child care, and so on from the advertisements on the radio.

Seventy-eight per cent of Palanpur women voted in the last elections (panchayat elections), which is quite a high participation rate. When asked if they have ever been to a government/panchayat office in their village, or in a government office outside the village, 86 per cent of them said no. The women were also asked whether they had ever attended a gram sabha or any such meeting in the village or ever gone for a public meeting/political meeting/rally outside the village, but there were no positive answers for the first question and only two for the second one.

[31] Women would go to fields outside the village to take meals to workers, to do farm work, to gather/cut grass for the cattle. Since there are very few households in Palanpur which have toilets, so women also have to go to the fields to relieve themselves.

There was a whole section about women's participation in any kind of associational activities, including self-help groups, mahila mandals, and so on. But none of the women reported being part of any association.

Based on whatever little data are available from the previous Palanpur surveys, it is seen that while there has been a positive change in women's status, it is probably not as much as is seen in other aspects of village life. Two aspects in which the change can be seen statistically is the age of marriage, which has increased, and schooling among girls, which has also increased significantly. On the other hand, while there are no comparable data, it is clear that on aspects such as mobility, decision-making, etc., women's lives are still very restricted. The same can be said also with regard to participation in the workforce and property rights.

Politics in the Village

As seen in the previous sections, the village society in Palanpur continues to have several inequalities in social and economic fronts. As a result of this, there are very few people in the village who are able to influence the village's collective agenda and are generally seen as 'spokespersons' with the outside world. It is this group of about 10–12 men who usually visit the government offices at the block or higher levels if there is something that the village needs; who influence the way different groups of people vote at the panchayat elections, and so on. It is also generally seen that anyone who has the support of these people can get away with a lot of wrongdoing as well (for example, the school teacher). This is of course a simplistic presentation; even within this group of persons, there are differences and power struggles, often determined by caste affiliations. The equation differs from time to time, depending on the issue and the personal interests of these individuals. When the issues in question are beneficial to all the castes, it is more likely that there is some collective action by villagers.

No political party has any significant presence in the village. There is some political consciousness among the Jatabs that they belong to the same caste as the then Chief Minister Mayawati. Many in the village (including Jatabs themselves) observed that the Jatabs had become more vocal and were generally more confident in voicing their opinions after the Bahujan Samaj Party (BSP) won with a big majority in 2007. However, there is no organized group or branch of the BSP in the village. Some villagers have access to some political leaders and, in case of any problems, approach them for help. For instance, some of the Muslims have access to a minister from the same caste and they approach him sometimes, even taking along villagers from other castes when they need help. The general feeling in the village is that, because it is a small village with not many votes, political parties are not interested in investing any time there.

During our period of stay in the village, there were two incidents, which can be seen as positive examples of collective action by the villagers. Both these incidents helped us understand how the power dynamics in the village work. These cases showed us some insights on what provokes people in the village to get together and take action. It also showed that such action can be effective.

Case Study 1: Removal and Re-election of the Pradhan

The first was the case where the existing pradhan was impeached by the village community. In the 2007 panchayat elections, the post of the pradhan of the gram panchayat in Palanpur was reserved for candidates from the SC community. While Jatabs are the majority SC group in Palanpur, the election was won by Mahesh[32] from the Valmiki community. It was widely understood that he won because of the support he had from the powerful people in the village, including those from the upper castes and Muslims.

However, in about two years this pradhan became very unpopular with the same people who were supporting him, leading a mobilization to get him removed. The charges against him were that he did not do anything for the village; he was very corrupt and usurped a large share of the funds that came to the village. The antagonism however was not purely because Mahesh did no development work, as the previous headmen did not do much either. Nor was it that he showed favouritism in allocating government benefits. This was also the practice earlier. For instance, many villagers reported that under the previous pradhan, one of the richest persons in the village owning a tractor, thresher, mentha plant, etc. got a grant under the IAY because of his proximity with the pradhan.

[32] All names have been changed.

Therefore, while it is not the case that the previous pradhans were not corrupt, what worked against this one was twofold. First, he did not include any of the powerful people in the village in what he was doing, not even those who propped him up as the pradhan in the first place. For instance, it was during his tenure that the school midday meal was completely stopped while most people knew that the foodgrains continued to be supplied for this purpose. It was rumoured that this was one of the main reasons for the fallout between the pradhan and the local school teacher, an influential member of the village. While corruption was the explicit reason given for the anger against the pradhan, it could also argued that there was such a mobilization also because he was from the SC and yet defied the local power structures.

Second, he also indulged in petty corruption with almost no patronage to anyone in the village. He asked for money or liquor even for petty jobs, such as signing a document or certificate. He was drunk most of the time and would pass lewd comments on women passing by. As a result, the level of anger among the entire village community was very high and when a campaign began that he should be impeached, there was widespread support. This became the topic of discussion in the village for a few weeks, with almost everyone except four or five households, being against the pradhan. Even the women were quite vocal about how he needed to be removed and there was an effective campaign amongst the women as well.

While a large number of people in the village wanted him removed, the process of impeachment was long-drawn-out and the result of a lot of effort by some of the villagers over more than four months. The villagers collected details of funds that came to the village using the Right to Information Act (RTI) and filed complaints against the pradhan at the BDO office with detailed charges of irregularities. An enquiry was ordered and the enquiry team found that even on the date of enquiry, no midday meal was served. Following this, an application for a no-confidence motion against Mahesh was submitted to the district magistrate in Moradabad, signed by 530 people from the village, including all the gram panchayat members. Simultaneously a similar process was undertaken towards the removal of the PDS dealer. The pradhan was finally impeached by an overwhelming majority of 416 to 27.

Elections were held for a new pradhan after three weeks, which Mahesh also contested again. While there were a few other candidates in the fray, once again the 'elders' decided who would have their support. Ranjit, the candidate who came a close second in the previous election, was the chosen candidate. He was the son of Lakshman, who is a good friend of Ganesh Maurya, who allegedly ensured that nobody else filed a nomination. There was intense campaigning by Mahesh, where he not only apologized for his previous misdeeds and promised to reform himself, but also distributed a lot of liquor and allegedly cash as well. Out of 491 votes cast, Mahesh got 90 while Ranjit got 401 votes.

At the end of Ranjit's term the pradhan's post was once again reserved, this time for a woman candidate. Other than formally filling the papers in a woman's name, the entire contest and campaign was for and by the husbands. While one of the active persons in the village (Naseem, a Muslim) with a reputation of being honest and hardworking, filed a nomination in his wife's name, the post was ultimately won by a Thakur woman who lives outside the village. Naseem claimed that although he was promised support by many of the powerful people in the village, who also worked with him closely for the removal of Mahesh, they ultimately ended up putting their weight behind an ex-army officer from the village who lives in Moradabad. In our discussions with some of the key people in the village, they said that they favoured the army officer because he lived outside, had worked in the army, and was already rich and therefore did not need to make money from the panchayat. In conversation with some of them, when we visited the village recently, they even let it slip out that Naseem was not supported because he was a Muslim. The Thakur's wife who lives outside won the election and the panchayat is now managed by her nephew. The impression some villagers have is that he also is corrupt and siphons off funds but at the same time is active and has helped make some improvements, such as the construction of pucca roads, concrete around wells, and a drainage system in the village.

Case Study 2: Dealing with the Monkey Menace

One of the problems that have been plaguing the village was that of monkeys. This was not a problem at the time of the previous survey held in 1993. Since then, over time a number of monkeys came into the village. The reasons given were that monkeys were attracted to Palanpur because of the presence of the station, resulting in people from trains passing by feeding them. It was also surmised that people from nearby villages stealthily diverted and brought monkeys from their villages and left them in Palanpur to get rid of them. While this appears to be a trivial issue, in fact, it was causing severe disruption to daily lives. The monkey menace changed the cropping pattern in Palanpur—people could no more grow vegetables or groundnuts, which used to be grown before. People needed to guard the farms all the time before the harvest. Someone had to stand guard all the time when women were cooking; this was the duty of children (with sticks). Eighty-four cases of monkey bites were reported in the one-year period before the survey. The monkeys were a constant source of menace for even those of us visiting the village for the survey and we had to always be careful if we were carrying any food with us.

In spite of such inconvenience, it was surprising to find that there was never any attempt to arrive at a collective solution to the problem. People did not even try to stop those from other villages coming and leaving monkeys in Palanpur. Some temporary solutions were worked out by those who could afford it. For instance, in some better-off upper-caste homes, they built barricades around the cooking area and in some farms, people bought big guard dogs.

After about a year of staying in the village, the research team suggested to the villagers that there was a possibility of contacting the forest department to come and round up the monkeys, take them away from the village, and release them in a natural habitat conducive for their survival. This motivated the village community to get together to solve the difficulties they were facing due to the monkey menace. Under the leadership of a few influential people, the village got together and collected funds from every household. A detailed formula was worked out where each family had to contribute according to their means. Many of the people from the village volunteered time and joined the professional monkey-trapping team that came to the village. Trapping was done under the supervision of forest department officials and a doctor. The whole operation went on for a few days and, according to the forest department's count, over 900 monkeys were caught by them and left in the forest.

* * *

Both these examples show that collective action is possible when the issue affects most of the village population and gets support from the influential people as well. In the case of the monkey menace, there was also the limited role played by the researchers in giving information and suggesting action.

This chapter makes two preliminary propositions. First, that a reason for the slow human development improvements in Palanpur is the failure of public services. Secondly, that the lack of collective action in the village towards improving public services is a result of high social fragmentation especially based on caste and gender. Overall, both these propositions are evident across the state of UP.

Much like the rest of UP, Palanpur has experienced some improvements in human development outcomes during the same period. There is improvement in literacy rates (although lower than in rest of the state and country) in the recent two decades, with health outcomes showing slower progress. There have been greater investments in education and health by central and state governments through various programmes, which are reflected in better buildings and infrastructure. However, there are large gaps in the functioning of public services. Both, the school and health centre are understaffed; absenteeism is a huge problem; and the quality of services are largely poor. In Palanpur, as in UP, it is found that there is hardly any public uproar against such poor services although people individually express dissatisfaction over the state of affairs. It is worth mentioning here that this is not the situation uniformly across the country. Particularly in states such as Kerala and Tamil Nadu, researchers have documented how there is pressure from below, where it is unacceptable for public services to be in such a poor condition. Further, in these states as well as others, the public services are of much better quality and see greater participation by people (for example, see Sinha 2013; Srinivasan 2014).

The high level of social fragmentation, especially based on caste and gender, makes it difficult for any issue to become a common concern for the majority of the people. Further, it has been seen that only when those who are powerful or have some voice within the village take up an issue that people are able to get mobilized around it. Such people in Palanpur are usually male and upper caste. In many ways these people drive the agenda of the village. They are the ones who are able to access officials and politicians outside the village and also influence opinion in the village.

The inadequate services of education and health in the village have until now failed to become important concerns. People who are able to afford it, use private services to overcome the lack of public facilities. Therefore, they have lower value toward improvement of public services in the village. Those who depend on public services are poorer socio-economic groups and unable to mobilize efforts to seek improvements. They also aspire to move away to the private sector as soon as they are able to afford it.

In some instances, the villagers have shown that they can mobilize themselves and get things done. They were able to fight a corrupt pradhan and ensure that he was removed. Similarly, they were able to come together to get rid of the monkeys in the village through the participation of almost everyone in the village. In both of these cases, the 'leaders' were the same and it is when they were convinced to act that some mobilization for change happened. While the identity of the 'leaders' has until now been largely determined by caste, gender, wealth, and education this is also dynamic. There are new entrants who are beginning to become influential in the village. With increasing literacy (amongst men and women), and more people going outside the village for work, we can expect that there will be some change in the village dynamics. At the same time, political developments in the state, such as the rising influence of the BSP, it has been seen, can make it possible for those from the most vulnerable groups (Jatabs) to feel encouraged and raise their voices.

It will be interesting to see in future rounds of surveys, how changes that are occurring in Palanpur in gender and caste relations, brought about by improvements in literacy and external political influences, might provide avenues for collective action in the village, if at all. As mentioned earlier, this chapter is only exploring these issues; further work is required to arrive at any firm conclusions. It is also reiterated that this story of social fragmentation, lack of collective action, and failure of public services are only some of the dimensions that explain the problem of slow human development improvements in Palanpur.

References

Bersier, Florian. 2009. 'Education in Rural India: Perspective from a North Indian Village', Report to Ecole Polytechnique, France.

Chakraborty, Achin. 2011. 'Human Development: How Not to Interpret Change?' *Economic and Political Weekly*, 46 (51): 16–19.

DISE (District Information System for Education). 2011. *Elementary Education in India: Progress towards UEE, Flash Statistics, 2010–11*. New Delhi: National University of Education Planning and Administration.

Drèze, Jean and Haris Gazdar. 1997. 'Uttar Pradesh: The Burden of Inertia', in Jean Drèze and Amartya Sen (eds), *Indian Development: Selected Regional Perspectives*, pp. 33–128. New Delhi: Oxford University Press.

Drèze, Jean and A.K. Sen. 2013. *An Uncertain Glory, India and Its Contradictions*. London: Penguin UK.

Drèze, Jean and Naresh Sharma. 1998. 'Palanpur: Population, Society Economy', in Peter Lanjouw and Nicholas Stern (eds), *Economic Development in Palanpur over Five Decades*, pp. 3–113. Oxford: Clarendon Press.

Drèze, Jean, Peter Lanjouw, and Naresh Sharma. 1998. 'Economic Development in Palanpur, 1957–93', in Peter Lanjouw and Nicholas Stern (eds), *Economic Development in Palanpur over Five Decades*, pp. 114–234. Oxford: Clarendon Press.

Government of India. 2011. *Sample Registration System Bulletin*, 45 (1). New Delhi: Office of the Registrar General.

Himanshu and Nicholas Stern. 2011. 'India and an Indian Village: 50 Years of Economic Development in Palanpur', Working Paper 43, Asia Research Centre, London School of Economics and Political Science, London.

Himanshu, Ishan Bakshi, and Camille Dufour. 2011. 'Poverty, Inequality and Mobility in Palanpur: Observations from Palanpur' Working Paper 45, Asia Research Centre, London School of Economics and Political Science, London.

IAMR (Institute of Applied Manpower Research). 2011. *India Human Development Report 2011, Towards Social Inclusion*. New Delhi: Government of India.

IIPS (International Institute for Population Sciences). 2007. *National Family Health Survey (NFHS 3): 2005–06*. Mumbai: IIPS.

Jejeebhoy, Shireen J. 2000. 'Women's Autonomy in Rural India: Its Dimensions, Determinants and Influence of Context', in Harriet Presser and Gita Sen (eds), *Female Empowerment and Demographic Processes*, pp. 204–38. Oxford: Clarendon Press.

Kabeer, Naila. 2001. 'Reflections on the Measurement of Women's Empowerment', in *Discussing Women's Empowerment: Theory and Practice*. Sida Studies No. 3, Stockholm: Novum Grafiska, AB.

Kattumuri, Ruth and Dinesh Tiwari. 2011. 'Developments in Education in Palanpur, a Village in Uttar Pradesh', Working Paper 49, Asia Research Centre, London School of Economics and Political Science, London.

Kundu, A. and J.M. Rao. 1986. 'Inequality in Education Development: Issues in Measurement Changing Structure and its Socio-Economic Correlates with

Special Reference to India', in Moonis Raza (ed.), *Educational Planning: A Long Term Perspective*, pp. 435–66. New Delhi: National Institute of Educational Planning and Administration (NIEPA).

Lanjouw Peter and Nicholas Stern. 1998. *Economic Development in Palanpur over Five Decades*. Oxford: Clarendon Press.

Mason, Karen Oppenheim. 1986. 'The Status of Women: Conceptual and Methodological Issues in Demographic Studies', *Sociological Forum*, 1 (2): 284–300.

———. 2005. 'Measuring Women's Empowerment: Learning from Cross-national Research', in D. Narayan (ed.), *Measuring Empowerment: Cross Disciplinary Perspectives*, pp. 89–102. Washington, DC: World Bank.

NSSO (National Sample Survey Office). 2005. *Morbidity, Health Care, and the Condition of the Aged*, Report No. 507. New Delhi: NSS 60th Round.

Parker, Barbara and Valerie Kozel. 2003. 'Profile and Diagnostic of Poverty in Uttar Pradesh,' *Economic and Political Weekly*, 38 (04): 385–403.

Pierre, Violain. 2011. 'Health Inequalities in Palanpur', Master's dissertation, Ecole Polytechnique, Paris.

Sen, Amartya. 1981. 'Public Action and the Quality of Life in Developing Countries', *Oxford Bulletin of Economics and Statistics*, 43: 287–319.

Sinha, Dipa and Rosalinda Coppoletta. 2011. 'The Invisible Half–Women's Status in Palanpur', in *India's Economic Revolution: A Perspective from Six Decades of Economic Development in Palanpur, A North Indian Village*, pp. 1–17. Report to DFID. London: Department for International Development.

Sinha, Dipa. 2013. 'Health and Human Development: Comparative Experiences of Tamil Nadu and Uttar Pradesh', PhD thesis, Jawaharlal Nehru University, New Delhi.

Srinivasan, Vivek. 2014. *Delivering Public Services Effectively: Tamil Nadu and Beyond*. New Delhi: Oxford University Press India.

Watine, Loic. 2008. 'Will We Have another Child? Fertility Behaviour in Rural Areas of North India, An Empirical Study of the Village of Palanpur', Master's dissertation, Ecole Polytechnique, Paris.

R. RAMAKUMAR

Caste and Land Distribution

Results from a Village Resurvey in Maharashtra, 1964–2007*

The nature of ownership and distribution of land is the starting point in the analysis of the standard of living of people in the rural areas. While land continues to be a central variable in the understanding of agrarian classes, the cleavages across caste groups also form an important reality in Indian villages. In other words, social oppression *and* class exploitation stand interlinked. Differentiations across class run through the systems of hierarchy that the caste system fosters.

This chapter discusses changes in the ownership and distribution of land across caste groups in one village between 1963–4 and 2006–7. The data used for this chapter comes from a detailed resurvey of one village, Dongargaon, in the Vidarbha region of the western state of Maharashtra in India. The chapter attempts to answer the following questions: what was the nature of distribution of land in the village

* I wish to express my gratitude to Aparajita Bakshi and Pallavi Chavan for comments, and Karan Raut, Tushar Kamble, and Awanish Kumar for research assistance. This article is part of a larger research project on agrarian change in rural Maharashtra. I am also grateful to the National Centre for Competence for Research (NCCR North-South), Bern for supporting the project.

in 1963–4? How did the nature of distribution of land change between 1963–4 and 2006–7? What was the nature of change in land distribution across caste groups? What were the impacts of demographic change on the changes in land distribution? How large was the land market in the village? Which caste groups were the gainers and losers in the nature of exchanges in the land market?

The Study Region and the Database

Dongargaon belongs to the Akola tehsil in Akola district, in the Vidarbha region of Maharashtra. The village is located at a distance of about 13 km from the town of Akola on the National Highway (NH) 6 that connects Akola to Amravati and Nagpur. The *gaothan* (village site) of Dongargaon extends less than 1 km off NH 6, towards the south. The market-town of Murtizapur is about 32 km away from the village, to the east. Dongargaon is surrounded by the villages of Sisa, Masa, Kumbhari, and Babulgaon, located at distances of between 3 to 5 km.

This chapter is based on data collected from the village of Dongargaon as part of a larger study of agrarian relations in eight villages of Maharashtra. Dongargaon was surveyed by a team of investigators led by the author in the summer of 2007, with the agricultural year 2006–7 as the reference year. At the time of the survey, there were 357 households in the village, and a census-type socio-economic survey was conducted of all 357 households using detailed questionnaires (see Table 16.1 for the demographic and agricultural details of the village). The survey began in the last week of April 2007 and was completed by the third week of May the same year. An earlier survey of Dongargaon had been conducted in 1963, by V.H. Joshi of the College of Agriculture, Akola (see Joshi 1967).

Dongargaon was a predominantly cotton-growing village in 2007. Two features of agricultural change in Dongargaon between 1963 and 2007 were notable. First, Dongargaon was primarily a rain-fed village in 1963. Only about 16 acres of land, accounting for 3.1 per cent of the net cropped area, was irrigated (Joshi 1967). In 2007, the village was no longer a dry village. Of all the land owned by inhabitants of the village, 33.5 per cent was irrigated. The expansion of irrigation had a major impact on the availability of employment in agriculture in Dongargaon.

TABLE 16.1 Some Basic Demographic and Agricultural Details—Dongargaon (2007) in Numbers, Acres, and Per cent

Item	Number/ Extent	Share in total population/ households/working population (%)
Total number of households	357	–
Total population	1,680	–
Number of men	855	51.0
Number of women	825	49.2
Total number of SC households	161	45.1
Total number of ST households	45	12.6
Total number of VJNT households	14	3.9
Population (> 6 years) who are fully literate	1,202	80.3
Population (> 6 years) who never went to school	258	17.2
Average household size	4.7	–
Number of workers with primary occupation as:		
Agricultural labourer	362	46.6
Cultivator	246	31.7
Total area under ownership holdings (acres)	630	–
Extent of area irrigated	270.5	40.5

Source: Survey data 2007.
Notes: SC = scheduled caste; ST = scheduled tribe; VJNT = Vimuktya Jati and Nomadic Tribes.

Secondly, the cropping pattern in the village witnessed major changes between 1963 and 2007. The cropping pattern in 1963 was predominated by *jowar*, followed by cotton. About 55 per cent of the total area owned was cultivated with jowar and 33.8 per cent with cotton. In 2007, the area under cotton was significantly larger than in 1963, and it exceeded the area under jowar by a large margin. Along with traditional and hybrid varieties of cotton, Bt-Cotton was also widely cultivated. Soybean had emerged as an important crop cultivated in the first season. There was a significant growth in the land area devoted to second-season crops, the most important of which was wheat, followed by vegetables. There was a major increase in the variety of vegetables grown in the second season, alongside a rise in the total land area under vegetables. The annual cultivation of a larger number of crops was a major feature of the change in the production environment, which in turn had an effect on the number of days of employment available to labourers.

There were five major caste groups among the households of Dongargaon: Maratha, Mali, Chambhar, Navbaudh, and Gowari. Of these, the Navbaudhs (Dalits/Scheduled Caste or SC) were the largest group, constituting 28.1 per cent of the population. Malis (OBC or other backward class) constituted 17.4 per cent, Chambhars (Dalits/SC) 13.8 per cent and Marathas (upper caste) 12 per cent of the population. The share in population of Gowaris (Adivasis/Scheduled Tribe or ST) was 8 per cent.[1]

Dongargaon is located in the Berar area of western Vidarbha, a region that has the highest incidence of agricultural labourers in India (see Reddy 1988).[2] The growth of a large population of landless agricultural workers in Berar began during the cotton boom of the 1860s and continued well into the twentieth century. Using two different sources and estimates, Reddy (1988) showed that, while in the 1860s, agricultural labourers in Berar accounted for between 14 to 33 per cent of the total workforce, by the 1881 Census, the proportion of agricultural labourers had risen sharply, to about 50 per cent. In conclusion, he noted that: '... right through the regime of agrarian expansion beginning from the 1860s and ending in the 1920s, there were processes which created a substantial "demand" for agricultural labour in Berar, while market forces and colonial regulations maintained a high 'supply' of landless labour.' (Reddy 1988: 202)

The two major features identified by Reddy, with regard to a large increase in the supply of landless agricultural labourers, were immigration and the dispossession of small peasantry that led to the concentration of large landholdings. The emergence of large landholdings,

[1] In the present chapter, I have used the term scheduled tribe (ST) when I refer to the category so defined in the Census of India. Otherwise, the term 'Adivasi' is preferred.

[2] In the contemporary period, the Berar region would include the districts of Buldhana, Akola, Washim, Wardha, Amravati, and Yavatmal in Maharashtra.

combined with the large labour demand in cotton cultivation, resulted in the overall expansion of labour demand in Berar. The heterogeneity within the class of agricultural labourers persisted throughout this period, though an overwhelming majority came from the backward and untouchable castes. By the 1920s, Berar had the highest incidence of agricultural labourers in the country.

Even when the 2001 Census took place, more than 50 years after India's Independence, Berar claimed the largest share of India's agricultural labourers (see Ramakumar, Raut, and Kumar 2009), showing that the supply of labour to Berar's agrarian economy proceeded unhindered over all these years. At the state level too, in 2001, the share of agricultural labourers in the workforce of Amravati division (which roughly comprises Berar and includes Akola district), at 53.7 per cent, was the highest in Maharashtra. Between 1961 and 2001, the share of agricultural labourers in Amravati division's workforce increased by 1.3 per cent, from 52.4 to 53.7 per cent. Among the female workforce, the rise in the share was higher: 65.4 per cent of the female workers in Amravati division were agricultural labourers in 2001, as opposed to 62.5 per cent in 1961. Among the SC workers of Amravati, 72.6 per cent were agricultural labourers in 2001; and the share of female SC agricultural labourers, at 82.1 per cent, was even higher.

In sum, Berar has historically been home to a large and growing population of agricultural labourers, and Dalits constituted a significant share of the agricultural labour force of the region.

The village of Dongargaon shares the above characteristics with Berar (see Ramakumar et al. 2009), as revealed by the following data: (a) The Census of India data show that there was a dramatic increase in the share of workers employed as agricultural labourers in the village between 1961 and 2001, from 47.7 per cent to 71.1 per cent; (b) During every inter-censal period between 1961 and 2001, except 1991–2001, the rate of increase in the number of agricultural labourers in the village was higher than the rate of increase of the population (see analysis given below). In other words, there were major changes in the internal composition of the workforce of Dongargaon between 1961 and 1971; (c) A comparison of data from the 2007 survey with Joshi's 1967 data shows that, between 1963–4 and 2006–7, Dongargaon registered a rise in the share of workers with agricultural labour as their primary occupation; (d) The dependence on agricultural employment in the village was higher for female workers as compared to male workers. In 2006–7, agricultural labour was the primary occupation for 37.2 per cent of the male workers, while the corresponding share for female workers was 60.8 per cent.

Changes in Land Ownership in Dongargaon, 1963–4 to 2006–7

Land Distribution in 1963–4

Data from V.H. Joshi's survey in 1963 show that land ownership in Dongargaon was marked by a few very large landholdings on the one hand, and a large number of small landholdings on the other. In 1963, the top 8 per cent of the households owned about 36 per cent of the total area owned by residents of the village. On the other hand, 27.7 per cent of households in the village were totally landless. From the bottom, about 52 per cent of the households owned just about 8 per cent of the total area. As Joshi's survey showed, tenancy was an insignificant phenomenon in Dongargaon in 1963, and as such, did not help alleviate the problem of landlessness in the village.

Joshi did not provide caste-wise ownership of land in the village in 1963. However, we collected detailed information on caste and land ownership in the village from the land revenue records of 1971, available at the office of the Tehsildar, Akola taluk (see Table 16.2). From the land records of 1971, which were provided for each plot of land, we tried to classify land owned according to the caste of the owners. However, we could not accurately identify the caste identity of the owners of 42 out of 173 plots of land in the records of 1971. Hence, the data for this set of 42 households were set aside and presented separately in Table 16.2. It is important to note that the data in Table 16.2 refer to plots of land situated within the geographical boundary of the village, and not land owned by the village residents; thus, the figures are not strictly comparable with other data provided in this chapter, which are based on land owned by households resident in the village.

The Maratha caste group (defined as comprising of Marathas and Kunbis) was the most dominant landowning group in Dongargaon in 1971, when they owned at least half (50.2 per cent) of the total area in the village. It is likely that the area of land recorded under members of

TABLE 16.2 Distribution of Land Owned across Caste Groups, Dongargaon, 1971, Village Records, in Acres and Per cent

Caste	Caste category	Area of land owned, 1971 (acres)	Share of land owned, 1971 (%)
Maratha	General	284.5	46.5
Mali	OBC	66.7	10.9
Chambhar	SC	62.5	10.2
Kunbi	OBC	22.7	3.7
Muslim	Muslim	9.4	1.5
Gond	ST	6.9	1.1
Baudh	SC	6.2	1.0
Brahmin	General	3.1	0.5
Marwari	General	2.0	0.3
Gowari	ST	1.2	0.2
NA	NA	146.9	24.0
Total	–	612.2	100.0

Source: Village land records, 1971.
Note: NA – Not Available.

the Maratha caste group in 1971 is an underestimate, and much of the land recorded as 'NA' also belonged to Maratha households. The second most important land owning group was the Malis, who owned 10.9 per cent of the total area. As per Joshi's 1963 survey, members of the Maratha, Kunbi, and Mali castes formed 51.4 per cent of Dongargaon's population; Joshi described them as the 'dominant and major caste [group] of the Dongargaon community' (Joshi 1967: 30). Together, members of these three caste groups owned at least 61.1 per cent of the total area in 1971.

The two major Dalit groups of the village were the Chambhars and Navbaudhs. According to Joshi, 'Harijans' and 'Navbaudhs' together formed 31.7 per cent of Dongargaon's population in 1963. In 1971, members of the Chambhar caste owned 10.2 per cent of the total area, and Navbaudhs owned one per cent of the total area. However, Joshi (1967) had also noted that the large-scale conversion of the Dalits of Dongargaon to Buddhism after 1956 had led to some improvement in their land ownership status. He noted that:

> When they were asked about the major changes that they have noticed since the change in their religion, they expressed that (a) each family had managed to purchase 2 to 3 acres of land, which provides them minimum food. They could also work on their farms when other suitable employment is not available to them... (Joshi 1967: 36)

Land Distribution in 2006–7

A striking feature of change in Dongargaon between 1963–71 and 2007 was the sharp rise in the extent of landlessness among households. If 27.7 per cent of households were landless in 1963, the share of landless households in 2007 was significantly higher at 63.6 per cent (Table 16.3). In other words, 227 out of 357 households were landless in 2007. By any measure, the rise in landlessness in Dongargaon between 1963 and 2007 was phenomenal.

TABLE **16.3** Distribution of Ownership Holdings and Area by Size-Classes, Dongargaon, 2007, in Acres and Per cent

Size-class of land	Number of ownership holdings		Area under ownership holdings	
	Number of holdings	Share of holdings (%)	Extent (acres)	Share of area (%)
Landless	227	63.6	0	0.0
< 2 acres	14	3.9	14	2.6
2 acres to < 5 acres	80	22.4	223	41.8
5 acres to < 10 acres	28	7.8	183	34.3
10 acres to < 20 acres	7	2.0	90	16.9
20 acres to < 100 acres	0	0.0	0	0.0
100 acres and more	1	0.3	120	19.0
Total	**357**	**100.0**	**630**	**100.0**
Share of area owned by the top 5 per cent of HHs (%)		46.0		
Share of area owned by the bottom 50 per cent of HHs (%)		0.0		

Source: Survey data 2007.
Note: HH – Household.

On the other hand, the concentration of land in a few hands continued to be a reality in the village even in 2007. The traditional landlord family of the village, a Deshmukh family, continued to retain much of its inherited holdings; this family held the largest single landholding in the village of 120 acres in 2007. In percentage terms, this implied that one household (0.3 per cent of the households) owned 19 per cent of the total area owned (Table 16.3). The earlier study by Joshi (1967) had severely underestimated the holdings of the Deshmukh household in 1964. It is also probable that the Deshmukh household had refused to divulge accurate information about its holdings in 1964, a period when the first efforts to implement the land reform legislation were initiated in Vidarbha. In an interview to us in 2009, Pratapsinh Deshmukh, the head of the household, told us that his family owned roughly 400 to 500 acres of land in the 1950s, spread over many villages of the district. By 2007, the Deshmukh household retained land only in Dongargaon and its surroundings, and had sold off land elsewhere.

The increase in the concentration of land ownership can be judged by another indicator. We arranged households in the ascending order of land owned and looked at the share of land area owned by the top five per cent and the bottom 50 per cent (see Table 16.3). While the top five per cent of households owned 46 per cent of the total area, the bottom 50 per cent in the village was completely landless.[3]

Land Distribution across Caste Groups, 2006–7

Across caste groups, the changes in the concentration of land ownership are interesting (Table 16.4). About 86 per cent of the population in Dongargaon in 2007 belonged to the Maratha, Kunbi, Mali, Chambhar, Navbaudh, or Gowari groups. First, in 2007, Marathas and Kunbis formed 18.1 per cent of the population, but owned a disproportionate 47.5 per cent of the total area owned. Secondly, Marathas, Kunbis, and Malis together formed 35.6 per cent of the population, but owned 66.2 per cent of the total area owned. Thirdly, members of the Chambhar caste formed 13.8 per cent of the population, but owned 18.1 per cent

[3] The idea of comparing the share in land owned by the top 5 per cent and the bottom 50 per cent of households is borrowed from Ramachandran, Rawal, and Swaminathan (2010).

of the total area. On the other hand, members of the Navbaudh religion formed 28.1 per cent of the population, but owned only 10.2 per cent of the total area. Finally, members of Gowari tribe formed 8 per cent of the population, but owned only 1.6 per cent of the total area.

Compared to Joshi's 1963 study, the demographic composition of Dongargaon underwent major changes. According to Joshi (1967), Marathas, Kunbis, and Malis formed 51.4 per cent of the population in 1963. In 2007, the corresponding share was only 35.6 per cent. The reasons for the reduction in the share of population of these prominent caste groups appears to be a sharp increase in the population of the Dalit groups (such as Chambhars and Navbaudhs), Adivasi groups (such as Gowaris and Gonds), and Vimuktya Jati Nomadic Tribes (VJNT) groups (such as Zingabhois) in the intervening period. It would appear that the sharp rise in labour demand generated by the spread and intensification of cotton cultivation, as well as availability of non-agricultural employment in the vicinity, attracted, over a period, a substantial number of landless Dalit, Adivasi, and VJNT labourers from outside the village.

TABLE 16.4 Distribution of Ownership Holdings and Area by Caste and Size-Classes, Dongargaon, 2007, in Acres and Per cent

Caste	Share in population (%)	Number of landless HHs	Caste-wise share of landless HHs (%)	Total area owned (acres)	Share of each caste in total area owned (%)
Maratha	12.0	19	41.3	250.0	39.7
Mali	17.4	32	52.5	118.0	18.7
Chambhar	13.8	17	34.7	114.0	18.1
Navbaudh	28.1	88	84.6	64.0	10.2
Kunbi	6.1	10	43.5	49.0	7.8
Zingabhoi	6.7	10	71.4	13.0	2.1
Gowari	8.0	27	84.4	10.0	1.6
Sonar	0.6	0	0.0	8.0	1.3
Gond	3.8	9	75.0	4.0	0.6
Mang	1.8	8	100.0	0.0	0.0
Others	1.6	7	100.0	0.0	0.0
All HHs	100.0	227	63.6	630.0	100.0

Source: Survey data, 2007.

Note: HH–Household.

In other words, demographic change driven largely by migration was an important explanatory variable in the analysis of landlessness in Dongargaon.

Immigration and Rise in Landlessness

Three major streams of immigration into the village could be identified between 1964 and 2007.

1. The first stream of migration was of the members of the Dalit caste groups. Data from the Census of India show that there was a major rise in the population of SCs in Dongargaon between 1961 and 1971 from 59 to 134 (Table 16.5). This rise represented a 127.1 per cent rise over a period of 10 years. In the same period, the total population of Dongargaon rose only by 42.1 per cent. As both the male SC and female SC population rose at comparable rates between 1961 and 1971, we can conclude that the migration was of households, and not individuals. The rate of growth of the SC population in the village remained more than double that of the general population in the following decade too; between 1971 and 1981, when the general population increased by 12.9 per cent, the SC population increased by 26.9 per cent. The immigration of Dalits into Dongargaon after 1981 appears to have tapered off; between 1981 and 1991. Between 1991 and 2001, the rates of growth of the SC population and the general population in Dongargaon were comparable.

   All the Dalit households that migrated into Dongargaon in the 1960s and 1970s were landless. These households came to Dongargaon in search of employment in the cotton cultivation sector from different backward regions of the district and the state. Between 1961 and 1971, the number of agricultural labourers rose by 79.4 per cent and the share of agricultural labourers in the workforce increased from 47.7 per cent to 69.7 per cent. Between 1971 and 1981, the number of agricultural labourers rose by 18.7 per cent.

   However, distress migration alone cannot explain the increase in the SC population of Dongargaon between the 1960s and 2000s. In Dongargaon, there has always been a practice among Dalit households where the sons-in-law are brought to the village after marriage and settled in a new household, rather than sending the daughter to

TABLE 16.5 Selected Features of Demographic Change between 1961 and 2001, Dongargaon Village, Census of India, in Number and Per cent

Item	1961	1971	1981	1991	2001
Total population	784	1114	1258	1605	1809
Scheduled caste population	59	134	170	215	241
Scheduled tribe population	0	0	34	76	37
Number of agricultural labourers	194	348	413	567	638
Decadal rate of change (%) in population between:					
	–	1961–71	1971–81	1981–91	1991–2001
Total population	–	42.1	12.9	27.6	12.7
Scheduled caste population	–	127.1	26.9	26.5	12.1
Scheduled tribe population	–	0.0	0.0	123.5	–51.3
Number of agricultural labourers	–	79.4	18.7	37.3	12.5

Source: Census of India, various years.

the in-law's village. In our interviews with Dalit elders in the village, this practice was repeatedly and consistently pointed out as a major reason behind the increase in the Dalit population. At the same time, the Dalit men who married from Dongargaon did not follow the practice of moving into the bride's village.

According to the Dalit elders, there were many reasons why the sons-in-law readily moved into Dongargaon, and all of them were related to a rise in employment opportunities in the village. First, the rise in the area on which cotton was cultivated had raised labour absorption in agriculture, thus increasing employment opportunities in the village. Secondly, with the spread of irrigation in the village and a second crop of wheat, employment opportunities in agriculture had further expanded. Thirdly, with the increasing sub-division of land over the years, the average size of holdings in the village had declined. This phenomenon had led to more intensive utilization of land; for instance, intercropping with vegetables had risen considerably. A further rise in the employment opportunities in agriculture was the outcome. Finally, the presence of the Maharashtra Industrial Development Corporation (MIDC) complex near the village had led to a rise in non-agricultural employment opportunities in the village's vicinity.

2. The second stream of migration into Dongargaon was of the Adivasi population. Joshi (1967) made no mention of any Adivasi household in the village in 1963. However, in 2007, there were 45 Adivasi households in the village, forming 12.6 per cent of the total number of households. Almost all the ST residents of the village belonged to the Gowari and Gond community.

   Census data also show that there was no Adivasi inhabitant in the village till 1971. As per the 1981 Census, there were 34 ST persons in Dongargaon; these were 20 men and 14 women. By the 1991 Census, the ST population had risen to 76 (38 men and 38 women), which represented a rise by 123.5 per cent.

   The 2001 Census shows an absolute fall in the ST population in Dongargaon, but we were told that most ST households were travelling outside the village for work during the census enumeration in 2001. In fact, there were more ST women than ST men in the village in 2001, a clear indication that most men were out of the village for work. While Census 2001 reported the presence of only 37 ST persons in the village, we found, in our 2007 survey, that there were 200 ST persons and 112 VJNT persons permanently residing in the village.

   There are two factors associated with the sharp rise of the ST population in Dongargaon. The first is that the increase in the Census ST population, particularly between 1971 and 1981, was largely a result of the new self-declared identities of people. It has been widely noted by scholars that, at the 1981 census, a large number of new households reported themselves as belonging to the ST in Maharashtra, in lieu of belonging to the Halba or Halbi tribe (Guha 2003; Kulkarni 1991). These new households belonged to the Koshti sub-caste in the State, which had been claiming ST status. The Government of Maharashtra had not yet accepted this demand, but during the 1981 Census surveys, most Koshti sub-caste members identified themselves as belonging to the Halba or Halbi tribe, and thus ST. For instance, in Maharashtra State, the population of the Halba or Halbi tribe rose from 7,205 persons in 1971 to 242,819 persons in 1981 (Kulkarni 1991).

   Of course, changes in the self-declared identities of people do not fully explain the rise in the ST population in the village. There has also been significant Adivasi immigration as a consequence of the expansion of employment opportunities in the village.

3. Like the Dalit and Adivasi immigrants, there was also a significant stream of VJNT immigration into Dongargaon after the 1960s.[4] The VJNT immigrants were universally landless. All the VJNT households in the village in 2007 belonged to the Zingabhoi community. According to the *Akola District Gazetteer*:

   > The Jhingabhois (*sic*) speak of themselves as quite a separate caste but are not distinguished from Bhois in the Census Reports. Members of the caste say they have no fixed home but divide themselves into small parties and wander about selling medicines, each party having a definite area assigned for its operations.

It is possible that the stream of migration into Dongargaon, and Akola as a whole, was also driven by the severe and recurrent droughts that affected large parts of Maharashtra in the early 1970s (see Oughton 1982). Studies on the Maharashtra drought show that Akola and other western Vidarbha districts were not severely affected, while many of the surrounding regions and districts were severely affected. According to Oughton, '... the cotton growing areas of Maharashtra were relatively less badly hit by the droughts' (1982: 191). On the other hand, within the drought-affected districts like Aurangabad and Ahmednagar, 'the most badly affected class were the labourers, who lost nearly one quarter of the value of their assets' (Oughton 1982: 190). Dyson and Maharatna (1992) examined data on population movements across Maharashtra and their relationship with the death rate and fertility rate across districts. According to them,

> The general tendency in the literature on the Maharashtra drought has been to play down, and even deny, the existence of significant population movement ... There is considerable evidence from various parts of India that populations in drought-prone zones have well established strategies of migration in the event of drought and production failure...
>
> ... Thus in the present context, it is noteworthy that the districts of Akola, Amravati, Buldana, and Yeotmal ... experienced comparatively large increases in death rates. There are reports for famines in the late nineteenth century of large numbers of people migrating into precisely these districts in search of work and food-who subsequently died there.... More generally, we posit that some of the more vulnerable sections of society may have moved towards areas of relative agricultural improvement

[4] See Bokil (2002) for a description on VJNT.

> in 1973, perhaps conditioned by long-standing routes for distress migration. There, some of them died. (Dyson and Maharatna 1992: 1330–1)

As mentioned earlier, the permanent immigration of landless labourers into Vidarbha was a phenomenon that existed from the beginning of the twentieth century itself (see Reddy 1988). According to Reddy, much of the expansion of the landless labour force in Vidarbha between 1891 and 1931 could be attributed to a sharp rise in the immigration of labourers 'who hoped to take in land for cultivation but were unable to do so' (Reddy 1988: 8).

In sum, the phenomenal rise in landlessness in Dongargaon between 1963 and 2007 can be primarily attributed to the inmigration of Dalit, Adivasi, and VJNT labourers into the village to gain wage employment in agriculture. Dalits, Adivasis, and VJNTs constituted the most populous group among agricultural labourers in Dongargaon in 2007. As Table 16.4 shows, the extent of landlessness among the backward caste groups, except Chambhars, was almost universal. All Mang households were landless; among Navbaudh households, 84.6 per cent were landless; among Gowari households, 84.4 per cent were landless; among Gond households, 75 per cent were landless; and among Zingabhoi households, 71.4 per cent were landless.

Immigration alone cannot fully explain the rise in landlessness in Dongargaon between 1963 and 2007. There were also exchanges in the land market that actively aided dispossession in the village.

The Land Market in Dongargaon

An important limitation of point-to-point comparison of data, over 44 years as in this chapter, is that the events in the intervening period are assumed to be linear in progression. For instance, one may tend to infer that there was a linear rise in landlessness in Dongargaon over every year between 1963 and 2007. Available information does not allow us to comment on the intervening period in the conclusion; however, we have attempted a simple method to corroborate the long-run result over the shorter-run. We collected data on land purchases and sales of resident households in Dongargaon for a period of 20 years preceding the date of our survey, that is, between 1987 and 2007. From this data set, we tried to understand the nature and extent of gain or loss of land among the village residents. We also tried to understand which social groups have gained or lost land in this period. While such an exercise does not fully address the concerns of linearity in the assumptions and interpretations, it can serve as a useful corroborative exercise.

The land market in Dongargaon would appear to be an active market, given that a significant extent of land was bought and sold between 1987 and 2007. Between 1987 and 2007, about 23 per cent of the total land owned by all households—147 acres out of 630 acres—was reported as sold. About 12 per cent of the total land owned by all households—74 acres out of 630 acres—was reported as purchased. The benchmark of total land owned by all households is only representational, as land sold, or purchased, need not be either to, or previously owned by, residents of the village. Prices of land in the village were high and rising; from the early-2000s, prices of irrigated land have been in the range of Rs 1 lakh to Rs 2 lakh per acre and unirrigated land in the range of Rs 30,000 and Rs 60,000 per acre. A few features of land sales and purchase in the village during the last 20 years (1987 to 2007) are interesting (see Tables 16.6 and 16.7):

- As mentioned, between 1987 and 2007, about 146 acres of land were sold by the residents, while only about 74 acres of land were purchased by the residents. In rough net terms, this implied a purchase of 72 acres of land by non-residents (Tables 16.6 and 16.7).
- Of the 146 acres of land sold between 1987 and 2007, only about 22 acres were irrigated and 124 acres was unirrigated.
- Of the 74 acres purchased between 1987 and 2007, only 14 acres were irrigated and about 60 acres were unirrigated.
- There were 37 households (10.4 per cent of all households) in the village who reported having sold land between 1987 and 2007. Of these 37 households, 12 households (32.4 per cent) were totally landless during our 2007 survey. Another 12 households reported less than 2 acres of owned land during our 2007 survey. There was no household that reported land sales between 1987 and 2007, and also reported more than 8 acres of owned land during our 2007 survey (Table 16.6).
- Let us now consider the caste-wise composition of land sellers and buyers.
    - Of the 146 acres of land sold by residents of the village between 1987 and 2007, 43.1 per cent was sold by Mali households and 24.6 per cent by Chambhar households. Land sold by Navbaudh

households accounted for 8.9 per cent of the total area (Table 16.6).

- Considered together, the share of the area of land sold by Dalit households (Chambhar and Navbaudh) accounted for 33.5 per cent of the total area of land sold between 1987 and 2007.
- When we asked the households about the caste of the persons to whom they sold land, many households could not respond, as the buyers were from outside the region, mainly from the towns of Akola or Amravati. The land sold, thus, to persons whose caste could not be recalled, accounted for 35.7 per cent of the total land area sold between 1987 and 2007. For Mali households that sold land, 48.0 per cent of the area of land sold was to persons whose caste could not be recalled.
- The area of land sold to Maratha, Kunbi, Marwari, and Brahmin persons accounted for 40.9 per cent of the total land area sold.
- In particular, members of the Marwari caste from Amravati and Akola were prominent buyers of land in the village. Between 1987 and 2007, there were five land sales that were reported where the buyer was a Marwari and the total extent of land sold was 18.3 acres.
- Of the 35.8 acres of land sold by Chambhar households between 1987 and 2007, 25.3 acres, or 70.6 per cent, was sold to Maratha, Kunbi, or Marwari persons.
- Of the 48.8 acres of land sold by Dalit households (Chambhar and Navbaudh) 30.3 acres was sold to Maratha, Kunbi, Marwari, or Brahmin persons.
- About 76 per cent of the total area of land sold by Mali households was sold to persons whose caste could not be recalled by the sellers—an indication of buyers who resided outside the region.
- Of the 73.9 acres of land bought by the residents of the village between 1987 and 2007, about 43 acres (57.6 per cent) were bought by Dalit households—30.5 per cent by Navbaudhs and 27.1 per cent by Chambhars (Table 16.7).
- However, an interesting feature of the land purchase of Dalit households between 1987 and 2007 was that 20.3 acres out of the 43 acres purchased (47.2 per cent) were *from other Dalit households*. Within this exchange, sales from Chambhars to Navbaudhs and Chambhars to Chambhars predominated, in that order. Thus,

Table 16.6 Matrix of Sale of Land by Residents of Dongargaon, 1987 to 2007, by Caste, in Acres and Per cent

Caste of the buyer	Extent of land (in acres) sold by the seller in Dongargaon, by caste									Share in total land sold (%)
	Butcher	Chambhar	Gowari	Kunbi	Mali	Maratha	Navbaudh	Nhavi	All	
Navbaudh	–	–	–	3.0	–	2.0	–	–	5.0	3.4
Brahmin	–	2.0	1.0	–	–	–	3.0	–	6.0	4.1
Chambhar	–	2.5	–	–	–	8.0	–	–	10.5	7.1
Dhangar	–	6.0	–	–	–	–	–	–	6.0	4.1
Gowari	–	–	1.0	–	–	–	–	–	1.0	0.7
Koshti	–	–	–	–	2.0	–	–	–	2.0	1.4
Kunbi	–	6.0	–	3.0	5.0	2.0	–	–	16.0	10.8
Mali	–	–	–	–	1.5	–	–	–	1.5	1.0
Maratha	0.0	9.3	–	–	5.0	3.0	–	2.0	19.3	13.1
Marwadi	–	10.0	1.0	–	1.3	4.0	2.0	–	18.3	12.4
Muslim	–	–	–	–	–	–	8.0	–	8.0	5.4
NA	–	–	4.0	–	48.0	2.0	–	–	54.0	36.6
All	0.0	35.8	7.0	6.0	62.7	21.0	13.0	2.0	147.5	100.0
Share in total land sold (%)	0.0	24.2	4.7	4.1	42.5	14.2	8.8	1.4	100.0	–

Source: Survey data 2007.

TABLE 16.7 Matrix of Purchase of Land by Residents of Dongargaon, 1987 to 2007, by Caste, in Acres and Per cent

Caste of the seller	Extent of land (in acres) bought by the buyer in Dongargaon, by caste									Share in total land bought (%)
	Chambhar	Kunbi	Mali	Maratha	Navbaudh	Nhavi	Sonar	Zingabhoi	All	
NA	3.0	–	–	0.8	2.0	–	–	–	5.8	7.9
Barber	–	–	2.0	–	–	–	–	–	2.0	2.7
Baudh	–	–	–	–	3.5	–	–	–	3.5	4.7
Chambhar	6.8	–	–	1.0	10.0	–	–	–	17.8	24.0
Dhangar	1.3	–	–	–	–	–	–	–	1.3	1.8
Kunbi	3.0	–	–	2.0	3.0	–	–	–	8.0	10.8
Mali	–	–	1.0	4.0	4.0	–	–	–	9.0	12.2
Maratha	6.0	2.0	3.0	7.5	–	2.0	2.0	2.0	24.5	33.2
Zingabhoi	–	–	–	–	–	–	–	2.0	2.0	2.7
All	20.1	2.0	6.0	15.3	22.5	2.0	2.0	4.0	73.9	100.0
Share in total land bought (%)	27.1	2.7	8.1	20.7	30.5	2.7	2.7	5.4	100.0	–

Source: Survey data 2007.

no significant land transfer from the upper castes to backward castes appeared to have taken place in Dongargaon between 1987 and 2007.

- Considering sales and purchases between 1987 and 2007 together, Chambhar households were net losers of land (35.8 acres sold and 20.1 acres bought) and Navbaudh households were net gainers of land (13 acres sold and 22.5 acres bought).

- If we consider the five-year periods between 1991 and 2006, the extent of land sales and purchases appear to have been more or less stable over the years. For land sales, the extent of land sold in the periods 1991–6, 1996–2001, and 2001–6 were respectively 44.5 acres, 42.5 acres, and 40.5 acres. For land purchases, the extent of land purchased in the three periods were respectively 16.8 acres, 23.8 acres, and 17.3 acres (Tables 16.6 and 16.7).

In sum, while the web of land purchase and sale in Dongargaon between 1987 and 2007 is extremely complicated, some tentative conclusions can be arrived at. One, the Chambhar and Mali households in the village were net losers of land between 1987 and 2007. Two, while Navbaudh households were net gainers of land between 1987 and 2007, this gain was largely inadequate given the sheer increase in the number of Navbaudh households over time. Three, among the Maratha-Kunbi households, both land sale and land purchase were common, and the data point to some form of differentiation progressing within the Maratha-Kunbi community.

Along with the immigration of landless labourers, the net loss of land among village residents was another important reason for the sharp rise in landlessness in Dongargaon between 1963 and 2007.

* * *

The most important feature of agrarian change in Dongargaon between 1964 and 2007 was a sharp rise in landlessness. If 27.7 per cent of households were landless in 1963, the share of landless households in 2007 was significantly higher at 63.6 per cent. Marathas and Kunbis were the most dominant land owners in 2007. In 2007, Marathas and Kunbis formed 18.1 per cent of the population, but owned 48 per cent of the total area owned. On the other hand, members of the Navbaudh religion formed 28.1 per cent of the population, but owned only 10.2 per cent of the total area. In other words, land ownership in Dongargaon was extremely unequal in 2007. In no terms could it be inferred that land and its ownership had ceased to be the bases of social and economic power in the village.

The rise in landlessness between 1963 and 2007 was due to two reasons. First, the demographic composition of Dongargaon appears to have undergone changes between 1963 and 2007. The sharp rise in the demand for labour generated by the spread and intensification of cotton cultivation in the village attracted, over a period, a substantial number of landless Dalit and Adivasi labourers from outside the village. The first stream of migration was of the members of the Dalit caste groups that began in the 1960s and continued thereafter. All the Dalit households that migrated into Dongargaon in the 1960s and 1970s were landless. The second stream of migration into Dongargaon was of the Adivasi population. There were no Adivasis in Dongargaon till the 1971 Census. The Adivasi migration began in the 1970s and these immigrants were also landless. It is possible that the stream of Adivasi and Dalit migration into Dongargaon, and Akola as a whole, was driven by the severe and recurrent droughts that affected large parts of Maharashtra in the early 1970s.

Secondly, there was a net loss of land among village residents between 1987 and 2007, which was another important reason for the sharp rise in landlessness. A significant extent of land was bought and sold between 1987 and 2007, and about 72 acres of land owned by the village residents were sold, on the net, to non-residents. The spread of cotton cultivation and the closeness of the village to the National Highway and the MIDC complex were the proximate reasons for the purchase of village land by non-residents. The complex web of exchanges in the land market also showed that Dalit households were net losers of land between 1987 and 2007. Among Maratha-Kunbi households, both land sale and land purchase were common, pointing to some form of growing differentiation within the landowning caste group.

In sum, the changes in the agrarian economy of Dongargaon between 1963 and 2007 were built on an extremely unequal agrarian structure. In 2007, land ownership in the village continued to be concentrated in the hands of a small share of households, which also typically belonged to the upper caste groups. The hold of upper caste groups on land ownership in Dongargaon had only got strengthened over a period of about four decades.

References

Bokil, Milind. 2002. 'De-notified and Nomadic Tribes: A Perspective', *Economic and Political Weekly*, 37 (2): 148–54.

Census of India. Various Years. 'Primary Census Abstract', Office of the Registrar General and Census Commissioner, Ministry of Home, Government of India, New Delhi.

Dyson, Tim and Arup Maharatna. 1992. 'Bihar Famine, 1966–67 and Maharashtra Drought, 1970–73', *Economic and Political Weekly*, 27 (26): 1325–32.

Guha, Sumit. 2003. 'The Politics of Identity and Enumeration in India c. 1600–1990', *Comparative Studies in Society and History*, 45 (1): 148–67.

Joshi, V.H. 1967. *Dongargaon: A Socio-economic Study*, Research Bulletin, Socio-economic Studies: Pune, 4, Department of Agriculture, Maharashtra.

Kulkarni, Sharad. 1991. 'Distortion of Census Data on Scheduled Tribes', *Economic and Political Weekly*, 26 (5): 205–8.

Oughton, E. 1982. 'The Maharashtra Drought of 1970–73: An Analysis of Scarcity', *Oxford Bulletin of Economics and Statistics*, 44 (3): 169–97.

Ramachandran, V.K., Vikas Rawal, and Madhura Swaminathan. 2010. *Socio-Economic Surveys of Three Villages in Andhra Pradesh: A Study of Agrarian Relations*. New Delhi: Tulika Books.

Ramakumar, R., Karankumar Raut, and Awanish Kumar. 2009. 'Agrarian Change in Rural Maharashtra: Resurveys of Selected Villages: A Resurvey of Dongargaon Village, Akola District', Maharashtra, Research Report, Tata Institute of Social Sciences, Mumbai.

Reddy, C. Rammanohar. 1988. 'The Incidence of Agricultural Labourers in India: Variations over Time and Space (With a Study of Varhad in Maharashtra)', PhD Thesis, Jawaharlal Nehru University, New Delhi.

17

BARBARA HARRISS-WHITE

Ideas and Substance in Rural–Urban Economic Relations

The Contribution of a Long-term Urban Study in South India

While India has long had the world's liveliest school of village-level studies,[1] long-term urban studies are a desert. Worldwide, there appear to be only two classes of studies addressing long-term urban studies and their many problems—and remarkably few examples. The first is global in scope and devoted to best practice in the study of urban poverty dynamics. This body of research engages with 'poor communities' as though they exist in 'original conditions' rather than as the outcomes of longstanding processes of production and reproduction; it focuses on households and incomes rather than firms, labour markets, and work-based relations of poverty. Methodological difficulties for this kind of long-term urban study include matching quantitative and qualitative evidence; the elusiveness of panel households (and the costliness of their pursuit over successive rounds)—both of which only

[1] Breman, Kloos, and Saith 1997; Harriss and Harriss-White 2007; Lanjouw and Stern 1998; Lindberg et al. 2011, Ramachandran, Swaminathan, and Rawal 2001, together with the chapters of this volume.

increase with the gap in revisits; 'household surveillance technologies' (how to watch the daily lives of urban families); the retro-fitting of new concepts to earlier field evidence; and shifts in the way knowledge is created and regarded as valid. What to do about hitherto neglected urban processes—about gendered labour markets, the role of civil society and the state and private provision of infrastructure and utilities for instance? What to do about urban energetics? (Moser 2003)

A second kind of contribution to long-term urban studies is exemplified by a study of Australian towns from 1981 to 2006 and the methodological miseries of their changing political boundaries, of census reclassifications (both of which make categories non-comparable), and of comparing economic data without knowledge of local price deflators (Courvisanos 2008). Neither of these examples has much to say about the theoretical contexts that frame the need to know about long-term urban change.

Born from an early village studies literature that critiqued the concept of the isolated village republic, this chapter will focus specifically on rural–urban relations and what a long-term Indian urban study may reveal about them that a focus on rural sites alone ignores at its peril.

The town concerned, Arni in northern Tamil Nadu, has been studied through three rounds of surveys of business histories in 1973–4, 1983–4, and 1993–5,[2] based on random samples of firms that have been stratified by neighbourhood and by occupation/sector and selected after the first-hand physical mapping of the entire town's economic activities (Basile 2013; Harriss 1981; Harriss-White 2003, 2015). Owners and managers of firms have provided narratives about the long cycle of accumulation: their apprenticeships; the origins of starting capital; the growth of their businesses (including agrarian and cultural seasonalities, shocks, and episodes of decline); and the destinations of investments; they have also explained the short cycle of profit-making: purchases; inventory and processing; maintenance; transport and sale; their labour relations; the social aspects of their families and political activity of all kinds. This method itself has laid constraints on the way knowledge has been produced. In particular, the interior economies of households and

[2] Eighty-eight firms in 1974, 114 firms in 1983–4, and 287 firms in 1993–4.

home-work are hard to identify and to know, as are the informal economies of government offices and courts; the night-time economy; mobile economic activity, such as that of sales agents, medical practitioners, the urban fire brigade (whose work is mainly rural), labour commuting, shifting site-specific sequential production practices (as in gold), or peripatetic trade (as in livestock). As the town has grown upwards as well as outwards, economic activity tucked away on the highest storeys of buildings is hard to spot. For insights here, field researchers have relied on case material. Further, influenced by political economy and institutional economics, the successive rounds of research did not examine the local state and local politics, other than that regulating the informal economy. Of particular inexcusability is our neglect of the political economy of urban land, and the local energy economy throughout the entire period until very recently.[3]

In the twenty-first century, the sheer size of the town compared with modest research resources has exceeded the possibilities of its being researched through surveys. While it has grown officially from about 30,000 in 1971 to 61,000 in 2001, in practice the organic settlement contains well over a lakh of people as the town surges over and engulfs villages unwilling to be incorporated into the municipality for a legitimate fear of increased taxes. In 2011, its surrounding taluk had 151,000.[4] Our ways of knowing this place had to change. Between 2002 and 2012, the town was studied partially, specifically, and continuously, using approaches to evidence mainly drawn from institutional economics.[5] By 2013, the town and its environs had generated 5 PhD and 3 MPhil theses, and a total of 52 publications. In this chapter, this body of work will be searched for what it has contributed to ideas and findings about

[3] Available at http://www.southasia.ox.ac.uk/resources-greenhouse-gases-technology-and-jobs-indias-informal-economy-case-rice (last acccessed 1 October 2015).

[4] Available at http://en.wikipedia.org/wiki/Aarani_Tamil_Nadu where it presents itself officially as a 'city' (last accessed 1 October 2015).

[5] Arivukkarasi (forthcoming): rural urban silk relations; Basile (2013): local capitalism, the corporatist regulation of the informal economy; Cavalcante (2015): rural food economy; Harriss-White (2013): rice mills, the materiality of local rice economy; Harriss-White and Rodrigo (2013): innovation in the informal economy; Polzin (2006): rural credit; Roman (2008): Innovation in silk; Srinivasan (2011): the local labour markets; Stanley (2002): the gold cluster.

rural–urban relations. We therefore omit some of the main concerns of the 1993–5 round of surveys—urban institutions (and rapid institutional change) and urban infrastructure. We also discard some research in the twenty-first century, for example clustered manufacturing (rice, silk, and gold), the regulation of informal capitalism and innovation in, and the physical materiality of Arni's only very partially state-regulated informal economy.[6]

A Brief History from Field Research

> 'Arni is not a poor town'. 'Arni's economy is in good shape.' (President of Arni's Chamber of Commerce, June 2012)

The town has always been a minor administrative centre, a major paddy marketplace, the site of a growing workshop industry producing hand-woven silk sarees, and of gold craft production. Like most market towns in what till 1990 was called the North Arcot District, the town had bristled for decades with 'commonplace' industrial clusters.

From 1973 to 1983, its population rose by 27 per cent, the rice production in its hinterland increased by 50 per cent, but commodity trade expanded by 6.5 in nominal terms: paddy-rice by a factor of 12 and silk by a factor of 15 (Harriss 1991). While big strides in the development of the national market took place in the wake of the new agricultural technology, multipliers from local agriculture were not the sole drivers of this transformation in scale and complexity. Officials of the state's administration supplied an estimated 14 per cent of total urban demand. The silk weaving and manufacturing cluster was not the product of local raw materials but rather of long distance flows of raw materials and products—for crafts developed in Arni in response to the cosmopolitan tastes of a local nineteenth-century jagirdar. In the immediate post-green revolution period, local business had made strides in gross value added and in the inequality of enterprise structure (Basile 2013). In each major economic sector, the latter took the form of oligopolies co-existing with a vast number of self-employed petty firms, not always able to compete freely with the larger business on which they depended

[6] Available at http://www.southasia.ox.ac.uk/resources-greenhouse-gases-technology-and-jobs-indias-informal-economy-case-rice (last acccessed 1 October 2015).

for premises, information, credit, transport, etc. By contrast, real wages for labour were found to be static though higher than in agriculture; and the distributive share (the relation between wages and profit) was swinging away from the wage component. Women provided merely 10 per cent of the workforce (Harriss 1991).

By the 1990s, the process of extinction of artisanal craft production had taken a severe toll. Handloom silk weaving, prey to its own cycles of boom and bust, was an exception however. Many crafts (from music-making to the craft production of paint from crushing shells) together with the whole of the livestock sector had been displaced, and the structure of industry and trade had concentrated and polarized further. At the apex, firms started to integrate their operations in a vertical and diagonal manner. But very few added manufacturing to their bases in trade. The economic base (fuel, rice mills, silk weaving, wholesale and general retail of food) became more complex, continuing to develop in both numbers of firms and concentration of scale while at the same time productive activity and retail trade also decentralized: spilling over into the countryside and shifting the urban economy towards its current wholesale entrepôt role. Meanwhile a massive wave of economic diversification also took place. And ownership of urban firms started to diversify socially: Dalits and women expanded their hold on the urban economy as owners rather than wage labour, though from very small starting points.

The twenty-first century has seen an unprecedented pace of adoptive innovation and institutional change, the obvious drivers—there may be others—being a) the metropolitanization and globalization of information, culture, tastes, and aspirations with profound implications for the acquisition of the technologies of mass communication in this small town (from video libraries and ubiquitous TV and mobile phones to instant bank transactions, insurance, and share dealing services); b) the rapid proliferation of fossil-energy-guzzling goods (from kerosene and calor gas stoves though scooters and motorbikes to commercial deep freezes, air conditioners, tempo trucks, SUVs, and all sizes of luxury buses); c) transformations in the spatial scale of work mobility (from long distance inmigration from Orissa to daily commuting out to the factories on the Chennai–Bangalore corridor); d) the revitalizing of the silk sector through rebranding to scoop a superior market segment; and e) the development of the 'knowledge economy' in the form of a substantial new private sector education hub (with seven colleges, over 100 private English medium schools and 25 English pre-schools)—together with the emergence of an extensive informal economy of private tuition. Among the young, a profound social desire to leave the grind of agriculture, escape patriarchal control in local family firms, and the parochialism of the town means that family labour is being replaced by wage work, not always local in origin, and that new kinds of subnational and national capital are waiting in the wings to transform the modern bazaar into a set of branch agencies, franchizes, and showrooms. Textiles, general retail, electronics, fertilizer, and cement are models of what is to come. That said, at the time of writing the overwhelming majority of firms are still small family businesses or self-employed. The average number of employees remains two, for the most part kin.

The economy weaves in and out of regulatory jurisdictions, almost entirely socially regulated through caste-corporatist business associations. Although it is a low-caste town, or because of it, its economy is moving towards caste cosmopolitanism rather than caste eradication; given sectors of the town are slowly diversifying in terms of caste while retaining their long-standing caste cores. The persistently oppressive role of caste in constraining economic choice is best seen in the labour markets and from a Dalit perspective (Harriss-White et al. 2014). On the whole, wages for labour do not keep pace with the prices of wage goods. At the loom, on the drying yard, as on the farm, work is being mechanized, and labour is being displaced, casualized, and feminized before being partially replaced by more skilled male labour. Female wages persist in being two-thirds those of male ones.

At 15 per cent of the population and mostly confined to fruit and vegetables, fish and meat, transport and portering, recycling and sanitary work, Dalits still operate at a distinct disadvantage in the labour markets, in entry to business and the operation of their firms. And yet, while Marwari and Jain moneylenders and pawnbrokers are confronting new 'finance companies' (small collectives of public servants with financial surpluses) in the informal money markets, and easier registration and instantaneous transactions through formal banks, the biggest moneylenders are widely reported to be a trio of Dalits. They have graduated in their single working lifetimes from head-loading through informal finance to possessing suburban walled mansions and swimming pools.

The state regulates this economy with strategically selective efficiency. In past decades, owners of firms wished to speak at length about the corrupt nexus of interest between state officials and local capital, knotted together in partially implemented regulative interventions (Harriss-White 1996). Now they speak not always approvingly, of state neglect, which they feel results from the prevailing ideology of free market efficiency. Regulative deficits (which may be caused by deliberate capture or by scarcities of staff or of essential equipment [transport, computers]) encourage informal activity. Whereas 'neglect' used to be deliberately brokered by collective political appeals and business association pressure (with or without bribery)[7] now the evidence points in two political directions. First, there appears to be a severe lack of state capacity and under-provision of many services (notably that of refuse collection) and second, a hybrid institutional ecosystem is emerging in which the informal economy parodies formal procedures (such as certification), while formal institutions are intimately meshed with informal ones (for example, the PWD, unable to hire directly due to a politically provoked recruitment freeze, is outsourcing work to networks of informally qualified engineering and construction firms). In turn, many firms have a selective engagement with the legal framework: being licenced, with a bank account or two, as well as private credit, but not paying taxes, and not complying with labour laws or environmental standards. All state policies edge their way through this matrix of institutional arrangements and micro-politics in their process of implementation or abandonment.

With the last four decades of Arni's economic history in mind, we can now turn to examine ideas about the evolution of those local rural–urban economic relations that have proved capable of being

[7] Bribery is theorized as the privatization of or creation of a market in public resources by officials (patrons) charging citizens (clients) (Krueger 1974; Wade 1984). In earlier field research, collective bribery was found to be initiated by business associations and powerful 'clients' to speed access to resources (licences, infrastructure), to waive obligations to the state (tax), to avoid disciplinary regulation (movement of goods, safety, labour rights, etc.) to delay or subvert the implementation of market regulation (packaging, transparent price formation, site, in a reversal of the orthodox theory's role of patron and client (White and Harriss-White 1996). Clearly both balances of power between the state and capital are possible.

explored through first hand fieldwork. Economic relations concern finance and capital, commodities and labour. In what follows, we juxtapose ideas about them with substantive findings over a 40-year time span.

Rural–Urban and Urban–Rural Relations of Finance and Investment

When it was still possible to equate the 'rural' and the 'village' with 'agriculture', before the late 1980s, the question of the relation between agricultural production and the town engaged with classic concerns of the agrarian question. Economic historians and geographers had distinguished a 'generative' model of urbanism, the corollary of a peasant model of accumulation in which the cycle of surplus and investment was driven by the transition of the strata of middle and rich peasants to the agrarian bourgeoisie, which proceeded to invest productively in the regional agricultural and non-agricultural economy. This path was distinguished from a 'parasitic' model of urbanism on the other hand, derived from a mercantile route to capitalist accumulation in which towns were sites of rentier or mercantile accumulation extracted from agricultural production—and of parasitic consumption rather than productive investment (Chattopadhyay 1965; Harriss and Harriss 1984).

Matters arising for Arni were: a) which of these two models did the economy of an agricultural market town more closely resemble and why?; and b) if the agricultural merchant class had its origins in agricultural surpluses, then how would towns be progressively unhitched from their agricultural hinterlands? The questions were answered in three rounds of detailed investment histories taken from local, randomly sampled businesses from 1973 to 1995 and reinforced by questions to the Presidents of the town's Business Associations in 1997 and 2012.

Despite massive agricultural growth in the hinterland, in the 1970s and 1980s, the post green revolutionary evidence suggested the town's economy tended towards parasitic rather than generative growth. We found the terms of trade went against agriculture. Flows of investment were increasingly dominated by mercantile firms trading within the town. New firms tended to be 'Junker' or mercantile capitalists—starting comparatively big in terms of assets, with, even then, remarkably little capital got from agricultural rents, profits, or from the state by way of loans. However, their own seasonal loan practices were key to their accumulation trajectories. In the1970s, informal production credit for agriculture was dominated by the paddy commission agencies, which lent to agriculture on terms and conditions that tied the marketed surplus and pushed rates of return below those obtained under contracts that were not interlocked. Consumption credit was confined by and large to retail trade with the urban middle classes, particularly with the households of employees of the local state. Meanwhile, pawnbrokers serviced the consumption needs of a segmented sector of poor producers at collusively high interest and with a low fraction of the jewel value as the loan.

By the early 1980s, moneylending was both more institutionally diversified and its control was more concentrated than a decade earlier. Loans circulated increasingly within the town relative to the countryside and at higher real interest than ten years before. In 1983, many new entrants to Arni's business economy were small. But their starting capital was not from agricultural savings: much featured a high incidence of loans and was the result of petty accumulation (at one remove from agriculture) from urban wage-work or from urban petty trade.

Investment in the reverse direction, from the profits of elite urban businesses into agricultural land, had atrophied too. The proportion of investment of urban profits into agriculture had halved over the decade and was low.

A study of the fine detail of credit and deposit ratios of nationalized and scheduled banks revealed that, within the North Arcot District, agriculturally backward regions supplied capital to agriculturally advanced regions; there were net flows between local rural banks and local urban banks and the entire district was witnessing a significant flight of capital to the metropolis (Harriss 1988). Rural savings through formal institutions were being drawn increasingly into metropolitan circulation. With respect to politics, however, the reverse was found (Harriss J. 1991) with increasingly 'ruralist' rhetoric, subsidies, and doles, and, pace Michael Lipton's 'urban bias' (Lipton 1977), no political organization or party representing an urban class.

In the 1990s, while agriculture stagnated, the rural economy diversified, a process driven by distress among petty producing and labouring class fractions and by voluntarist, 'speculative' investment by agrarian elites. Local agricultural markets started to be formally deregulated (having in practice been long out of the direct control of the state). The processes of urban accumulation consolidated themselves. The main sources of capital were from the investor's family and from own savings from previous businesses: a third of the firms had been inherited. Agricultural rent and profit disappeared as sources of starting capital. The principal spatial origin of the capital invested in Arni was within the town itself, while only a small fraction came from the surrounding district (and that too from smaller urban centres rather than villages); and the contribution of the rest of Tamil Nadu and other Indian states was negligible.

This increasingly self-generated capital met with a dramatic challenge in the twenty-first century, when a large tract of land north of the town, long sequestered from agriculture by a local politician, was sown using metropolitan finance to a perennial crop of educational colleges and schools, whose market is state-wide.[8]

In sum: the rural–urban–rural financial relations of this small town are more complex than theoretical schemas allow for—having elements of urban bias and parasitic urbanism but not for the reasons theorized—in which the circulation of money inside the town itself becomes a material force in the delinking of agricultural profit from urban starting capitals. Agricultural surpluses come to be increasingly invested in private education. In turn peri-urban land is urbanized so that education can develop as a new component of the urban economic base—but using metropolitan finance and political intermediation.

Growth and Rural–Urban Development

Rural–urban development has also been theorized in terms of 'growth': a) growth centres or poles where supply is the main driver; and b) growth linkages in which the dynamic force comes from demand. In the 1970s, regional planners at the National Institute of Rural Development (NIRD) and their US advisers—asking, in their own version of the

[8] These investment conditions had resulted from two opposite trends: first, the town's growing financial intricacy and its integration with the jurisdictions of a growing number of nationally regulated banks and second, the loosening of financial linkages with the immediate agrarian hinterland.

agrarian question, how surpluses from the green revolution technology were to be generated, physically distributed, and productively circulated—decided to apply the German geographer Walter Christaller's theories of abstract spatial economic hierarchies and the French geographer Francois Perroux's practical concept of growth poles to the arrangements of Indian agriculture (Andrade 1972; Ensminger 1972; Sen 1972). The Indian state would invest with public–private synergy in selected services and in towns, which would plug the access gaps in the supply of inputs and finance, the marketing of products, and the consumer goods and services needed by agricultural populations—also now known as forward and backward linkages. If successful, this planning concept would also obstruct migration to the cities. The idea has stood the test of time, its embers smouldering through decades at the International Food Policy Research Institute (IFPRI) (Diao and Yanoma 2003; Wanmali and Ramasamy 1994) before being recently fanned to life by the National Commission for Enterprises in the Unorganized Sector (NCEUS) in an application of its principles of equitable access to inclusive development for small producers in the informal economy (NCEUS 2009).

The Arni business histories elicited detailed descriptions of the origins and destinations of raw materials, products, and services and were supplemented by field studies of the populations of traders in all the weekly marketplaces in the region around the town. These provided evidence, which exposed the intricacy of the regional economy and the crudity of growth centre theory. The rural hinterland for trade in individual agricultural goods and services was not only commodity-specific but also socially specific. While trade in agricultural investment goods could by-pass the market town altogether, the town was nonetheless a place for the transactions of local rural elites. In contrast, periodic market places were for low-caste and poor traders, agricultural producers, and consumers—and sites of agency for women. The spatiality of economic markets was gendered—the town's labour market being a male fortress while women were able to trade independently in periodic markets. The average rural–urban expenditure gap was huge—a factor of 6.

With prescience, John Mellor commented that '[d]espite its intellectual appeal the market town concept has in general failed because the basic strategy of growth did not provide the essential foundation for raising rural incomes. With change, the market town can become the corner stone of the development effort' (Mellor 1976: 18). Not thinking of parasitic urbanism, or the need for female and male growth centres or low and high caste ones, Mellor's 'change' required the substitution of a demand-led theory of growth for the supply-led one. This was and is the theory known as 'growth linkages from agriculture', a theory of the multiplier effects of the income/consumption linkages without which small-scale labour-intensive non-(internationally) tradable goods and services would not be produced. According to the growth linkages theory, growth centres would be driven by hinterland demand from a technologically dynamic agricultural sector. Successful ones would also stem metropolitan migration.

One way of testing this theory is by defining and constructing regional social accounts and input-output tables, and testing a partial equilibrium model against a counterfactual of no green revolution, an extraordinary feat achieved by Hazell and Ramasamy (1991). The theory can also be interrogated using commodity flow data, which were part of the Arni business histories. From an analysis of commodity flows in the early 1980s, it was concluded that production links *to* (intermediate inputs for) agriculture were weak—at 8 per cent of commodity flows from the town. Production links *from* local agriculture, at 15 per cent, were weaker than anticipated. Some by-passed the town. Meanwhile trade in consumption goods was strong: 28 per cent of all flows. And while the distribution of rural–urban income inequality was exacerbated by a sharp rise in top urban incomes, rises in rural incomes resulted in the difference between estimated average rural and urban demand halving in a decade to a factor of 3.

But the generative multipliers from growth linkages assume that the structure of rural demand would not change and would favour labour intensive goods and services. Mellor's assumption proved false. Rural demand was metropolitanizing. So, despite attempts to ruralize them through industrial estates, were sources of goods. The prime movers of growth were not just agriculture but work-shop manufacturing industry, silk, and this local industry served metropolitan markets rather than local ones. While agriculture was a net beneficiary of the revenue and expenditure relations of the local state, 70 per cent of the agriculture budget went to the urban salaries of Agriculture Department officials. While Mellor's growth linkages dynamized the town they were not exclusively from agriculture; as seen earlier here, the town had a dynamism of its own neglected in growth linkages theory. In practice, rather than acting as a hub for the regional economy, it was increasingly bolted into the national market.

In sum: research on growth linkages from agriculture revealed the town as a location for expenditure derived from increased agricultural incomes, but not of demand for goods and services produced under Mellorian conditions of development and *not* being the sole location for such expenditure. The town already had much else besides growth linkages from agriculture to power the urban economy. As for being a supply-led growth centre, the town behaved in a theoretically compliant way for consumer goods but was completely bypassed for many other growth-inducing transactions.

Rural–Urban Commodity Flows

In this part of India, rural–urban economic interactions have long taken the commodity form. Rural–urban economic accounts can be used to generate a set of commodity flow matrices. The latter have been assembled (originating in practices in the US) and published as precursors of the inter-industry, interregional input-output models on the basis of which the sectoral (rather than the spatial) impact of new investment or policy adjustments can be modelled—or the minimum investment to achieve regional income, output, or employment goals can be computed.[9] Since urban centres and their spatio-economic hinterlands are not conventional accounting units, such exercises have thrown down a very basic challenge concerning the nature of 'regions'. The identification of regions is not made easier by the existence of radically different spatial hinterlands for different goods: not a phenomenon of central place hierarchies so much as of marketing technology, advertising, and of the social relations of exchange. For Arni, a regional grid (comprising the town itself, the rural district, rural or urban sites within the state, and the rest of the world) was superimposed on the commodity flow data and compared over the decades.

[9] Accepting their heroic assumptions of fixed factor proportions.

In 1973, two-thirds of the commodity flows passing through Arni originated and finished within the district, and 10 per cent within the town itself. Trade was highly localized. The fact that 18 per cent of all flows were to non-final destinations within the district, to itinerant traders, to periodic marketplace traders, and to village retailers; and that a further 21 per cent went to non-final wholesale destinations within the state was an unexpected pointer to the town's emerging wholesale role. A decade onwards and commodity flows were marked by spatial diversification; by the increased long-distance metropolitanization of sources and destinations of goods and by the greater importance both of exports and of the wholesale role of the town. In the 1990s, the trend towards the creation of a southern regional market intensified with the increased contribution of inputs from other sources in urban Tamil Nadu and outside the state, in particular for food, farm inputs, silk, and general merchants' provisions. Meanwhile Chennai came to supply or broker almost all the inputs for general merchants and a high percentage of raw materials for silk production. As for the *destination* of goods, Arni increasingly reinforced its role as an entrepôt market town. In the 1990s (with the exception of paddy-rice firms and silk wholesaling—which both sold their products increasingly to other towns in Tamil Nadu and outside the state), the bulk of Arni's remaining sales went to the town and its surrounding villages, while other destinations received a negligible proportion of the commodities and services produced (Basile 2014; Harriss B. 1991).

Globalization has had an indirect impact on urban–rural commodity flows: first through an expanded scale of circulation of labour from the town and suburban villages—ranging from the daily commuting to the Nokia estate on the Madras–Bangalore industrial corridor to skilled emigration to the USA; second, through exports brokered first through Arni and then through Chennai, as in cases of de-oiled bran cake which go as fodder to the European Union (EU), sarees to south-east Asia, silk goods to the Middle East and even, it was reported, to China; third, through financial technology, notably the advent of electronic transfers, which has revolutionized the speed of urban transactions as well as globalizing their spatial reach and has differentiated exchange relations along urban–rural fault lines according to access to electronic technology; fourthly by images and aspirations mediated through global telecommunications networks and technology; and lastly by threat. So far it is the 'threat of

Walmart' and of legislation regulating foreign multi-brand retail rather than their reality that has provoked the pre-emptive transformation of retail practices. Tiny family firms are now packaging and branding, stamping goods with expiry dates, and setting fixed prices.

Rural–Urban Labour Relations

It is a basic tenet of economics that labour moves from low-wage to higher-wage activity. Other dualities accompany this intuition: labour migrates from traditional to modern, from primary to secondary sectors, from agriculture to the non-farm (rural) economy, and from rural to urban sites.[10] The study of the informal economy has led to formal and informal subsectors being distinguished in the 'modern' urban economy. The study of labour market segmentation has confirmed that the informal unregulated labour market is not transitory and that within it gender, caste, and occupational sector are remarkably rigid and persistent agents of segmentation and stratification. In 1985, Deshpande concluded influentially that the segmentation of the labour market starts in the villages (Deshpande 1985).

In the Arni region, in the 1980s and 1990s, the overall spatial trend in the labour force was quite the opposite to that of capital. The share of the urban workforce originating from within the town was declining in favour of workers commuting from local villages. (The contribution of migrant labourers from further afield was negligible. Even in 2012 there were but a few score reported from Orissa, negotiating the babble of 'meals hotels' and rice mills.) There seems to have been remarkable continuity in the rural–urban flux of labour.

And since the mid-1990s, the objective conditions for local rural–urban migration have been consolidated. In the twenty-first century, a new wave of enclosures has privatized and commercialized common property resources, leaving ever less for the poor. Rental markets have rapidly developed for land—with instances of sharecropping, hitherto unheard-of, at extortionate rates. So have rental markets for water, machinery, and rural houses—following the exodus to Arni and

[10] Harris and Todaro, Lewis, Scoville and others, all reviewed in Srinivasan (2015).

beyond of village elites and the growing ubiquity not just of absentee ownership of rural assets but of absentee governance of village panchayats (Harriss 2007).

Landlessness in silk handloom-weaving households doubled in the decade from 1995 and in non-weaving households it trebled (Arivukkarasi forthcoming). Rural economic inequalities continued to rise in the twenty-first century while poverty took a more specific form than it had done three decades earlier: in particular workers handicapped by occupational hazards and diseases pitch their households into poverty and force women and children in their families onto the labour market (Erb and Harriss-White 2003). Rural, casual female wage labour continues to get paupers' returns; scheduled caste paupers forego meals in certain villages in the town's hinterland; itinerant scheduled tribal paupers still pursue socially and spatially excluded lives picking waste alongside the pigs and camping in any site they can.

In the twenty-first century however, while the villages peripheral to Arni are indeed epicentres of casual labour commuting to work in the town, while the urban casual labour market reflects the caste and gender segmentation 'starting in the villages' and while the town is integrated with national economic markets, it is also developing social entry barriers This is not due to the activities of labour unions. It is due to the domination of self-employment and own account enterprise which, by under cutting the wage form, 'mutes' the development of the urban labour market (Bharadwaj 1999). This muting takes place in three main ways. First, attenuated periods of skill formation through apprenticeships in a given sector of the urban economy mean work is performed at costs below the prevailing wage for qualified labour. Second, unpaid family labour substitutes intensively for wage-work—and 85 per cent of unpaid family labour is done by women. Third, petty production and trade can and does operate way past the point at which returns equal the wage to a point where incremental returns approximate zero—production is maximized rather than profit.

When Srinivasan made the first rigorous field study of Arni's labour markets in 2000,[11] he found that 66 per cent of the 'workforce' was in

[11] Srinivasan (2011, 2015). Srinivasan researched the histories of 287 businesses in 1994 and 219 labour households in 1999–2000.

self-employment or petty commodity production and trade; only 30 per cent consisted of casual labour, while regular salaried work was a mere 4 per cent. There is a clear fault-line between wage work and self-employment, with little to no mobility between the two forms. Self-employment is neither residual nor transitory; it is remarkably persistent and it reproduces itself across generations and within given sectors of the urban economy. 'Industrial' sectors are highly differentiated by earnings and yet it is next to impossible for self-employed people to move between them. Despite evidence of social cosmopolitanism in the town, caste is still deployed to immobilize the self-employed. The alignment between caste and occupation is most rigid among the larger firms with small wage labour forces and most flexible among unstable, small low-caste enterprises. Low-caste entrants face hostility across the board—in skilling, in sites and rental arrangements, in demands for unrealistic money advances, and in the terms and conditions of tied credit. Caste screens entry most aggressively in silk and least aggressively in general trade.

So Arni's urban economy expands by dual trajectories: on the one hand through the accumulation and concentration of capital (rice processing) and on the other through the multiplication of firms—units—of self-employment (trade). Caste still segments the workforce; yet it works simultaneously in contradictory ways—being dissolved (trade) while also persistently structuring (silk, gold). The major fault line however remains in work: between firms employing (rural migrant) labour and self-employed, own account enterprises.

The significance of this finding is that self-employment is regarded as (disguised) wage labour in India's labour laws. If it is disguised in Arni it is well-disguised, for it does not allow any mobility to and from the wage form. Claims for breaches of labour laws require an employer to be identified. But without an identifiable employer or with *many* intermediaries who might be termed employers under the law, no court claim can be brought about work conditions so that petty producers are effectively disenfranchised under India's labour law (Sankaran 2008). And they also differ from wage workers in the economic sites of their exploitation: whereas casual labour is exploited and oppressed on labour markets, the petty producer is exploited through exchange relations—on rental and money markets, in the terms and conditions on which their raw materials are purchased, and their finished product is sold. The evidence from Arni is supportive of the conclusion that petty production cannot be assumed to be disguised wage labour wherever it is found but instead exists in a continuum from disguised wage labour lacking in economic autonomy to independent firms embodying both capital and labour.

* * *

Urban–rural relations have changed over the four decades of growth and transformation during which a local economy in Tamil Nadu has been being researched. Profit and rent from the agrarian economy have atrophied as sources of investment, with financial resources increasingly mobilized within the town itself or through the national banking system. Commodity flows have greatly expanded and complexified. They have integrated what was a small agricultural marketplace with a national market and indirectly with global ones. The rural hinterland became a significant source of local urban labour before being pushed by the expansion of petty production and own-account enterprise in the town or pulled by non-agricultural demand at long distance. The rural economy has become a major source of demand for the commodities and services of the town—which are increasingly being wholesaled there. Meanwhile the town developed new services, notably health, transport, and energy together with (private, English medium) school and college education, providing both urban and rural entrants to the workforce with capabilities that are reported to enable many to quit agriculture, quit family businesses, and quit the town.

Responses to the generalized labour shortage have taken the forms of mechanization and further displacement of wage labour, the feminization of self-employment, a proliferation of homeworking and the organization of inmigration from north India (Guerin 2009; Harriss-White and Rodrigo 2013).

There is solid evidence from the rounds of North Arcot surveys that the villages themselves have also undergone extensive diversification. By the mid-1990s the local population-land ratio had halved. Into the twenty-first century, land use has been moved away from rice and towards labour- and water-sparing crops, tree crops, and income-elastic condiments, flowers, and luxury fruits and vegetables. Returns to agricultural production, demand for agricultural labour, and relative wages in agriculture have all declined relative to those of the non-farm economy. Not only diversification but also differentiation have expanded rural assets distributions, increasing rural inequality and influencing the livelihood and employment structures of households in the direction of multi-sited, multi-sector, multi-occupations in which agriculture is a part-time component.[12]

While part of the non-farm workforce has sought to engage in non-farm activities in the villages, another part commuted to Arni as well as other local towns to supply wage labour for the growth of trade and manufacturing activities. In the twenty-first century however, the exit from agriculture has developed scale and reach and much outmigration by-passes the town.

What we know is the product of how we come to know: theories drive methods, which drive evidence and results, which enable reflections upon theory. In this chapter, we have shown how the interrogation of theories: of parasitic and generative urbanism, of urban bias, of demand- and supply-led theories of growth, and of labour markets, spatial, and social mobility, have led to fresh insights about rural–urban economic relations. The economy of the small town of Arni and its rural–urban–rural relations are altogether more complex than any of these theoretical schemas allow for. But without the latter, we would never have known this.

Our findings from over four decades of first-hand field research call for conceptions of the economy not just in terms of markets but as an instituted phenomenon. The institutions of capitalism need to be central to an understanding of the dynamics of an economy, but institutional change needs to be theorized as embodying the re-working of certain non-class institutions alongside the destruction and creation of others. And the phenomenon of institutional persistence needs to be conceived not only as the possible result of stasis and absence of change but also as the possible outcome of a balance of force between destructive and creative agency. It is first-hand field research alone that will distinguish these relationships. This research is the more necessary because at one level these dynamics endow an economy with its character—they are

[12] Jayaraj estimates that in 1993–4 around 40 per cent of male workers and 16 per cent of female workers reported non-farm activities as their primary occupation (2004: 185–6, Tables 4 and 5). See also Harriss-White, Janakarajan, and Colatei (2004: 38–9).

also the institutional mesh all policy has to pass through during the course of implementation—while at another level their study drives progress in understanding the co-evolution of economic institutions.

References

Andrade, P.C. 1972. 'Pilot Research Projects in Growth Centres', in L.K. Sen (ed.) *Readings on Microlevel Planning and Rural Growth Centres*. Hyderabad: National Institute of Community Development (NICD).

Arivukkarasi N.A. forthcoming. 'Structural changes in a Household Industry in Tamilnadu—The case of silk weaving in the Arni region', PhD Thesis, Madras University, Chennai, India.

Basile, E. 2013. *Capitalist Development in India's Informal Economy*. London: Routledge.

———. 2014. 'A Heterodox Analysis of Capitalism: Insights from a Market Town in South India,' in B. Harriss-White and J. Heyer (eds), *India's Capitalism in Development*, pp. 170–89. London: Routledge.

Bharadwaj, K. 1999. 'On the Formation of the Labour Market', in K. Bharadwaj (ed.), *Essays on Indian Economy*. New Delhi: SAGE Publications.

Breman, J., P. Kloos, and A. Saith. 1997. *The Village in Asia Revisited*. New Delhi: Oxford University Press.

Cavalcante, M. 2015. 'Feeling Rich on an Empty Stomach: Agrarian Crisis and Rural Consumption Choices', in B Harriss-White (ed.), *Middle India and Urban-Rural Dynamism: Four Decades of Change*, pp. 251–73. New Delhi: Springer India.

Chattopadhyay, B. 1965. 'Marx and India's Crisis', in P.C. Joshi (ed.), *Homage to Karl Marx*. Delhi: Peoples' Publishing House.

Courvisanos, J. 2008. 'Towns in Time: Methodology,' unpublished report, Department of Planning and Community Development, University of Ballarat, Australia.

Deshpande, L.K. 1985. 'Segmentation of Labour Market: A Case Study of Bombay', Kunda Datar Memorial Lecture, Gokhale Institute of Politics and Economics, Orient Longman Ltd., Hyderabad.

Diao, X. and Y. Yanoma. 2003. 'Exploring regional dynamics in Sub-Saharan African Agriculture', *DSDG Discussion Paper 02*, IFPRI, Washington, DC, available at http://www.ifpri.org/publication/exploring-regional-dynamics-sub-saharan-african-agriculture?print (last accessed 1 October 2015).

Ensminger, D. 1972. *Rural India in Transition*. New Delhi: All India Panchayat Parishad.

Erb, S. and B. Harriss-White. 2003. *Outcast from Social Welfare: Adult Disability in Rural India*. Bangalore: Books for Change.

Guérin, I. 2009. 'Bonded Labour in the Rice Mills: Fate or Opportunity?' in J. Breman, I. Guérin, and A. Prakash (eds), *India's Unfree Workforce. Old and New Practices of Labour Bondage*, pp. 284–311. New Delhi: Oxford University Press.

Harriss, B. 1981. *Transitional Trade and Rural Development.* New Delhi: Vikas.

———. 1988. 'Government Revenue and Expenditure in an Agrarian District of South India', *Journal of Public Administration and Development,* 8 (4): 437–57.

———. 1991. 'The Arni Studies: Changes in the Private Sector of a Market Town, 1971–1983', in P. Hazell and C. Ramasamy (eds), *The Green Revolution Reconsidered. The Impact of High-Yielding Varieties in South India*, pp. 181–212. Baltimore: Johns Hopkins University Press.

Harriss, B. and J. Harriss. 1984. '"Generative" or "Parasitic" Urbanism? Some Observations from the Recent History of a South Indian Market Town', *The Journal of Development Studies,* 3 (20): 82–101.

Harriss J. 1991. 'Economic Mobility and the Politics of an Awkward Class', in P. Hazell and C. Ramasamy (eds), *The Green Revolution Reconsidered. The Impact of High-Yielding Varieties in South India*, pp. 29–56. Baltimore: John Hopkins University Press.

———. 2007. 'Postscript: North Arcot Papers', in J Harriss (ed.), *Power Matters: Essays on Institutions, Politics and Society in India*, pp. 161–68. New Delhi: Oxford University Press.

Harriss, J. and B. Harriss-White. 2007. 'The "North Arcot Papers"', Working Paper Series No 146, Queen Elizabeth House, Oxford University, UK.

Harriss-White, B. 1996. *A Political Economy of Agricultural Markets in South India: Masters of the Countryside* New Delhi: SAGE Publications.

———. 2003. *India Working: Essays on Economy and Society*. Cambridge: Cambridge University Press.

———. 2013. 'The Foodgrains Economy in Northern Tamil Nadu, 1973–2010: Local Capitalist Transformations', available at http://www.southasia.ox.ac.uk/working-papers-resources-greenhouse-gases-technology-and-jobs-indias-informal-economy-case-rice#sthash.ajumoaUF.dpuf (last accessed 1 October 2015).

———. (ed.). 2015. *Middle India and Urban-Rural Dynamism : Four Decades of Change*. New Delhi: Springer India.

Harriss-White, B., S. Janakarajan, and D. Colatei. 2004. 'Heavy Agriculture and Light Industry in South Indian Villages', in B. Harriss-White and S. Janakarajan (eds), *Rural India facing the 21st Century*, pp. 3–47. London: Anthem.

Harriss-White, B., E. Basile, A. Dixit, P. Joddar, A. Prakash, and K. Vidyarthee. 2014. *Dalits and Adivasis in India's Business Economy*. New Delhi: Three Essays Press.

Harriss-White, B. and G. Rodrigo. 2013. 'Pudumai—Innovation and Institutional Churning in India's Informal Economy: A Report from the Field', available at http://www.southasia.ox.ac.uk/sites/sias/files/documents/PUDUMAI%20-%20INNOVATION%20AND%20INSTITUTIONAL%20CHURNING%20IN%20INDIA%E2%80%99S%20INFORMAL%20ECONOMY%20a%20report%20from%20the%20field.pdf (last accessed 1 October 2015).

Harriss-White, B. and J. Heyer. (eds). 2014. *India's Capitalism in Development*. London: Routledge.

Hazell, P. and C. Ramasamy (eds). 1991. *The Green Revolution Reconsidered. The Impact of High-Yielding Varieties in South India*. Baltimore: Johns Hopkins University Press.

Jayaraj, D. 2004. 'Social Institutions and the Structural Transformation of the Rural Economy', in Barbara Harriss-White and S. Janakarajan (eds), *Rural India Facing the 21st Century: Essays on Long Term Village Change and Recent Development Policy*, pp. 175–94. London: Anthem.

Krueger, A. 1974. 'The Political Economy of the Rent-seeking Society,' *American Economic Review*, 64 (3): 291–303.

Lanjouw, P. and N.H. Stern (eds).1998. *Economic Development in Palanpur over Five Decades*. Oxford: Oxford University Press.

Lindberg, S., V.B. Athreya, R. Vidyasagar, G. Djurfeldt, and A. Rajagopal. 2011. 'A Silent "Revolution"? Women's Empowerment in Rural Tamil Nadu', *Economic and Political Weekly*, 44 (13): 111–20.

Lipton, M. 1977. *Why Poor People Stay Poor: Urban Bias in World Development*. London: Maurice Temple Smith.

Mellor, J. 1976. *The New Economics of Growth*. Baltimore: John Hopkins University Press.

Moser, C. 2003. *Urban Longitudinal Research Methodology*. London: University College.

NCEUS (National Commission for Enterprises in the Unorganized Sector). 2009. *Growth Pole Programme for Unorganised Sector Enterprise Development*. New Delhi: NCEUS.

Polzin, C. 2006. 'Credit in South India—An Empirical Critique of Competing Frameworks of Institutional Change', MPhil Thesis, Queen Elizabeth House, Oxford University, UK.

Ramachandran, V.K., M. Swaminathan, and V. Rawal. 2001. 'How Have Hired Workers Fared? A Case Study of Women Workers from an Indian Village, 1977 to 1999', Trivandrum Working Papers 323, Centre for Development Studies, Trivandrum.

Roman, C. 2008. 'Learning and Innovation in Clusters: Case Studies from the Indian Silk Industry', DPhil thesis, Oxford University, UK.

Sen, L.K. (ed.). 1972. *Readings on Microlevel Planning and Rural Growth Centres*. Hyderabad: National Institute of Rural Development (NIRD).

Sankaran, K. 2008. 'Informal Economy, Own Account Workers and the Law: An Overview', WIEGO Law Pilot Project on the Informal Economy. Available at http://wiego.org/sites/wiego.org/files/resources/files/fow_background_note.pdf (last accessed 29 May 2012).

Srinivasan M.V. 2011. 'Segmentation of Urban Labour Markets in India: A Case Study of Arni Tamil Nadu', PhD Thesis, Jawaharlal Nehru University, New Delhi, India.

———. 2015. 'Arni's Workforce: Segmentation Processes, Labour Market Mobility, Self-employment and Caste', in B. Harriss-White (ed.), *Middle India and Urban-Rural Dynamism: Four Decades of Change*, pp. 65–96. New Delhi: Springer India.

Stanley, J. 2002. *A Common Cluster in a Crowded Market: The Gold Ornaments Cluster in Arni, Tamil Nadu, India*, MPhil thesis, Oxford University, UK.

Wade, R. 1984. 'The Market for Public Office: Why the Indian State is Not Better at Development', *World Development*, 18 (4): 467–97.

Wanmali, S. and C. Ramasamy. 1994. *Developing Rural Infrastructure for Poor People: Studies from North Arcot, Tamil Nadu, India*. New Delhi and Washington: ICAR and IFPRI.

White, G. and B. Harriss-White. 1996. 'Corruption, Liberalisation and Democracy,' *Bulletin Institute of Development Studies*, 27 (2): 1–5.

Index

About the Editors and Contributors

Editors

Himanshu is Associate Professor of Economics at the Centre for Economic Studies and Planning, School of Social Sciences, Jawaharlal Nehru University (JNU), New Delhi, India. His areas of research include issues related to poverty, inequality, employment, food security, and agrarian change. He has been involved with various government committees including the Expert Group on Measurement of Poverty (Tendulkar Committee), National Statistical Commission, and the Ministry of Rural Development. He has received the Sanjay Thakur Young Economist Award of the Indian Society of Labour Economics and Personnalité d' Avenir of the French Ministry of Foreign Affairs. Himanshu received his PhD in economics from JNU, New Delhi, India.

Praveen Jha is Professor of Economics and Chairperson of the Centre for Economic Studies and Planning, School of Social Sciences, JNU, New Delhi, India. He is one of the editors of a tri-continental journal, *Agrarian South: Journal of Political Economy*. His major area of research and teaching is political economy of development with a focus on Indian economy, labour economics, agricultural economics, the economics of education, public finance, and history of economic thought. He has authored and edited a number of books and monographs.

Gerry Rodgers is presently Visiting Professor at the Institute for Human Development, New Delhi, India. Previously, he worked at the International Labour Office in a variety of positions, including as Director of International Institute for Labour Studies. His work has mainly been concerned with poverty, inequality, labour, and employment, especially in India and Latin America. He has a long-term interest in rural development in Bihar. His current research includes a comparative study of labour market inequality in Brazil and India.

Contributors

Shapan Adnan is an independent academic educated at University of Cambridge, UK and University of Sussex, Brighton, UK. He has taught at National University of Singapore, Singapore, University of Dhaka, Bangladesh, and University of Chittagong, Bangladesh. He has been a visiting Research Fellow at the University of Oxford, UK and is an associate of its Contemporary South Asian Studies Programme. He is on the international advisory board of *The Journal of Peasant Studies*. The topics of his research and publications extend across political economy, sociology, anthropology, and development.

Ruchira Bhattacharya is a Research Scholar at the Centre for Study of Regional Development, School of Social Sciences, JNU, New Delhi, India. She is currently pursuing her PhD on the Public Distribution System in India and its impact on welfare of households. She was awarded the Ruddar Dutta Memorial Prize for best paper at the 55th Annual Conference of Indian Society of Labour Economics in 2013.

Amrita Datta is an Associate Fellow at the Institute for Human Development, New Delhi, India and a PhD researcher at the International Institute of Social Studies, Erasmus University Rotterdam, the Netherlands. Her research interests are in the areas of migration, gender, and village and longitudinal studies.

John Harriss is Professor of International Studies at the Simon Fraser University, Vancouver, Canada. He has researched and written on different aspects of Indian society, politics, and political economy, and is currently working on a book on rural society.

Barbara Harriss-White is Emeritus Professor of development studies and Fellow of the Wolfson College, University of Oxford, UK. She founded University of Oxford's MPhil programme in development studies, the masters in contemporary India, and directed Queen Elizabeth House. Her research has three streams: rural markets, markets and deprivation, and regional development round the hub of a local town, studied through fieldwork over 40 years.

Judith Heyer held a post in the economics department of the University of Oxford, UK, from 1975 to 2005, prior to which she was with University of Nairobi, Kenya. Heyer is now an Emeritus Fellow of Somerville College, Oxford, UK. A specialist in rural development, much of her earlier work focused on Kenya. Her recent work has drawn on fieldwork in western Tamil Nadu over more than three decades, focusing first on the role of Dalits in the rural economy and now on the role of the landowning castes.

Patricia Jeffery is Professor of Sociology in the School of Social and Political Science, University of Edinburgh, UK. Her work focuses on women's reproductive rights, social demography, gender and communal politics, education, and the reproduction of inequality in rural Uttar Pradesh. In 2009–10, she held a British Academy/Leverhulme Trust Senior Research Fellowship. Currently, she is Chair of the British Association for South Asian Studies, UK.

J. Jeyaranjan is Director of Institute of Development Alternatives, Chennai, India. After his doctoral research on agrarian transition, he has been working on several economic and social issues concerning Tamil Nadu. His areas of interest include village studies, rural labour, industrial organization, and gender relations. He has authored several papers and reports based on research undertaken by him. He also writes in popular magazines in his native language, Tamil. He has taught economics for five years.

Surinder S. Jodhka is Professor of Sociology at JNU, New Delhi, India. He is also an affiliate senior fellow at Centre for Humanities and Social Sciences, New Delhi. He researches on different dimensions of social inequalities—old and new—and the processes of their reproduction.

The empirical focus of his work has been the dynamics of caste and the varied modes of its articulation with the nature of social and economic change in 'neo-liberal' India; studies of agrarian social change and contemporary rural India; and the political sociology community identities.

Ruth Kattumuri is Co-director of India Observatory and the Asia Research Centre at the London School of Economics (LSE), UK. She holds a PhD from LSE and is a Cambridge Commonwealth Fellow. Prior to joining the LSE, she taught statistics and computer science in Chennai, India. Her research and policy engagement extends across many areas of sustainable and equitable growth and development. With over twenty-five years of experience, she has pioneered several innovative education, research, and skills development programmes in the UK and India.

Peter Lanjouw is Professor of Development Economics at VU University Amsterdam, the Netherlands since January 2015. Prior to this, he was research manager of the Poverty Team in the Development Economics Research Group of the World Bank. His research focuses on the analysis of poverty and inequality as well as on rural development, notably the study of village economy in rural India and the broader analysis of rural non-farm diversification. He has taught at University of California, Berkeley, US; University of Namur, Belgium; Foundation for the Advanced Study of International Development, Tokyo, Japan; and he is also an honorary fellow of the Amsterdam Institute of International Development, the Netherlands.

Sunil Kumar Mishra is presently working as an associate fellow at the Institute for Human Development, New Delhi, India. He has done his post-graduation and MPhil in economics from Sambalpur University, Odisha. He is an ICSSR research fellow at Govind Ballabh Pant Social Science Institute, Allahabad, Uttar Pradesh. He has worked extensively in the area of livelihood, child deprivation, food security, and poverty. Presently, he is working in the project 'Growth, Urbanization Rural–Urban Linkages in Bihar' sponsored by IGC International Growth Centre, UK. He has authored two books and published around 15 papers or chapters in journals and edited books.

Rinku Murgai is a lead economist in the World Bank's South Asia Poverty Reduction and Economic Management Unit. She holds a PhD in agricultural and resource economics from University of California at Berkeley, USA. Murgai has worked on a range of issues in the areas of poverty measurement, impact evaluation of public programmes, social protection, and functioning of rural land and water markets.

R. Ramakumar is Professor at the Centre for Study of Developing Economies, School of Development Studies, Tata Institute of Social Studies (TISS), Mumbai, India. He has done MSc in agricultural economics from Tamil Nadu Agricultural University, Coimbatore, Tamil Nadu and PhD in economics from the Indian Statistical Institute, Kolkata. His areas of research include agrarian change in rural India and rural Maharashtra, economic reforms and changes in rural livelihoods, and fiscal policy in India. He is also closely associated with Foundation for Agrarian Studies, India.

Janine Rodgers is a development economist who specializes in gender and labour market issues. She has been Deputy Executive Secretary of European Association of Development Research and Training Institutes (EADI), worked at the International Labour Office, and is currently visiting research fellow at the Institute for Human Development, New Delhi. She has been conducting research in rural Bihar since the 1970s.

Alakh N. Sharma is Professor and Director of Institute for Human Development (IHD), New Delhi, India. Earlier he has worked as faculty in Institute of Economic Growth, New Delhi; V.V. Giri National Labour Institute, Noida, Uttar Pradesh; Shri Ram Centre for Industrial Relations, New Delhi; and A.N. Sinha Institute of Social Studies, Patna, Bihar. He has directed or coordinated more than 30 research projects in various areas such as livelihoods, poverty, employment, and labour markets. He has authored, edited, and co-edited 18 books and published around 50 research papers in various journals. He is also editor of *Indian Journal of Labour Economics* (*IJLE*)—the quarterly journal of the Indian Society of Labour Economics, and IHD's bi-annual journal, *Indian Journal of Human Development*.

Dipa Sinha is an independent researcher and activist working on issues of food rights, nutrition, and public health. She has worked with the Office of Commissioners to the Supreme Court (on the Right to Food) and continues to be associated with the office as an Adviser. She is also part of the research team for the Palanpur Village Survey—a longitudinal village survey being conducted by the London School of Economics in collaboration with the Centre de Sciences Humaines, New Delhi. As a health and population fellow of the Population Council, she has worked at the grassroots level on maternal and child health and nutrition. She has done her MA in economics from JNU, New Delhi; MSc in development studies from School of Oriental and African Studies (SOAS), London; and PhD from JNU.

Ravi Srivastava is Professor of Economics at Centre for the Study of Regional Development, JNU, New Delhi, India, since 1999. Prior to this, he had served in the University of Allahabad, Uttar Pradesh and Govind Ballabh Pant Social Science Institute, Allahabad, Uttar Pradesh, for over two decades. His main areas of research and publication include human development, rural poverty and rural development, decentralization, and labour markets and migration. In 2001, he was given the University Grant Commission's award in economics for innovative research on poverty. He is a member of the Editorial Board of *Social Concern*, *Journal of Agrarian Change*, *Indian Journal of Labour Economics*, and *Sarvekshana*, and acts as a referee to a large number of international journals.

Nicholas Stern is I.G. Patel Professor of Economics and Government, Chairman of Grantham Research Institute on Climate Change and the Environment, and Head of India Observatory at the London School of Economics, UK. He is President of British Academy (since July 2013), and was elected Fellow of the Royal Society (June 2014). He was knighted for services to economics in 2004 and made a cross-bench life peer as Baron Stern of Brentford in 2007. His research and publications have focused on the economics of climate change, economic development and growth, economic theory, tax reform, public policy, and the role of the state and economies in transition.

Avanindra Nath Thakur teaches economics at Bhim Rao Ambedkar College, University of Delhi, India. He has completed his PhD from

JNU, New Delhi. His research interests include issues related to labour and agriculture, with special focus on employment, migration, agrarian conditions, government policies and its implications.

Dinesh Kumar Tiwari is Associate Fellow at the National Council of Applied Economic Research (NCAER), New Delhi. He has a doctorate in anthropology from Sagar University, Madhya Pradesh. He has worked on many field surveys for the Indian Statistical Institute (ISI), New Delhi and the World Bank on experimental economics and run experiments in field in the past. In recent years he has worked extensively on data collection and supervision and was mainly responsible for the management of the Palanpur Survey conducted by London School of Economics (LSE) and Center de Sciences Humaines. Currently, Tiwari is working with Sonalde Desai on India Human Develoment Survey project on data processing and was in-charge of field monitoring and supervision for the India Human Development.